THE EVERYTHING® LARGE-PRINT CROSSWORDS BOOK VOLUME III

Dear Reader,

Maybe they can't break our bones, but words are still powerful. With the right words we can express our deepest emotions, or explain the most complicated concepts. Crossword puzzles are for those of us who love to find just the right words. That is what I like about these puzzles—they give us a playful way to boost our mastery of language.

It was a joy putting this book together for you. I hope you have as much fun solving these crosswords as I had creating them. We used large print because bigger letters are better; it makes the solving less tedious. Your brain will be tested, not your vision.

Words are almost magical. They can even send messages across time and space, from one person to another. Here is my message to you: may you find these crossword puzzles to be both entertaining and educational; and may your word power grow stronger!

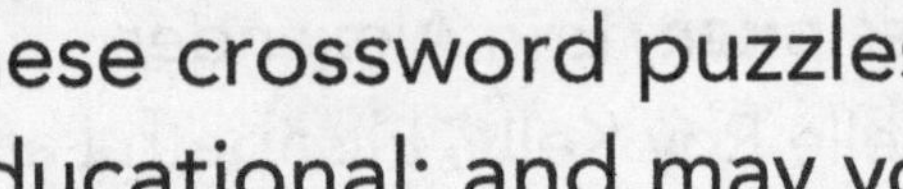

Welcome to the EVERYTHING® Series!

These handy, accessible books give you all you need to tackle a difficult project, gain a new hobby, comprehend a fascinating topic, prepare for an exam, or even brush up on something you learned back in school but have since forgotten.

You can choose to read an Everything® book from cover to cover or just pick out the information you want from our four useful boxes: e-questions, e-facts, e-alerts, and e-ssentials. We give you everything you need to know on the subject, but throw in a lot of fun stuff along the way, too.

We now have more than 400 Everything® books in print, spanning such wide-ranging categories as weddings, pregnancy, cooking, music instruction, foreign language, crafts, pets, New Age, and so much more. When you're done reading them all, you can finally say you know Everything®!

PUBLISHER Karen Cooper

MANAGING EDITOR, EVERYTHING® SERIES Lisa Laing

COPY CHIEF Casey Ebert

ASSISTANT PRODUCTION EDITOR Melanie Cordova

ACQUISITIONS EDITOR Lisa Laing

EDITORIAL ASSISTANT Matthew Kane

EVERYTHING® SERIES COVER DESIGNER Erin Alexander

LAYOUT DESIGNERS Erin Dawson, Michelle Roy Kelly, Elisabeth Lariviere

THE EVERYTHING® LARGE-PRINT CROSSWORDS BOOK

VOLUME III

150 jumbo crossword puzzles for easier reading & solving

Charles Timmerman
Founder of Funster.com

Adams Media
New York London Toronto Sydney New Delhi

Adams Media
An Imprint of Simon & Schuster, Inc.
100 Technology Center Drive
Stoughton, Massachusetts 02072

Manufactured in the United States of America

16 2022

Library of Congress Cataloging-in-Publication Data has been applied for.

ISBN 978-1-4405-3890-2

To Suzanne, Calla, and Meryl

Acknowledgments

I would like to thank each and every one of the more than half a million people who have visited my website, *www.funster.com*, to play word games and puzzles. You have shown me how much fun puzzles can be and how addictive they can become!

It is a pleasure to acknowledge the folks at Adams Media who made this book possible. I particularly want to thank my editor, Lisa Laing, for so skillfully managing the many projects we have worked on together.

Contents

Introduction

What do Rosa Parks, Richard Nixon, Jesse Owens, and crossword puzzles have in common? They were all born in the year 1913. In that year, a journalist named Arthur Wynne published a "word-cross" puzzle in the *New York World's* Sunday newspaper. Though it was diamond-shaped, it had all of the features of the crossword puzzles that we know and love today. The name evolved into *Crossword* as the paper continued to publish the popular word puzzles.

It wasn't until 1924 that the first book of crossword puzzles was published. That was when the crossword craze really began. It joined other fads of the Roaring Twenties like goldfish-swallowing, flagpole sitting, yo-yos, and pogo sticks. Of course, not all of these fads survived (perhaps fortunately). Besides crossword puzzles, some really beautiful things came out of the 1920s. In music, jazz surged in popularity and George Gershwin's *Rhapsody in Blue* was performed for the first time. In literature, F. Scott Fitzgerald published some of his most enduring novels including *The Great Gatsby.* In design, it was the beginning of Art Deco. That's how the world was shifting when crossword puzzles came of age.

Crossword puzzles became popular closer to a time when entertainment required *active* participation. In those days, people actually played sports rather than watched them, told each other stories rather than turning on the television, and even sang songs rather than listening to an MP3. Like entertainment of yesteryear, crossword puzzles require your active participation. And this is a refreshing change for those of us who still enjoy a mental workout.

Today, nearly every major newspaper runs a crossword puzzle. Entire sections of bookstores are devoted to crossword puzzle books. (Thanks for choosing this one!) Indeed, crosswords are the most common word puzzle in the world.

Why do crossword puzzles continue to be so popular? Only you can answer that question since there are as many reasons to work a crossword puzzle as there are solvers. But perhaps it has something to do with the convenient marriage of fun and learning that crossword puzzles offer.

Puzzles

ACROSS

1. Dose amt.
4. Talk online
8. Pot-bellied critter
11. Wednesday's child is full of it
12. Skillfully
13. ___ Major (constellation)
14. ___ Gang comedies
15. Betsy or Diana
16. Showy display
17. Baseball's Bambino
19. Partner of aahs
21. Chinese cooking vessel
23. Poverty-stricken
26. Made a getaway
30. Pub perch
32. Half a quartet
33. "___ Are My Sunshine"
35. Three: Prefix
36. City-related
39. Accumulated
42. Went out, as the tide
44. Engine additive letters
45. Follow, as advice
47. "The Battle ___ of the Republic"
50. "Round and Round" singer Perry
53. Sidewalk eatery
55. Look through the crosshairs
57. Are you coming ___ not?
58. Ken or Lena
59. Nova subj.
60. Mom's mate
61. Deli breads
62. Voodoo doctor's doing

DOWN

1. A pair
2. Like a lime
3. Llama country
4. Server at a drive-in
5. "Big Love" airer
6. ___-ran: loser
7. Boxing's "Iron Mike"
8. Paid player
9. Doctrine: Suffix
10. Noticeable opening
13. Unexpected sports outcome
18. Up, up, and away defunct flier
20. For ___ a jolly good . . .
22. Door opener
24. Periods
25. Olden times
26. University URL ending
27. Be glad to
28. Ty or Lee J.
29. ___ one-eighty
31. Pot's top
34. Hesitant sounds
37. Really hate
38. Previously named
40. Greek metropolis

Puzzle 1

Solution on Page 314

41. Undercover agent
43. Interior designer's concern
46. Tyne of "Cagney & Lacey"
48. Alan Alda series
49. Delightful
50. Scotland Yard div.
51. "Cat ___ Hot Tin Roof"
52. Stylish, 1960s-style
54. What foolishness!
56. Blender setting

ACROSS

1. Propel a dinghy
4. Moms
7. Rudely overlook
11. Prefix with center or cycle
12. Capote, for short
13. Frontiersman Daniel
14. Web address: Abbr.
15. Maple syrup source
16. Fort Knox bar
17. Rocket launch site
18. Plant with fronds
20. [snicker]
22. Noah's craft
23. PC innards: Abbr.
26. Opposite of fore
28. Make a minister of
31. Wrecking-ball swinger
34. Buildings with lofts
35. Hound
37. Indistinct
38. Library admonition
39. Hardship
41. Nova network
44. Animal parks
45. Sighs of contentment
47. "___ Doesn't Live Here Anymore"
51. Chelsea "Z"
53. ___ many cooks . . .
54. Mary Tyler ___
55. Make a boo-boo
56. Caveman Alley
57. Pint-sized
58. Muddy enclosure
59. To the ___ degree

DOWN

1. Do another hitch
2. TV host Winfrey
3. Oscar who wrote "The Picture of Dorian Gray"
4. Rockies, e.g.
5. Palestinian leader
6. Fantastic!
7. Bush 43, to Bush 41
8. Christmas drink
9. Mattel card game
10. Place a wager
13. Storage box
19. "King Kong" studio
21. ___ Christian Andersen
23. Ford or Lincoln
24. ATM code
25. Young ___ (kids)
27. Lawyer's payment
29. Sacrifice fly stat.
30. In need of dehumidification
31. Letterman's employer
32. Pep rally yell
33. Blaze remnant
36. Duet number
37. Gobi or Mojave
40. Falls through the cracks?

Puzzle 2

Solution on Page 314

42. Conductor's stick
43. Fire a gun
44. Letter after wye
46. Junior-to-be
47. What a guitar may be hooked up to
48. Mary's TV boss
49. Tiny charged particle
50. Boo-hoo
52. Desertlike

ACROSS

1. Racetrack stops
5. Dah's partner
8. Tennis great Arthur
12. Molecule building block
13. Deer female
14. Imposter
15. Word form for "trillion"
16. Former "Grand Ole Opry Live" network
17. Small children
18. Stop and ___ the roses
20. Ongoing TV show
22. Inc., in Britain
24. Blowup letters?
25. Passes, as time
29. Discarded metal
33. Prefix with hertz
34. ___ Na Na
36. It's where the heart is
37. Thrill to death
39. Least difficult
41. Eighth mo.
43. Barnyard cackler
44. Houston nine
47. Book of maps
51. Car
52. Tiebreaker rounds: abbr.
54. What ___ become of me?
55. Not false
56. You don't ___!
57. Postal delivery
58. Places for experiments
59. Suffix with north
60. Suffix with luncheon

DOWN

1. Butter servings
2. Unit on a list
3. Verbally attacked, with "into"
4. Something of trivial importance
5. Insecticide banned since 1973
6. Cyclotron particles
7. Church belief
8. Saver of nine
9. Nursery rhyme home of many children
10. They may be tossed in the ring
11. Typesetter's units
19. They rank below capts.
21. M.D.'s associates
23. ___ Plaines, IL
25. Scratch (out), as a living
26. Abner adjective
27. Chicken ___ King
28. "___ Drives Me Crazy" (Fine Young Cannibals hit)
30. Fish eggs
31. Pro-___ (some tourneys)
32. Household animal
35. Ooh's partner
38. The Continent: Abbr.

Puzzle 3

Solution on Page 314

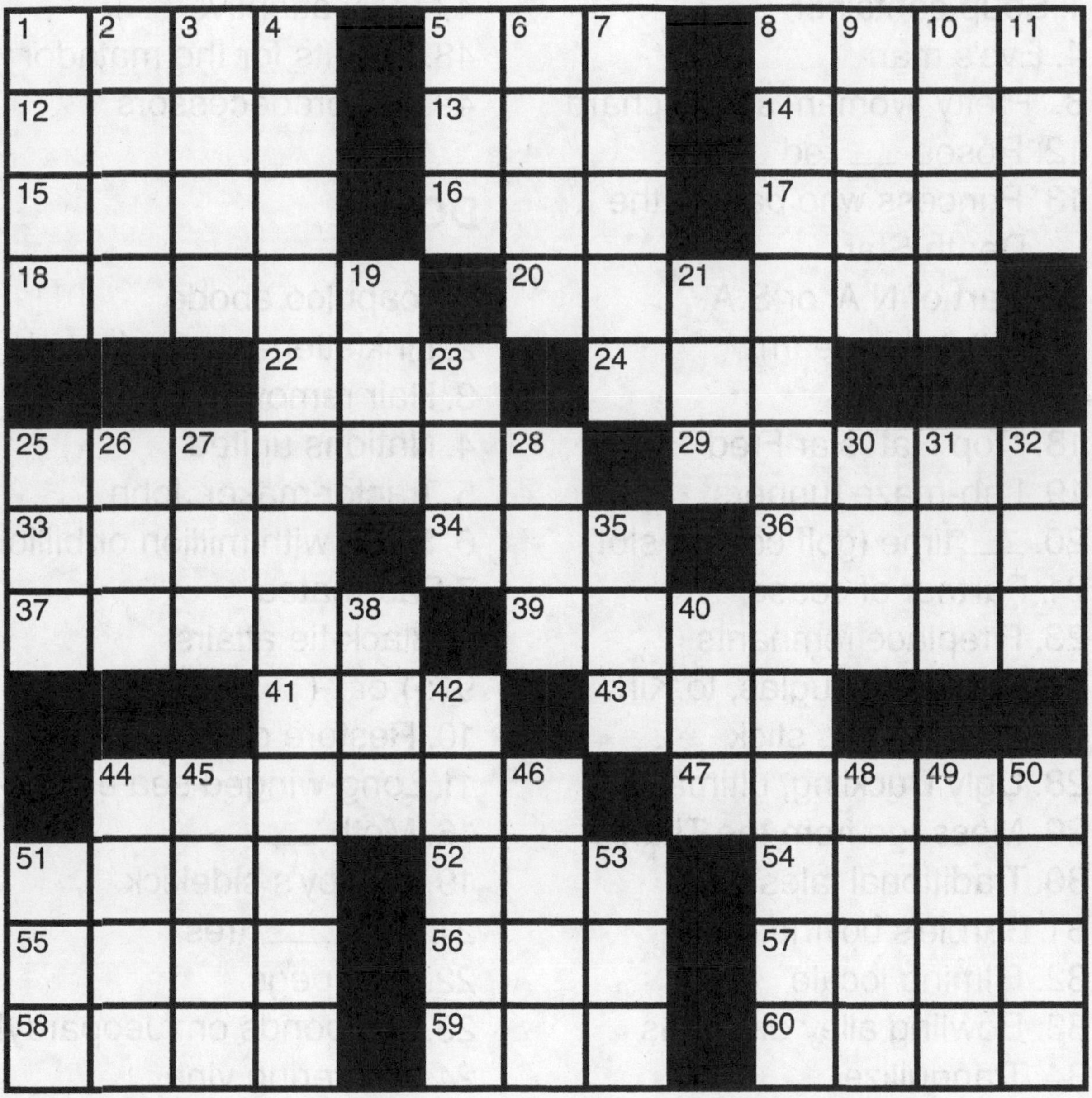

40. Dead ___ Scrolls
42. Barnyard honker
44. Radiant glow
45. Hit, as one's toe
46. Symbol on the Hollywood Walk of Fame
48. Future D.A.'s exam
49. Going ___ tooth and nail
50. ___ survivor
51. U.S./Eur. divider
53. Opp. of ant.

ACROSS

1. Soup container
4. Eve's man
8. "Pretty Woman" star Richard
12. Roses ___ red . . .
13. Princess who battles the Death Star
14. Part of N.A. or S.A.
15. Pittsburgh team
17. Bank offer
18. "Top Hat" star Fred
19. Lab-maze runners
20. ___ time (golf course slot)
21. Partner of cease
23. Fireplace remnants
26. Michael Douglas, to Kirk
27. Pool player's stick
28. Ugly Duckling, ultimately
29. Message from the Titanic
30. Traditional tales
31. Barbie's boyfriend
32. Filming locale
33. Bowling alley divisions
34. Tranquilize
36. Uncle ___
37. Helpful hints
38. They're in your apartment building
42. Pet adoption org.
43. Not abstract
44. "All in the Family" producer Norman
45. If all ___ fails . . .
46. Depressed
47. Fully attentive
48. Shouts for the matador
49. CD predecessors

DOWN

1. Acapulco abode
2. Linkletter and Garfunkel
3. Hair removal brand
4. Nations united
5. Tractor-maker John
6. Suffix with million or billion
7. Pas' mates
8. Black-tie affairs
9. :-) or :-(
10. Restore confidence to
11. Long-winged sea eagle
16. Moth-___
19. Stimpy's sidekick
21. Uno, ___, tres
22. Golf pegs
23. Responds on "Jeopardy!"
24. Flowering vine
25. Equalizer on the links
26. Heavy drinker
29. Visualize
30. Tennessee Senator Alexander
32. Elm and Main: abbr.
33. Knights' weapons
35. Off to one side

Puzzle 4

Solution on Page 314

36. Taste or smell
38. Driver's payment
39. "Ain't Misbehavin'" star Carter
40. Sporty auto roof
41. Uses a Singer
42. Camera type, briefly
43. Top of the corp. ladder

ACROSS

1. Chemists' workshops
5. Succulent houseplant
9. Idiot boxes
12. Cousin of the bassoon
13. Jets, Mets, or Nets
14. The Third
15. . . . or ___! (threat)
16. India and indelible
17. Coffee order: Abbr.
18. Sunset direction
19. Auction grouping
20. Already stitched
21. "The Cat in the ___"
23. Q-U connection
25. Great Lakes Indians
28. Announce
32. Model builder's purchase
33. 2000 candidate Ralph
35. Sprint
36. Nail polishes
38. Pointed a pistol
40. La la lead-in
41. Downing St. residents
42. Part of a home entertainment system
45. Quilting party
47. Cries of triumph
51. Solemn wedding words
52. Knight's lady
53. Auto with a four-ring logo
54. Tool with teeth
55. Arabian prince
56. Family group
57. Wd. in Roget's
58. Cushions for tumblers
59. Identical

DOWN

1. MGM mogul Marcus
2. Having sufficient skill
3. Bruce Springsteen, with "The"
4. Be really mad
5. Like the Leaning Tower of Pisa
6. Jay of NBC
7. Symbol of sturdiness
8. Dash widths
9. Michelin product
10. Panorama
11. Speak with one's hands
20. Mo. metropolis
22. Ed of "Lou Grant"
24. Get out of here!
25. ___ out (barely make)
26. ___ Tin Tin (old TV dog)
27. Let's call ___ day
28. Tooth pro's deg.
29. Elbow's place
30. ___ the day
31. ___ of the line
34. Mobile home?
37. "The Real World" network
39. Newton and Stern

Puzzle 5

Solution on Page 315

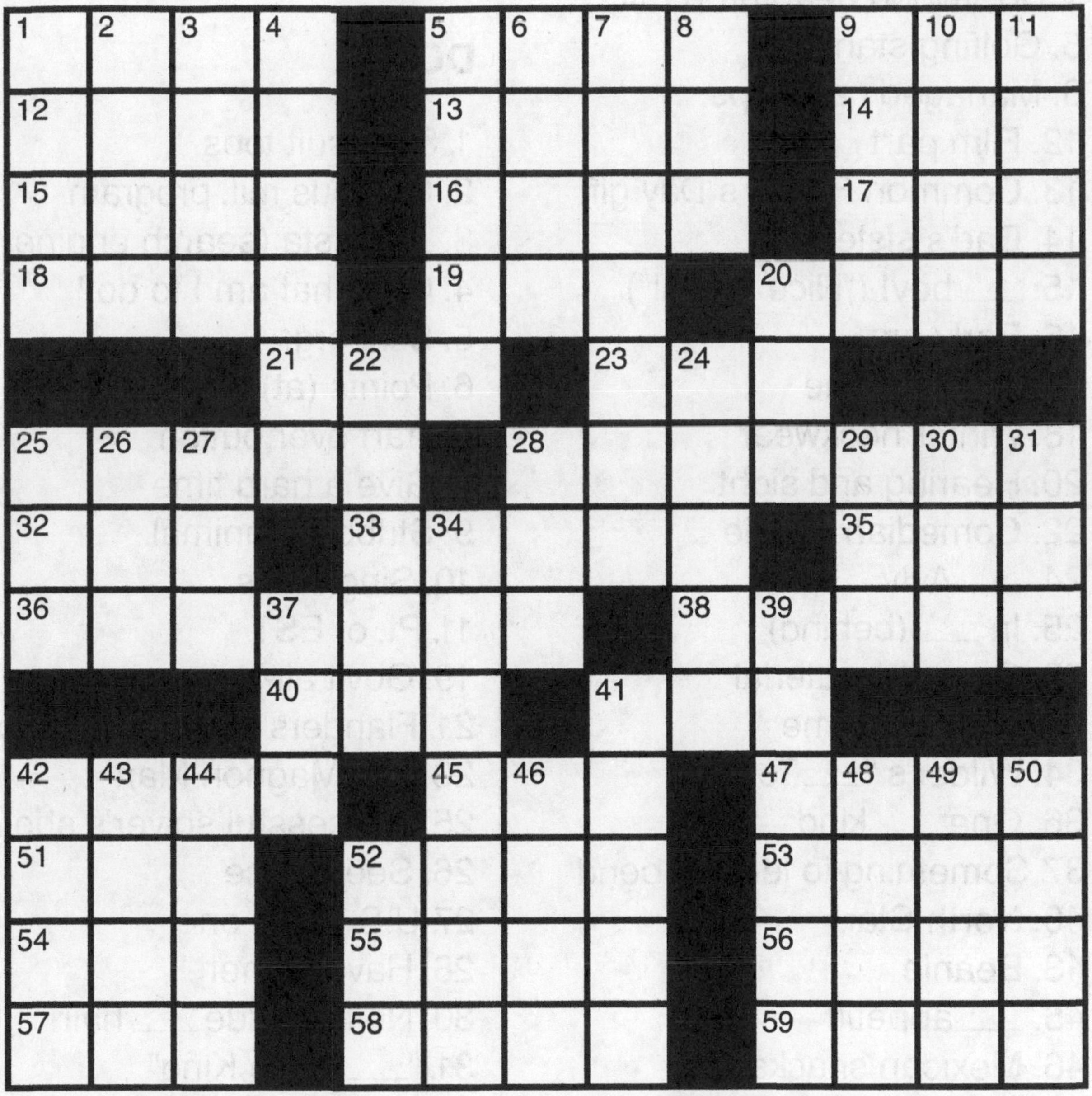

41. Lords and ladies
42. Snake's sound
43. W.W. II turning point
44. Word after boom or Bean
46. Send out, as rays
48. Dance in a grass skirt
49. Sandler of "Big Daddy"
50. Right triangle ratio
52. Rep.'s opponent

ACROSS

1. Hollywood heartthrob Pitt
5. Golfing standard
8. Managed care grps.
12. Film part
13. Common Father's Day gift
14. Dad's sister
15. ___ boy! ("Nice going!")
16. Early hrs.
17. Luge, for one
18. Winter neckwear
20. Hearing and sight
22. Comedian Bernie
24. ___ Aviv
25. In ___ (behind)
29. Overalls material
33. Humble home
34. Wilder's "___ Town"
36. One ___ kind
37. Something to lend or bend
40. North Star
43. Beanie
45. ___ appétit!
46. Mexican snacks
49. Calls a spade a thpade
53. Oliver Twist's request
54. Singing group ___ Na Na
56. Castle encircler
57. Has dinner
58. Comic Conway
59. Friend in war
60. ___ and wherefores
61. Hot springs site
62. Be defeated

DOWN

1. Swimsuit tops
2. Campus mil. program
3. ___ Vista (search engine)
4. Oh, what am I to do?
5. Sch. org.
6. Points (at)
7. Start over button
8. Give a hard time
9. Stubborn animal
10. Singletons
11. Pt. of EST
19. Gov't air-safety org.
21. Flanders of "The Simpsons"
23. ___-Magnon Man
25. Successful solver's shout
26. Seek office
27. U.S. 1, for one
28. Have dinner
30. Neither hide ___ hair
31. "___ Were King"
32. Pas' partners
35. Lowe or Reiner
38. Passwords provide it
39. Word of cheer
41. Texter's guffaw
42. Orwell's "___ Farm"
44. Fence supports
46. Wordwise Webster

Puzzle 6

Solution on Page 315

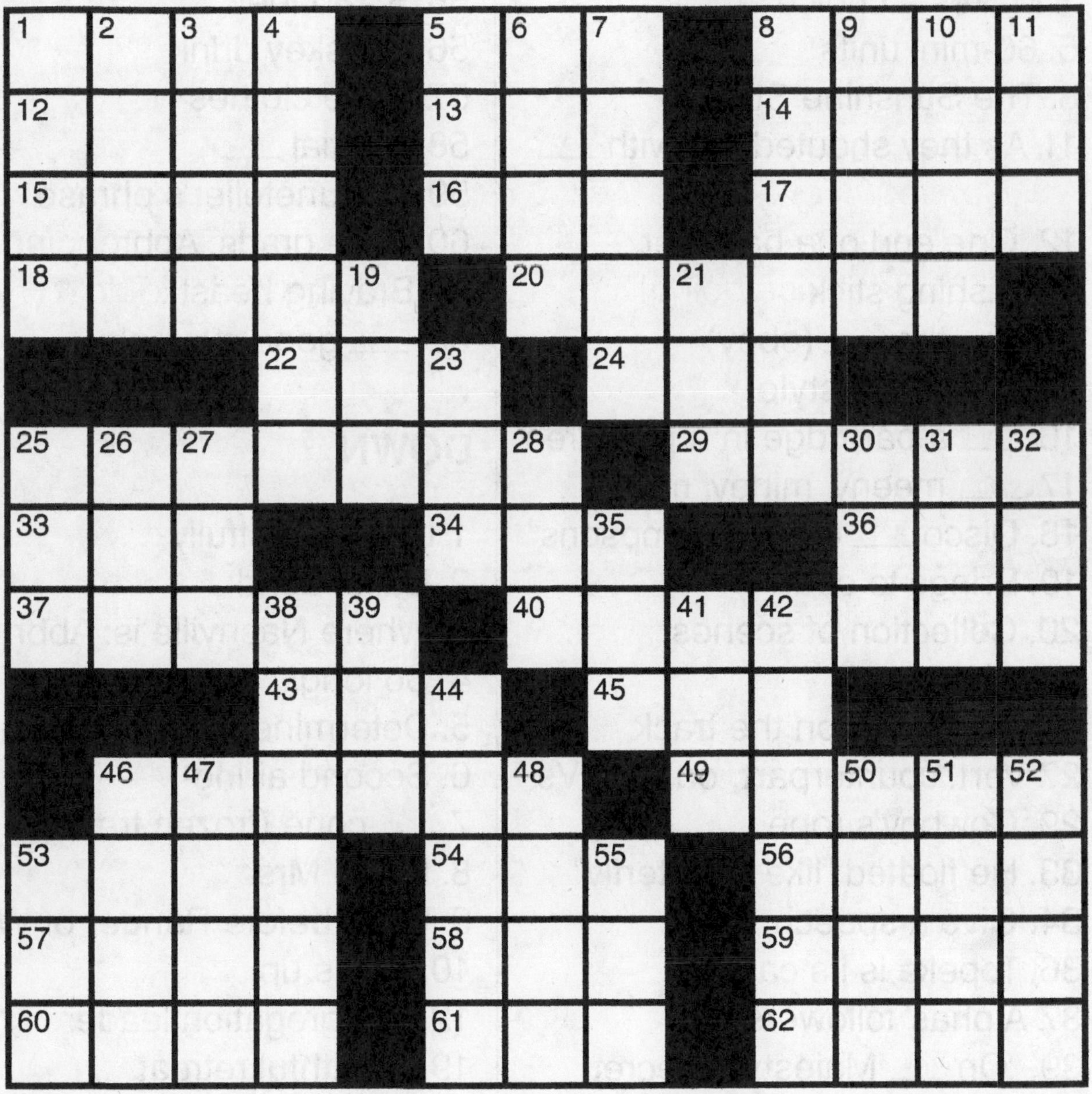

47. Superficially cultured
48. Use UPS, e.g.
50. Unaccompanied performance
51. Buddies
52. Eyelid trouble
53. Kitten's plaint
55. Doctors' grp.

ACROSS

1. Makes a choice
5. 60-min. units
8. The Sunshine St.
11. As they shouted out with ___ . . .
12. One end of a hammer
13. Fishing stick
14. Toe the ___ (obey)
15. Bushy hairstyle
16. ___ a partridge in a pear tree
17. ___, meeny, miney, moe . . .
18. Disco ___ of "The Simpsons"
19. Brings to court
20. Collection of scenes
22. Siesta
24. Full circle, on the track
27. Vert. counterpart, on old TVs
29. Cowboy's rope
33. He floated "like a butterfly"
34. Give a speech
36. Topeka is its cap.
37. Alphas' followers
39. "On ___ Majesty's Secret Service"
40. Stock debut, for short
41. Hairstyling goo
43. From ___ Z (the gamut)
45. Job for Perry Mason
48. Crunched muscles
50. Hawkeye player on "M*A*S*H"
54. "Fourscore and seven years ___ . . ."
55. 5,280 feet
56. Whiskey drink
57. Make clothes
58. Martial ___
59. Fortuneteller's phrase
60. June grads: Abbr.
61. Braying beast
62. ___ good example

DOWN

1. Look at lustfully
2. Ballet bend
3. Where Nashville is: Abbr.
4. So long!
5. Determine weight by lifting
6. Second airing
7. ___-cone (frozen treat)
8. Berlin Mrs.
9. Word before Ranger or Wolf
10. Totals up
12. Congregation leader
19. Healthful retreat
21. Picked
23. Notify
24. Chem class component
25. Drink by the dartboard
26. Cherry seed
28. Stadium cry
30. Glide over snow
31. Gullible person

Puzzle 7

Solution on Page 315

32. The woman of Lennon's 'Woman'
35. Makes fun of
38. Advance in years
42. Lions' dens
44. Desert spring
45. Mama of the Mamas and the Papas
46. Ending for "teen"
47. Scatters, as seed
49. Layered sandwiches, for short
51. Come in last
52. Song for two
53. Side squared, for a square
55. Lamb's bleat

ACROSS

1. Physics particle
4. Barnyard sound
7. Takes too much of a drug
10. Absolutely the best
12. Fuse rating unit
13. Song for a diva
14. Naysayers' words
15. Blouse or shirt
16. Not straight
17. Knotted neckwear
19. Red-tag events
20. Keys in, as data
23. Greyhound vehicle
24. Scorches
25. Most sensible
28. Winter hrs. in L.A.
29. Boy king of Egypt
30. "The Man Who Knew ___ Much"
32. Calm, cool, and collected
35. From another planet
37. CPR expert
38. Thinly populated
39. They're sometimes loaded on the field
42. Knights' titles
43. Lincoln and Vigoda
44. Sink in the middle
45. Leader opposed by the Bolsheviks
49. Vocal pitch
50. A in German 101?
51. Daughters' counterparts
52. Grass in strips
53. Commercials, for example
54. Drill attachment

DOWN

1. Fleming who created 007
2. XXX counterpart
3. U-turn from SSW
4. Spouses
5. Famous cookie maker
6. Software program, for short
7. Hershiser on the mound
8. Eat fancily
9. College entrance exams
11. Perfume compound
13. Lower in esteem
18. Tax agency: Abbr.
19. "Here Comes the ___"
20. Sixth sense, initially
21. Loch ___ monster
22. London's ___ Gallery
23. Cave dweller
25. Take to court
26. Mix (up)
27. Tot's "little piggies"
29. Big bang initials
31. Early afternoon hour
33. Witherspoon of "Walk the Line"
34. Dorothy's aunt and others

Puzzle 8

Solution on Page 315

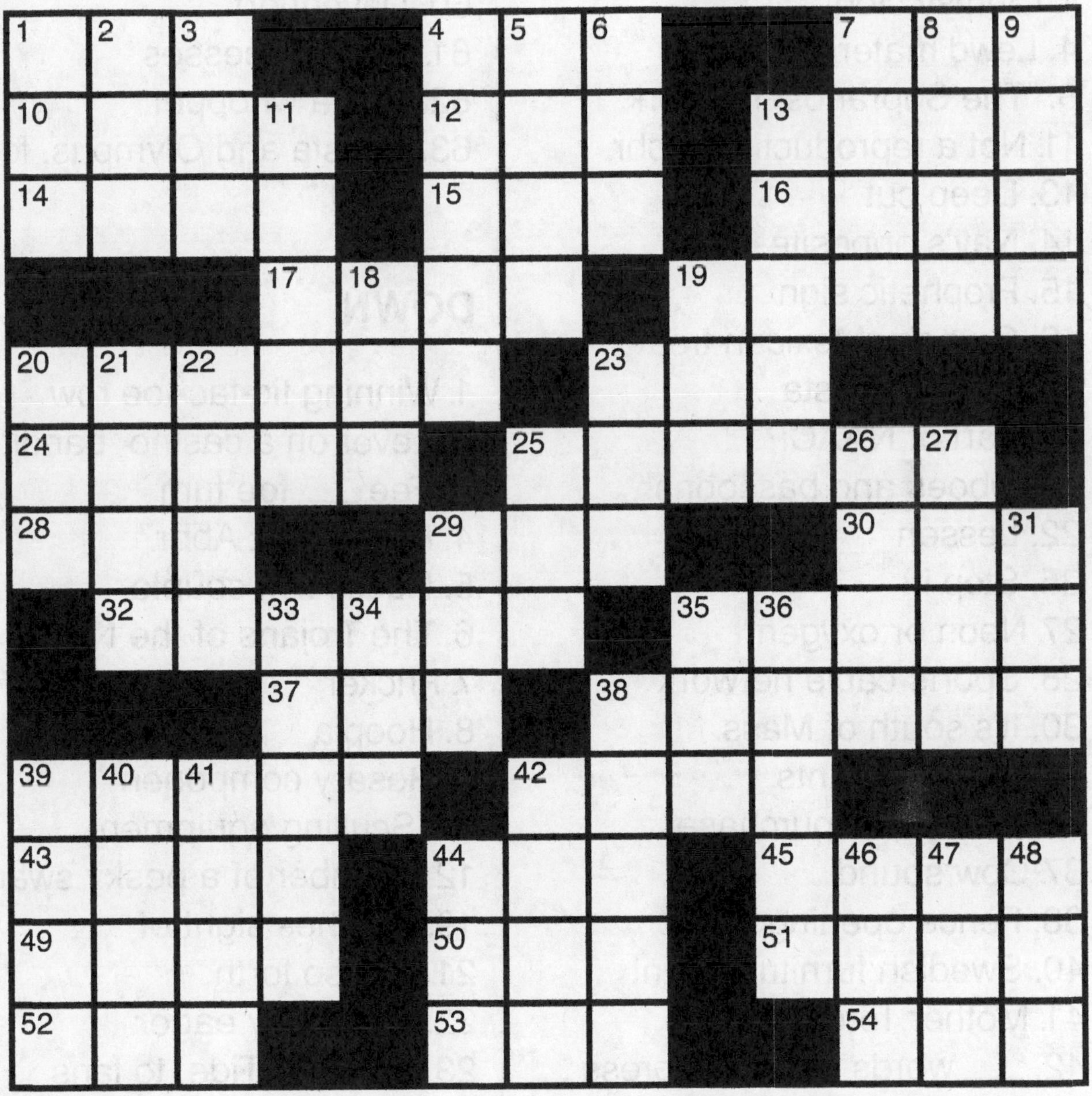

35. Mar. follower
36. Goes on and on
38. Leo and Libra
39. Belfry residents
40. Ending with peek or bug
41. Put in a mailbox
42. Declared
44. Poseidon's realm
46. Cry loudly
47. "Wheel of Fortune" purchase, perhaps
48. Letters after Q

ACROSS

1. Clumsy clod
4. Lewd material
8. "The Sopranos" network
11. Not a reproduction: Abbr.
13. Deep cut
14. Nay's opposite
15. Prophetic sign
16. Crunchy Mexican treat
17. 72, at Augusta
18. Part of NAACP
20. Oboes and bassoons
22. Lessen
25. Stop it!
27. Neon or oxygen
28. Sports cable network
30. It's south of Mass.
34. Mantra chants
35. Post office purchase
37. Cow sound
38. Fence opening
40. Swedish furniture giant
41. Mother Teresa, e.g.
42. ___ words cannot express . . .
44. German wine valley
46. Peacock's walk
49. "The Wizard of Oz" dog
51. "The Raven" poet
52. Internet address opener
54. Pyramid scheme, e.g.
58. Chime in
59. George W. Bush's alma mater
60. Davenport
61. QB's successes
62. Told a whopper
63. Shasta and Olympus, for short

DOWN

1. Winning tic-tac-toe row
2. Lever on a casino "bandit"
3. Fee ___ foe fum
4. Bilko et al.: Abbr.
5. Rustic film couple
6. The Trojans of the N.C.A.A.
7. Pricker
8. Hoopla
9. Rosary component
10. Sculling equipment
12. Member of a pesky swarm
19. Catches sight of
21. And so forth
22. Obviously eager
23. Crimson Tide, to fans
24. Aide: Abbr.
26. This round's ___!
29. Mix together
31. Prefix with present or potent
32. Gerund, e.g.
33. ___ of your business!
36. Role to play
39. Flightless Australian bird

Puzzle 9

Solution on Page 316

43. Gas additive
45. A Ponderosa son
46. Minor quarrel
47. Rocker Rundgren
48. Cincinnati baseball team
50. Newspaper essayist's page
53. Mai ___ cocktail
55. End of many URLs
56. Back, at sea
57. Bell and Kettle, e.g.

ACROSS

1. Supplies with weapons
5. Freudian ___
9. Kitten call
12. Pig in the movies
13. Filly's brother
14. Tree-ring indication
15. Healthful grain
16. Big-eyed birds
17. Mafia
18. Ashes, e.g.
20. Own (up to)
21. Hockey legend Bobby
22. Scoundrel
24. Chicago terminal
27. Fencing call
31. Cuba's ___ of Pigs
32. Gleamed
34. Needle hole
35. Child by marriage
37. Belly button
39. Strong alkali
40. Capts.' subordinates
41. Dramatic presentation
44. Droopy-eared hounds
48. Outdoor parking area
49. No longer worth debating
51. Tennis great Nastase
52. Have supper
53. Abrasive particles
54. Seattle ___ (Triple Crown winner)
55. Grammy winner Winehouse
56. 1/500 of the Indianapolis 500
57. Paves

DOWN

1. Etc., for one
2. Pink, as a steak
3. Degrees for CEOs
4. 12th grader
5. Use an SOS pad
6. Rob of "St. Elmo's Fire"
7. Running a temperature, say
8. Scoreboard nos.
9. Auntie of Broadway
10. They're sometimes inflated
11. Spiders' creations
19. Fancy, as clothes
20. Pharmaceutical watchdog grp.
22. Larry King Live channel
23. Insurance sellers
24. Delivery docs, for short
25. Derby or bowler
26. Affirmative at sea
27. Unit of time
28. Minister: Abbr.
29. Redhead maker
30. Snaky swimmer
33. Garden tool
36. Tissue layer
38. Aid
40. Caffè with hot milk

Puzzle 10

Solution on Page 316

41. Bit of begging
42. Gardener's soil
43. Trial fig.
44. Bring to 212 degrees
45. Jazz great Fitzgerald
46. Part of a wedding cake
47. Makes clothes
49. Leo's studio
50. Either you do it, ___ will!

ACROSS

1. So there!
4. Nurses a drink
8. Give this for that
12. "Wayne's World" negative
13. St. Louis's Gateway ___
14. When tripled, a WWII movie
15. Golly!
16. California's Golden ___ Bridge
17. Cockeyed
18. Will be, to Doris Day
20. Chem. or bio.
22. Puts to work
25. Rigorous exams
29. It's tall when exaggerated
32. Prince's "___ Go Crazy"
34. Grassy field
35. Cheer for a bullfighter
36. Golf shoe gripper
37. Beer keg insert
38. ___ Dieu! (French exclamation)
39. Lyricist with Rodgers
40. Atlas contents
41. Put away for later
43. Swedish auto
45. Surgery sites, for short
47. Condé ___ Publications
50. Farewells
53. H.S. junior's hurdle
56. "___ a Rock": Simon and Garfunkel
58. At ___, soldier!
59. Actress Bancroft
60. Second Amendment rights org.
61. Examines closely
62. Cargo weights
63. Not straight

DOWN

1. Filmmaker Lee
2. Tilling tools
3. Suit to ___
4. Long, drawn-out stories
5. Songwriter Gershwin
6. Agts. usually get 10
7. "___ All That": 1999 film
8. ___-climber (exercise machine)
9. I'm impressed!
10. Incoming flight: Abbr.
11. Salary
19. Golden Girl McClanahan
21. Price to pay
23. Fitzgerald of song
24. Crystal ball users
26. ___ Vista (Internet search engine)
27. Look before you ___
28. Maple fluids
29. Male turkeys
30. That makes ___ of sense
31. Funnyman Jay
33. Toodle-oo

Puzzle 11

Solution on Page 316

36. Sonny's partner, once
40. Wharton degree
42. Kentucky Derby flowers
44. Opening bets
46. Lover's quarrel
48. Croon
49. "Gone with the Wind" estate
50. Spelling competition
51. ___, team!
52. Opposite of WNW
54. ___-cone (summer treat)
55. Advice-giver Landers
57. Indy 500 month

ACROSS

1. Singer Kristofferson
5. Level out the lawn
8. They may be parallel or uneven
12. "___ Rock" (Simon & Garfunkel hit)
13. Mai ___ (tropical drink)
14. Wait just ___!
15. December 24 and 31
16. Part of CST
17. Express relief
18. Dog docs
19. Radiator emanation
21. Kennel sound
24. Arctic barkers
28. Trio before O
31. Clues, to a detective
34. Icky, sticky stuff
35. Wide shoe spec
36. Wigwam relative
37. Negotiator with GM
38. Part of TGIF: Abbr.
39. Make changes to
40. McMahon and Sullivan
41. Voice below alto
43. Quart divs.
45. Gorbachev was its last leader: abbr.
48. Fizzling-out sound
52. Small pieces
55. Sound of a punch
57. That's ___! ("Not true!")
58. ___ of arms
59. Big part of an elephant
60. Word repeated after "Que" in a song
61. Bombs that don't explode
62. Lacking moisture
63. Military lunchroom

DOWN

1. Ukraine's capital
2. Glowing review
3. "How ___ Your Mother": CBS sitcom
4. Smart-mouthed
5. Everest and St. Helens
6. Courtroom pledge
7. Ample, as a doorway
8. Moisten while cooking
9. Do ___ say, . . .
10. Alternative to unleaded (abbr.)
11. Jr. high, e.g.
20. State with confidence
22. Sacrificial sites
23. Orange throwaway
25. Flulike symptoms
26. Put bullets in
27. Spreads seed
28. Not right
29. A ___ pittance: very little
30. Opposite of "ja"

Puzzle 12

Solution on Page 316

32. It may have 2 BRs
33. Not shallow
42. Removes from office
44. Involuntary twitch
46. Risked a ticket
47. Crowd noise
49. Turn tail
50. Needle-bearing trees
51. 4:00 socials
52. String after A
53. Promissory initials
54. Itsy bit
56. Twisted, as humor

ACROSS

1. Sizable sandwich
4. Every little bit
7. State frankly
11. Breakfasted, e.g.
12. Canoe or kayak
14. Beep with a beeper
15. ___ and caboodle
16. Feel the ___
17. Sword handle
18. Pass, as time
20. Flared skirts
22. Cooped clucker
23. Writing tablet
24. Check someone's ID
27. "The ___ Squad" of 1960s/1970s TV
28. Menagerie
31. Magnum ___: great work
32. Except that
33. Stick-shift selection
34. Tent pin
35. Land of ___
36. Whistle blowers
37. Rock's ___ Lobos
38. Cell "messenger," briefly
40. Tibetans and Thais
43. A large quantity
47. Angry outburst
48. Prefix with distant or lateral
50. John Denver's 'Thank God ___ Country Boy'
51. Bygone picture weekly
52. Studio stages
53. Meditative sounds
54. Landfill's emanation
55. Susan of "The Partridge Family"
56. Bill ___, TV's Science Guy

DOWN

1. Hot Japanese drink
2. Power co.
3. Alpha, ___, gamma
4. Treat badly
5. "Two Women" star Sophia
6. Fall (behind)
7. Garden insect
8. Conceited
9. Look at amorously
10. Soaks
13. Kitchen whistler
19. Advanced degrees
21. Young guy
24. Speeder stopper
25. Tarzan raiser
26. Alternative to a bare floor
27. Wet ground
28. Closing letter
29. Clumsy type
30. Sterile hosp. areas
32. Supervisors
33. Cap and gown wearer

Puzzle 13

Solution on Page 317

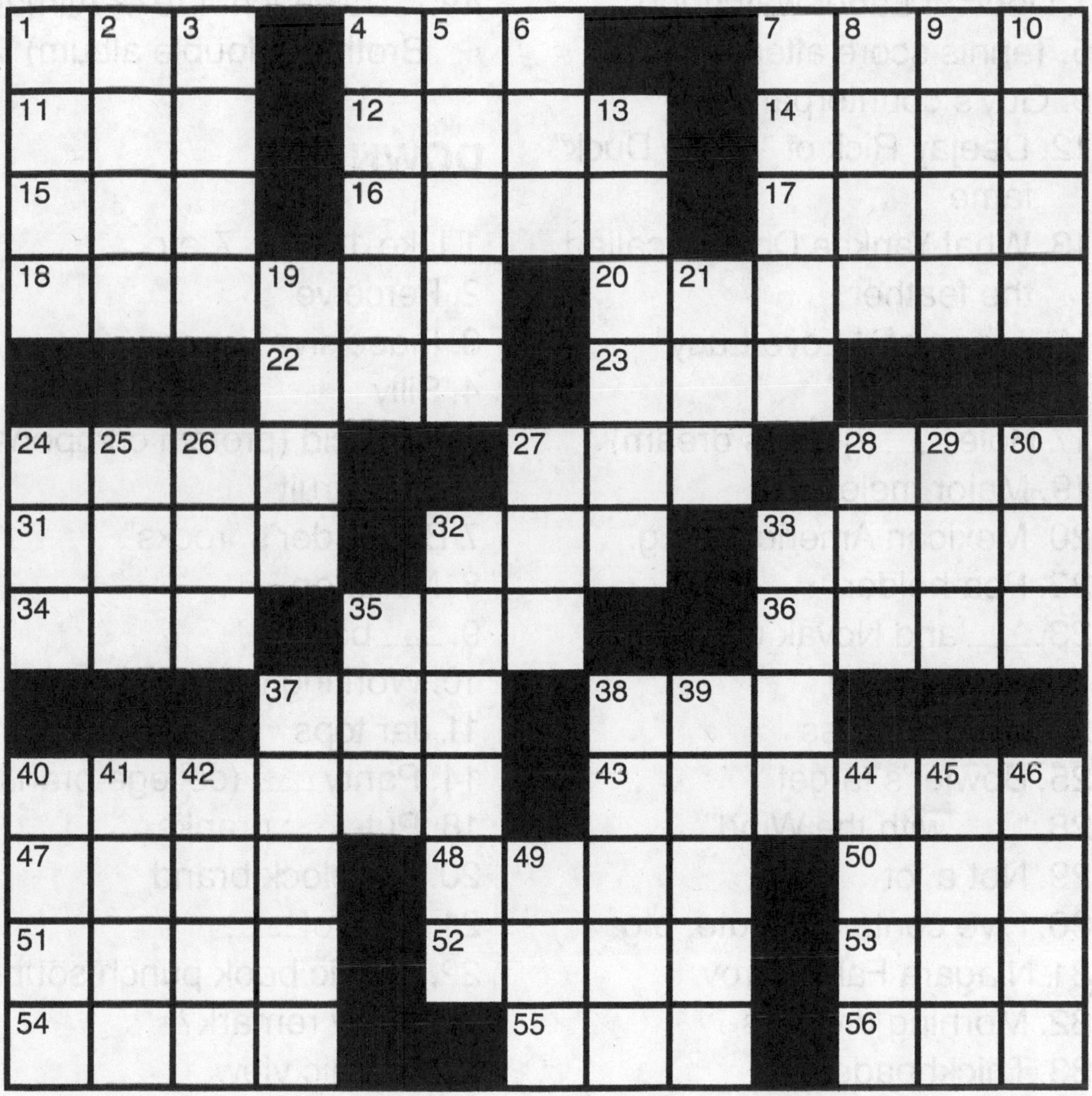

35. Smoking or ___? (waiter's query)
37. Bye for now
38. MapQuest offering
39. Clamorous
40. Woody Guthrie's son
41. Verbalized
42. Data
44. Animal on England's shield
45. Television award
46. Submission encl.
49. End of a proof

ACROSS

1. Dept. of Labor watchdog
5. Tennis score after deuce
9. Guy's counterpart
12. Deejay Rick of "Disco Duck" fame
13. What Yankee Doodle called the feather
15. Arnaz of "I Love Lucy"
16. Repeated
17. Hole ___ (golfer's dream)
19. Major melees
20. Mexican American, e.g.
22. Pea holder
23. ___ and Novak (old news partnership)
24. Cut the grass
25. Bowler's target
28. "___ with the Wind"
29. Not a lot
30. Five cents a minute, e.g.
31. Niagara Falls's prov.
32. Morning droplets
33. Thickheaded
34. Yank's war foe
35. Put in more ammo
36. Sink outlet
39. Laser printer powder
40. Breathers
42. Org. for those 50+
45. Greasy spoons
46. Self-satisfied
47. Wedding vow
48. Prefix with potent or present
49. "___ Peach" (1972 Allman Brothers double album)

DOWN

1. Like 1, 3, 5, 7, etc.
2. Perceive
3. Indecisive
4. Silly
5. ___ acid (protein component)
6. Palm fruit
7. Bartender's "rocks"
8. Not wide
9. ___ bat for
10. Working without ___
11. Jar tops
14. Panty ___ (college prank)
18. Put-___: pranks
20. Toy block brand
21. Bard of ___
22. Comic book punch sound
24. Catty remark?
25. Scenic view
26. "___ Wonderful Life"
27. If ___ be
29. Leap day's mo.
30. Let go
32. Robert of "Goodfellas"
33. Lion's lair
34. Ready to harvest
35. Martini & ___ vermouth

Puzzle 14

Solution on Page 317

36. Three, in Bonn
37. Enjoy a book
38. Marching ___ war
39. Adult-to-be
41. Actor Robbins
43. Wagon track
44. Tiger Woods' grp.

ACROSS

1. Go by plane
4. Tell all
8. Meat inspection org.
12. Gambling cube
13. Score before 15
14. Sentence subject, usually
15. Materialized
17. Combination ___
18. Marvel Comics group
19. Ship of Columbus
20. Glide on the ice
23. Coated with gold
25. Crown prince, e.g.
26. McEntire of country music
27. Day-___: pigment brand
30. Make one's blood boil
32. Like slanted type
34. Myrna of "Love Crazy"
35. Comic Foxx
37. Make the acquaintance of
38. Rouse from slumber
39. Enthusiastic, as an attitude
40. Liable to make one scratch
43. Grand Canyon St.
45. Round roof
46. Guards
50. Frankenstein's assistant
51. Honeybee's home
52. The Windy City, for short
53. Sold, to an auctioneer
54. Owner's proof
55. Tea holder

DOWN

1. Govt. watchdog
2. Fresh talk
3. Slangy affirmative
4. Point the finger at
5. Handed-down stories
6. Exact retribution for
7. Fourposter, e.g.
8. Not yet burning
9. In a minute
10. Air passage
11. "Puppy Love" singer Paul
16. Movie crowd member
19. Developer's map
20. Poet Silverstein
21. Game similar to lotto
22. Breezy
24. Term paper abbr.
26. Smell horrible
27. Campbell of country
28. Emulated Pinocchio
29. Prefix with -pus
31. Battleship shade
33. Astound
36. Honeybunch
38. . . . ___ angels fear to tread
39. Referred to
40. Beatnik's "Gotcha!"

Puzzle 15

Solution on Page 317

41. Like takeout orders
42. Let's go!
44. Wander about
46. Grad student's goal, perhaps
47. L times VI
48. Day before Fri.
49. Imbibe slowly

ACROSS

1. Rolls of bills
5. Rather of news
8. Be with you in a coupla ___
12. Farming unit
13. "One Day ___ Time"
14. Salty drop
15. Not imaginary
16. Have we ___?
17. Four-footed friends
18. U2 guitarist (with "The")
19. Get caught in ___
21. Tools with teeth
24. Shoulder bag feature
28. Sawyer or Seaver
31. Director Spike
32. Capital of South Korea
33. Eats away
35. Terrapin, e.g.
36. Word before and after say
37. Buzzer in a hive
38. Not even
39. Refine, as metal
40. One more thing . . .
42. Fox Sports alternative
44. Put blacktop on
48. Gofer: Abbr.
51. Listening organ
53. Dry, as a desert
54. Enclosure with a MS.
55. Genetic material, for short
56. "Penny ___" (1967 Beatles chart-topper)
57. Gorillas
58. Off one's rocker
59. British weapon of WWII

DOWN

1. Suffix with hard or soft
2. Got a perfect score on
3. Race for hot rods
4. Tennis great Monica
5. River blocker
6. Relax, soldier!
7. Part of NBC: Abbr.
8. Heaven's gatekeeper
9. Wide shoe width
10. Manx or Siamese
11. Soon-to-be grads: Abbr.
20. Debate topics
22. Warnings
23. Thriller director Craven
25. ___-Rooter
26. "___ Lang Syne"
27. Answered a charge in court
28. ___ of thousands
29. City NNW of Provo
30. Change location
34. Removes
35. Address book no.
37. Monkey treat
41. Iridescent gems

Puzzle 16

Solution on Page 317

43. Salon job, informally
45. Smell ___ (be leery)
46. Tarzan's transport
47. Barbara of "I Dream of Jeannie"
48. Gentle ___ lamb
49. Tree liquid
50. Opposite of NNW
52. Awesome, dude!

ACROSS

1. NNW opposite
4. Palindromic Gardner
7. Cousin of a frog
11. Raised railways
12. Eyelid attachment
14. Hold ___ your hat!
15. Developer's land unit
16. Dog food brand
17. Color lightly
18. J. Edgar Hoover's gp.
19. Christmas greenery
21. Word before ring or swing
23. Tiny Dickens boy
24. Dressed (in)
26. Color shade
27. Mind-reading ability, for short
30. Take painful steps
34. Go after in court
35. Floor application
36. D.C. fund-raisers
37. Former Russian space station
38. Mix, as a salad
40. Cinderella stepsister
44. Part of an iceberg that's visible
47. Cooking grease
48. Get out of here!
49. Billy Joel's "___ to Extremes"
50. Get ___ shape
51. Having no doubt
52. KFC's Sanders, e.g.
53. Santa's sackful
54. "___ Boot" (1981 war film)
55. Arch city: Abbr.

DOWN

1. Egotist's love
2. Messy type
3. Body shop figure
4. Remember the ___!
5. Legitimate
6. Venomous snakes
7. Pole carving
8. Words after step or sleep
9. ___ point (never)
10. Lavish affection (on)
13. Sociable soaking spot
20. In ___ of (replacing)
22. Poem of praise
24. "48 Hours" network
25. "Ally McBeal" actress Lucy
26. Put a spell on
27. Stretchables
28. 1/60 of a min.
29. Score components: Abbr.
31. Twerp
32. Bother continually
33. Precursor of CDs
37. Forerunner of Windows
38. Pageant crown
39. Singers Hall and ___
40. Landed (on)

Puzzle 17

Solution on Page 318

41. iPod type
42. Like many independent films
43. Mideast missile
45. Gershwin's "___ Rhythm"
46. Gallup specialty

ACROSS

1. "Monday Night Football" network
4. Halloween's mo.
7. Conniptions
11. Fan's rebuke
12. Middling grades
14. One-spot cards
15. URL ending
16. Gomer Pyle's org.
17. Lighter-___-air
18. Makes tough
20. Stock page heading: Abbr.
22. Alda of "What Women Want"
23. Here's to you! and others
27. Sweater wool
29. Skin art
30. Feathered neckwear
31. It's boring to be in one
32. Brings together
36. Nasty looks
39. Renter
40. Le Pew of skunkdom
41. Fish-to-be
42. Christie of mystery
45. Pre-calc course
48. Poet Pound
50. Gear part
51. Sweep under the rug
52. Walt Whitman, for one
53. Civil War prez
54. Leave out
55. ___ to Billie Joe
56. Reel partner

DOWN

1. Grade-school basics
2. Cowboy's footwear
3. Say what?
4. Eye-related
5. Big name in small planes
6. President pro ___
7. Rich dude
8. Freud's "I"
9. Drink "for two"
10. IRS ID
13. Actor George C.
19. "Telephone Line" rock grp.
21. ___ man: unanimously
24. San Francisco transport
25. Military stint
26. Tipplers
27. Be adjacent to
28. ___ of the above
33. Dartboard, for one
34. Brian of rock music
35. Prepare, as tea
36. Dealt leniently with
37. Make null and void
38. Fed. pollution monitor
43. Boxcar rider
44. Got older

Puzzle 18

Solution on Page 318

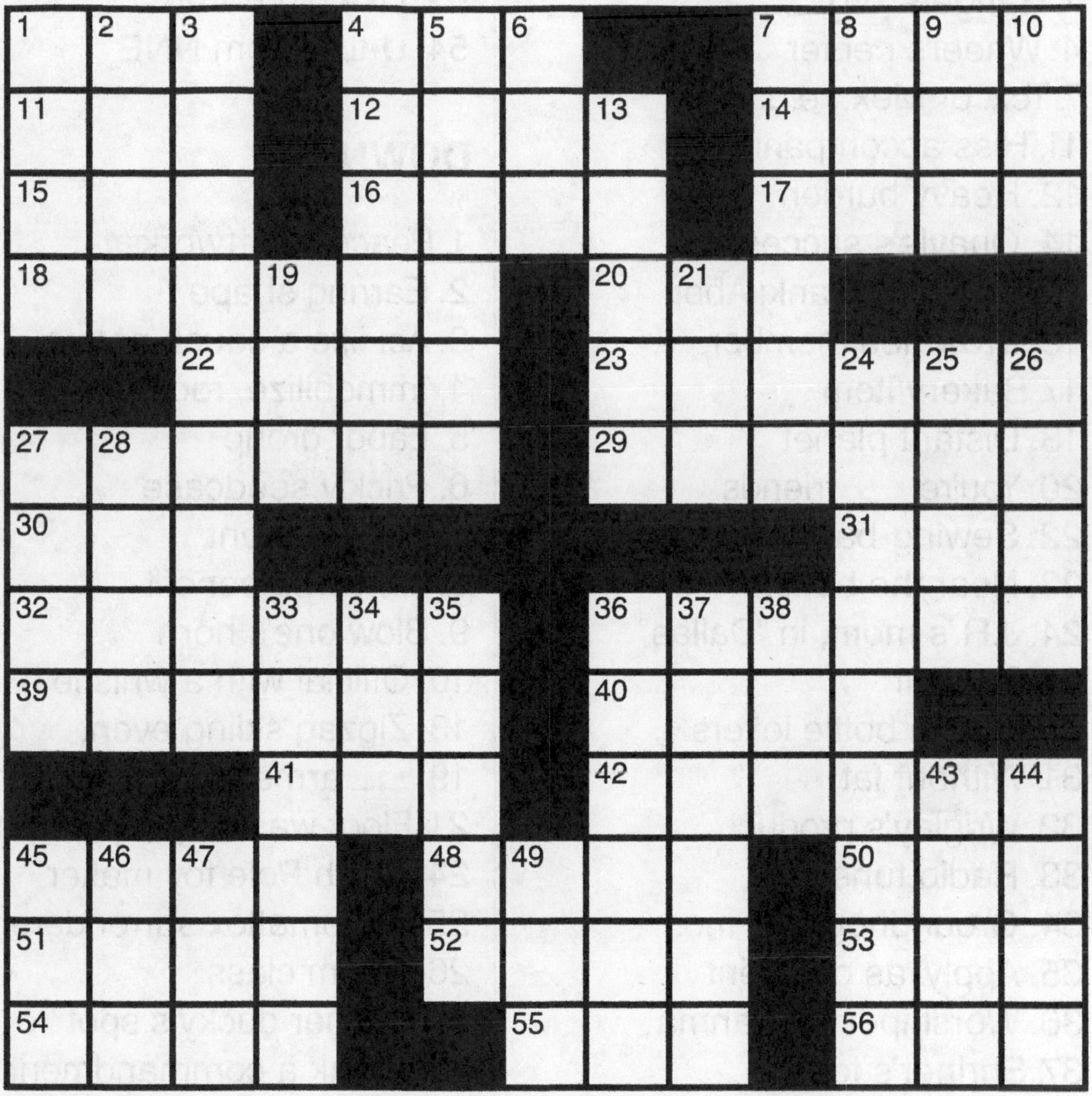

45. Even if, informally
46. What an air ball doesn't touch
47. General Amin
49. Dr. Seuss' "If I Ran the ___"

ACROSS

1. Rangers' org.
4. Wheel's center
7. Tex. or Mex., e.g.
11. Hiss accompanier
12. Heavy burden
14. Quayle's successor
15. Mustard's rank: Abbr.
16. Brownies member
17. Bakery item
18. Distant planet
20. You're ___ friends
22. Sewing-basket item
23. Near the bottom
24. J.R.'s mom, in "Dallas"
27. Summit
28. Beach bottle letters
31. Without fat
32. Wrigley's product
33. Radio tuner
34. Groundhog Day mo.
35. Apply, as ointment
36. Worshiper of Brahma
37. Shriner's topper
38. Mediocre mark
39. Moon stage
41. ___ in the court!
44. Group voting the same way
45. Cute porker of film fame
47. Trim
49. Price paid
50. Yours and mine
51. CEO's degree, maybe
52. Salon colorings
53. Like old Paree
54. U-turn from NNE

DOWN

1. Peacock network
2. Earring shape
3. Act like a couch potato
4. Immobilize, rodeo-style
5. Labor group
6. Prickly seedcase
7. Incandescent
8. Welcome benefit
9. Blow one's horn
10. Official with a whistle
13. Zigzag skiing event
19. ___ arms
21. Floor-washing implement
24. North Pole toy maker
25. Appomattox surrenderer
26. Chem class
27. Rubber ducky's spot
28. Break a commandment
29. Paper holder
30. Wintertime bug
32. Garden structure
33. Fizzled out
35. ___ Moines
36. Religious dissent
37. Sergeant Friday's request
38. Snake charmer's snake

Puzzle 19

Solution on Page 318

39. Clever tactic
40. Socks and such
42. Shady giants
43. Steals from
44. Alphabetic trio
46. Mo. without a holiday
48. Cat's foot

ACROSS

1. Stuff (in)
5. Ale server
8. Homecoming attender
12. Filly's father
13. 180° from WNW
14. Completely demolish
15. Look-alike
18. Window framework
19. Wire measurement
20. "___ Lang Syne"
23. Nasty looks
27. Halloween word
30. Tranquilizer gun projectile
32. Shredded side dish
33. Works
35. Agreeable response
36. Dreamcast game company
37. The "A" of I.R.A.: Abbr.
38. Swedish car
40. Fido's doc
41. Grain bundle
43. Talking equine of TV
45. "___ Sawyer"
47. Speak highly of
50. Coin motto
56. King of Shakespeare
57. 1960s war zone, briefly
58. Chinese: Comb. form
59. Fortune's partner
60. Double-curve letter
61. Crammer's concern

DOWN

1. CBS police series
2. Clears (of)
3. Carpeting calculation
4. High-I.Q. group
5. I. M. the architect
6. The Trojans of the NCAA
7. Smile from ear to ear
8. Lacking guile
9. Attorney's profession
10. Israeli arm
11. Stag party attendees
16. Dull impact sound
17. Rapper ___ Wayne
21. Puts down
22. Bedtime story?
24. Abbr. on a contour map
25. All the ___: widely popular
26. Whack
27. Arm: Fr.
28. Toe stubber's cry
29. ___ upon a time
31. Ivan the Terrible, e.g.
34. Level of achievement
39. Gamblers place them
42. Part of F.Y.I.
44. Put out, as a fire
46. Selfish one's exclamation
48. Operating system developed at Bell Labs
49. Bluefin, for one
50. Santa's helper

Puzzle 20

Solution on Page 318

51. Shooter pellet
52. On the ___: fleeing
53. Kind of relief
54. Vocal stumbles
55. Hi ___! (fan's message)

ACROSS

1. Mega- or giga- ending
5. Flow back, as the tide
8. Ten to one, e.g.
12. Luminous radiation
13. Educators' org.
14. Choo-choo's sound
15. Med. care choices
16. Diner's bill
17. Turnpike charge
18. Literary spoof
20. Cognizant (of)
22. Continent north of Afr.
23. Use an oar
24. Appetizer
28. Artist's prop
32. Sort of suffix
33. Potato chip accompaniment
35. Deli bread
36. Mexican moolah
39. Holy
42. Org. in Tom Clancy books
44. Approximate no.
45. Ringo of the Beatles
47. Horizontally
51. Oahu wreaths
52. Negatives
54. Oops!
55. Roof's edge
56. Reverent respect
57. "The Simpsons" girl
58. Ex-QB Aikman
59. A's opposite, in England
60. Weaver's apparatus

DOWN

1. Scroogean outbursts
2. City WSW of Phoenix
3. Harness race gait
4. Less difficult
5. Came in
6. Arthur of "Maude"
7. Elephant of children's lit
8. Canada's capital
9. Place for a peephole
10. Loser to Clinton in 1996
11. Cardinals' home: Abbr.
19. Tiresome grind
21. Deep distress
24. Nurse a drink
25. When doubled, an African fly
26. Relieved sounds
27. Chest protector
29. Former jrs.
30. Optometrist's interest
31. Paved the way
34. Delighted
37. Irish dramatist Sean
38. "To ___, with Love"
40. PC "Go back!" key
41. Leisurely walk
43. "I Love Lucy" star
45. Blacken, as a steak
46. DVR brand

Puzzle 21

Solution on Page 319

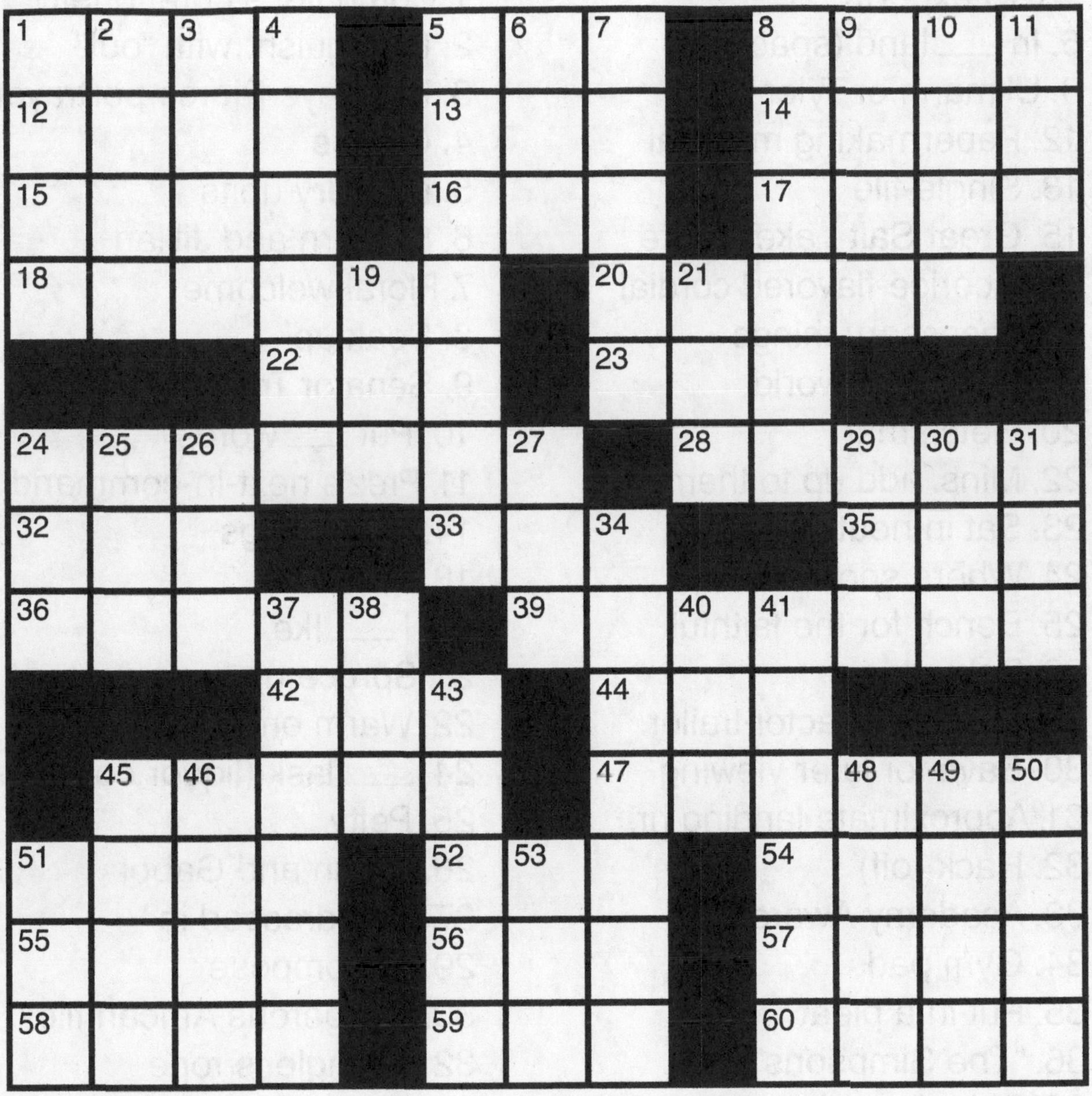

48. Home of the Buckeyes
49. Just okay
50. Sam the ___ and the Pharaohs
51. The Beatles' "___ It Be"
53. Have debts

ACROSS

1. IRS experts
5. In ___ land (spacey)
9. Ullmann or Tyler
12. Papermaking material
13. Single-file
15. Great Salt Lake's state
16. Licorice-flavored cordial
17. Necessary things
19. ___ of the world
20. Gets smart
22. Mins. add up to them
23. Sat in neutral
24. Where spokes meet
25. Bench for the faithful
28. Baby goats
29. Trucker's tractor-trailer
30. Save for later viewing
31. Approximate landing hr.
32. Hack (off)
33. Academy Award
34. Gym pad
35. Put in a pleat
36. "The Simpsons" dad
39. Shindig
40. Quick joke
42. Takes to court
45. Place to pull over
46. That green feeling
47. Disease research org.
48. Pucker-producing
49. . . . ___ and not heard

DOWN

1. Computer's core, briefly
2. Extinguish, with "out"
3. Hawkeye Pierce portrayer
4. Globes
5. Laundry units
6. Sothern and Jillian
7. Floral welcome
8. Soak up
9. Senator Trent
10. Put ___ words
11. Prez's next-in-command
14. Hankerings
18. Finish up
20. I ___ Ike
21. Spruce up a manuscript
22. Warm embrace
24. ___ flask (liquor container)
25. Petty
26. Braun and Gabor
27. Was dressed in
29. Decompose
30. Dangerous African flies
32. Wrangler's rope
33. Bruin Bobby
34. Unfreeze
35. Diamond weight
36. Traffic jam honker
37. "The ___ Love" (R.E.M. hit)
38. Open-textured fabric
39. Use a spyglass
41. Gun owners' org.

Puzzle 22

Solution on Page 319

43. Night before a holiday
44. Opposite of ant.

ACROSS

1. Just misses, as a putt
5. Source of PIN money?
8. Jackson 5 hairdo
12. Don't worry about me
13. Revolutionary Guevara
14. Picnic side dish
15. Sandy hill
16. Visibly embarrassed
17. In one's right mind
18. Alaska native
20. Changes, as the Constitution
22. Catch, as a criminal
23. Football's Dawson
24. Victoria's Secret purchase
27. Boxer's punch
29. Face-valued, as stocks
33. Oxen coupler
35. Wed. preceder
37. Big hauler
38. Pass, as legislation
40. Old horse
42. Engine speed, for short
43. The "L" of L.A.
45. R-V link
47. Slot-machine site
50. Throat extract, at times
54. Right away, on a memo
55. SSW's opposite
57. ___ cost (free)
58. PIN points
59. Berlin's land: Abbr.
60. Ladder step
61. Winning margin, sometimes
62. ___ Luis Obispo
63. Retailer's gds.

DOWN

1. Hitchhiker's need
2. Radio talk show host Don
3. Man in a robe
4. Coil of yarn
5. Circus performer
6. "For Whom ___ Bell Tolls"
7. Olympic award
8. Says yes
9. Custard dessert
10. ___ McNally (atlas publisher)
11. Is in debt
19. Capt.'s superior
21. ___ culpa (my fault)
24. See you later
25. Howard of "Happy Days"
26. Letters before a pseudonym
28. Hamburger holder
30. The "p" in m.p.g.
31. Stereo component
32. Canyon edge
34. Lunar or solar event
36. Part of EDT
39. Like a ___ of bricks
41. Classic Pontiac
44. Musical numbers
46. Deprive of weapons

Puzzle 23

Solution on Page 319

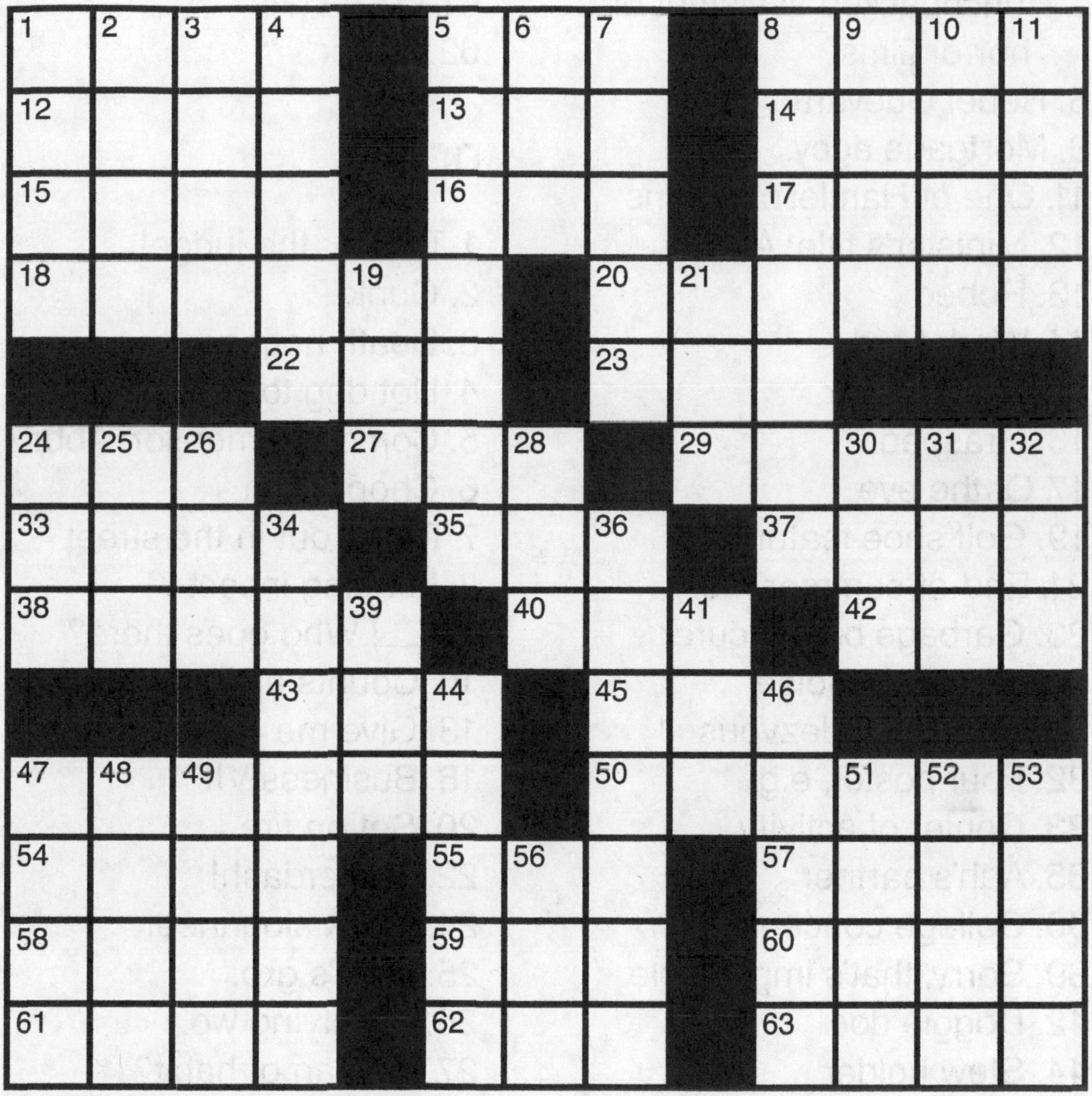

47. Misery costar James
48. Concerning, in a memo
49. ___ Club (retail chain)
51. Poker variety
52. B&Bs
53. Part of the mezzanine
56. Cultural support org.

ACROSS

1. Hunchbacked assistant of horror films
5. Rebel Guevara
8. Mortgage agcy.
11. One of Hamlet's options
12. Minister's title: Abbr.
13. Robed
14. Work hard
15. Light starter
16. Grasped
17. Of the eye
19. Golf shoe features
21. End-of-summer mo.
23. Garbage bag securer
24. Man from Boise
28. Lovers' rendezvous
32. Four-poster, e.g.
33. Center of activity
35. Aah's partner
36. College concentration
39. Sorry, that's impossible
42. Doggie doc
44. Stew holder
45. Cornell's home
48. Samuel with a code
52. Pop singer Collins
53. Studio that made "Notorious"
56. Treadmill unit
57. On the ___ (bickering)
58. What Eve was formed from
59. Optimistic words
60. Letters after a cavity filler's name
61. QB's stats
62. Xerox

DOWN

1. Tell ___ the judge!
2. Gunk
3. Death notice
4. Hot dog topper
5. Computer monitor: Abbr.
6. Chop down
7. Throw out in the street
8. Leaping insect
9. ___! Who goes there?
10. Counts up
13. Give me an A . . . , e.g.
18. Business VIP
20. Set on fire
22. Balderdash!
24. Think sloganeer
25. Narc's grp.
26. Modifying wd.
27. Woman of habit?
29. Over there, poetically
30. Lawn base
31. Nevertheless
34. Hit on the head
37. Racetrack shapes
38. Kind of room or hall
40. Dot-___ (Internet company)
41. Part of AEC

Puzzle 24

Solution on Page 319

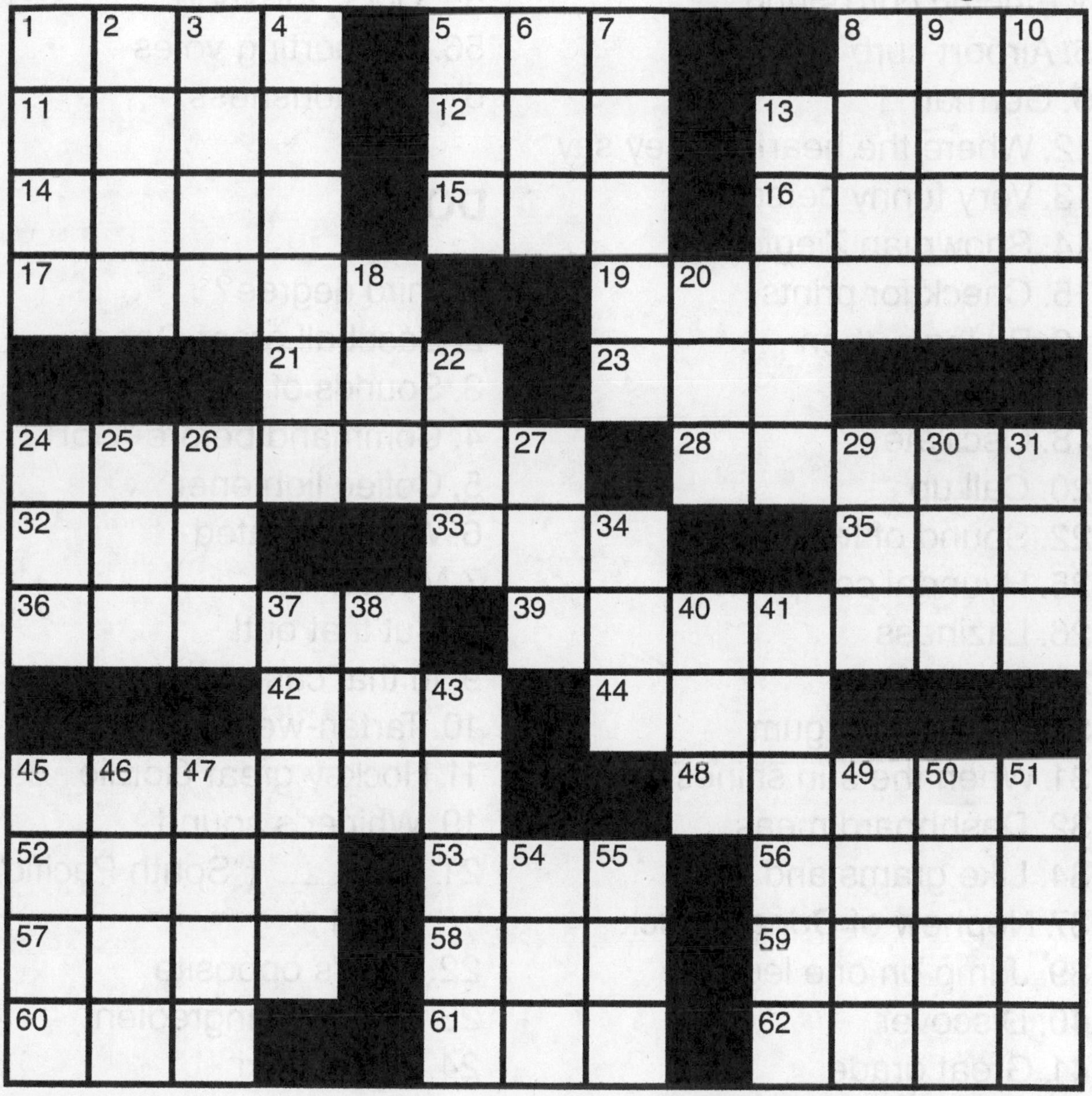

43. Loiter
45. Apple MP3 player
46. Impact sound
47. Top 40 songs
49. Puerto follower
50. Sharp blow
51. ___, meeny, miney, mo
54. Young goat
55. Docs for pregnant women

ACROSS

1. Electric cord's end
5. Airport curb queue
9. German "I"
12. Where the heart is, they say
13. Very funny person
14. Showman Ziegfeld
15. Check for prints
16. By logic, then . . .
17. Logging tool
18. Oscillate
20. Call up
22. Sound of fright
25. Hyundai competitor
26. Laziness
27. Small size
30. Mouthful of gum
31. When the sun shines
32. Dashboard meas.
34. Like grams and liters
37. Nephew of Donald Duck
39. Jump on one leg
40. Discover
41. Great grade
44. Cold war defense grp.
45. "Back to the Future" actress Thompson
46. A bit cracked?
48. Abide by
52. Brain wave reading: Abbr.
53. Noose material
54. Far-side-of-the-moon photographer of 1959
55. Docs, for short
56. Supporting votes
57. Covetousness

DOWN

1. Third degree?
2. Baseball great Gehrig
3. Sounds of indecision
4. Command before "Go!"
5. Coffee lightener
6. Well-ventilated
7. Morass
8. Cut that out!
9. In that case
10. Tartan-wearing group
11. Hockey great Gordie
19. Whiner's sound
21. "Bali ___" ("South Pacific" song)
22. NNE's opposite
23. Chowder ingredient
24. Took a taxi
25. B flat, for one
27. Campaign contributor, maybe
28. T on a test
29. DeMille-like film
31. Quick swim
33. He earns his pay at Shea
35. Cal. heading
36. Prayer beads

Puzzle 25

Solution on Page 320

37. Give permission
38. Peter of "My Favorite Year"
40. Tempts fate
41. Shake ___!
42. Chick's cry
43. Falls behind
44. California wine valley
47. Montana or Louis
49. Prim do
50. SASE part
51. Yippee!

ACROSS

1. Pvts.' bosses
5. Lassies' partners
9. Cut off, as branches
12. Guinness who played Obi-Wan Kenobi
13. Cain's brother
14. One thing ___ time
15. Lymph bump
16. The Bruins of the Pac Ten
17. ___ Pan Alley
18. Yes signal
20. God ___ America
22. Become narrower
25. ___ it seems . . .
27. Put ___ good word for
28. "Ali ___ and the Forty Thieves"
30. Country crooner McEntire
34. Say no to
36. Thanksgiving mo.
37. Oh, heck!
38. Suffix with marion
39. Near-failing grades
41. Cleanse (of)
42. Hawaiian neckwear
44. Actress Moorehead
46. Talks hoarsely
49. Big bird from Down Under
50. Pub draught
51. Where Anna met the king
54. Perón and Gabor
58. Writing implement
59. Legal rights grp.
60. Scotch and ___
61. Rank above cpl.
62. Thumbs-up votes
63. Like molasses

DOWN

1. ___ Fernando Valley
2. Mop & ___: floor cleaner
3. Mack or Koppel
4. Movie division
5. Shower with praise
6. Alphabetical network
7. Tierra ___ Fuego
8. Thick chunks
9. Better ___ than never
10. Elevator company
11. Thumbs-down reviews
19. Celestial body
21. "___ of the Flies"
22. It waits for no man
23. Operating without ___ (taking risks)
24. Breathe hard
25. Double reeds
26. Great review
29. Me, myself, ___
31. Make, as an income
32. Cheese with a moldy rind
33. No ifs, ___, or buts
35. Sharp bark

Puzzle 26

Solution on Page 320

40. TV reporter Donaldson
43. High-school composition
45. Surmise
46. Performs like Ice-T
47. Words after shake or break
48. Put in the mail
49. Grounded Australian birds
52. Freezer cubes
53. Pie ___ mode
55. TV control abbr.
56. Noisy commotion
57. Logger's tool

ACROSS

1. It might say WELCOME
4. Wastes, in mob slang
8. Ladder rung
12. Bread for a ham sandwich
13. "___ Ha'i" ("South Pacific" song)
14. Early late-night host
15. Poster paints
17. Palo ___, Calif.
18. Hurricane centers
19. Use an iron
20. Sail holders
23. Tortoise's race opponent
25. I can't believe ___ the whole thing!
26. Trig term
27. Gun rights org.
30. Pleasantly concise
33. 180 degrees from NNE
34. Tetra- doubled
35. Radio letters
36. Frat recruiting event
37. Actress Glenn
38. Modern surgical tool
41. Great Caesar's ghost!
43. Landers and Sothern
44. Sitcom segments
48. Funny sketch
49. Bygone days
50. Exerciser's unit
51. Maple syrup fluids
52. Poker starter
53. Cloud backdrop

DOWN

1. "The A-Team" star
2. Favorable vote
3. Pro ___: for now
4. Follows directions
5. Price of a ride
6. Short-lived success
7. Lisa, to Bart Simpson
8. Extra tire
9. A fisherman may spin one
10. Breaks bread
11. Major-leaguers
16. Actor Ustinov
19. White House VIP
20. Young lady
21. Oohs' companions
22. Store (away)
24. Shave-haircut link
26. Anatomical pouches
27. Pixar fish
28. Football officials
29. Look ___ when I'm talking to you!
31. ___ de France
32. Ralph ___ Emerson
36. Catches one's breath
37. Hindu social division
38. Scottish girl
39. Paul who wrote "My Way"

Puzzle 27

Solution on Page 320

40. Scissors cut
42. Essential meaning
44. Clean Air Act org.
45. Welby and Kildare: Abbr.
46. Mouse hater's cry
47. Finder of secrets

ACROSS

1. Eminem's genre
4. School basics
8. Kennedy and Turner
12. California's Santa ___ River
13. Nightclub in a Manilow tune
14. ___ vera
15. Availability extremes
18. Quartet minus one
19. Sixth-sense letters
20. Plunge
23. Proverbial waste maker
27. Can ___ true?
30. Donate
32. Civil War general
33. Cold War symbol
36. Boy
37. Gas in advertising signs
38. Hole-punching tools
39. Shoppers' reminders
41. Celestial Seasonings selections
43. Not at home
45. Bottom-row PC key
48. Technologically advanced
54. Hydrant attachment
55. Undercooked
56. Moon jumper of rhyme
57. Kennel cries
58. No votes
59. Ambient music pioneer Brian

DOWN

1. British fliers: Abbr.
2. Work without ___ (take risks)
3. Old TV host Jack
4. Thespian
5. Ghost's greeting
6. Class for EMTs
7. Bank fixture
8. Home of the N.F.L.'s Buccaneers
9. Inventor Whitney
10. Crime boss
11. Get a look at
16. Flip of a hit single
17. White with fright
21. "Shrek," for one
22. 747 flier
24. Cole ___
25. Rat (on)
26. Lampreys, e.g.
27. ___ be a cold day in July . . .
28. Bangkok citizen
29. Garden plots
31. Ivy, for one
34. Follow as a consequence
35. ___ not, want not
40. Carries
42. Partner of pains
44. In tatters
46. Marathon, e.g.
47. Scientologist ___ Hubbard

Puzzle 28

Solution on Page 320

48. Not outgoing
49. Suit ___ T
50. Egyptian viper
51. Airport overseer: Abbr.
52. Make an effort
53. Toddler's age

ACROSS

1. ___ one's time (wait)
5. Infamous Roman emperor
9. ___ and away
12. Like Darth Vader
13. Implication
15. NASDAQ competitor
16. Distinct
17. Flies off the handle
19. Fainthearted
20. High on something other than life?
22. Red or White team
23. Ann ___, Mich.
24. Gymnastics device
25. Pampering, for short
28. Traveling type
29. Something to do in a suit
30. Flower pot filler
31. Half-brother of Tom Sawyer
32. Perry Mason's profession
33. Laughing animal
34. Oath
35. Took five
36. Parade sight
39. Mottled bean
40. Unevenly balanced
42. Inscribe with acid
45. Completely paired
46. Brood
47. The "p" of m.p.h.
48. Tiny criticisms
49. Stitched line

DOWN

1. Gentle bear
2. Wall climber
3. Stripped
4. Franklin's First Lady
5. Snooped, with "about"
6. Nights before holidays
7. Dem.'s opponent
8. Rhetorician
9. Lather
10. The "A" in ABM
11. Sax vibrator
14. Cereal that's "for kids"
18. Berlin's country: Abbr.
20. Gives in to gravity
21. "Star Trek: T.N.G." counselor
22. Give in to gravity
24. Arrow shooter
25. Direct, as a confrontation
26. "Come here often?" is one
27. Decked out (in)
29. Argue vehemently
30. All ___ go!
32. Skin soother
33. Egg layer
34. Like the universe
35. Disney World attractions
36. Big failure

Puzzle 29

Solution on Page 321

37. Companionless
38. Switchboard worker: Abbr.
39. Locked (up)
41. ___ have to?
43. Book balancer, briefly
44. Skirt bottom

ACROSS

1. Recommend
5. Belief suffix
8. Baseball stat
12. Poison ivy symptom
13. "Morning Edition" airer
14. Lighten, as a burden
15. Love ___ leave it
16. Caboodle's partner
17. Exhilaration
18. Sunup direction
20. Leers at
21. Assailed on all sides
24. Garr or Hatcher
26. Slip through the clutches of
27. Most frigid
30. El ___, weather phenomenon
31. Yoko of music
32. The slammer
34. Holiday quaff
36. Countesses' spouses
37. Classic soda brand
38. Burn badly
39. Allow in
42. Part of a Halloween costume
44. Calc prerequisite
45. Kilmer who played Batman
46. "___ in the Clowns"
50. Ruler division
51. Nest item
52. Had payments due
53. Frost or Burns
54. Boston ___ Party
55. Former House Speaker Gingrich

DOWN

1. Prefix with angle
2. Feed seed
3. Grp. that entertains troops
4. "Joy to the World" group
5. Calligraphers' supplies
6. Look-alike
7. Mohawk-sporting actor
8. Baseball's "Mr. October"
9. Play ___!
10. Shrink's reply
11. Views
19. Gobbled down
20. Either you say it ___ will
21. Jerry's ice-cream partner
22. Peace Nobelist Wiesel
23. Vocalized
25. ___-friendly (green)
28. ___ Lee (cake company)
29. Money drawer
31. ___ and aah
33. It was dropped in the 1960s
35. Tennis court divider
36. Letter after ar
39. Let me give you ___
40. First 007 film
41. Cheese nibblers
43. Fish tank organism

Puzzle 30

Solution on Page 321

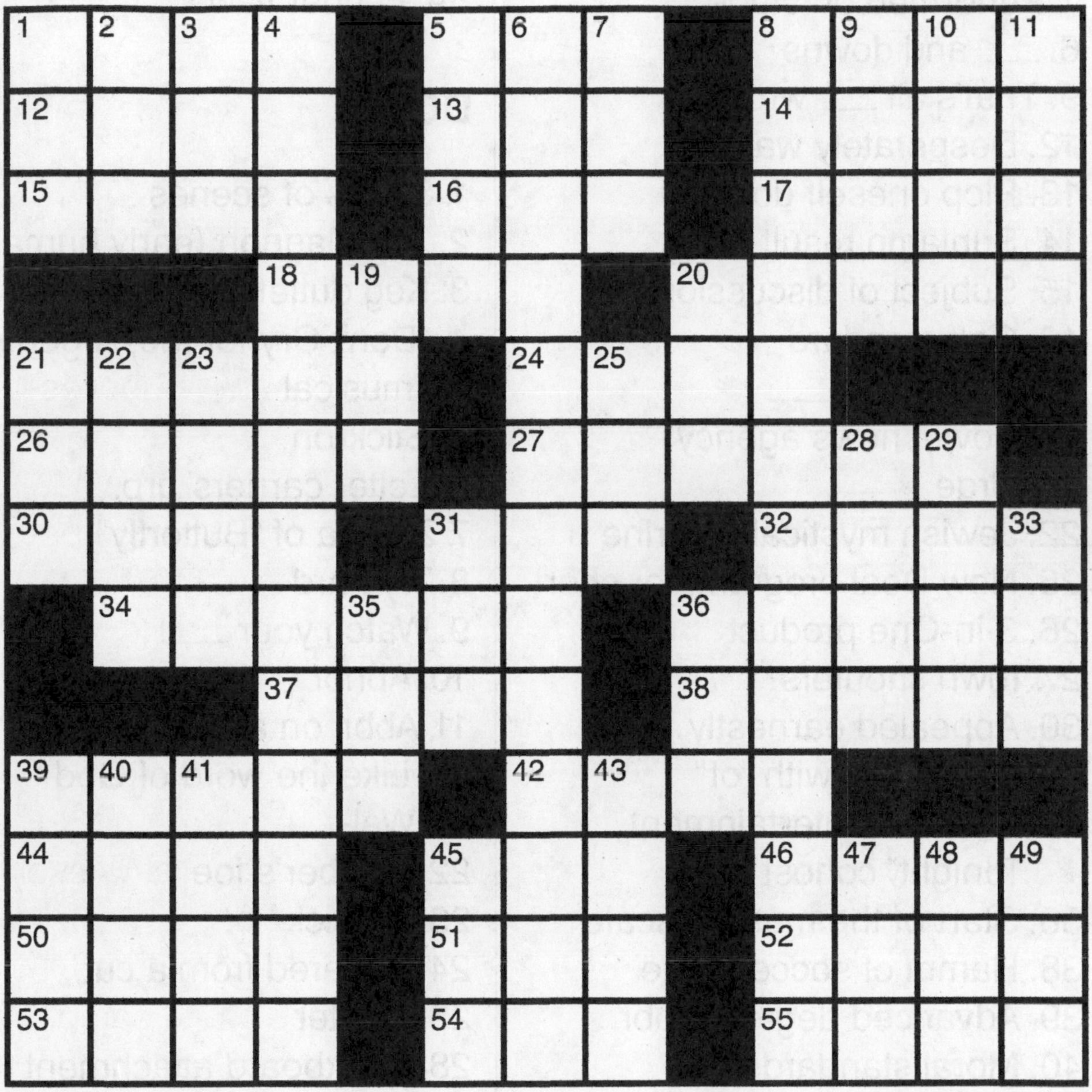

45. Dog doc
47. Female with a wool coat
48. Still in the wrapper
49. Banned bug spray

ACROSS

1. Performed on stage
6. ___ and downs
9. That's all ___ wrote
12. Desperately want
13. Plop oneself down
14. Sunlamp result
15. Subject of discussion
16. Golf standard
17. Mail Boxes ___
18. Soviet news agency
20. Urge
22. Jewish mystical doctrine
25. New Deal program, for short
26. 3-in-One product
27. Town shouters
30. Appealed earnestly
32. Free from, with "of"
33. Former "Entertainment Tonight" cohost John
36. Start of the musical scale
38. Hamm of soccer fame
39. Advanced degree: Abbr.
40. Moral standards
43. Actor Sal
46. Soft French cheese
47. Big bird down under
48. Hoops grp.
50. Synagogue leader
54. Persona ___ grata
55. ___ Jones Industrial Average
56. Perrier competitor
57. Young ___: tykes, in dialect
58. Hole-punching tool
59. Fender flaws

DOWN

1. Series of scenes
2. ___-Magnon (early human)
3. Keg outlet
4. "Don't Cry for Me, Argentina" musical
5. Stick-on
6. Letter carriers' grp.
7. Zadora of "Butterfly"
8. Try hard
9. Watch your ___!
10. Abhor
11. Abbr. on a business letter
19. Like the word of God
21. Wal-___
22. Robber's foe
23. Be sick
24. Suffered from a cut
25. Neater
28. Backboard attachment
29. Big truck, for short
31. Latest news, slangily
34. "Attack!," to Rover
35. Elvis ___ left the building
37. Girl in a Beach Boys song
41. Worn out
42. Throw with great effort
43. List of choices

Puzzle 31

Solution on Page 321

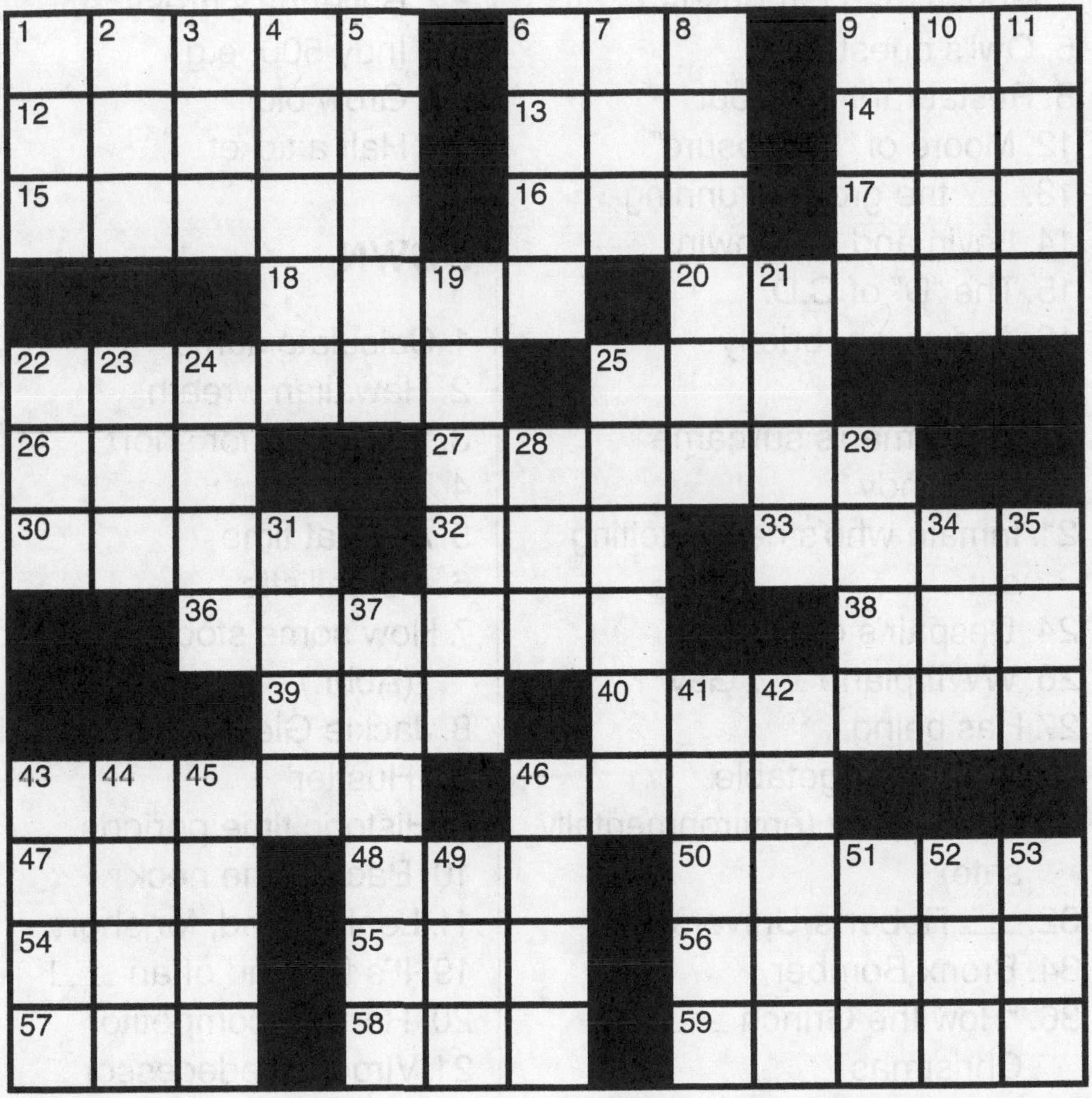

44. ___ my way
45. Habit wearers
46. Cry one's eyes out
49. Ship's front
51. Place for coal
52. Face the pitcher
53. Shoo-___ (certain winners)

ACROSS

1. Money man Greenspan
5. Owl's question?
8. Restaurant handout
12. Moore of "Disclosure"
13. ___ the ground running
14. Levin and Gershwin
15. The "D" of C.D.
16. And so on, briefly
17. Tots' rests
18. Superman's surname
20. Al of Indy
21. Inmate who's never getting out
24. Despair's opposite
26. WWII plane ___ Gay
27. Has being
30. Gumbo vegetable
31. ___-friendly (environmentally safe)
32. ___ Roberts University
34. Bronx Bomber
36. "How the Grinch ___ Christmas"
37. Sandwich seller
38. Despised
39. Run-down in appearance, as a motel
42. Bit of foliage
44. Cab
45. Bit of eBay action
46. Shortened wd.
50. Line-___ veto
51. London's land: Abbr.
52. Ballerina's dress
53. Indy 500, e.g.
54. Grow old
55. Half a ticket

DOWN

1. Calculate sums
2. Hawaiian wreath
3. Mornings, for short
4. Trivial
5. At what time
6. Go ballistic
7. How some stocks are sold (Abbr.)
8. Jackie Gleason role in "The Hustler"
9. Historic time periods
10. Back of the neck
11. Lenin's land, for short
19. It's the end of an ___!
20. Reuters competitor
21. Virgo's predecessor
22. Like printers' fingers
23. "___ Few Dollars More"
25. Losing tic-tac-toe row
28. Horse's gait
29. Reduced-price event
31. Moray, e.g.
33. Was ahead
35. F major or E minor

Puzzle 32

Solution on Page 321

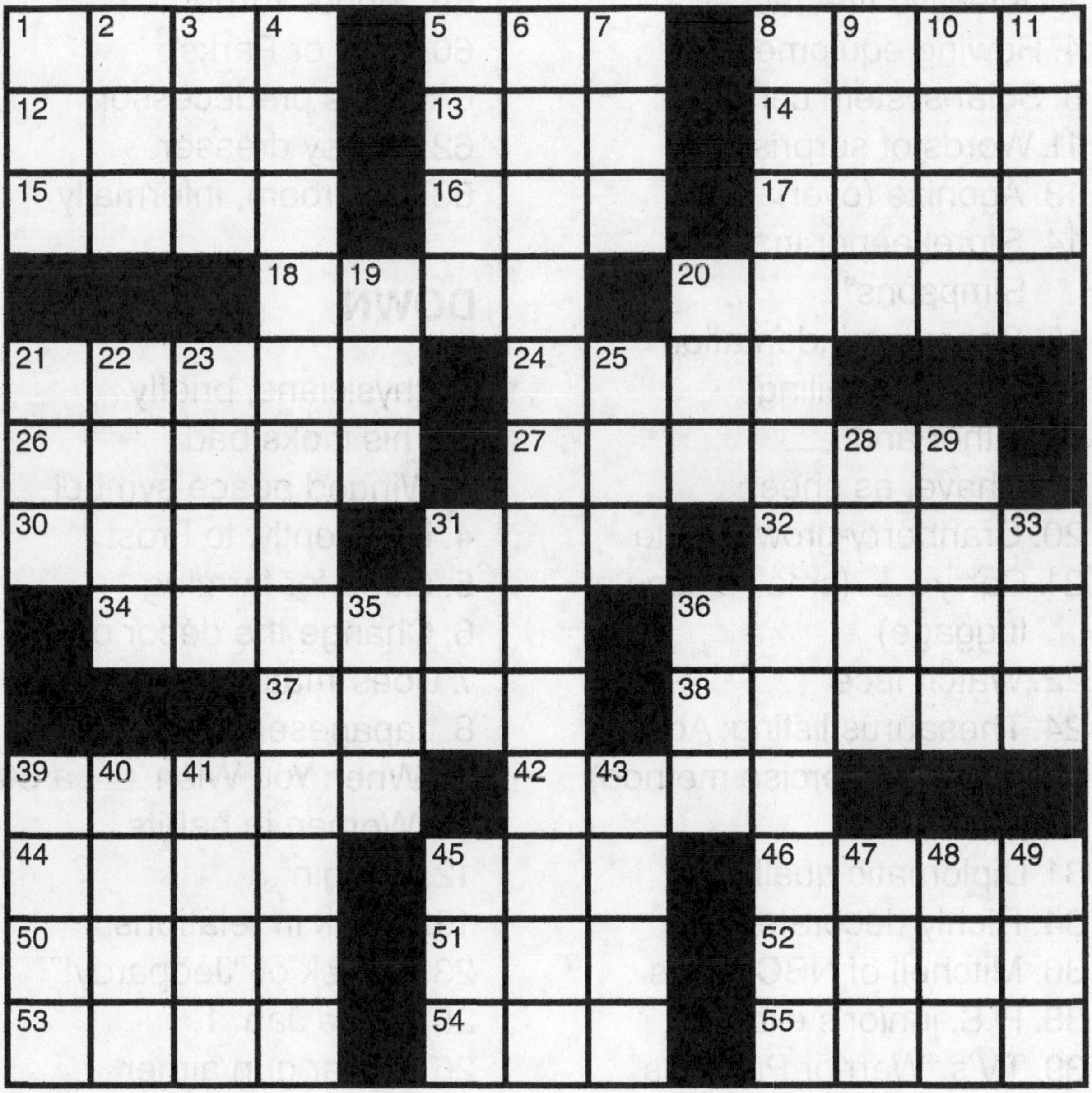

36. TV's "___ Na Na"
39. Blend
40. I could ___ horse!
41. Company bigwig
43. Sharp side of a knife
45. Don't ___ stranger
47. However . . .
48. A/C measure
49. Hamlet's catch

ACROSS

1. Defective firecracker
4. Rowing equipment
8. Solar-system center
11. Words of surprise
13. Agonize (over)
14. Storekeeper in "The Simpsons"
15. Shoreline indentation
16. Cry of unveiling
17. Hither and ___
18. Shave, as sheep
20. Cranberry-growing site
21. Carry-___ (small pieces of luggage)
22. Watch face
24. Thesaurus listing: Abbr.
26. Tai ___ (exercise method)
29. Aviated
31. Diplomatic quality
34. Richly decorated
36. Mitchell of NBC News
38. H.S. junior's exam
39. TV's "Warrior Princess"
41. Height: Abbr.
42. Baglike structure
44. Pants parts
46. Revolutionist Guevara
48. Have in hand
50. Hide for future use
54. Solo in "Star Wars"
55. Articulated
57. Abruptly dismissed
58. Question's opposite: Abbr.
59. Singer Turner
60. Lahr or Parks
61. JFK's predecessor
62. Messy dresser
63. Restroom, informally

DOWN

1. Physicians, briefly
2. This looks bad
3. Winged peace symbol
4. Frequently, to Frost
5. Good for farming
6. Change the décor of
7. Does' mates
8. Japanese farewell
9. "When You Wish ___ a Star"
10. Women in habits
12. Noggin
19. Break in relations
23. Trebek of "Jeopardy!"
25. Since Jan. 1
26. Radar gun aimer
27. "48 ___" (Nick Nolte film)
28. Looking at it one way
30. Grow dim
32. Cartoon frame
33. "I tawt I taw a puddy ___!"
35. ___ standstill (motionless)
37. Pesters persistently
40. Pacific weather phenomenon

Puzzle 33

Solution on Page 322

43. Prices
45. Attack with a knife
46. Neighbor of Niger
47. Something to shake with
49. Cry out
51. "Beverly Hills Cop" character Foley
52. Will be, in a Doris Day song
53. Modern RCA offering
56. Small amount, as of hair cream

ACROSS

1. Pull a scam
4. Fissures
8. ___ in a day's work
11. Underground deposits
13. Remove the wrinkles from
14. Generous ___ fault
15. Gull-like bird
16. River where baby Moses was found
17. Coffee-to-go topper
18. Couches
20. Chilean fish
22. Football kick
24. Cub Scout group
25. Rice Krispies sound
28. Give out cards
30. Variety of poker
33. Moody
35. Clothing
37. Storage building
38. Place for a ship to come in
40. [Not my mistake]
41. Reagan-era mil. program
43. Co. honchos
45. Blot on the landscape
48. Reduce drastically, as prices
52. Commandment count
53. Detach from a source of dependence
55. Not home, on a sports schedule
56. Lion or leopard
57. ___ Nicole Smith
58. Repair
59. 60-min. periods
60. Intrusively curious
61. President before JFK

DOWN

1. Foldable beds
2. Crème-filled cookie
3. Squishy ball brand
4. Martini liquor
5. Competitor of Capitol and Epic
6. Barbershop emblem
7. Golfer Sam
8. Legendary sunken island
9. Lane of "The Daily Planet"
10. Ones wearing knickers
12. Rice Krispies sound
19. Lather
21. Second to none
23. "All You ___ Is Love"
25. Evening hrs.
26. ___ and aah
27. Things kept under wraps?
29. "Arsenic and Old ___"
31. Debunked mentalist Geller
32. New Year's Eve mo.
34. ___ and ends
36. Boxing wins, for short
39. Indian and Arctic
42. Des Moines native

Puzzle 34

Solution on Page 322

44. Close angrily
45. Carve in stone
46. January to December
47. Nevada city
49. Impressed mightily
50. Beach surface
51. Jekyll's bad side
54. Yea's opposite

ACROSS

1. Jackass's sound
5. Ave. crossers
8. Potatoes' partner
12. The Eternal City
13. Former Pan Am rival
14. European mountains
15. Vanderbilt and Grant
16. OPEC product
17. "Pirates of the Caribbean" star Johnny
18. Taxpayer's ID
20. Political pamphlets
22. Like seawater
25. Dr. Seuss's "Sam ___"
26. Be crazy about
27. Toronto's loc.
28. CBS forensic series
31. Snorkeling accessory
32. Venomous snake
34. Extra play periods, for short
35. London's locale: Abbr.
36. Tease playfully
37. Mr. T series, with "The"
39. ___ Aviv
40. Perfumes
41. Strive
44. Proverbial sword beater
45. Happy as a ___
46. Letters after L
48. Legal action
52. Old instrument that's strummed
53. Was introduced to
54. Frozen waffle brand
55. Sounds of displeasure
56. Washboard muscles
57. Broadway offering

DOWN

1. Playtex item
2. Computer storage acronym
3. "The Joy Luck Club" writer Tan
4. Assent accompanying a salute
5. Rosetta ___
6. Prefix for light
7. Soup cracker
8. Lady's title
9. Power co. product
10. Datebook entry: Abbr.
11. Recipe measures: Abbr.
19. Athletic shoe
21. Nine-to-five grind
22. Opposite of out
23. Deuce follower, in tennis
24. ___ time no see
27. Strange
28. Either "Fargo" co-director
29. Ballpark figure?
30. Belief systems
33. Perplexing problem
38. Past, present, and future

Puzzle 35

Solution on Page 322

39. Multiplied by
40. Leopard features
41. Civil rights org.
42. Powerful punch
43. Way through the woods
47. Omaha's state: Abbr.
49. That's disgusting!
50. Here ___ again
51. Aid for a stranded auto

ACROSS

1. Signed off on
5. Theory suffix
8. ___ dunk
12. Magnitude
13. Compete in a slalom
14. Actress Spelling
15. German mister
16. Secreted
17. Tracks in mud
18. To no ___ (useless)
20. Soundness of mind
22. Group of Cub Scouts
24. Have a late meal
25. Incited
29. Contract provisions
33. Live and ___ live
34. Eggy beverage
36. Wine barrel wood
37. Straight from the garden
40. Front porch
43. One of the tides
45. W.C.
46. Pay no mind to
49. Holy city of Islam
53. State with a panhandle: Abbr.
54. Nonprofit's U.R.L. ending
56. Paper towel unit
57. Furnace output
58. The Monkees' "___ Believer"
59. Mouse catcher
60. ___-to-order (custom)
61. Set down
62. Puts in a hem

DOWN

1. Worker protection org.
2. Chicken ___
3. Book after II Chronicles
4. Scoff at
5. Suffix like -like
6. Cross-country equipment
7. Golden touch king
8. American flag feature
9. Clumsy one
10. Pretentiously showy
11. Prefix with place or print
19. ___ Zeppelin
21. Pecan or cashew
23. Oui's opposite
25. North Pole toymaker
26. Aus. neighbor
27. A Verizon predecessor
28. Oct. follower
30. Hollywood's Howard
31. Irate
32. Jamaican music
35. Hair goop
38. Part of Congress
39. "True Blood" airer
41. Aries animal
42. Turns away
44. Oven setting

Puzzle 36

Solution on Page 322

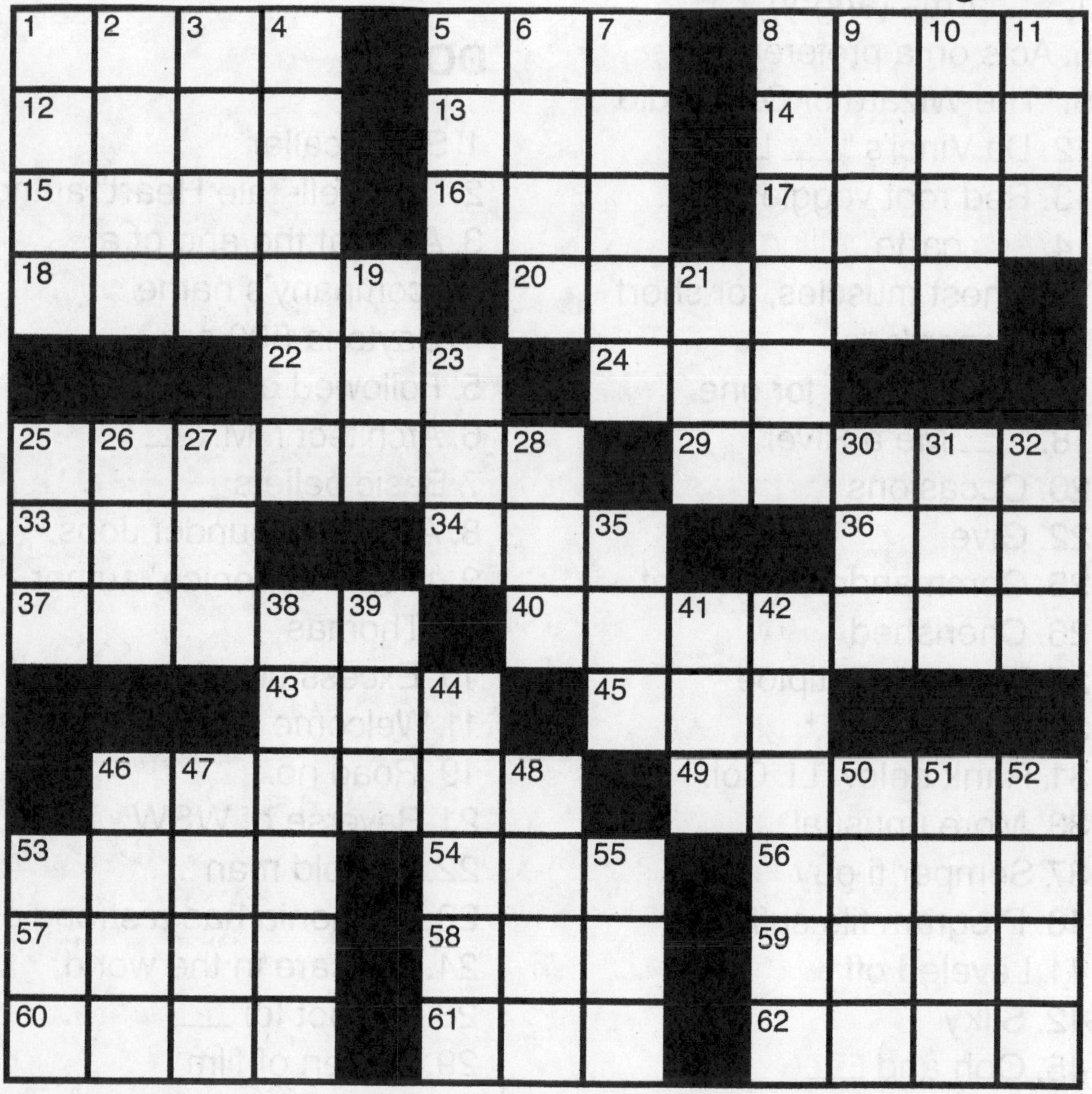

46. Furniture company named partly for its founder Ingvar Kamprad
47. Trash bag brand
48. Columnist Bombeck
50. Apple throwaway
51. Crab's grabber
52. Swiss skiing site
53. Resistance unit that sounds like a meditation word
55. In a merry mood

ACROSS

1. ___ arms (angry)
5. Acts on a preference
9. "The Wizard of Oz" studio
12. Da Vinci's "___ Lisa"
13. Red root veggie
14. ___ carte
15. Chest muscles, for short
16. Mozart's "a"
17. Macadamia, for one
18. "___ Me a River"
20. Occasions
22. Give
25. Commandments count
26. Cherished
27. Proceed on tiptoe
30. i topper
31. Rank below Lt. Col.
33. More unusual
37. Semper fi guy
40. Program file suffix
41. Leveled off
42. Silky
45. Ooh and ___
46. Academic URL ender
47. Snakelike fish
49. Incubator items
53. N.Y.C. hrs.
54. Carpentry fastener
55. That was ___ of fun!
56. ___ Moines
57. Deuce topper, in cards
58. Broadway's "Sweeney ___"

DOWN

1. Strike caller
2. "The Tell-Tale Heart" author
3. Abbr. at the end of a company's name
4. Daytona 500 org.
5. Followed orders
6. Architect I. M. ___
7. Basic beliefs
8. Apple co-founder Jobs
9. "Death in Venice" author Thomas
10. Excess supply
11. Welcome sites
19. Road no.
21. Reverse of WSW
22. The old man
23. Ammonia has a strong one
24. ___ care in the world
28. Despot Idi ___
29. Citizen of film
32. ___ Bartlet, president on "The West Wing"
34. Speed Wagon maker
35. Full range
36. Listen to again, as arguments
37. Pathetically small

Puzzle 37

Solution on Page 323

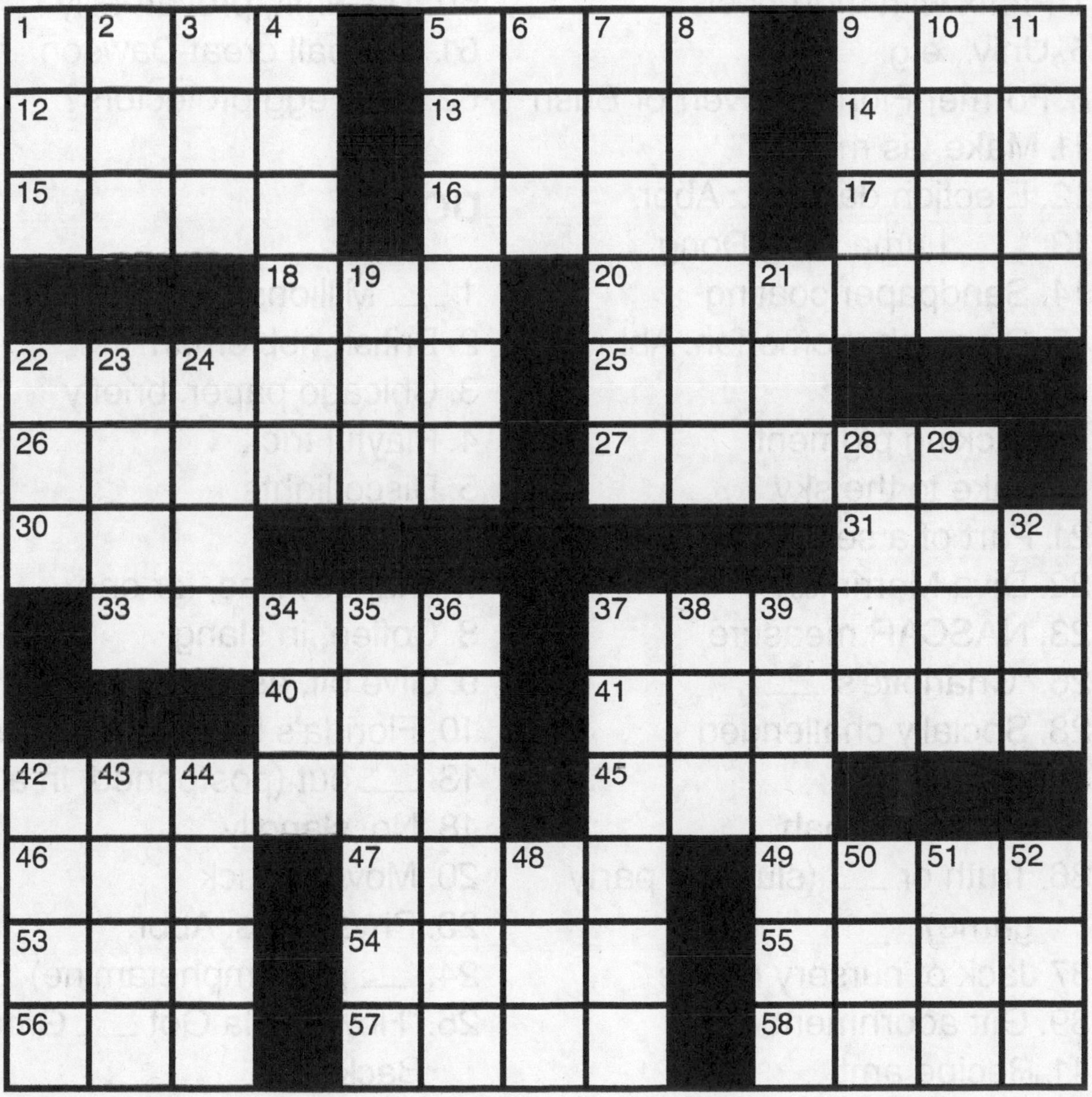

38. Gardner of Hollywood
39. Microwave, perhaps
42. Gardener's spring purchase
43. Store goods: Abbr.
44. On the ___ (not speaking)
48. Fib
50. Day-___ paint
51. Deity
52. Part of CST: Abbr.

ACROSS

1. Prefix with morphosis
5. Univ., e.g.
8. Former Florida governor Bush
11. Make, as money
12. Election day, e.g.: Abbr.
13. "___ Lama Ding Dong"
14. Sandpaper coating
15. Sleep phenomenon: Abbr.
16. Enthusiastic
17. Lacking pigment
19. Take to the sky
21. Part of a semi
22. Diva Merriman
23. NASCAR measure
26. "Charlotte's ___"
28. Socially challenged
32. Regard as
34. ___-boom-bah
36. Truth or ___ (slumber party game)
37. Jack of nursery rhyme
39. Gift adornment
41. Recipe amt.
42. Stewart or Steiger
44. PC linkup
46. Masthead title
49. Starting point
53. H.S. subject
54. PC maker
56. ___ bene
57. ___ Minor (constellation)
58. August 1 sign
59. "Iliad" setting
60. The limit, proverbially
61. Football great Dawson
62. Nest egg protectors?

DOWN

1. ___ Millions (lottery)
2. British nobleman
3. Chicago paper, briefly
4. Playful trick
5. Disco lights
6. Pool stick
7. Charles Atlas, for one
8. Coffee, in slang
9. Give off, as light
10. Florida's Miami- ___ County
13. ___ out (postponed, in a way)
18. No, slangily
20. Moving truck
23. Physicians: Abbr.
24. ___ pill (amphetamine)
25. "How Stella Got ___ Groove Back"
27. Baby's neckwear
29. Urban vermin
30. E.R. workers
31. Cowboy's assent
33. Mrs. Washington
35. Wise king of Israel
38. This ___ shall pass
40. Armed conflict

Puzzle 38

Solution on Page 323

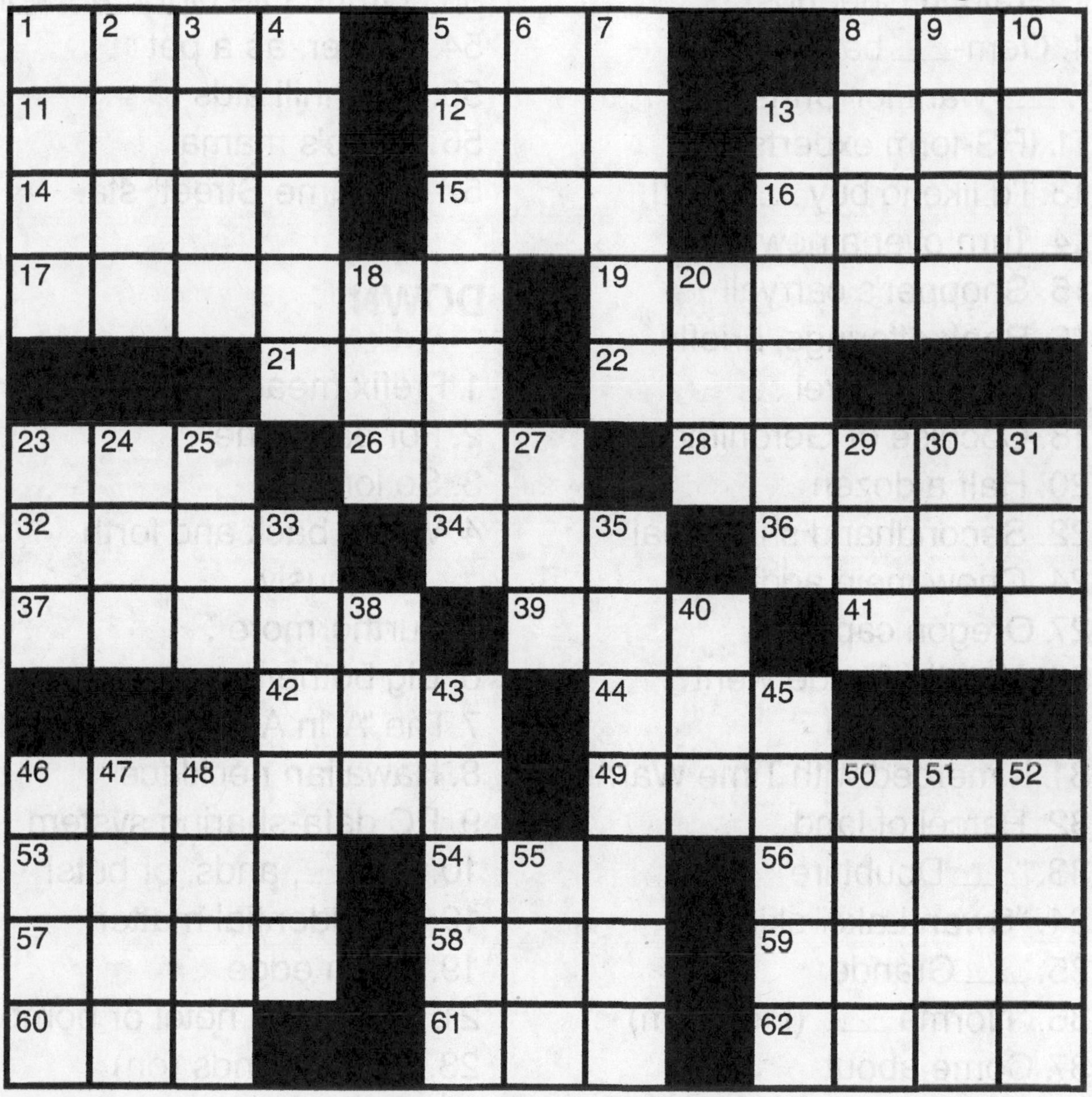

43. Dentist's tool
45. Final inning, usually
46. Aussie birds
47. Like the night
48. Teensy
50. Al or Tipper
51. Lay ___ the line
52. Anti votes
55. Honey maker

ACROSS

1. Grain in Cheerios
4. Oom-___ band
7. ___ want for Christmas . . .
11. IRS-form experts
13. I'd like to buy ___, Pat!
14. Turn over a new ___
15. Shopper's carryall
16. Bank offerings, briefly
17. ___, zwei, drei . . .
18. Cochise or Geronimo
20. Half a dozen
22. Secondhand shop deal
24. Chow mein additive
27. Oregon capital
30. Nat. that underwent reunification
31. It merged with Time Warner
32. Parcel of land
33. "___ Doubtfire"
34. "Swan Lake" skirt
35. ___ Grande
36. "Norma ___" (Field film)
37. Come about
38. Informal affirmative
39. Deficiency of red blood cells
41. From Jan. 1 until now, in accounting
42. New Balance competitor
46. Tiny pest
49. "Gimme ___!" (Indiana cheerleaders' cry)
51. Roman tyrant
52. ___ unrelated note . . .
53. "Grand Ole Opry" network
54. Neuter, as a pet
55. Downhill aids
56. Lamb's mama
57. "Sesame Street" sta.

DOWN

1. Prefix meaning "eight"
2. For each one
3. So long!
4. Walks back and forth nervously
5. Furthermore . . .
6. Big bothers
7. The "A" in A-Rod
8. Hawaiian necklace
9. PC data-sharing system
10. No ___, ands, or buts!
12. Confidential matter
19. Sewn edge
21. Suffix with hotel or bombard
23. Shake hands (on)
24. Hawaii's second-largest island
25. Drunkards
26. Rubber cement, e.g.
27. Quick on one's feet
28. I cannot tell ___
29. Chicago locale, with "the"
33. Authoritative order

Puzzle 39

Solution on Page 323

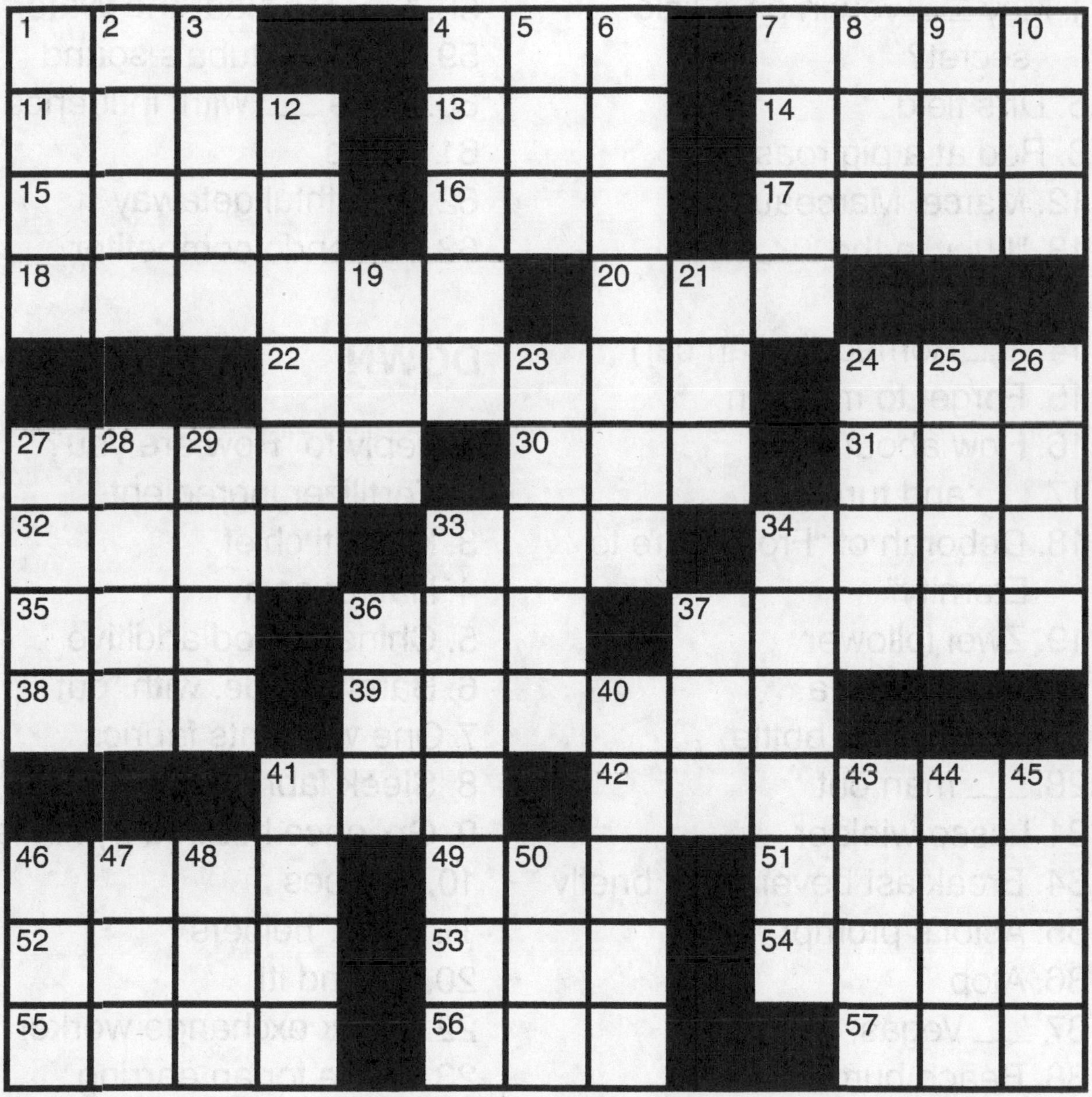

34. Choo-choos
36. You dirty ___!
37. Samaritan's offer
40. L.L. Bean's home
41. Strong longings
43. Scissorhands portrayer Johnny
44. Part of U.A.E.
45. High-protein beans
46. Year divs.
47. Bic filler
48. ___ chi: martial art
50. Opposite of SSE

ACROSS

1. May ___ you in on a little secret?
5. Dr.'s field
8. Rod at a pig roast
12. Marcel Marceau
13. "Lucy in the ___ with Diamonds"
14. ___ Romeo (Italian car)
15. Forget to mention
16. How about that!
17. ___ and turn
18. Deborah of "From Here to Eternity"
19. Zwei follower
21. Capital of Ga.
24. Open, as a bottle
28. ___ man out
31. Lasso wielder
34. Breakfast beverages, briefly
35. Actor's prompt
36. Atop
37. ___ Vegas, NV
38. Beach bum's shade
39. Bo of "10"
40. Gallery display
41. Seaweed
43. Eminem's music
45. Web addresses, for short
48. Warhead weapon, for short
52. "September ___" (Neil Diamond hit)
55. Relative of Ltd.
57. British Conservative
58. "___ Go Near the Water"
59. Part of a tuba's sound
60. Have ___ with: influence
61. Baths
62. Healthful getaway
63. Nintendo competitor

DOWN

1. Reply to "How are you?"
2. Fertilizer ingredient
3. Kuwaiti chief
4. Half of octa-
5. Chinese food additive
6. Barely made, with "out"
7. One who tints fabrics
8. Sleek fabric
9. Gp. once headed by Arafat
10. Maybes
11. Profs.' helpers
20. I found it!
22. Stock exchange worker
23. Place for an earring
25. Pepsi, for one
26. Partially open
27. Hissed "Hey!"
28. Penta- plus three
29. Like some exhausts
30. China's ___ Xiaoping
32. ___ favor: Sp.
33. Next-to-last fairy tale word

Puzzle 40

Solution on Page 323

42. Uncles' mates
44. Breads with pockets
46. They're kissable
47. Crackle and pop's partner
49. Dunce cap, geometrically
50. Ship's prison
51. Talking bird
52. RNs' coworkers
53. Alley ___
54. Genetic info
56. When repeated, a ballroom dance

ACROSS

1. Bruin legend Bobby
4. Playtex products
8. Cable TV's C-___
12. Classic auto
13. Acting Anderson
14. "Mary ___ Little Lamb"
15. Letterman dental feature
16. Abbr. before a name on an envelope
17. Artist Warhol
18. Chest muscles, briefly
20. Alley-___
22. Cash dispensers, for short
25. Jokes
29. "The Simpsons" son
32. Boat paddles
34. Early d. of the wk.
35. Center of the eye
36. ___ la-la
37. Diva Horne
38. Holliday of the Old West
39. Rug variety
40. McGregor of "Down with Love"
41. Stockholm resident
43. Roll call reply
45. Paul Bunyan's tool
47. 401(k) alternatives
50. Go away!
53. Score-producing stats
56. [Not my error]
58. ___ of the party
59. Constructed
60. Give ___ shot
61. Quaker ___
62. Solvers' shouts
63. Use needle and thread

DOWN

1. Part of NATO: Abbr.
2. . . . so shall ye ___
3. Piece of rodeo gear
4. ___ from the past
5. Undergo decomposition
6. Tiny hill dweller
7. ___ -Japanese War
8. Circle or square
9. Pie holder
10. Total (up)
11. Aye's opposite
19. Andrew Lloyd Webber smash
21. IHOP beverages
23. One drawn to a flame
24. Jazz singer Vaughan
26. Soup of a sort
27. Chicken of the Sea product
28. Connery of the cinema
29. Actions at Sotheby's
30. And pretty maids all in ___
31. Serving with chop suey
33. Extreme anger
37. Look slyly
39. Topic for Dr. Ruth

Puzzle 41

Solution on Page 324

42. Sees romantically
44. Greets the day
46. Writer Bombeck
48. Buyer beware phrase
49. Builder's area
50. ___-mo (instant replay feature)
51. Espionage org.
52. Back, on a ship
54. ___! Humbug!
55. Boise's state: Abbr.
57. Crow's call

ACROSS

1. San ___ Obispo, California
5. Long sandwich
8. Kaput sound
12. Prefix with -valent
13. Medical care grp.
14. It's ___ big mistake!
15. "The Pajama ___" Doris Day film
16. NYPD alert
17. Fava or lima
18. Ewes' mates
20. Lost buoyancy
21. South Dakota's capital
24. Mental quickness
26. Sir ___ Newton
27. "What's up, ___?"
28. Spanish hero
31. ___-tac-toe
32. Dateless
34. John Cougar Mellencamp's "R.O.C.K. in the ___"
35. Camp residue
36. Morse code bit
37. Bitterly pungent
39. Singing cowboy Ritter
40. Wading birds
41. Lo-fat
44. Swiss artist Paul ___
45. Arthur ___ Stadium
46. Jack Sprat's bane
47. Coal waste
51. Like a bully
52. "Don't Bring Me Down" band, for short
53. Animator's creation
54. Where hymnals are stored
55. Method of meditation
56. "Star Trek" helmsman

DOWN

1. Time delay
2. Thurman of film
3. ThinkPad developer
4. Word before Nevada or Leone
5. Humiliation
6. Strike callers
7. 1996 candidate Dole
8. Blue Ribbon beer brewer
9. Kind of market or circus
10. Sweet Spanish dessert
11. Combat vehicle
19. Hangout for pinball wizards
21. Falafel bread
22. Egyptian goddess
23. Per person
24. Was victorious
25. Frigid epoch
27. Play-___ (kiddie clay)
28. Healing treatment
29. ___ just me, or . . .
30. Family men
33. Lenient
38. Reaches the highest level

Puzzle 42

Solution on Page 324

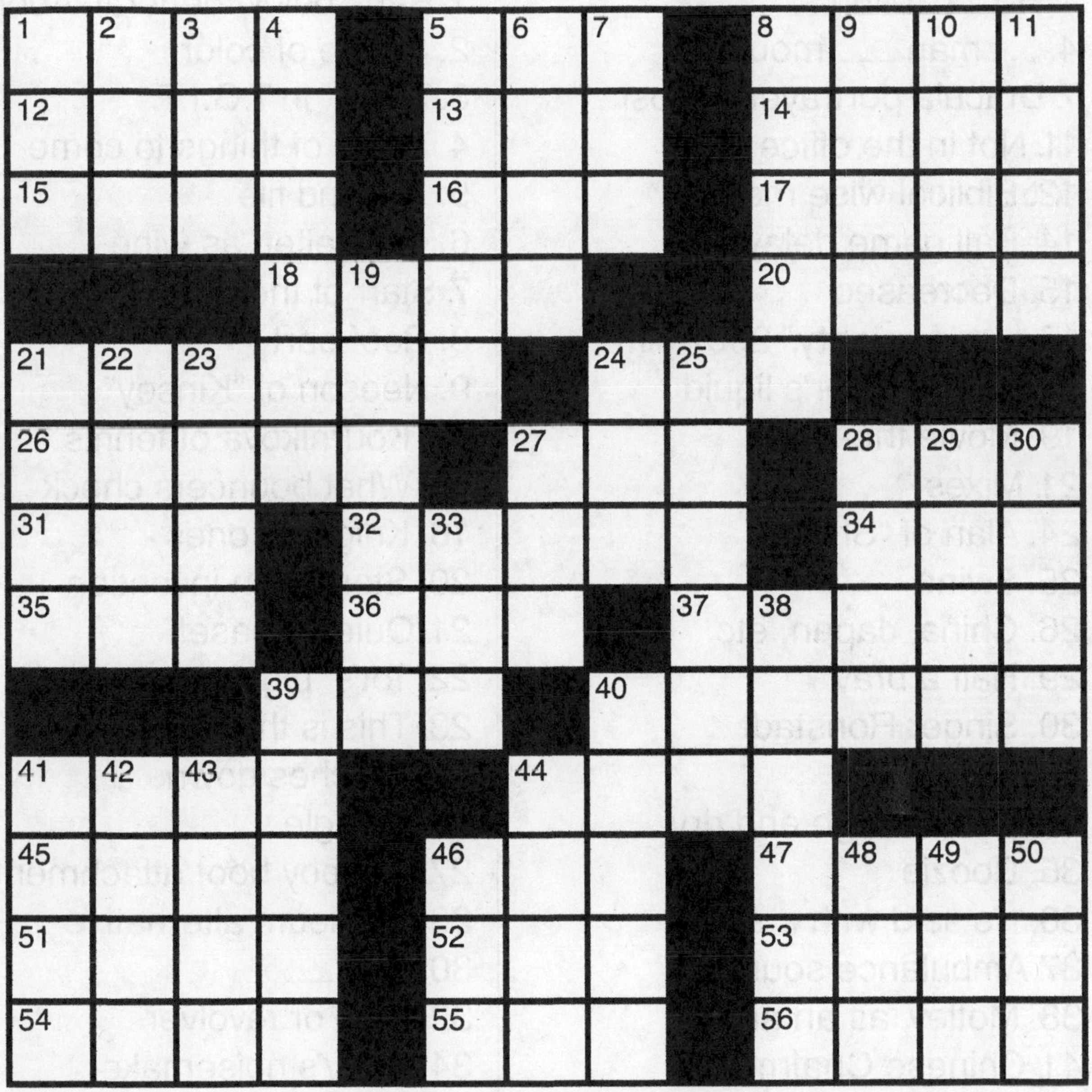

39. They're coming of age
40. Rock's ___ John
41. Genie's home
42. ___ the light!
43. Unfreeze
44. Leafy green vegetable
46. Turk's topper
48. Singer Rawls or Reed
49. Co. that merged with Time Warner
50. Bearded antelope

ACROSS

1. Ho ___ Minh
4. . . . man ___ mouse?
7. Dracula portrayer Lugosi
11. Not in the office
12. Biblical wise men
14. Ball game delayer
15. Decreased
17. "___ Almighty," 2007 film
18. Calligrapher's liquid
19. Movie theater
21. Mixes
24. Alan of "Shane"
25. Swine
26. China, Japan, etc.
29. Half a bray
30. Singer Ronstadt
31. Oinker
33. Leaves high and dry
35. Doozie
36. It's said with a sigh
37. Ambulance sound
38. Motley, as an army
41. Chinese Chairman
42. Death notice for short
43. Students
48. Steeple feature
49. Fitzgerald of jazz
50. Snake that squeezes its prey
51. Model MacPherson
52. "Real ___ Don't Eat Quiche"
53. "Monty Python" airer

DOWN

1. Rank below general: Abbr.
2. Shade of color
3. The "I" in T.G.I.F.
4. Signs of things to come
5. ___ and file
6. Get better, as wine
7. Starr of the comics
8. Roof part
9. Neeson of "Kinsey"
10. Kournikova of tennis
13. What bouncers check
16. Knighted ones
20. Start of an invention
21. Quiet, please!
22. Tot's "piggies"
23. This is the thanks ___?
24. Touches down
26. Wangle
27. Cowboy boot attachment
28. Linoleum alternative
30. Tra-___
32. Rifle or revolver
34. Baby's noisemaker
35. MGM symbol
37. Brand of wrap
38. Justice's attire
39. One slain by Cain
40. Fish's breathing organ
41. Boy or man
44. Nightmare street of film
45. Outward flow

Puzzle 43

Solution on Page 324

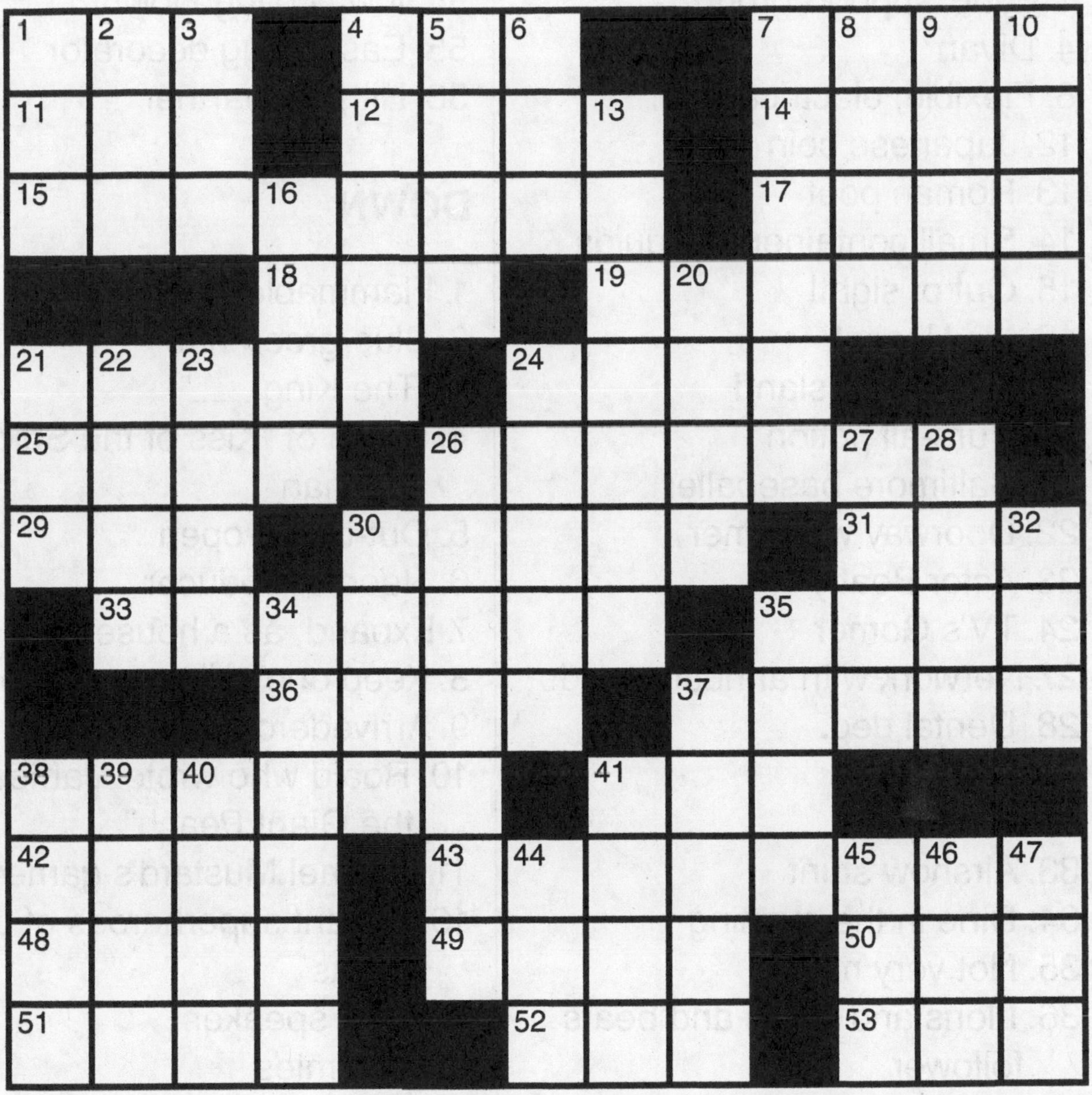

46. Filch
47. Possum's pouch

ACROSS

1. Educ. support group
4. Divan
8. Flexible, electrically
12. Japanese coin
13. Roman poet
14. Small container for liquids
15. Out of sight!
16. Mr. Uncool
17. Honolulu's island
18. Cure-all potion
20. Baltimore baseballer
22. Doorway welcomer
23. Actor Beatty
24. TV's Gomer
27. Network with annual awards
28. Dental deg.
31. ___ of Arc
32. Zodiac lion
33. Airshow stunt
34. Dine in the evening
35. Not very many
36. Lions and tigers and bears follower
37. Cow comment
38. Winter malady
40. All I got was this lousy ___
43. Rat or squirrel
47. Go ___ smoke
48. Hymn word
50. How about that?!
51. Lie in the sun
52. Seen once in a blue moon
53. Canine warning
54. Iowa college town
55. Easter egg decorator
56. Hither's partner

DOWN

1. Flammable pile
2. Blue-green hue
3. "The King ___"
4. Braga of "Kiss of the Spider Woman"
5. Out-in-the-open
6. Needle producer
7. Expand, as a house
8. Keep one's distance from
9. Arrivederci
10. Roald who wrote "James and the Giant Peach"
11. Colonel Mustard's game
19. Mutant superheroes of comic books
21. Sun. speaker
24. Jammies
25. "___ Light up My Life"
26. Once around the track
27. Kitten's sound
28. Homer Simpson outburst
29. Title for Pierre Perignon
30. Work under cover
32. Dancer's bodysuit
33. Ear-busting

Puzzle 44

Solution on Page 324

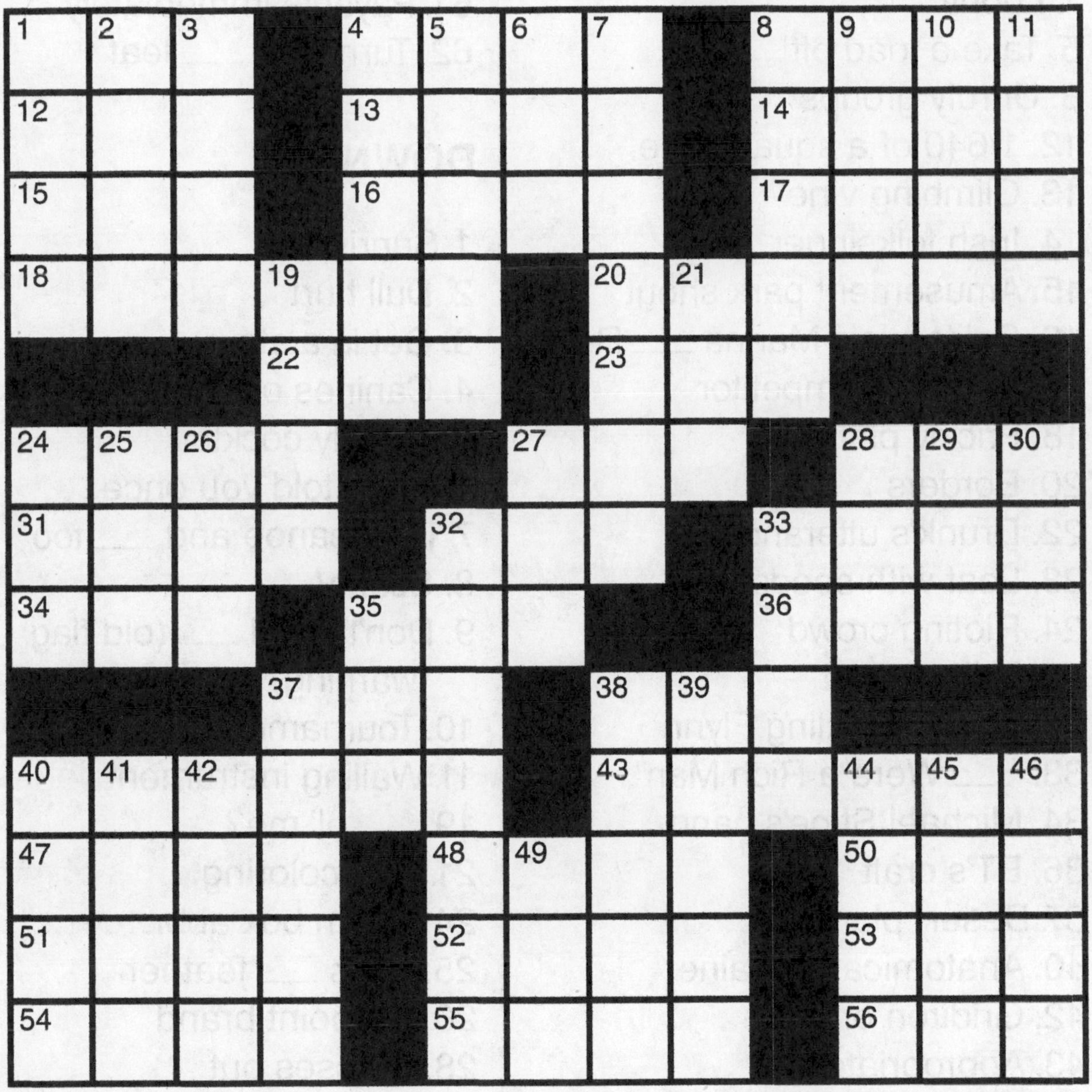

35. "A Bell ___ Adano"
37. Explosive devices
38. "___ Jacques" (children's song)
39. Asocial type
40. Oompah band instrument
41. Inbox junk
42. Take to the trail
44. Like an omelet
45. Roman "fiddler"
46. Bird with a forked tail
49. Memorial Day month

ACROSS

1. Loony
5. Take a load off!
8. Unruly groups
12. 1/640 of a square mile
13. Climbing vine
14. Irish folksinger
15. Amusement park shout
16. California's Marina ___ Rey
17. N.Y.S.E. competitor
18. Prickly plant
20. Borders
22. Drunk's utterance
23. Loaf with seeds
24. Rioting crowd
27. Calif. airport
29. Swashbuckling Flynn
33. "___ Were a Rich Man"
34. Michael Stipe's band
36. ET's craft
37. Desert plants
40. Anatomical container
42. Gridiron org.
43. Appropriate
45. Record collector's platters
47. Enjoy the taste of
49. Alternatives to tricks
53. Sandy slope
54. Hurricane hub
56. Scientology founder Hubbard
57. Ruler of Qatar
58. Negative replies
59. The "M" in MSG
60. State south of Mass.
61. Payable immediately
62. Turn over ___ leaf

DOWN

1. Sunrise
2. Dull hurt
3. Get in a stew
4. Canines or bicuspids
5. Brandy cocktail
6. If ___ told you once . . .
7. Tippecanoe and ___ too
8. Scanty
9. Don't tread ___ (old flag warning)
10. Tournament passes
11. Wailing instrument
19. ___ ol' me?
21. Hair coloring
24. Boom box abbr.
25. Birds ___ feather
26. Ballpoint brand
28. Crosses out
30. Hurry
31. "Ferris Bueller's Day ___"
32. Online guffaw
35. "The ___ Falcon"
38. Alehouse
39. Stock mkt. debut
41. EMS procedure
44. The way things are going

Puzzle 45

Solution on Page 325

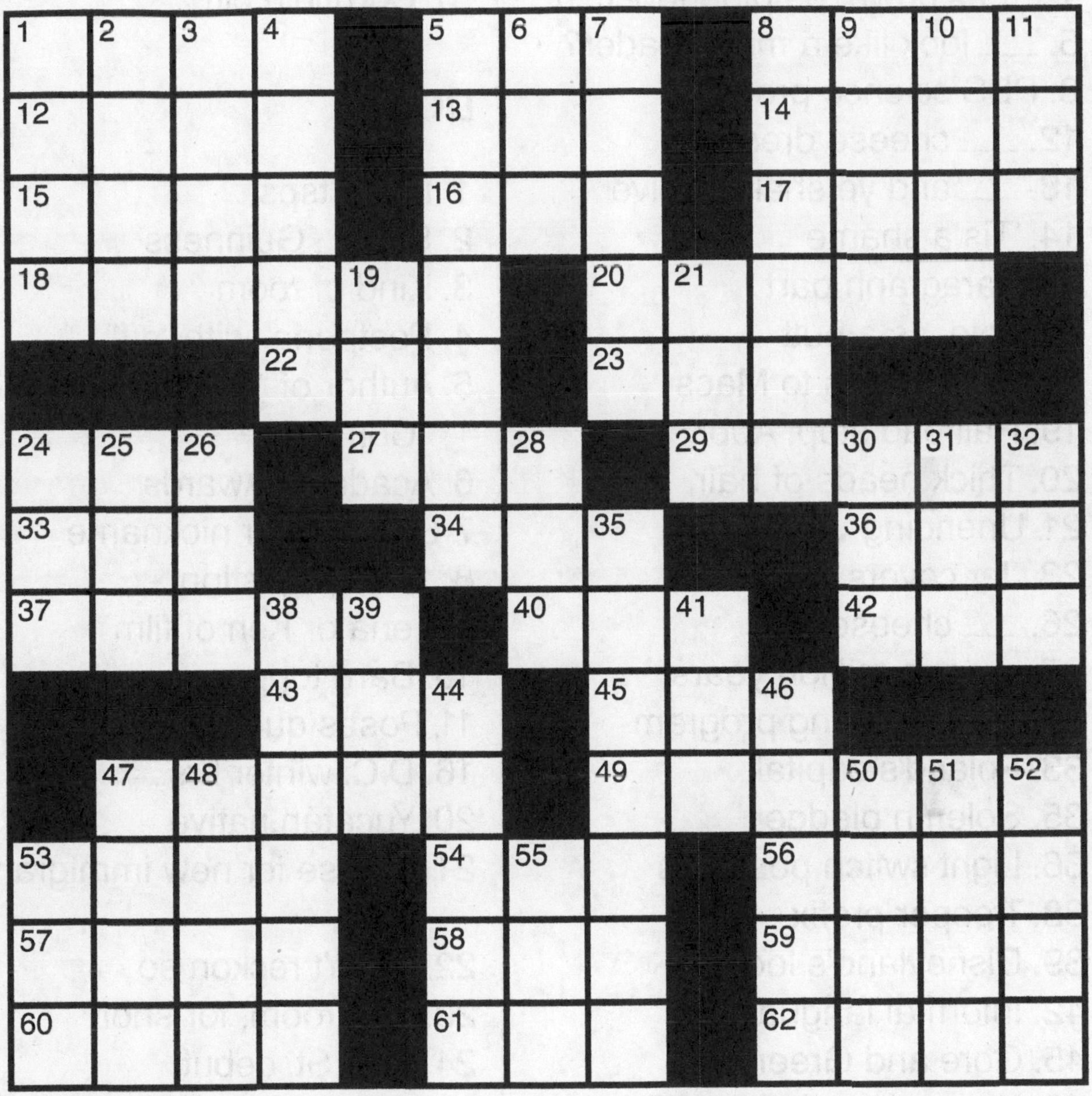

46. 1965 Alabama march site
47. Battle of beefy combatants
48. Has ___: has connections
50. Schoenberg opera "Moses und ___"
51. Dial ___
52. Chilly powder?
53. Christmas's mo.
55. ___ don't say!

ACROSS

1. Press down, as pipe tobacco
5. ___ look like a mind reader?
8. PBS science program
12. ___ cheese dressing
13. ___ and ye shall receive
14. 'Tis a shame
15. Paragraph part
17. Hole, as a putt
18. Alternatives to Macs
19. Railroad stop: Abbr.
20. Thick heads of hair
21. Unending
23. Jar covers
26. ___ cheese!
27. ___ in a million years!
30. Moon-landing program
33. Poland's capital
35. Solemn pledge
36. Light switch positions
38. Trooper prefix
39. Disneyland's locale
42. Informal language
45. Gore and Green
46. Nonprofit website suffix
49. Snake dancers of the Southwest
50. New York hockey player
52. Cheers for the matador
53. Numbered hwy.
54. Pro ___ (like some legal work)
55. Merrie ___ England
56. Okla. neighbor
57. Cornfield bird

DOWN

1. Three tsps.
2. Sir ___ Guinness
3. Kind of room
4. Postpone, with "off"
5. Author of "The Divine Comedy"
6. Academy Awards
7. Eisenhower nickname
8. ___ congestion
9. Lena or Ken of film
10. Barn topper
11. Poses questions
16. D.C. winter hrs.
20. Yucatán native
21. Course for new immigrants: abbr.
22. I don't reckon so
23. Restroom, for short
24. Wall St. debut
25. ___ Jones industrials
27. Cryptologic grp.
28. Boater's blade
29. Howard Hughes's airline
31. Like a hippie's hair
32. ___ roll (lucky)
34. LP speed
37. California peak

Puzzle 46

Solution on Page 325

39. Licorice-like flavoring
40. Comic DeGeneres
41. "Happiness ___ Warm Puppy"
42. Scat!
43. Lounge around
44. Modeled oneself on
46. Nose tickler
47. City near Lake Tahoe
48. Expand
50. Get on one's nerves
51. "The West Wing" network

ACROSS

1. . . . ___ quit!
4. Car for hire
7. Knight's protection
12. Harsh review
13. Blessed ___ the meek . . .
14. Africa's Sierra ___
15. New Deal dam-building org.
16. Near the center of
17. Bathroom powders
18. "___ I Fell for You"
20. Eight-member ensemble
21. Feathery wrap
23. Ore. clock setting
24. Murders, mob-style
27. Bemoan
29. Riverbed deposit
33. Gun lobby, briefly
34. Biblical beast
35. Glimpsed
36. Awfully long time
38. Wager
39. Mock words of understanding
40. "Killing Me Softly with ___ Song"
42. Boston Red ___
44. Turn red, perhaps
47. Draws nigh
51. Fancy goodbye
52. Part of L.A.
54. Baltic or Bering
55. Track contests
56. ___-inspiring
57. Rowboat blade
58. Dissect grammatically
59. The best is ___ to come
60. Pharmaceuticals watchdog agcy.

DOWN

1. Chooses (to)
2. Sitar player Shankar
3. Put ___ appearance
4. Small part played by a big name
5. Magnate Onassis
6. Part of B&B
7. Voices above tenors
8. Does a double take, e.g.
9. Shed one's skin
10. First word in a fairy tale
11. Repose
19. Network with an eye logo
22. Saudis and Iraqis
23. Exterminator's targets
24. Lonely number
25. Back, once you go to
26. Air blower
28. ___ only as directed
30. Kind of: Suffix
31. ___ Cruces, N.M.
32. What it takes to tango
37. Three ___ to the wind
39. Lumberjack's tool

Puzzle 47

Solution on Page 325

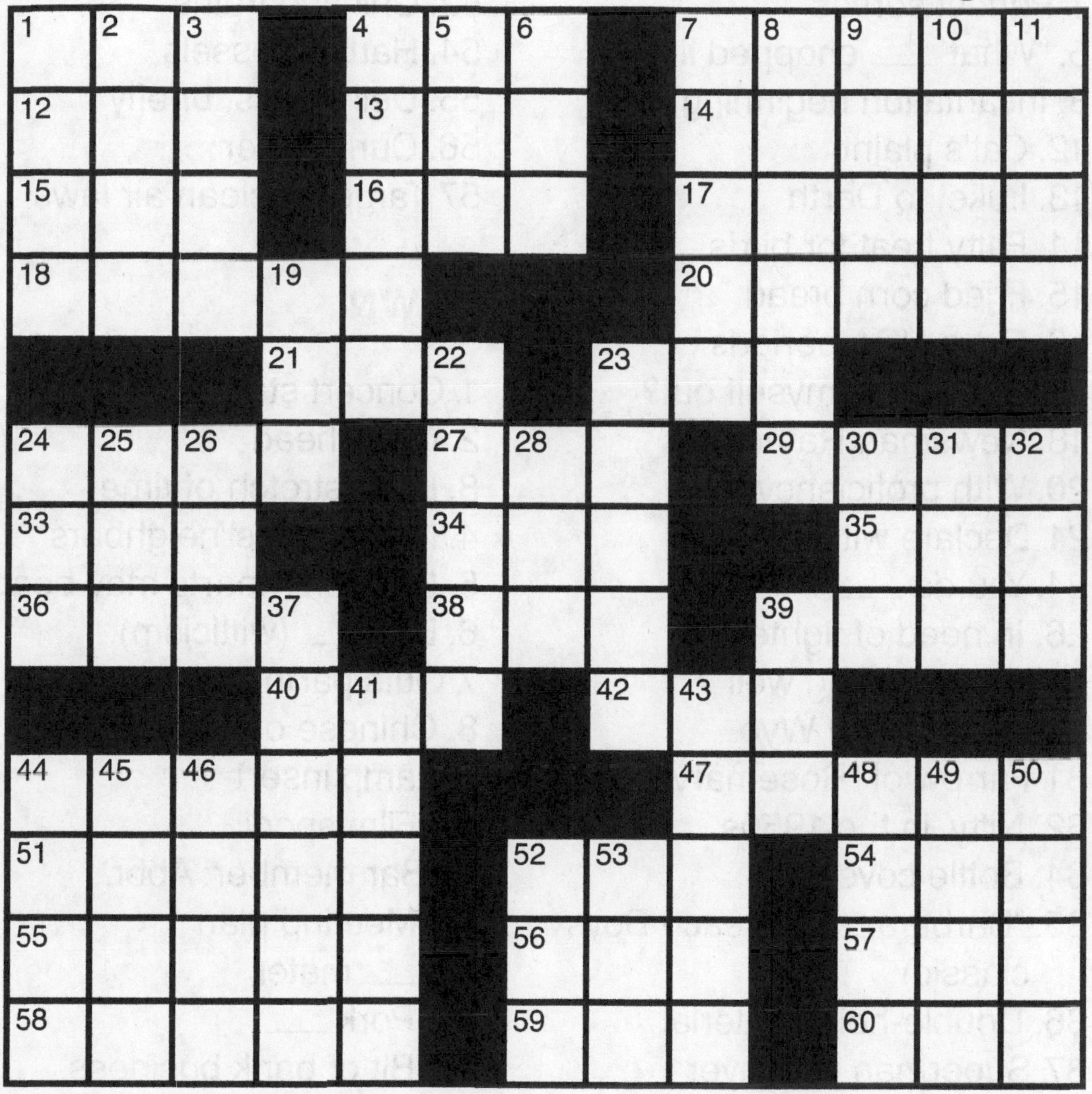

41. Occupied, as a lavatory
43. First appearance, as of symptoms
44. Wheelchair access
45. It's just a thought
46. Waterfront walkway
48. ___ now (immediately)
49. ___ 'em and weep!
50. ___ Lee cakes
52. Now I ___ me down . . .
53. Part of IOU

ACROSS

1. Perfect serves
5. "What ___, chopped liver?"
8. Incantation beginning
12. Cat's plaint
13. Luke, to Darth
14. Fatty treat for birds
15. Fried corn bread
16. Extra NBA periods
17. Okay if ___ myself out?
18. Newsman Rather
20. With proficiency
21. Declare without proof
24. You da ___!
26. In need of tightening
27. Not behaving well
28. Neighbor of Wyo.
31. Farrow of "Rosemary's Baby"
32. Nifty, in the 1950s
34. Bottle cover
35. "Barbara ___" (Beach Boys classic)
36. Double-helix material
37. Superman portrayer Christopher
39. I've ___ it!
40. Telescope parts
41. Mafia boss
44. Mesozoic or Cenozoic
45. Has debts
46. Valedictorian's pride, for short
48. Study feverishly
52. It goes with a nut
53. Chicago trains
54. Harbor vessels
55. Deli orders, briefly
56. Curly poker
57. Target of clean air laws

DOWN

1. Concert stage item
2. Corp. head
3. Long stretch of time
4. Norwegians' neighbors
5. How two hearts may beat
6. Bon ___ (witticism)
7. Outs partners
8. Chinese or Japanese
9. Lamp insert
10. Film spool
11. Bar member: Abbr.
19. Meeting plan
21. ___ mater
22. Pork ___
23. Bit of bank business
24. Place to wipe your shoes
25. Worshipful one
27. Sheep's bleat
28. Chills, as champagne
29. Pulitzer-winning humorist Barry
30. "Planet of the ___"
33. Go off the deep ___

Puzzle 48

Solution on Page 325

38. Passes, as a law
39. Party givers
40. Renter's paper
41. Baseball great Ty
42. Missing from the Marines, say
43. Animal skin
46. Jewel
47. Arafat's group: Abbr.
49. ___ and Coke
50. In times past
51. No ___ (Chinese menu notation)

ACROSS

1. Lobbying grp.
4. Cavity filler's deg.
7. Drunk's sound
10. Clickable screen symbol
12. Sailor's yes
13. Radius or rib
14. Conference-goer
16. ___ about (roughly)
17. Compete (for)
18. Apply, as pressure
19. Place for a squirting flower
22. Construction ___
24. Dr. Frankenstein's helper
25. Citizen Kane's real-life model
28. Writing tools
29. Part of m.p.h.
30. Connery of Bond films
32. Shut tight
34. Loser to the tortoise
35. Strong urges
36. "All That Jazz" choreographer Bob
37. Black card
40. ___ favor (please, in Spanish)
41. Jeans purveyor Strauss
42. Partridge's perch, in song
47. Nobelist Wiesel
48. Curse you, ___ Baron!
49. Belted out, as a tune
50. Join in holy matrimony
51. Gives the green light
52. Say "pretty please"

DOWN

1. Actress Zadora
2. Perform on stage
3. Army bed
4. Miami-___ County, Fla.
5. Cover the gray
6. Lay eyes on
7. Sharpen, as skills
8. Are you ___ out?
9. Part of CPA: Abbr.
11. Keep going!
13. Alternative to briefs
15. Zero
18. When a plane is due in: Abbr.
19. Place to apply gloss
20. Gets on in years
21. Corn bread
22. Outbuildings
23. Suffix with cash
26. Pirates roam them
27. ___ and feathers
29. Animal enclosure
31. Miss-named?
33. Filmmaker Spike
36. ___ Pete's sake!
37. Did away with, as a dragon
38. Brazilian soccer great
39. Like big fans
40. Cushions

Puzzle 49

Solution on Page 326

42. Major leaguer
43. Mouse-spotter's cry
44. Massage
45. WSW's reverse
46. Omelet ingredient

ACROSS

1. Entreat
4. Noun modifier: Abbr.
7. Amorphous mass
11. WWII foe, with "the"
13. British john
14. Ready for the pickin'
15. Joke
16. Place for beakers
17. ___ a man with seven wives
18. Very perceptive
20. Striped equine
21. Where the Yukon is
24. Formal decree
27. Three ___ Night
28. Chang's Siamese twin
31. Number-picker's game
32. Bend over forward
33. Triathlon leg
34. Horned animal
35. Undersea prowler
36. Hapless
37. Magician's cry
39. Bookcase part
43. Simoleons
47. "Les Misérables" author
48. Farrow of films
50. Prince Charles's sport
51. Frozen breakfast brand
52. Naval initials
53. Window box location
54. Cubicle fixture
55. Speed limit abbr.
56. Blurt out

DOWN

1. Cabo's peninsula
2. Former significant others
3. Main idea
4. Filmmaker Woody
5. ___ good deed daily
6. Applicant's goal
7. Runny French cheese
8. Tree branch
9. Letters on a phone's "0" button
10. Alpha follower
12. Plaster work
19. Bit of body art, for short
20. Move after a zig
22. Clay brick
23. Part of DJIA
24. Barely make, with "out"
25. The First State: Abbr.
26. Octopus's defense
28. She sheep
29. Bit of a chill
30. It's eight hours later than PST
32. Prickle
33. Pokes around
35. Tanning-lotion letters
36. What was ___ do?

Puzzle 50

Solution on Page 326

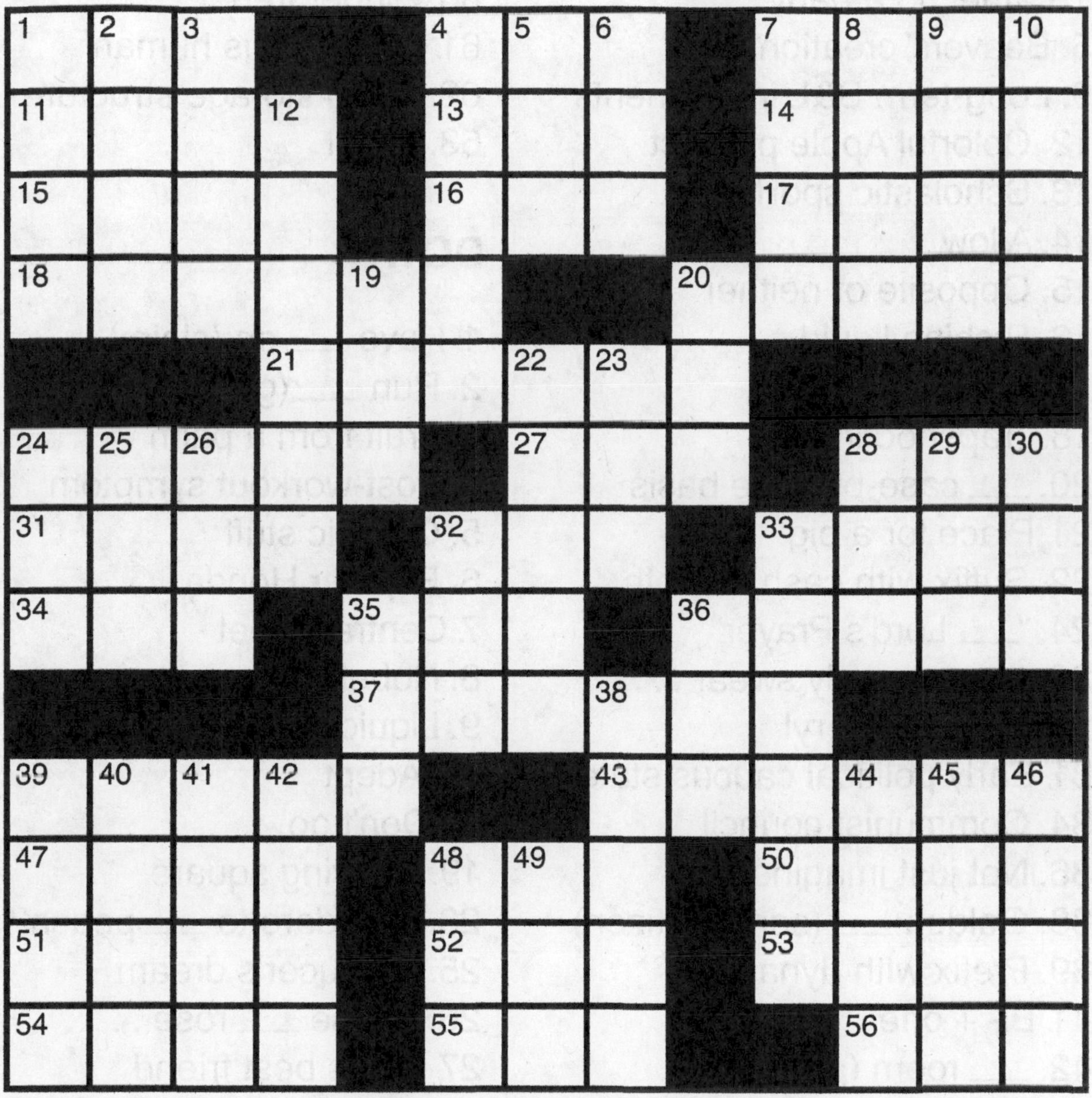

38. Huge hit
39. Tool house
40. Enormous
41. Urges (on)
42. Take a gander
44. Lane of "Superman"
45. It was ___ mistake
46. ___ cow!
48. Not talking
49. AOL, for one

ACROSS

1. Father, to a baby
5. Beavers' creations
9. Long-term S&L investments
12. Colorful Apple product
13. Scholastic sports grp.
14. Allow
15. Opposite of neither
16. Etching liquid
17. Son ___ gun
18. Trapshooting
20. ___ case-by-case basis
21. Place for a pig
22. Suffix with cash or cloth
24. "___ Lord's Prayer"
26. ___ solemnly swear . . .
29. Alan or Cheryl
31. Early political caucus state
34. Communist council
36. Not just imagined
38. Golden ___ (senior citizen)
39. Prefix with dynamic
41. Bi- + one
42. ___ room (play area)
44. "A Few Good ___"
45. Satisfied sounds
47. Letter carrier's assignment: Abbr.
49. Epsom ___
54. Tee-___
55. Snobbish mannerisms
57. Later, to Luigi
58. West of the silver screen
59. Body covering
60. Singer Irene
61. To do this is human
62. Grain storage structure
63. Pitfall

DOWN

1. Have ___ on (claim)
2. Run ___ (go wild)
3. Fruit from a palm
4. Post-workout symptom
5. Genetic stuff
6. Popular Honda
7. Central street
8. Nobelist Anwar
9. Liquidation sale
10. Adept
11. Don't go
19. Flooring square
23. Do I dare to ___ peach?
25. Producer's dream
26. A rose ___ rose . . .
27. Man's best friend
28. Manager
30. How ___ you!
32. ___ of 1812
33. Float like a butterfly, sting like a bee boxer
35. Annoyance
37. Hoodwinks

Puzzle 51

Solution on Page 326

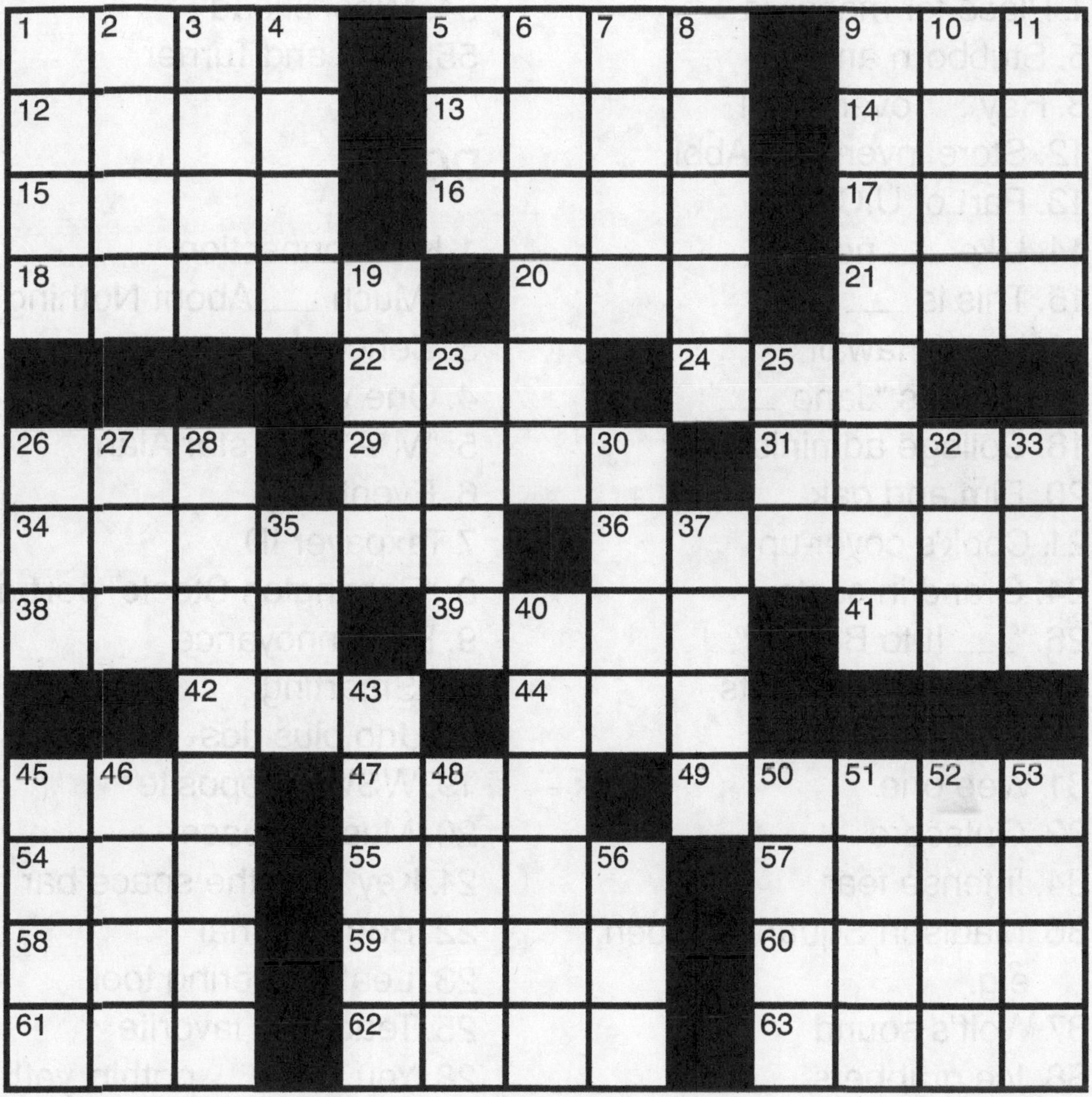

40. Lagasse of the Food Network
43. Lacking refinement
45. Whatever shall I do?
46. "See No Evil, ___ No Evil" (1989)
48. Kind of torch on "Survivor"
50. Bank no.
51. Word repeated before "pants on fire"
52. Scarlett O'Hara's plantation
53. Ivory or Coast
56. ___ Balls: Hostess snacks

ACROSS

1. Place for mascara
5. Stubborn animal
8. Hey . . . over here!
12. Store inventory: Abbr.
13. Part of U.C.L.A.
14. Like ___ not
15. This is ___ toy
16. Ho of Hawaii
17. Bronte's "Jane ___"
18. College administrator
20. Elm and oak
21. Cook's cover-up
24. Grand in scale
26. "___ It to Beaver"
27. Break for students
30. Seize
31. Wee one
32. Outscore
34. Intense fear
36. Madison Square Garden, e.g.
37. Wolf's sound
38. Ice grabbers
39. War horse
42. "A Farewell to ___"
44. Uneaten part of an apple
45. School support org.
46. Shuttle-launching org.
50. Electric or water co.
51. Member of the fam.
52. Ugandan dictator
53. Bucks' mates
54. Miner's load
55. Cole and Turner

DOWN

1. K-O connection
2. "Much ___ About Nothing"
3. Concorde, e.g.
4. One way to fall in love
5. "M*A*S*H" star Alan
6. Eventually
7. Taxpayer ID
8. "Remington Steele" portrayer
9. Eye annoyance
10. Smarting
11. Uno plus dos
19. WSW's opposite
20. Muscle spasm
21. Key near the space bar
22. Bog material
23. Leaf-gathering tool
25. Teacher's favorite
28. You ain't ___ nothin' yet!
29. Crooned
31. Disabled vehicle's need
33. Coll. helpers
35. Serling of "The Twilight Zone"
36. Dispenser of 20s
39. Soviet ballistic missile

Puzzle 52

Solution on Page 326

40. Dog on the Yellow Brick Road
41. . . . fifteen miles on the ___ Canal
43. Rattling breath
45. PGA player
47. "I ___ Rock" (Simon and Garfunkel hit)
48. Command for Fido
49. Reply to a ques.

ACROSS

1. Nightwear, for short
4. Run ___ (go crazy)
8. Bridge declaration
11. Bettors' promises, e.g.
13. Nevada gambling mecca
14. Singer Yoko
15. Actor Sean
16. Part of U.S.A.: Abbr.
17. "Star Wars" mil. project
18. ___ no good: plotting
20. Disney World's ___ Center
22. Native American group
25. Vintner's container
26. Go like a bunny
27. "Sexual Healing" singer Marvin
30. Date with an M.D.
34. ___ Z (the gamut)
35. Lay out cash
37. Shout from the bleachers
38. Rock's Rundgren
40. Opening stake
41. End ___ high note
42. Dot-com's address
44. It's accessed via a manhole
46. Machine shop tool
49. Slide on ice
51. Mensa members have high ones
52. Fit of fever
54. 100-yard ___
58. Break bread
59. Dice throw
60. Family rec facility
61. Prof's aides, briefly
62. "Duck ___" (Marx Brothers film)
63. Yang's complement

DOWN

1. Playing card dot
2. Baseball's DiMaggio
3. Subject of "worship"
4. I smell ___
5. Short note
6. Last number in a countdown
7. Seoul's home
8. Popular pear
9. ___-European (language group)
10. Just ___: Nike slogan
12. Rebuff
19. Cribbage markers
21. Educational org. founded in 1897
22. How about ___?!
23. Newspaper section
24. Apple's portable music player
25. Let it all out
28. C'mon, be ___ ("Do it for me")
29. Tokyo money
31. Ship's front
32. Window section
33. Where she blows

Puzzle 53

Solution on Page 327

36. Lucy's partner
39. Well, that's obvious!
43. Opposite of fronts
45. Small whirlpool
46. "Schindler's ___"
47. Greenish blue
48. Cookbook measures: Abbr.
49. "Star Trek" navigator
50. Kind of seaweed
53. Guck or gunk
55. First daughter Carter
56. Chem. or phys.
57. Solo of "Star Wars"

ACROSS

1. Env. abbr.
5. Rockers ___ Jovi
8. Both: prefix
12. Not exiting, as traffic
13. Wall St. opening
14. Stopped working, as an engine
15. Adolescent
17. . . . ___ I'm told
18. "Little Women" woman
19. Took the blue ribbon
20. Guitar bars
21. Retaliate
23. Brad of "Troy"
26. Telegraph signal
27. Carry on, as a trade
30. Cut some slack
33. Space streaker
35. Calligrapher's purchase
36. Bon ___: witticism
38. Movers' trucks
39. Pertinent
42. Comes to an end
45. Use blades on blades
46. Over-easy item
49. Heavenly music maker
50. Follow too closely
52. Sportscaster Hershiser
53. ___ only me
54. The shoe ___ the other foot
55. Not feral
56. Curly and Larry's cohort
57. AMEX counterpart

DOWN

1. Intro for boy or girl
2. It's us against ___
3. Deuce beater
4. Convent resident
5. Intolerant person
6. Performed prior to the main act
7. Neither rain ___ sleet . . .
8. Decorate
9. Swampy ground
10. Brief letter sign-off
11. Wedding-ceremony exchanges
16. Knock the socks off of
20. Gala gathering
21. Old telecom giant
22. Get-up-and-go
23. Province east of N.B.
24. James Bond creator Fleming
25. Sound of disappointment
27. Split ___ soup
28. Chaney of horror films
29. 52-wk. periods
31. Baseball officials
32. ___ favor: please (Sp.)
34. Family room items
37. BLT need
39. iPhone maker

Puzzle 54

Solution on Page 327

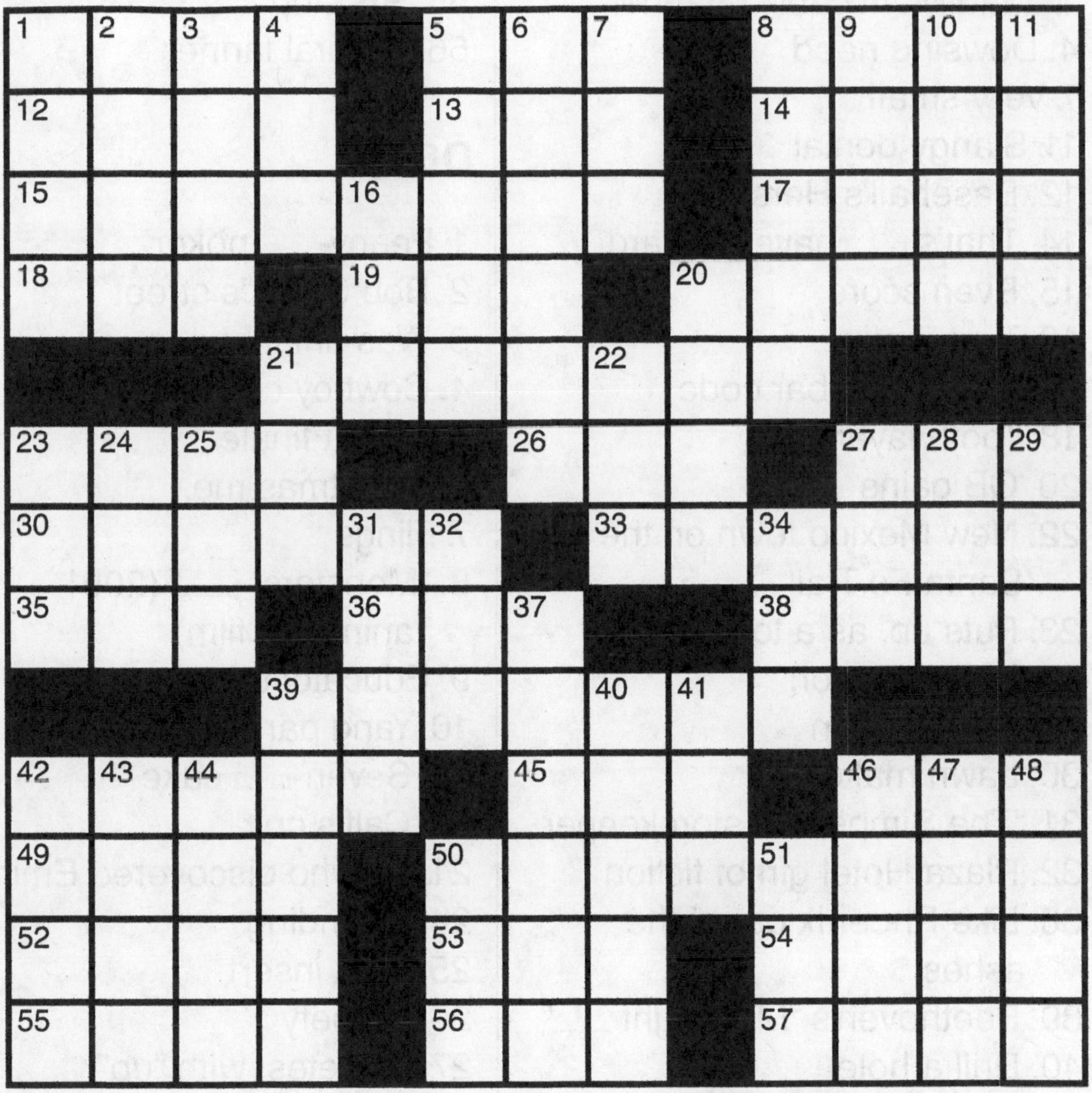

40. Grace under pressure
41. Bird that gives a hoot
42. Pulled the trigger
43. The O'Hara homestead
44. Utah city near Provo
46. Piece of cake!
47. Old Pontiac muscle cars
48. Chromosome part
50. Treasury secretary Geithner
51. Gimlet ingredient

ACROSS

1. "Mad Men" cable channel
4. Dowsing need
7. Very small
11. Slangy denial
12. Baseball's Hershiser
14. That's ___ haven't heard
15. Even score
16. Ten: Prefix
17. Read, as a bar code
18. Tooth layer
20. QB gains
22. New Mexico town on the Santa Fe Trail
23. Puts up, as a tower
27. Apprehension
29. Usher again
30. Lawn makeup
31. "The Simpsons" storekeeper
32. Plaza Hotel girl of fiction
36. Like Phoenix out of the ashes
39. Beethoven's "Moonlight ___"
40. Drill a hole
41. That's my ___ feeling
42. "A Streetcar Named Desire" woman
45. They worshipped from ___
48. ___ a Kick Out of You
50. Part of E.U.: Abbr.
51. Peel, as an apple
52. Cat-o'- ___ -tails
53. ___ Paulo
54. Annual theater award
55. RR stop
56. Natural tanner

DOWN

1. Penny-___ poker
2. Bob Seger's street
3. Was unfaithful to
4. Cowboy contests
5. Threat finale
6. Christmas mo.
7. Flings
8. "Monsters, ___" (2001 animated film)
9. Educator's org.
10. Yang partner
13. Seven-___ cake
19. Calf's cry
21. Dr. who discovered Eminem
24. Unending
25. VCR insert
26. Stupefy
27. Depletes, with "up"
28. ___ contendere: court plea
33. Words of concurrence
34. ___ Sutcliffe, early Beatle
35. Have dinner at home
36. Not present
37. Spoiled
38. Feeling of rage
43. Hawaiian cookout

Puzzle 55

Solution on Page 327

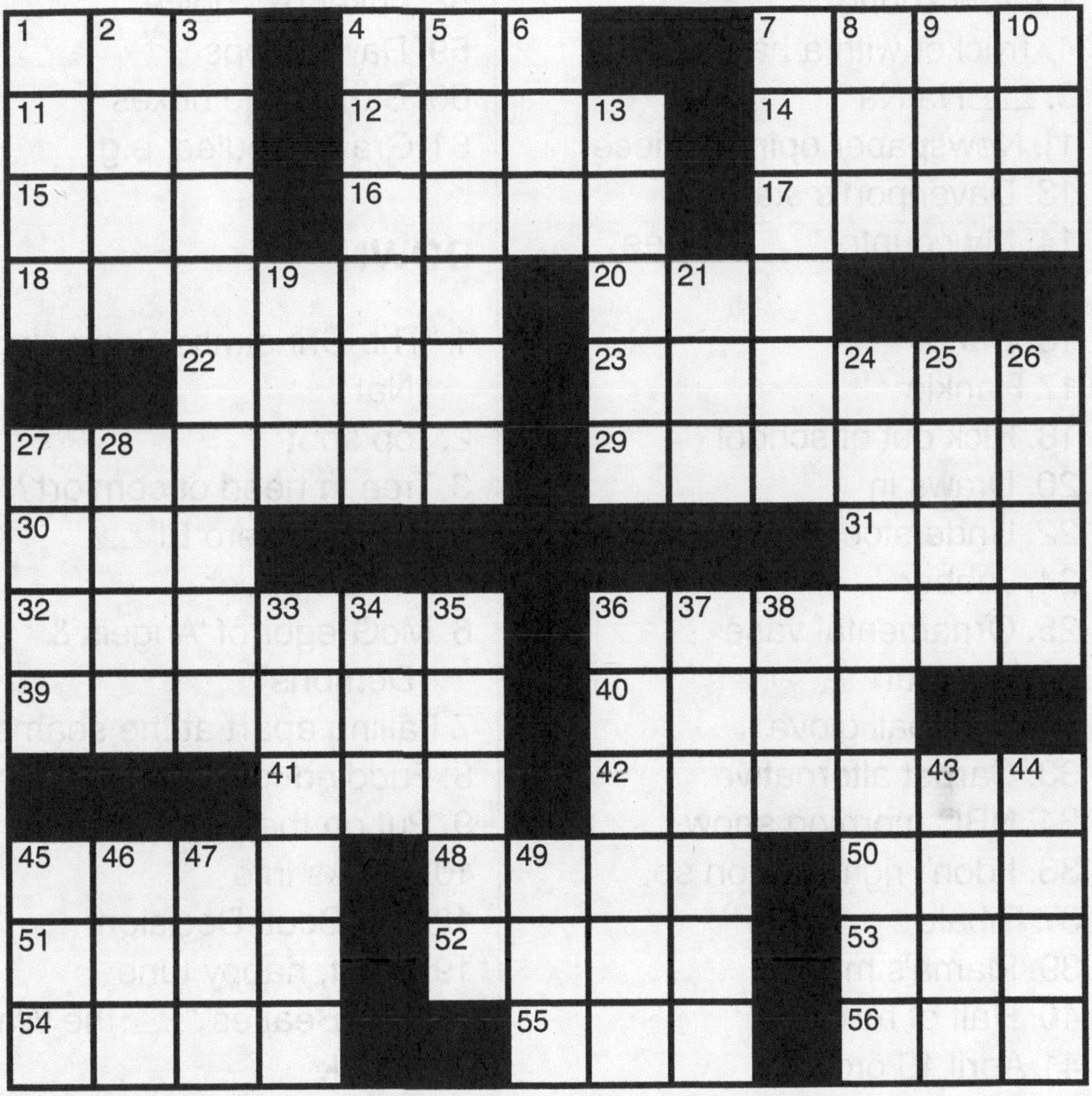

44. Elvis Presley's middle name
45. Part of a GI's address
46. ___ Four (Beatles)
47. Former White House spokesman Fleischer
49. Amer. soldiers

ACROSS

1. Crow sound
4. Trucker with a handle
8. ___ Na Na
11. Newspaper opinion piece
13. Davenport's state
14. My country, ___ of thee
15. Lusty look
16. Dang!
17. Rankle
18. Kick out of school
20. Draws in
22. Understood, hippie-style
24. Jabber
25. Ornamental vase
27. Pork cut
30. Baseball glove
33. Carpet alternative
34. NBC morning show
36. I don't right reckon so
37. Ribald
39. Mama's mate
40. Half of hex-
41. April 15 org.
43. Rainbow shape
45. Something new in LA?
49. Christmas carols
52. Encyc. book
53. "___, Nanette"
55. Dirty reading
56. Nasdaq debut: Abbr.
57. Chicago paper, for short, with "the"
58. Jukebox choice
59. Dawn drops
60. Bandstand boxes
61. Grand Coulee, e.g.

DOWN

1. "The Christmas Song singer" Nat
2. Top spot
3. Tree in need of comfort?
4. Spanish hero El ___
5. Yawn inducer
6. McGregor of "Angels & Demons"
7. Falling apart at the seams
8. Fuddy-duddy
9. Put on the payroll
10. Seeks info
12. ___ Scott Decision
19. Light, happy tune
21. The Beatles' "___ the Walrus"
23. Muck
25. Web address, for short
26. Feel sorry about
28. Where Boise is: Abbr.
29. Wine region near Sacramento
31. ___ and feather
32. Prefix with night or light
35. Tar's tale

Puzzle 56

Solution on Page 327

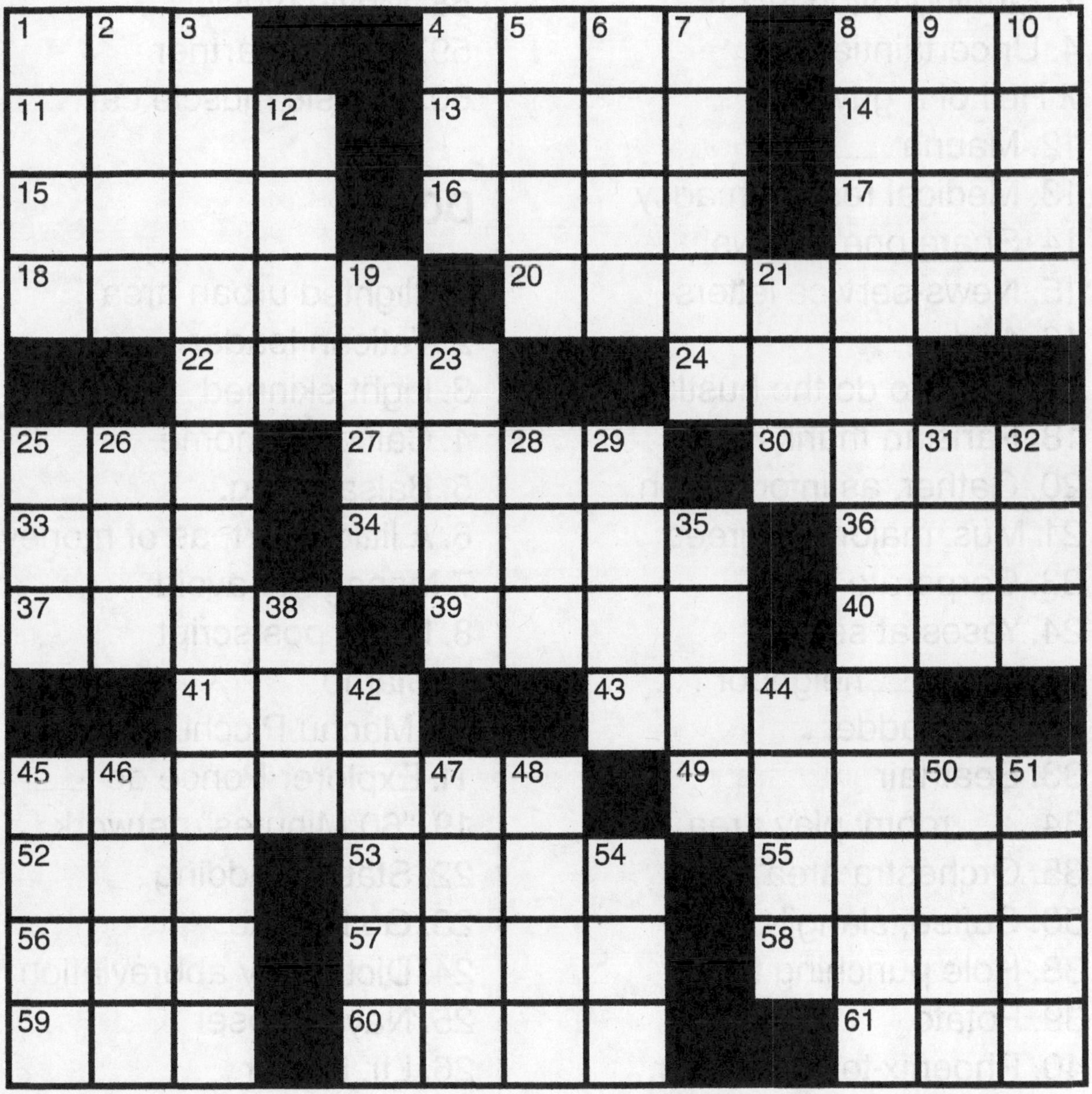

38. Rap's Dr.
42. Ho ho ho crier
44. Retail price
45. Roman love poet
46. Lariat material
47. 100, IQ-wise
48. Quick cut
50. Moon goddess
51. Flower part
54. No longer used: Abbr.

ACROSS

1. Tanning lotion letters
4. Uncertainties
7. Hell of a guy?
12. Mauna ___
13. Medical research agcy.
14. Share one's views
15. News-service letters
16. Arid
17. Place to do the hustle
18. Parisian thanks
20. Gather, as information
21. Mus. majors' degrees
23. Corporate V.I.P.
24. Yeses at sea
27. Love ___ neighbor . . .
29. ___ bladder
33. Bear lair
34. ___ room: play area
35. Orchestra area
36. Coffee, slangily
38. Hole punching tool
39. Potato
40. Phoenix-to-Seattle dir.
42. Cry of fear
44. Kemo Sabe's companion
47. Far-reaching view
51. Bikini Island, e.g.
52. Tournament exemption
54. No. on a business card
55. Stanford-___ test
56. ___ voyage!
57. Egyptian reptile
58. Movie music
59. Paste's partner
60. Classic muscle car

DOWN

1. Blighted urban area
2. Vatican leader
3. Light-skinned
4. Calcutta's home
5. Balsam, e.g.
6. A little short, as of money
7. Manage to avoid
8. Novel postscript
9. Clamp
10. Machu Picchu builder
11. Explorer Ponce de ___
19. "60 Minutes" network
22. Stable bedding
23. Go by bike
24. Dictionary abbreviation
25. Nay opposer
26. Ltr. holder
28. Chop
30. Killer computer program
31. Brooklyn campus: Abbr.
32. Inc., in England
37. Buck's defense
39. Go down a slippery slope

Puzzle 57

Solution on Page 328

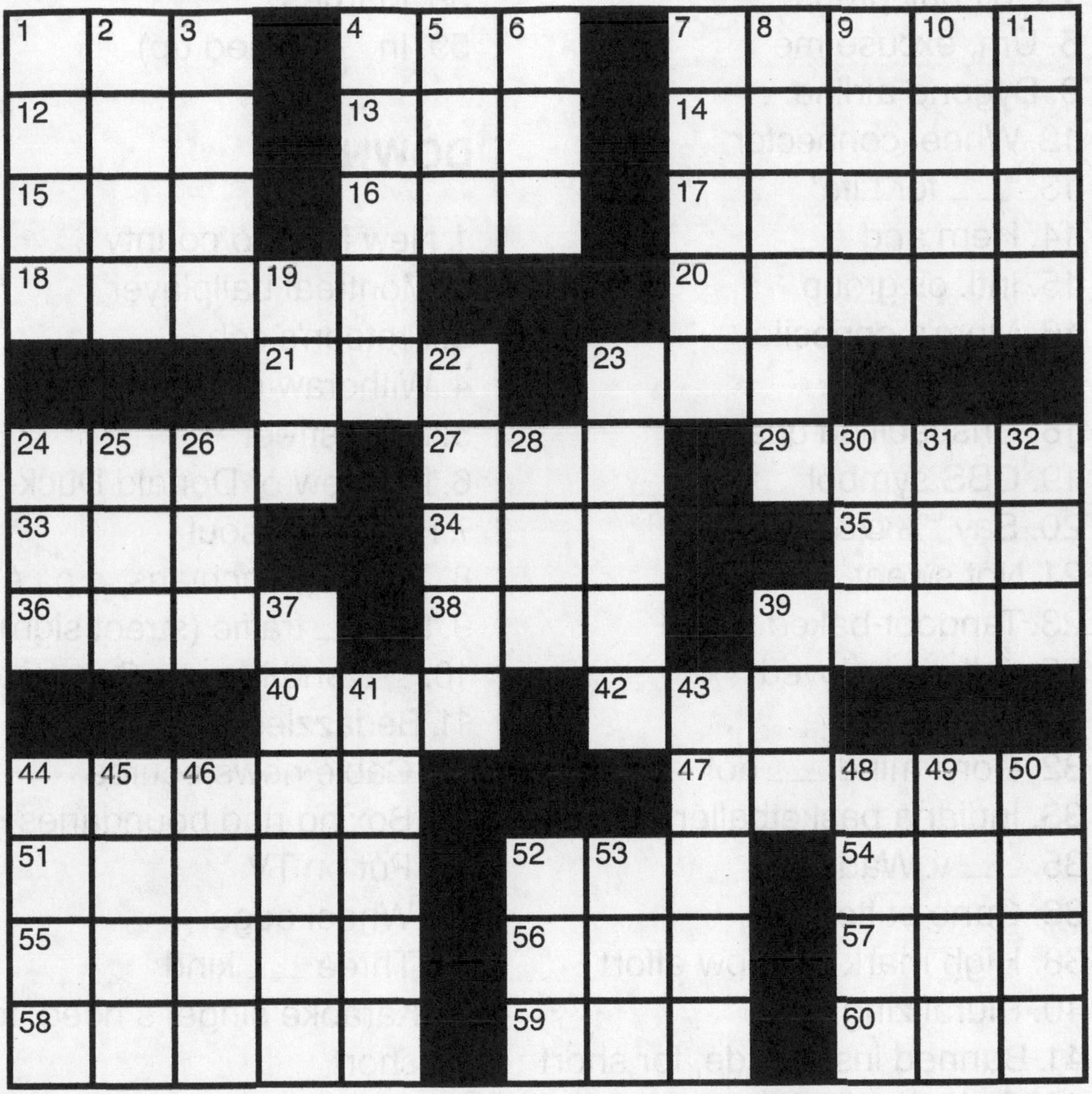

41. "The Prince of Tides" star Nick
43. Episode
44. Keep ___ on (watch)
45. Hearing-related
46. Faux pas
48. Fawn's father
49. Final or midterm
50. Brand for Fido
52. U.K. television network
53. Golden Rule pronoun

ACROSS

1. Golf ball props
5. Um, excuse me
9. Bygone airline
12. Wheel connector
13. "___ for Life"
14. Hem and ___
15. Intl. oil group
16. More's opposite
17. Ham on ___
18. Unspecified quantity
19. CBS symbol
20. Say "%@&#!"
21. Not sweet, as wine
23. Tandoor-baked bread
25. Juliet's beloved
28. Frigidity
32. Don't mind ___ do!
33. Indiana basketballer
35. ___ v. Wade
36. Cane cutter
38. High mark with low effort
40. Pluralizing letter
41. Banned insecticide, for short
42. Swing in the breeze
45. Day of the wk.
47. A lot
51. Advanced degree
52. Florist's vessel
53. ___ the Terrible
54. Tic-tac-toe victory
55. Approved
56. Jay who does "Jaywalking"
57. Prof's helpers
58. Marries
59. In ___ (lined up)

DOWN

1. New Mexico county
2. Montreal ballplayer
3. Preteen's sch.
4. Withdraw (from)
5. Back street
6. Nephew of Donald Duck
7. Heart and soul
8. The Appalachians, e.g.: Abbr.
9. No ___ traffic (street sign)
10. ___ and Means Committee
11. Bedazzles
20. Cable news source
22. Boxing ring boundaries
24. Put on TV
25. Wheel edge
26. Three ___ kind
27. Karaoke singer's need, for short
28. Freezer trayful
29. Ambulance destinations, for short
30. Wok-user's sauce
31. Adriatic or Aegean
34. Being risked
37. You, over there!
39. King of the Huns

Puzzle 58

Solution on Page 328

41. Owners' documents
42. Dick and Jane's dog
43. Stop!
44. Bustles
46. Like Goodwill goods
48. Eggs ___ easy
49. One billionth: Prefix
50. Falling flakes
52. I do, for one

ACROSS

1. ___ fun at (ridicule)
5. Edinburgh native
9. ABBA's "Mamma ___"
12. Barely manages, with "out"
13. Task list heading
14. ___ in the bag
15. Pecan and pumpkin
16. Pink, as cheeks
17. Educ. institution
18. Makes very happy
20. Sore all over
21. Talk, talk, talk
22. "Oedipus ___"
24. Deep gorge
27. Heredity-related
31. School transportation
32. Like an eagle in flight
34. Hosp. area for emergency cases
35. Like a clear night sky
37. Sprinted
39. Minister, slangily
40. So ___, so good
41. Detroit products
44. Truman who wrote "Breakfast at Tiffany's"
47. Chimp or gorilla
48. What the "ten" of "hang ten" refers to
50. ___ Lisa
52. Game show host Sajak
53. Litter weakling
54. Circle segments
55. Like octogenarians
56. Music, ballet, sculpture, etc.
57. Polio vaccine developer

DOWN

1. Liven (up)
2. Muskogee native
3. On an even ___ (stable)
4. School papers
5. Throat ailment
6. Dove or love murmurs
7. Pigs out (on), briefly
8. Kind of poodle
9. Various: Abbr.
10. Something to scratch
11. Like a fireplace floor
19. Tex-Mex snack
20. Logger's tool
22. N.B.A. official
23. Lure into crime
24. "60 Minutes" airer
25. Quonset ___
26. Smart ___ whip
27. "I ___ You Babe"
28. ___ Tac (breath freshener)
29. Skater's surface
30. What a cow chews
33. Actress Tyler of "Armageddon"
36. Train lines: Abbr.

Puzzle 59

Solution on Page 328

38. Inviting smells
40. Abstains from eating
41. Aria da ___
42. Be ___ . . . : "Help me"
43. AARP part: Abbr.
44. Coin with Lincoln's profile
45. When said three times, a 1970 war film
46. SASE, e.g.
48. Syllable before "la la"
49. First word of the Lord's Prayer
51. Query

ACROSS

1. Spoiled kid
5. Talk show host Dr. ___
9. ___ up or shut up!
12. Misplace
13. Boorish
14. Geller with a psychic act
15. Use the Selectric
16. RPI or MIT
17. Bobby's wife on "Dallas"
18. Silent
20. Syrup flavor
22. Holey cheese
25. Itsy-bitsy
27. Wrestling success
28. Iowa crop
30. Hollywood's Ken or Lena
33. American mil. fliers
35. ___ center (community facility)
36. Joint point
37. Pastrami purveyor
38. Hay bundle
40. W–Z, e.g., in an encyc.
41. Uneasy feeling
43. Turtle cover
45. And Jill came tumbling ___
47. Don't ___ fool!
48. Comic strip cry
49. Partner in war
52. Estrangement
56. Perjure oneself
57. Chimney sweep's target
58. 50-50
59. Camera initials
60. Newspaper unit
61. Mended

DOWN

1. Three-letter sandwich
2. Crying singer Orbison
3. Nile snake
4. Swarms (with)
5. ___ and proper
6. Attila or one of his followers
7. Driver's lic. and such
8. ___ tell you something . . .
9. Adolescent infatuation
10. ___ Mountains: Europe/Asia border range
11. Person of the Year magazine
19. O.J.'s alma mater
21. Author unknown: Abbr.
22. Potato, informally
23. Sensible
24. All worked up
25. Trick or ___
26. Letter accompanier: Abbr.
29. Heavenly bodies
31. Fox TV's "American ___"
32. Carter of "Gimme a Break!"
34. Jaywalker's punishment
39. WNW's opposite
42. Take hold of

Puzzle 60

Solution on Page 328

44. Jackrabbits, actually
45. Pointy tools
46. Pass alternative
47. Data unit
50. Hawaii's Mauna ___
51. Nautical journal
53. "___ Got the World on a String"
54. Handful
55. Former "Grand Ole Opry" network

ACROSS

1. Loose ___ sink ships
5. Oscar Madison, for one
9. Hair styles
12. Guilty or not guilty
13. Barber's focus
14. Checkout bars: Abbr.
15. Happy
16. Christmas season
17. Govt. narcotics watchdog
18. No questions ___
20. Put back in office
22. Work too hard
24. "Private Practice" network
27. Voice-master Blanc
28. Bag
32. Comb-over alternative
34. Dinosaur remnant
36. Contrived
37. "Raiders of the Lost ___"
38. Lunch meat
39. Singer Newton-John
42. Smeltery input
45. Sing in the Alps
50. At this moment
51. Containers
53. Paddy crop
54. Fawn's mother
55. ___ Velva
56. "___ Fire" (Springsteen hit)
57. Paycheck stub letters
58. Committed perjury
59. Lady's man

DOWN

1. Women's links org.
2. Woes
3. Summit
4. Infamous marquis
5. Unassertive
6. Winner's wreath
7. Edmonton hockey player
8. Kennel club classification
9. City slicker
10. Assn. with many Gulf members
11. Jazzy improv style
19. Stadium cover
21. At a ___ for words
23. Peace sign shape
24. 24-hr. banking convenience
25. Squeezing snake
26. Twice-chewed food
29. Cigarette residue
30. Espionage gp.
31. SAS competitor
33. Menial laborer
34. Part of T.G.I.F.: Abbr.
35. Authorize
37. Street
40. From around here
41. Baghdad resident
42. Archaeologist Jones, for short

Puzzle 61

Solution on Page 329

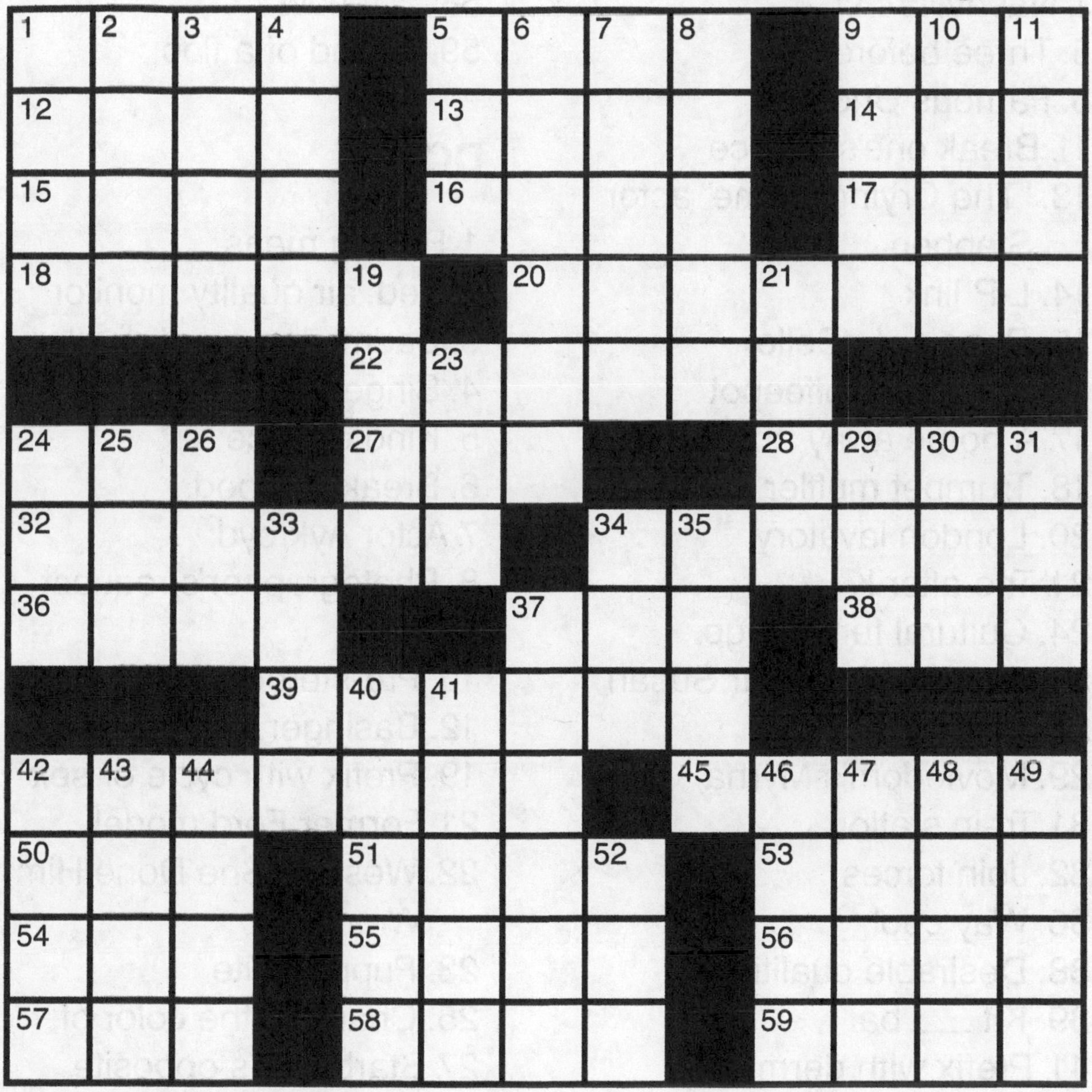

43. ___ canal (dental operation)
44. Was in debt to
46. Not a copy: Abbr.
47. Ten-cent piece
48. Subj. for Keynes
49. Loaned
52. ___ but true

ACROSS

1. Nashville's st.
5. Three before E
8. Famous Uncle
11. Break one's silence
13. "The Crying Game" actor Stephen
14. L-P link
15. Page or LaBelle
16. Caterer's coffeepot
17. A home away from home
18. Trumpet muffler
20. London lavatory
21. Trio after K
24. Cultural funding gp.
25. "L.A. Law" co-star Susan
26. Taiwan's capital
29. Moviedom's Myrna
31. Train station
32. Join forces
36. Way cool
38. Desirable qualities
39. Kit ___ bar
41. Prefix with dermal
43. Break, as a balloon
44. Not Rep. or Dem.
45. Apple carrier
47. Beatty of film
48. Hosp. diagnostic
49. Mine passage
54. Garfield, e.g.
55. Paper Mate product
56. Furry marsupial
57. "Without further ___ . . ."
58. ___-haw
59. Sound of a flop

DOWN

1. Baking meas.
2. Fed. air quality monitor
3. Badminton court divider
4. Singer ___ King Cole
5. Kind of force
6. Breakfast food
7. Actor Aykroyd
8. Photographer's request
9. Pester
10. Pre-stereo sound
12. Basinger of "Batman"
19. Prefix with cycle or sex
21. Former Ford model
22. West of "She Done Him Wrong"
23. Puppy's bite
25. Changes the color of
27. Starboard's opposite
28. Pilot's prediction, for short
30. Some chants
33. House member, for short
34. Powerful Pontiac
35. Sixth sense: Abbr.
37. Formal order
38. USAF part
39. Work, as dough

Puzzle 62

Solution on Page 329

40. Build on
42. Revolutionary pamphleteer Thomas
44. Peruvian of old
46. Tongue-clucking sound
48. Dashboard abbr.
50. Steamy
51. That hits the spot!
52. Cold and ___ season
53. Just a ___

ACROSS

1. Affectionate embraces
5. Tabloid fliers
9. Mustache site
12. Words before uproar or instant
13. Snare
14. Zsa Zsa's sister
15. Card game for one
17. Floor covering
18. Obviously!
19. Carbon copy
21. Sticky problem
24. Welles or Bean
26. Provide weapons for
27. Just dandy
29. ___ Romeo: sports car
32. Like some tea
34. Last letter
35. Seriously injure
36. Over hill and ___
37. Acorn producers
39. Dryly humorous
40. Tennis great Ivan
42. Sniffers
44. Arcade game maker
46. What golfers try to break
47. Prickly husk
48. Kitchen gadget that turns
54. Paleozoic, for one
55. Barely earned, with "out"
56. Do as directed
57. Blasting stuff
58. Pied Piper followers
59. Drink with unagi

DOWN

1. ___ and hers
2. Numero ___
3. "My ___ Sal"
4. Nasty, as a remark
5. 2002 Winter Olympics locale
6. TGIF day
7. Boat mover
8. Glasses, informally
9. Car buyers' protection
10. As a czar, he was terrible
11. Chopped liver spread
16. Surf and ___
20. Good farm soil
21. Picked up the tab
22. Willy of "Free Willy"
23. Suspect dishonesty
24. Ryan of "Love Story"
25. Smell strongly
28. Polo Ralph Lauren competitor
30. Cannoneer's command
31. Writers Lowell and Tan
33. Bambi's kin
38. Attention-getting sound
41. More friendly
43. Nabisco cookies
44. Aid and ___

Puzzle 63

Solution on Page 329

45. Chance to play in a game
46. Pea holders
49. Alias letters
50. Butterfly catcher's tool
51. Wizards and Magic org.
52. Mouse sighter's cry
53. Bread with seeds

ACROSS

1. Roadside rest
4. Crows' cries
8. Stage scenery
11. Plumber's concern
13. Going ___: fighting
14. Holiday preceder
15. ___ duck
16. Bond's first film foe
17. Bygone Russian space station
18. Animal in a roundup
20. Tel Aviv native
22. Writing points
24. Banquet hosts: Abbr.
25. Fast plane: Abbr.
28. Disneyland's Enchanted ___ Room
30. Website address starter
33. Ride a seesaw
35. Magician's hiding place
37. Univ. sports org.
38. Carnegie or Evans
40. Uncooked
41. "It's a Wonderful Life" studio
43. Apartment payment
45. Biology or chemistry
48. Salon jobs
52. Actor Chaney
53. Adds (up)
55. Neato!
56. Ft. above sea level, to a pilot
57. Many are about nothing
58. Pro or con, in a debate
59. Pontiac in a 1960s hit song
60. Unskilled laborer
61. Column crosser

DOWN

1. Aches and pains
2. Uncluttered
3. Partner of rank and serial number
4. Real heel
5. In harm's way
6. Successes
7. Lightning and thunder event
8. School period
9. Satan's work
10. Hatcher of "Desperate Housewives"
12. Like an eagle's vision
19. Baptism or bar mitzvah
21. Feel sore
23. Feathered friend
25. Depot: Abbr.
26. Triple ___ (orange-flavored liqueur)
27. Rip open
29. ___ of Wight
31. Dam-building agcy.
32. Cathedral seat
34. ___ it or leave it!
36. Period after Mardi Gras

Puzzle 64

Solution on Page 329

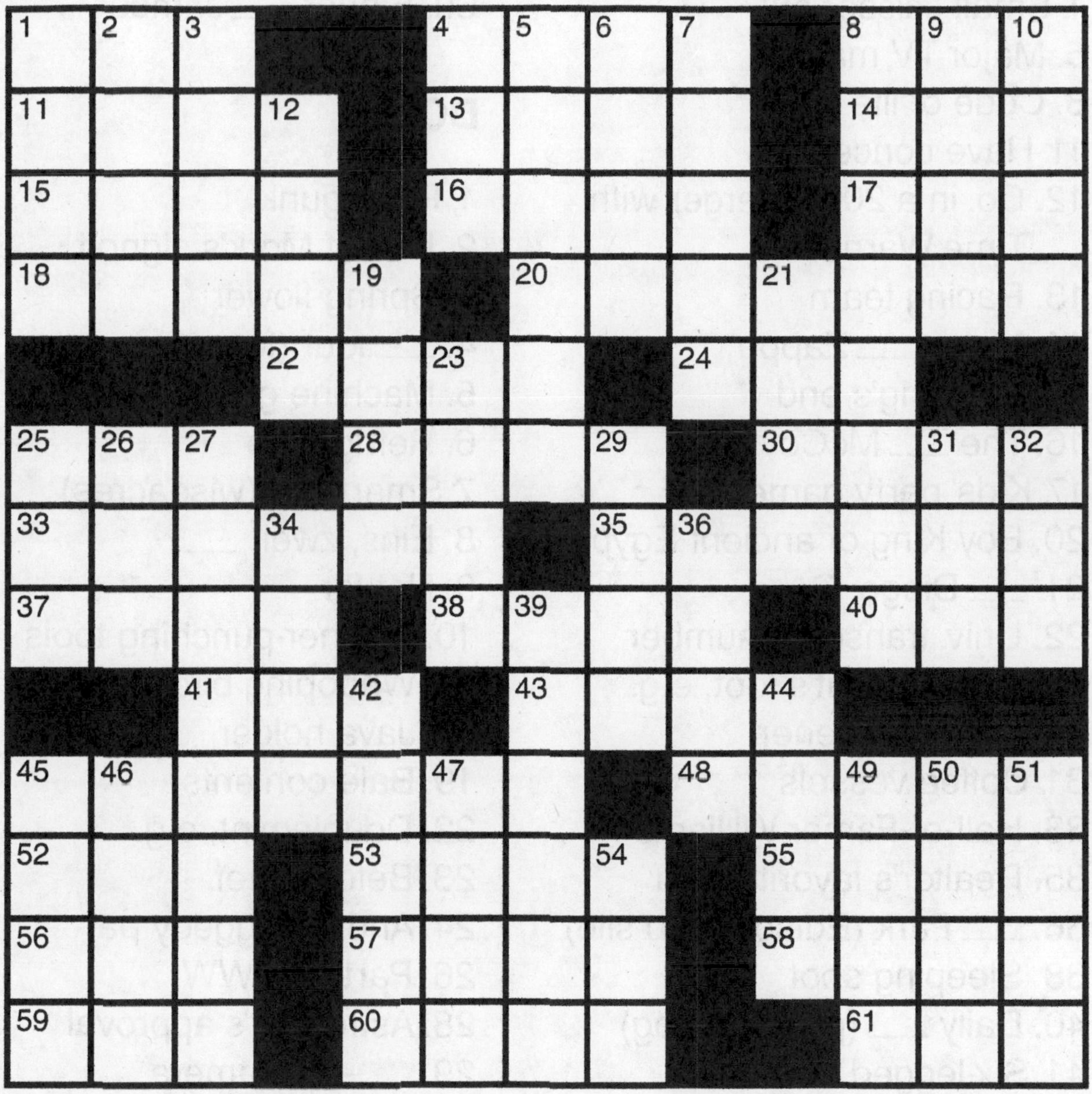

39. Am not! rejoinder
42. Ready to serve, as beer
44. Uncontrollable movements
45. Smelter residue
46. Future stallion
47. Morse ___
49. Film ___ (movie genre)
50. Chore list heading
51. Dispatched, as a dragon
54. Payroll ID

ACROSS

1. Small scissor cut
5. Major TV maker
8. Code of life
11. Have concern
12. Co. in a 2001 merger with Time Warner
13. Racing team
14. Moon ___ Zappa
15. Stocking's end
16. The ___ McCoy
17. Kids' party game
20. Boy King of ancient Egypt
21. ___ Diego, CA
22. Univ. transcript number
25. Lucky rabbit's foot, e.g.
27. Dough leavener
31. Coffee vessels
33. Hall-of-Famer Williams
35. Realtor's favorite sign
36. ___ Park (Edison's lab site)
38. Sleeping spot
40. Daily ___ (political blog)
41. Six-legged worker
43. Solar system center
45. Not a city child
52. Heloise offering
53. D.C.'s Pennsylvania, for one
54. Country music's McEntire
55. Tiny hill dwellers
56. Fellows
57. Moved very fast
58. Bout ender, briefly
59. Nev. clock setting
60. Singer ___ James

DOWN

1. Pond gunk
2. Half of Mork's signoff
3. Spring flower
4. ___ four (teacake)
5. Machine gun sound
6. Refrigerate
7. Smart ___ (wiseacres)
8. Eins, zwei, ___
9. Not far
10. Leather-punching tools
13. Whooping birds
18. Java holder
19. Bale contents
22. Doublemint, e.g.
23. Before: Pref.
24. Andy's raggedy pal
26. Part of WWW
28. Astronaut's approval
29. ___-mo camera
30. QB's scores
32. Leans
34. Drop
37. Niagara Falls' prov.
39. Batman and Robin
42. "Lady and the ___"
44. Nightingale or Barton, e.g.
45. Swap words on the web

Puzzle 65

Solution on Page 330

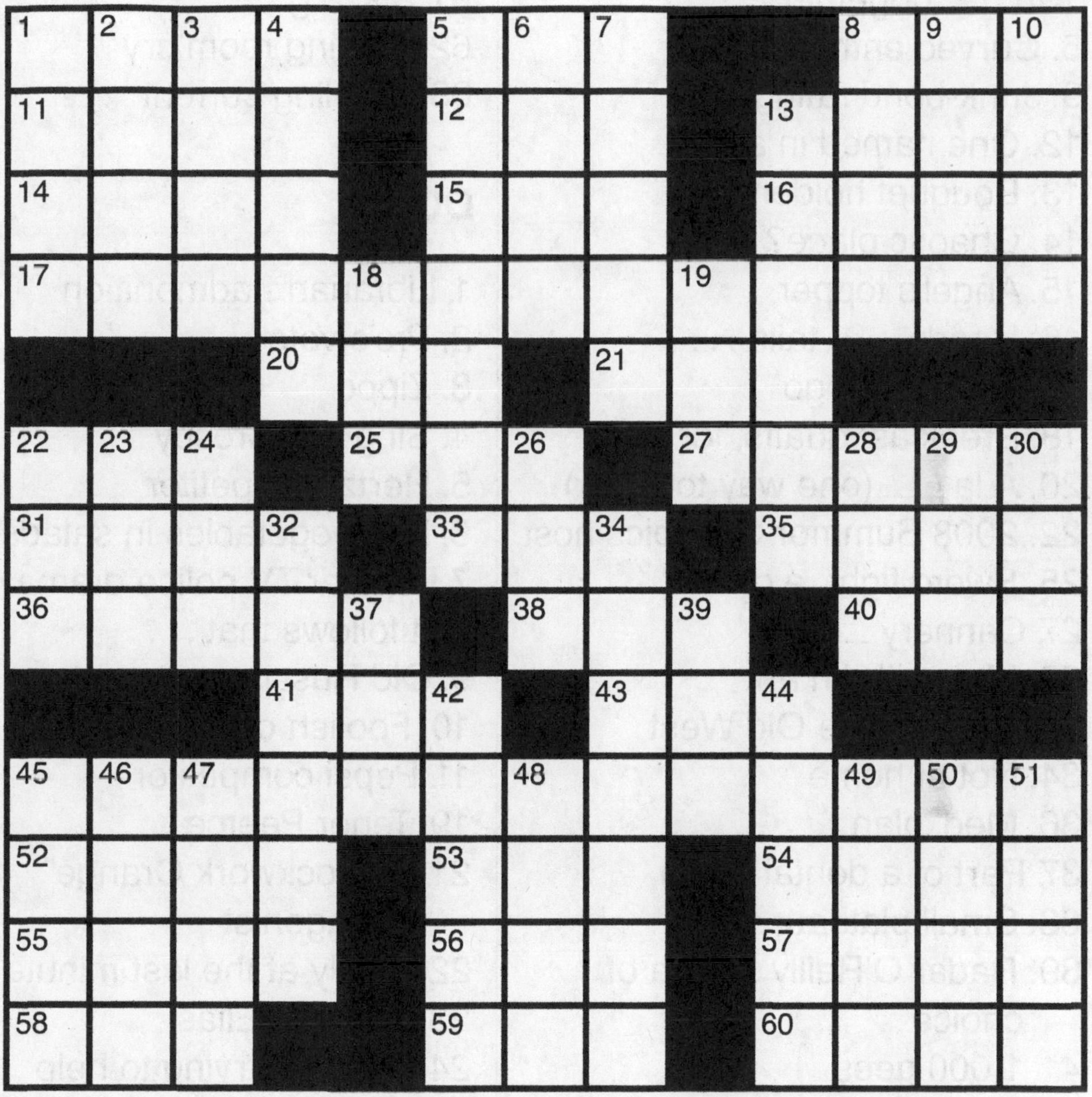

46. Sty sound
47. Render ___ Caesar . . .
48. ___ St. Laurent
49. Equinox mo.
50. Sarcastic agreement
51. Zilch, to Pedro

ACROSS

1. In ___ (together)
5. Curved entranceway
9. Junk-bond rating
12. One named in a will
13. Bouquet holder
14. Chaotic place?
15. Angel's topper
16. Heads ___, tails . . .
17. All systems go
18. Breakfast quaffs, for short
20. À la ___ (one way to order)
22. 2008 Summer Olympics host
25. Sword fight, e.g.
27. Cannery ___
28. Man with an ark
30. Wyatt of the Old West
34. Not at home
36. Med. plan
37. Part of a dental exam
38. Small plateau
39. Radar O'Reilly's soda of choice
41. 1,000 gees
42. Country abutting Vietnam
44. Hair arrangement
46. Lucy's best friend
49. Half a dance name
50. Quilters' gathering
51. Lazily
54. Actor Pitt
58. It's c-c-cold!
59. Pop music's Bee ___
60. Wolf's shelter
61. Sis, e.g.
62. Waiting room cry
63. Whirling current

DOWN

1. Librarian's admonition
2. Pro's vote
3. Zippo
4. Sing like Crosby
5. Hertz competitor
6. Like vegetables in salads
7. Popular TV police drama
8. It follows that . . .
9. Old Russian autocrat
10. Foolish one
11. Pepsi competitor
19. Tenor Peerce
21. "A Clockwork Orange" protagonist
22. Study at the last minute
23. Inventor Elias
24. ___ only trying to help
25. Knights' ladies
26. Now we're in trouble!
29. This looks bad!
31. West Point team
32. Train track part
33. Ernie or Gomer
35. Connecticut campus
40. Suffix with devil

Puzzle 66

Solution on Page 330

43. Arrange in a row
45. Billiards furniture
46. Falls away
47. Bond girl Hatcher
48. Parsley, sage, rosemary, or thyme
49. Bodily sac
52. Sandra or Ruby
53. Superman foe ___ Luthor
55. Groovy!
56. Partner of abet
57. Like some martinis

ACROSS

1. ___ and now
5. "___ Na Na"
8. Twirl
12. Man in Eden
13. May and June: Abbr.
14. ___-Cola
15. Local bond, familiarly
16. Two-by-two vessel
17. Give the thumbs-up
18. Gretzky's grp.
20. Eyeglass part
21. Sex ___
24. Puddle gunk
26. Mama Judd
27. Fix illegally
28. Small amount
31. Chip go-with
32. "The Mary Tyler Moore Show" spin-off
34. Post-op locale
35. 1999 and 2000: Abbr.
36. Wall Street index, with "the"
37. Sans clothing
39. Part of a gearwheel
40. Look up to
41. Peter the Great, for one
44. China's Chairman ___
45. Missing a deadline
46. ___ Guevara
48. Small screen award
52. Don't count ___!
53. Try to get elected
54. Born and ___
55. Le Pew of cartoons
56. Balance sheet abbr.
57. Helps

DOWN

1. Sandwich meat
2. University web address suffix
3. Fled the scene
4. "8 Mile" rapper
5. Wee
6. Vert. opposite
7. Pose a question
8. Give a tongue-lashing
9. Place for a pig?
10. Sammy Davis Jr.'s "Yes ___"
11. Thumbs-down votes
19. Bob or beehive
21. Raggedy doll
22. Duo
23. Boston ___
24. Prefix with shipman
25. Where Idi Amin ruled
27. Use the oars
28. Hawaiian carving
29. Skillful server on the court
30. Fellow, slangily
33. Greedy type
38. One-celled protozoan

Puzzle 67

Solution on Page 330

39. Largest Greek island
40. Revise
41. Horse hoof sound
42. Writer Grey
43. Eagerly expecting
46. "When Doves ___" (Prince)
47. Primitive home
49. Hosp. test
50. Club ___ (resort)
51. Football gains: Abbr.

ACROSS

1. Fem. opposite
5. Biol. or anat.
8. One of the five Ws
12. Word form for "eight"
13. It'll be ___ little secret
14. Bonanza son
15. Money in Mexico
16. 76ers' org.
17. The Hawkeye State
18. Women's golf org.
20. Playful aquatic animal
21. High-class tie
24. Clinton's veep
26. ___ on (pressures)
27. Selects from the menu
30. Wise man
31. Take more than one's share of
32. Loads
34. Took for a trial run
36. Discourage from proceeding
37. LP-playing system
38. Begins on Broadway
39. Twin Mary-Kate or Ashley
42. Poet Ogden
44. ___ of thumb
45. Gross!
46. "___ Love Her"
50. Bondsman's security
51. Bedwear, informally
52. Popular lunch hour
53. Soapy froth
54. Magnon start
55. Voyage with Captain Kirk

DOWN

1. Floor-washing aid
2. ___ Ventura (Jim Carrey role)
3. Rds. or aves.
4. Be kept waiting
5. Ballad, for example
6. "Jerry Maguire" Oscar winner
7. Lyricist Gershwin
8. Unwanted possession
9. Owl sound
10. R.E.M.'s "It's the End of the World ___ Know It"
11. Ivan or Nicholas
19. Quart parts: Abbr.
20. Run-of-the-mill: Abbr.
21. Capone and Pacino
22. By the ___ of one's pants
23. Zoo unit
25. Alternative to .com or .edu
28. Mechanical routine
29. WWII submachine gun
31. Playboy Mansion guy
33. Sophs., two years later
35. Can metal
36. MS-___
39. Spherical shapes

Puzzle 68

Solution on Page 330

40. Hawaiian feast
41. Lost control on ice
43. I get it, humorously
45. It's scanned at checkout: Abbr.
47. "The world will little note, ___ long remember, what we say here" (Lincoln)
48. Unidentified John
49. Printer's need

ACROSS

1. Hwys.
4. Chair part
7. Epic story
11. Nope's opposite
12. Soothing agent
14. Similar (to)
15. November event
17. Turns bronze
18. Scented pouch
19. Former rival of Pan Am
21. PC application file extension
22. Takes an apartment
25. Grant and Carter
28. Doberman's doc
29. 18-wheeler
31. Pod veggies
32. Membership charge
33. Mechanical teeth
34. Friend
35. Opposite of post-
36. Tolstoy's "___ Karenina"
37. Make fun of
39. "The Simpsons" shopkeeper
41. Suit accessory
42. Spoke roughly
46. Fair to middling
49. Caveman's era
51. Yoked beasts
52. Hanks and Cruise
53. This weighs a ___!
54. Simpleton
55. Hurrah!
56. Letter before tee

DOWN

1. Deli loaves
2. Boxer Oscar ___ Hoya
3. Job detail, briefly
4. Lab glove material
5. Best of the best
6. Slime
7. The devil
8. Alias, for short
9. Cotton ___
10. Response to a ques.
13. Main order in a restaurant
16. Fischer's forte
20. Dampen
23. 1982 sci-fi film
24. Aries or Libra
25. iPhone download
26. Vegetarians avoid it
27. The Clintons' alma mater
28. Geese formation
30. Govt. property overseer
32. Least restrained
33. ___ célèbre
35. Tire pressure abbr.
38. Make amends (for)
39. Inviting smell
40. Colorful violet
43. Hors d'oeuvre spread
44. Self-images

Puzzle 69

Solution on Page 331

45. Family rooms
46. Piece of turf
47. Nonwinning tic-tac-toe line
48. Labor Day mo.
50. Cracker Jack bonus

ACROSS

1. Lower, as the lights
4. Walked (on)
8. Carbonated drink
12. Grand ___ Opry
13. Went on horseback
14. Semi-convertible auto roof
15. Tiny criticism
16. Alan of "The West Wing"
17. Mozart's "___ Kleine Nachtmusik"
18. Hand-holding, spirit-raising get-together
20. Shoestrings
21. Tie-breaking periods: Abbr.
22. Moo goo gai pan pan
23. Hoist
26. Paper or plastic? item
27. Musician's date
30. Arguer's state?
34. Camera choice, in brief
35. Capote, on Broadway
36. Neighbor on
37. RR terminal
38. Muscles to crunch
40. Follower of Socrates
43. Manet or Monet
47. Waikiki Beach locale
48. ___ song (cheaply)
50. Science Guy Bill
51. Bakery fixture
52. Nuptial exchanges
53. Country music cable sta.
54. Amateur radio operators
55. Change of a twenty
56. Digital readout, for short

DOWN

1. Meredith and Shula
2. Tennis champ Nastase
3. "I never ___ man I didn't like" (Will Rogers)
4. Piece of land
5. Parts to play
6. Not divisible by two
7. Anti-narcotics grp.
8. T-bone, e.g.
9. Suffix with psych-
10. Taken care of
11. Chimps and orangutans
19. Middle C, e.g.
20. Theater section
22. Baby's bawl
23. Lots of oz.
24. Running a fever
25. Mink or ermine
26. Heat measure: Abbr.
27. Chew the rag
28. Hospital area with many IVs
29. ___ lost!
31. Leave ___ me
32. Right to bear arms grp.
33. Abstain from food
37. Astonishes

Puzzle 70

Solution on Page 331

38. Vice President Burr
39. Word with tacks or knuckles
40. Tush!
41. Volcano output
42. Throat clearer
44. The "I" in IHOP: Abbr.
45. In ___ (coordinated)
46. Be inclined (to)
48. Like a fiddle
49. Beethoven's "___ to Joy"

ACROSS

1. Roman 300
4. Oil treatment letters
7. Mail off
11. Military mail drop: Abbr.
12. Neckwear
14. Metamorphoses poet
15. Used a stool
16. Welder's gas
18. ___ Martin (James Bond car)
20. ___ Scotia
21. Non-Rx
22. Loewe's partner on Broadway
26. Comics orphan
28. Director Craven
29. "Evil Woman" band
30. Mediterranean fruits
31. NFL Hall-of-Famer Dawson
32. Carpenter's fastener
33. Folk rocker DiFranco
34. Sch. near Harvard
35. In base eight
36. Alamo offering
38. Brit. fliers
39. Periods in history
41. Waterproof covers
44. "Jimmy Crack Corn" sentiment
48. Ich bin ___ Berliner
49. Lumberjacks' tools
50. Hit with the fist
51. Storekeeper on "The Simpsons"
52. Gomer of TV
53. Alternative to coffee
54. Beer barrel

DOWN

1. Spanish house
2. Tax pros: Abbr.
3. Eli Whitney invention
4. Batter's position
5. Quirky habit
6. Hammerhead part
7. Renewable energy type
8. New Year's ___
9. Collages author Anaïs
10. Ike's monogram
13. Ripped off
17. Designer St. Laurent
19. Soul singer Redding
23. Compulsive cleaner
24. Film director Kazan
25. Bread basket choice
26. It's ___ cry from . . .
27. Cloud number
28. More than damp
31. Purple flowers
32. Final Four inits.
34. "Who Needs the Kwik-E-___?" (song from "The Simpsons")
35. Sandinista leader Daniel

Puzzle 71

Solution on Page 331

37. All wound up
40. Shaker contents
42. Sherlock Holmes item
43. Skintight
44. AOL or Earthlink, for example: Abbr.
45. "The ___ of the Jackal"
46. Wise bird
47. Feel regret over

ACROSS

1. Antoine Domino's nickname
5. Easy as letters
8. Valentine sentiment
12. Inlet
13. Un momento, ___ favor
14. Cyberauction site
15. Put one's hands together
16. Links org.
17. Fork feature
18. Let's call ___ day!
20. Space occupier
22. Oblong cream puff
25. Cutie ___
26. Day- ___: pigment brand
27. Just off the assembly line
29. Theater school study
33. Comic's bit
34. On the ___ (fleeing)
36. Like carrots that crunch
37. Animal nose
40. British WWII fliers
42. Tiny Tim strummed one
43. Pooh's middle name?
45. Filled with joy
47. Upstream swimmer
50. Second-stringer
51. Giant fair
52. Banned bug killer
54. Like a clear sky
58. Chair supports
59. ___ Father, who art . . .
60. I dropped it!
61. No longer fizzy
62. Question of identity
63. Slave away

DOWN

1. TV watchdog: Abbr.
2. "You've got mail" co.
3. Dam-building org.
4. Brown-toned old photo
5. Clothing
6. Where cranberries grow
7. Muscle malady
8. A, B, or C
9. Memorial news item
10. Weathercock
11. Looker
19. Sn, chemically speaking
21. Helping hand
22. Breakfast choice
23. Group with a common ancestor
24. McDonald's arches, e.g.
28. All's fair in it
30. In ___ (routine-bound)
31. ___ my day!
32. Really impressed
35. Eminent conductor
38. Maximum extent
39. Notwithstanding that, briefly

Puzzle 72

Solution on Page 331

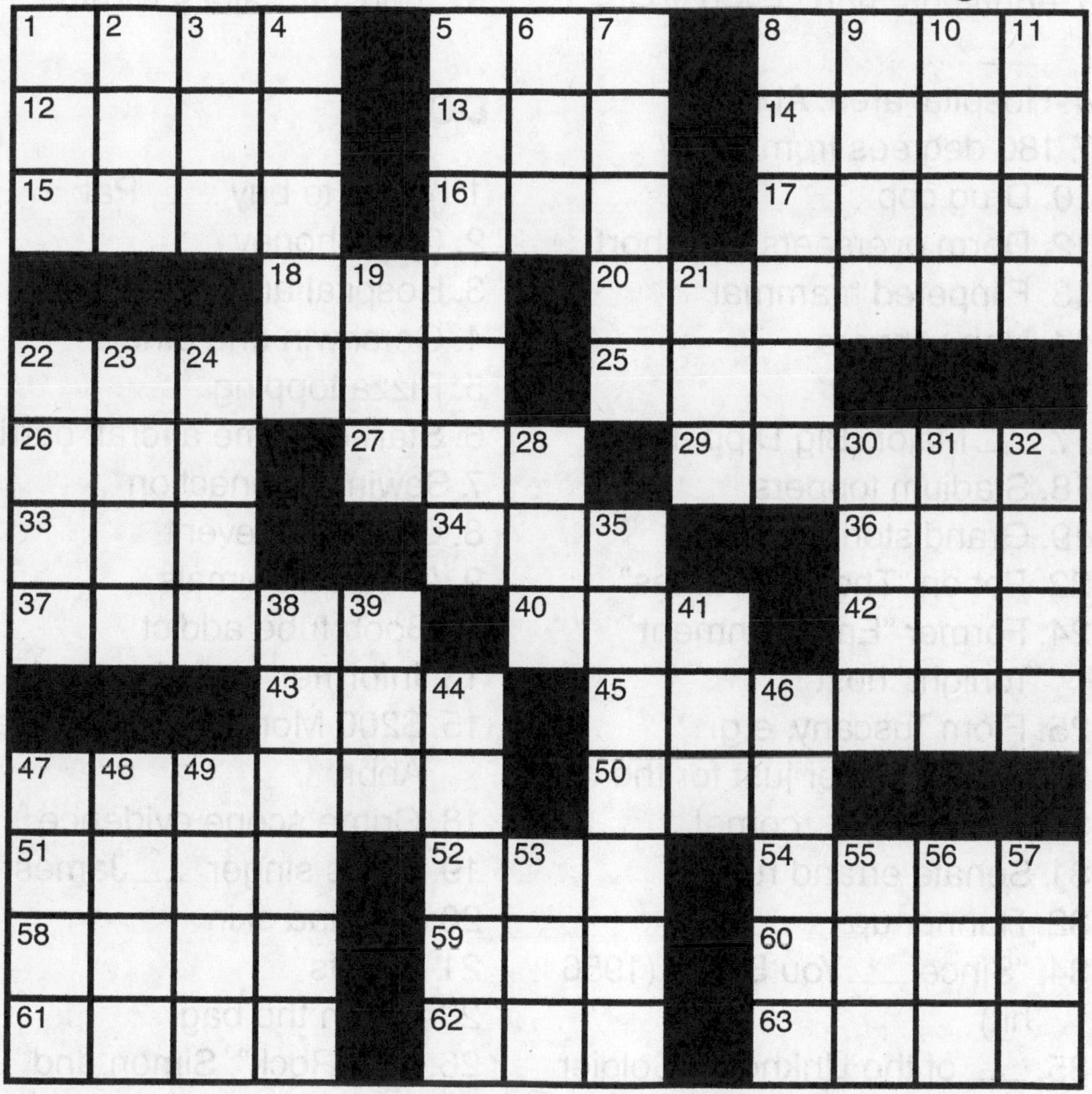

41. Winter bug
44. Fund, as one's alma mater
46. Monastery head
47. To thine own ___ be true
48. Rink leap
49. Org. for Annika Sorenstam
53. I am such a dope!
55. London lav
56. News org. created in 1958
57. Subj. for immigrants, perhaps

ACROSS

1. Fourscore and seven years ___ . . .
4. Hospital area: Abbr.
7. 180 degrees from NNW
10. Drug cop
12. Dorm overseers, for short
13. Flippered mammal
14. Non-winners
16. Have a chat
17. ___ Major (Big Dipper)
18. Stadium toppers
19. Grand stories
22. Pet on "The Flintstones"
24. Former "Entertainment Tonight" host
25. From Tuscany, e.g.
29. Office worker just for the day
30. The time ___ come!
31. Senate errand runner
32. Runner-up
34. "Since ___ You Baby" (1956 hit)
35. ___ of the Unknown Soldier
36. Antiquated exclamation
37. Aerosol
40. Teenage woe
42. Café au ___
43. Large sailing vessel
47. Songwriter Guthrie
48. Oft-stubbed digit
49. Scruff of the neck
50. When doubled, a nasty fly
51. Picnic intruder
52. Lobster eater's wear

DOWN

1. I'd like to buy ___, Pat
2. Guy's honey
3. Hospital areas: Abbr.
4. Gershwin and others
5. Pizza topping
6. Start of some aircraft carriers
7. Sewing connection
8. Clearance event
9. Antlered animals
11. Boob tube addict
13. Informer
15. $200 Monopoly properties: Abbr.
18. Crime scene evidence
19. Blues singer ___ James
20. Banana skin
21. Beliefs
23. ___ in the bag!
26. "___ Rock": Simon and Garfunkel hit
27. Grew older
28. Butterfly catchers
30. Popular Easter dish
33. Trigger's rider
36. Former Roxy Music member Brian
37. Venetian blind part

Puzzle 73

Solution on Page 332

38. Scores to shoot for
39. Anger, with "up"
41. Atkins of country music
43. RR depot
44. Catch in the act
45. Prefix with dermis
46. Confederate soldier

ACROSS

1. N.F.L. six-pointers
4. XXX times X
7. Soup pod
11. Cry of surprise
13. Pitch in for
14. Docking spot
15. Christmas carol
16. Helpers for profs
17. Big-ticket ___
18. Again!
20. Coral ridges
21. Event with floats
24. Monastery
27. Tupperware topper
28. Attila the ___
31. Promissory notes
32. What to do to hats and waiters
33. Food that's "slung"
34. Scale abbr.
35. Hold the deed to
36. Flower feature
37. Cinco de Mayo party
39. Personnel
43. Airport surface
47. Cabbage's kin
48. Ain't ___ shame?
50. Donkey pin-on
51. ___ hands are the devil's tools
52. Happy
53. Storage for forage
54. Magazine publisher Condé
55. Takes too much, for short
56. Chop suey additive

DOWN

1. Newcastle-upon-___, England
2. Singer Celine
3. Design detail
4. Supply party food for
5. Spy's org.
6. S & L offerings
7. Sheriff Taylor's son
8. Paper-and-string flier
9. Coral ridge
10. Up in ___ (outraged)
12. Splits to get hitched
19. Comic actor Romano
20. Color of embarrassment
22. Draw ___ in the sand
23. Slight downturn
24. Feel under the weather
25. Dylan or Dole
26. Public vehicle
28. Stetson or sombrero
29. It's between Can. and Mex.
30. Stanley Cup org.
32. Prefix with light or night
33. Red suit
35. Light switch position
36. School support gp.
38. Sticks around

Puzzle 74

Solution on Page 332

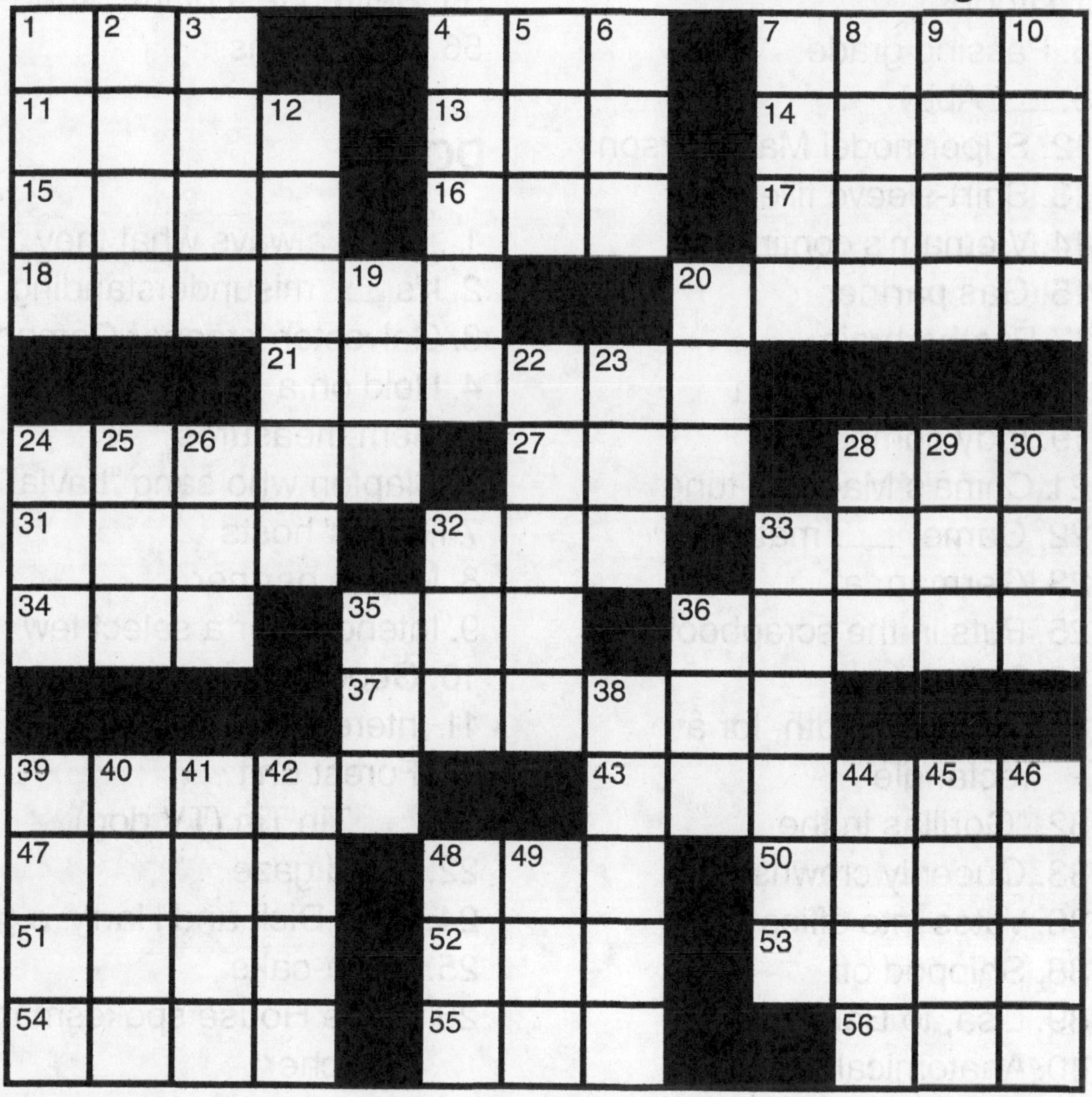

39. Birthday suit
40. Bit of verbal fanfare
41. ___ fair in love . . .
42. Units of length
44. Injure seriously
45. Needs medicine
46. Heavy shoe
48. Here ___ again!
49. Just a ___ (slightly)-

ACROSS

1. Droops
5. Passing grade
8. ___ Abby
12. Supermodel Macpherson
13. Shirt-sleeve filler
14. Vietnam's continent
15. Gas partner
17. Featherbrain
18. Million ___ March
19. Indy competitor
21. China's Mao ___-tung
22. Game, ___, match!
23. German "a"
25. Puts in the scrapbook
28. Entraps
31. Length x width, for a rectangle
32. "Gorillas in the ___"
33. Queenly crowns
36. Votes into office
38. Shipped off
39. Lisa, to Bart
40. Anatomical pouch
42. Draw an outline of
44. Word with punching or sleeping
47. Annual checkup
49. Stretch
51. Dog food once hawked by Ed McMahon
52. Kind of camera: Abbr.
53. Bed board
54. Leak slowly
55. Retired fast plane: Abbr.
56. Does sums

DOWN

1. . . . not always what they ___
2. It's ___ misunderstanding
3. Galveston crooner Campbell
4. Hold on a ___!
5. Gem measures
6. Clapton who sang "Layla"
7. Roasts' hosts
8. Mom's partner
9. Intended for a select few
10. Good for what ___ you
11. Interest figure
16. Forest unit
20. ___ Tin Tin (TV dog)
22. Fixed gaze
24. Tom, Dick and Harry, e.g.
25. ___-a-cake
26. White House spokesman Fleischer
27. Shore scene
29. Best guess: Abbr.
30. Thoroughfares: Abbr.
34. Insect on a hill
35. Emphasize
36. Accompany to a party
37. Claim on property

Puzzle 75

Solution on Page 332

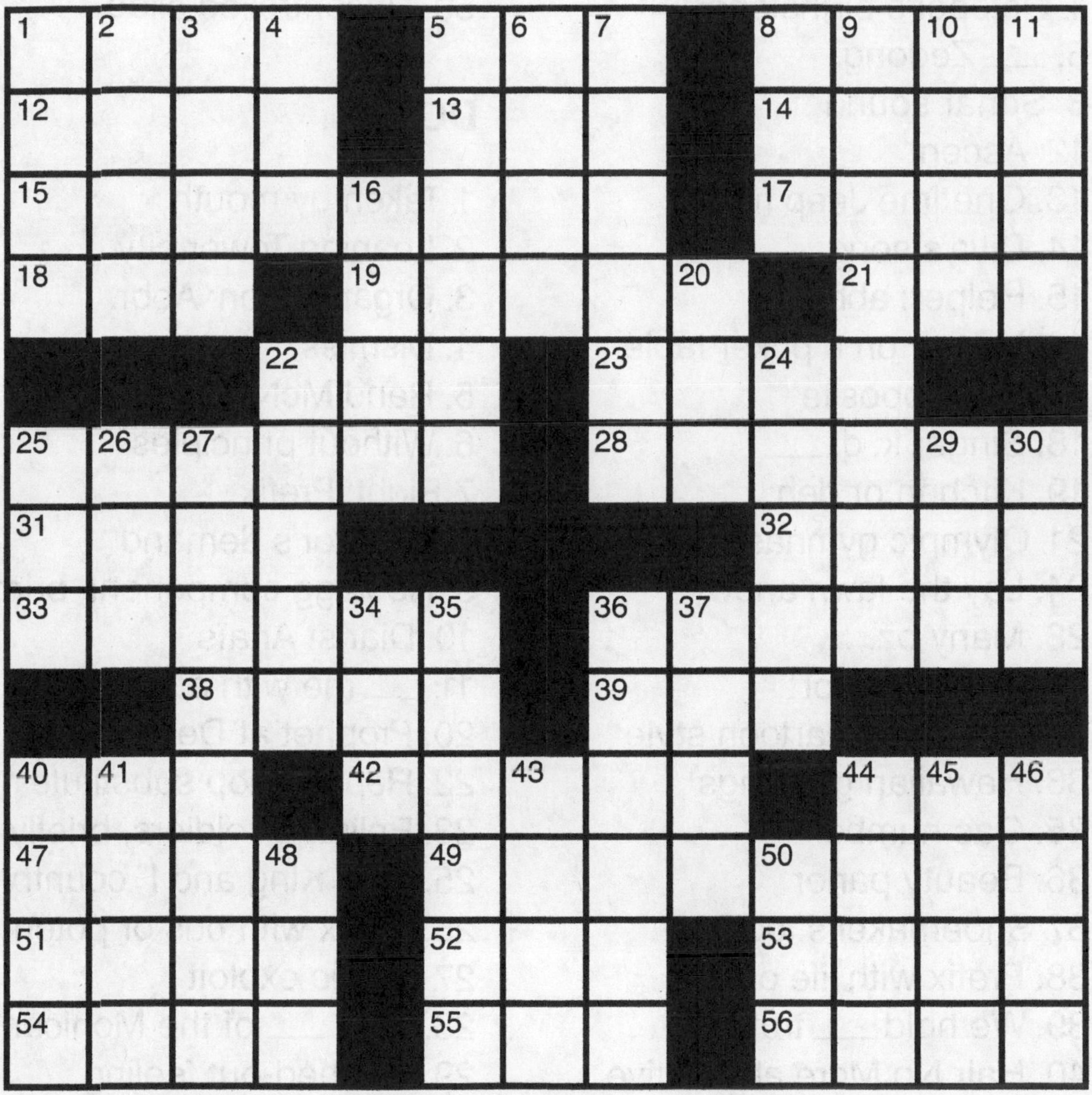

40. Caribbean and Mediterranean
41. Wheels connection
43. "___ Well That Ends . . ."
44. Having no need for a comb
45. Not very much
46. "Smoke ___ in Your Eyes"
48. Floor cleaner
50. Fed. property overseer

ACROSS

1. October's birthstone
5. ___ Zedong
8. Sonar sound
12. Ascent
13. Onetime Jeep mfr.
14. Diva's song
15. Helper: abbr.
16. Money on a poker table
17. Yin's opposite
18. Singer k. d. ___
19. Kitchen or den
21. Olympic gymnast Korbut
24. Lay the lawn anew
28. Many oz.
31. Kuwaiti export
32. Japanese cartoon style
33. Hawaiian greetings
35. Gas number
36. Beauty parlor
37. Shoemaker's tool
38. Prefix with life or wife
39. We hold ___ truths . . .
40. Hair No More alternative
42. Buffet meal carrier
44. Actor Foxx
48. Thin coin
51. Captain's journal
53. Up, Up, and ___
54. Peron and Braun
55. Young ___ (tots)
56. Barbershop symbol
57. Caustic compounds
58. Oh, give ___ home . . .
59. Uncontrolled slide

DOWN

1. Taken by mouth
2. Leaning Tower city
3. Organization: Abbr.
4. Dismiss
5. Rand McNally product
6. Without principles
7. Eight: Prefix
8. Creditor's demand
9. Nestegg component, briefly
10. Diarist Anaïs
11. ___ me with a spoon!
20. Prophet at Delphi
22. Repair shop substitute
23. Enlisted soldiers, briefly
25. "The King and I" country
26. Prefix with bus or potent
27. Heroic exploit
28. "The ___ of the Mohicans"
29. Washed-out feeling
30. Fillet of ___
34. It's her party
35. Be indebted to
37. Nobody in particular
41. Snares
43. Reunion attendee, for short
45. Cuddly "Return of the Jedi" creature

Puzzle 76

Solution on Page 332

46. Artist Salvador
47. Turned blonde, say
48. Dover's state: Abbr.
49. Yale's league
50. Daisy ___ of "Li'l Abner"
52. Cookie-selling org.

ACROSS

1. Heavenly body
4. Show the effects of weight
7. "Kiss Me, ___"
11. Harper who wrote "To Kill a Mockingbird"
12. Fine with me
14. Hungry for more
15. "Zip-A-___-Doo-Dah"
16. Hankering
17. ___ one's time: wait
18. Texas border town
20. Undo, as laces
22. Delivery vehicle
23. Scientist's milieu
24. Spanish artist Joan
27. Chinese cookware
28. Hair arrangements
31. Kitchen hot spot
32. ___ about that?!
33. Car scar
34. Popeye's Olive
35. ___ voyage party
36. Gazed at
37. Ballpoint, e.g.
38. Hoover ___
40. Military greeting
43. Arched foot part
47. Burn a bit
48. Catch in a stocking
50. Kitchen gadget brand
51. Sale tag words
52. Newcastle upon ___, England
53. "___ Lobo" (John Wayne film)
54. Lymph ___ (immune system part)
55. Snakelike swimmer
56. Final degree?

DOWN

1. Ye ___ Tea Shoppe
2. Fishing line winder
3. Horn sound
4. Composer of marches
5. Ohio tire city
6. Comedian's bit
7. Shish ___
8. Budget competitor
9. It ebbs and flows
10. Genesis garden
13. Coward's color
19. Stratford-upon-___
21. Mighty tree
24. Cattle call
25. Princeton greenery
26. Prot. or Cath.
27. Took the pennant
28. "The Partridge Family" actress Susan
29. ___ of a kind
30. Part of PST: Abbr.
32. Like Abe
33. Reps.' foes

Puzzle 77

Solution on Page 333

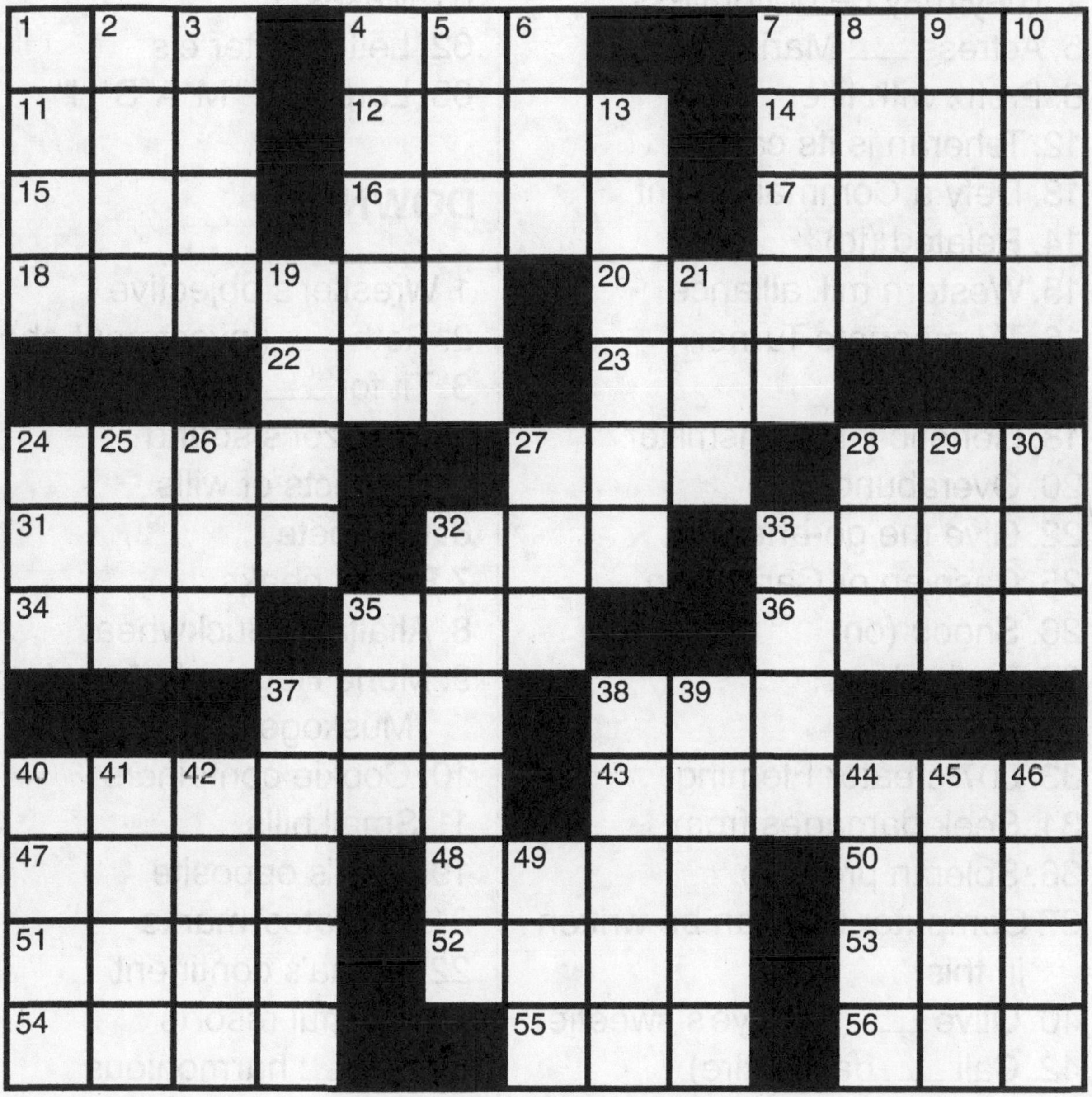

35. Put money (on)
37. Derby prize
38. Sawyer of TV
39. One with a halo
40. Read bar codes
41. Charlie Chan's comment
42. Let go, with "off"
44. Shredded
45. Emergency door sign
46. Milne bear
49. Bill the Science Guy

ACROSS

1. They may be bottomless
5. Actress ___ Marie Saint
8. Prefix with tiller
12. Teheran is its capital
13. Defy a Commandment
14. Related (to)
15. Western mil. alliance
16. TV magnate Turner
17. Wave type
18. Genetic info transmitter
20. Overabundance
22. Give the go-ahead
25. Caspian or Caribbean
26. Snoop (on)
27. Tie the knot
29. Toboggans
33. 007 creator Fleming
34. Seek damages from
36. Solemn promise
37. Computer text can be written in this
40. Olive ___ (Popeye's sweetie)
42. Call ___ day (retire)
43. Not even one
45. Shoelace hole
47. The puck stops here?
50. ___ Luthor of "Superman"
51. Basic desire
52. J.F.K.'s predecessor
54. Arthur of tennis
58. Native of Glasgow
59. Obtained
60. Sir's counterpart
61. Makes "It"
62. Letters after els
63. Loretta of "M*A*S*H"

DOWN

1. Wrestler's objective
2. Roth ___ (investment choice)
3. Tit for ___
4. Snoozer's sound
5. Subjects of wills
6. Compete
7. Peru's peaks
8. Alfalfa or Buckwheat
9. Merle Haggard's "___ from Muskogee"
10. Cookie containers
11. Small bills
19. SSE's opposite
21. Illiterates' marks
22. China's continent
23. Restful resorts
24. In ___: harmonious
28. Twosome
30. Devil's work
31. Shower affection (on)
32. Sultan of ___ (Babe Ruth)
35. Shoe features
38. Small bays
39. 3:00, on a sundial
41. Strong alkaline

Puzzle 78

Solution on Page 333

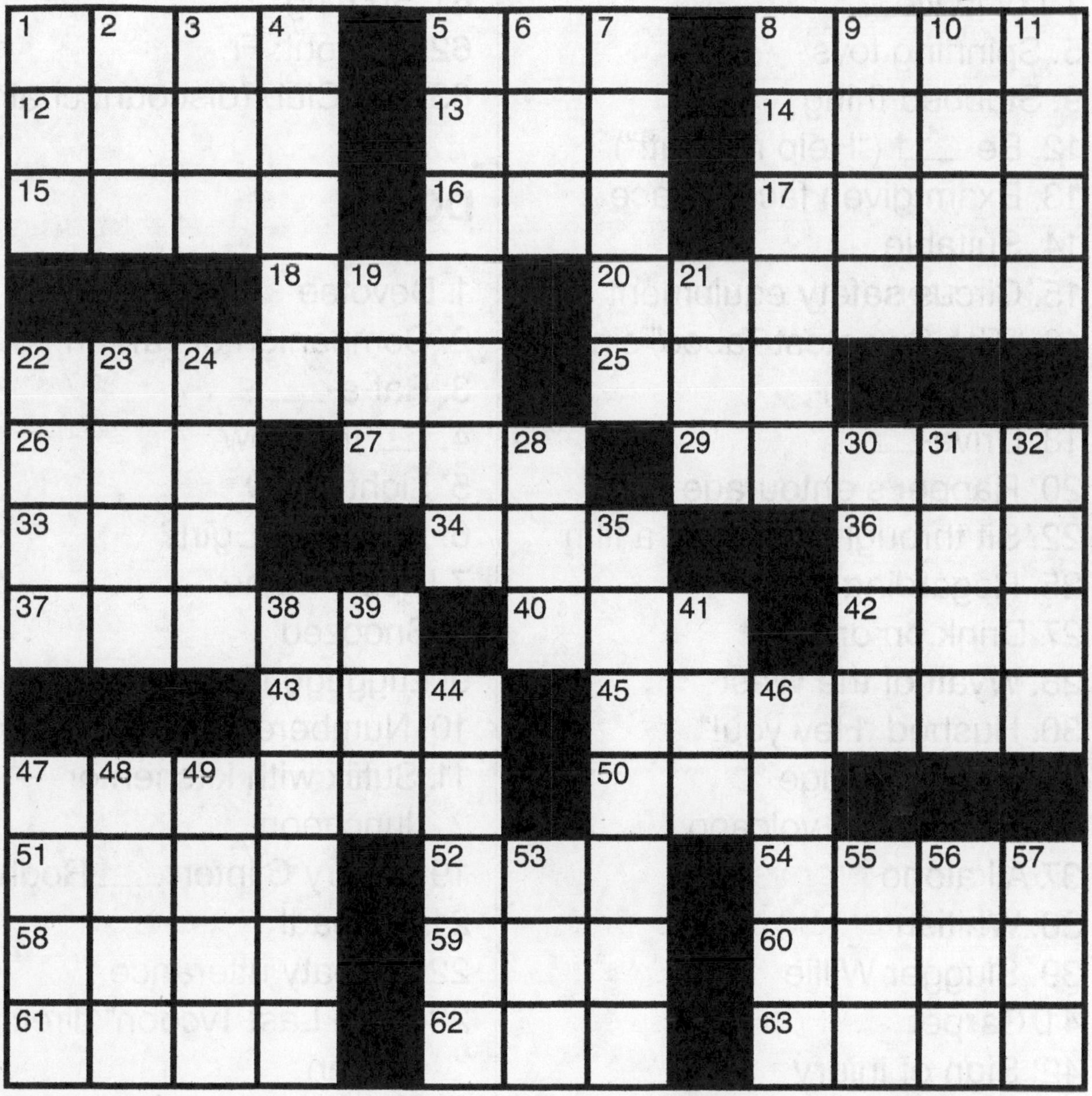

44. Window sill
46. Midterms and finals
47. Sudden wind
48. SeaWorld performer
49. Entranced
53. Comic DeLuise
55. Toothed tool
56. "Bali ___" ("South Pacific" song)
57. C.P.R. expert

ACROSS

1. Lot in life
5. Spinning toys
9. Stubbed thing
12. Be ___! ("Help me out!")
13. Exam given face-to-face
14. Suitable
15. Circus safety equipment
16. "The Sweetest Taboo" singer
17. ___ reaction
18. Drive-___
20. Rapper's entourage
22. Sit through again, as a film
25. Regarding
27. Drink on draught
28. Wyatt of the West
30. Hushed "Hey you!"
34. Window ledge
36. Mauna ___ volcano
37. All alone
38. Whitish
39. Slugger Willie
41. Carpet
42. Sign of injury
44. Prefix with physics
46. Tex-Mex sauce
49. Absorb with up
50. Capp and Gore
51. Lee of cakes
54. Partner of ready and willing
58. Depot: Abbr.
59. Santa ___ (hot California winds)
60. "___ Window": Hitchcock thriller
61. Sizzling
62. Without: Fr.
63. ___ Club (discount chain)

DOWN

1. Devotee
2. Companion of Tarzan
3. Rat-a-___
4. ___ the Cow
5. Light throw
6. . . . boy ___ girl?
7. Hippie home
8. Snoozed
9. Luggage IDs
10. Numbered musical work
11. Suffix with kitchen or luncheon
19. Hillary Clinton ___ Rodham
21. My bad!
22. Throaty utterance
23. "The Last Tycoon" director Kazan
24. Auction off
25. Like a raucous stadium crowd
26. Fix, as a cat
29. ___ mater
31. Put in alphabetical order
32. Nasty remark
33. Like drive-thru orders
35. More or ___

Puzzle 79

Solution on Page 333

40. ___ Paulo, Brazil
43. Spanish houses
45. Practices jabs and hooks
46. Part of Miss America's attire
47. Sax type
48. Future DA's exam
49. Impudent talk
52. Santa ___ winds
53. Competed in a marathon
55. "Luck ___ Lady Tonight"
56. On the ___ (escaping)
57. Hosp. trauma centers

ACROSS

1. Animal that beats its chest
4. ___ sesame
8. Wind-driven spray
12. Morse code word
13. Maxi's opposite
14. Sit for a photo
15. Lah-di-___!
16. Sorry if ___ you down
17. Portentous sign
18. Go inside
20. Sonnets and such
21. Makes yawn
23. Young woman
25. Fleecy females
26. Big Board inits.
27. 1960s records
30. The 49th state
32. Dozing
34. Step up from dial-up
35. Memorial Day weekend race, to fans
37. Mechanical learning
38. Hint for Holmes
39. ___ down (softened)
40. Oak-to-be
43. Sweat spot
45. Port or claret
46. Marx with a manifesto
47. Cleanup hitter's stat
50. Dobbin's dinner
51. ___ want for Christmas . . .
52. Rickles or Knotts
53. Ill-gotten goods
54. Auto roof option
55. Photo ___ (picture-taking times)

DOWN

1. Contribute to the conversation
2. Entertainer Zadora
3. Celestial
4. Leaves out
5. Big stack
6. The E in Einstein's formula
7. Annual coll. basketball competition
8. Thread holder
9. Ready or not, here I ___!
10. Puts into play
11. Contradict
19. Prohibition agent Eliot
20. Air Force One passenger: Abbr.
21. Drop of sweat
22. Avian symbols of wisdom
24. ___, old chap!
26. Half of Mork's goodbye
27. Kate's "Titanic" co-star
28. Tennis great Sampras
29. Hurried
31. Ceramist's oven
33. Scientologist Hubbard
36. Make potable, as sea water

Puzzle 80

Solution on Page 333

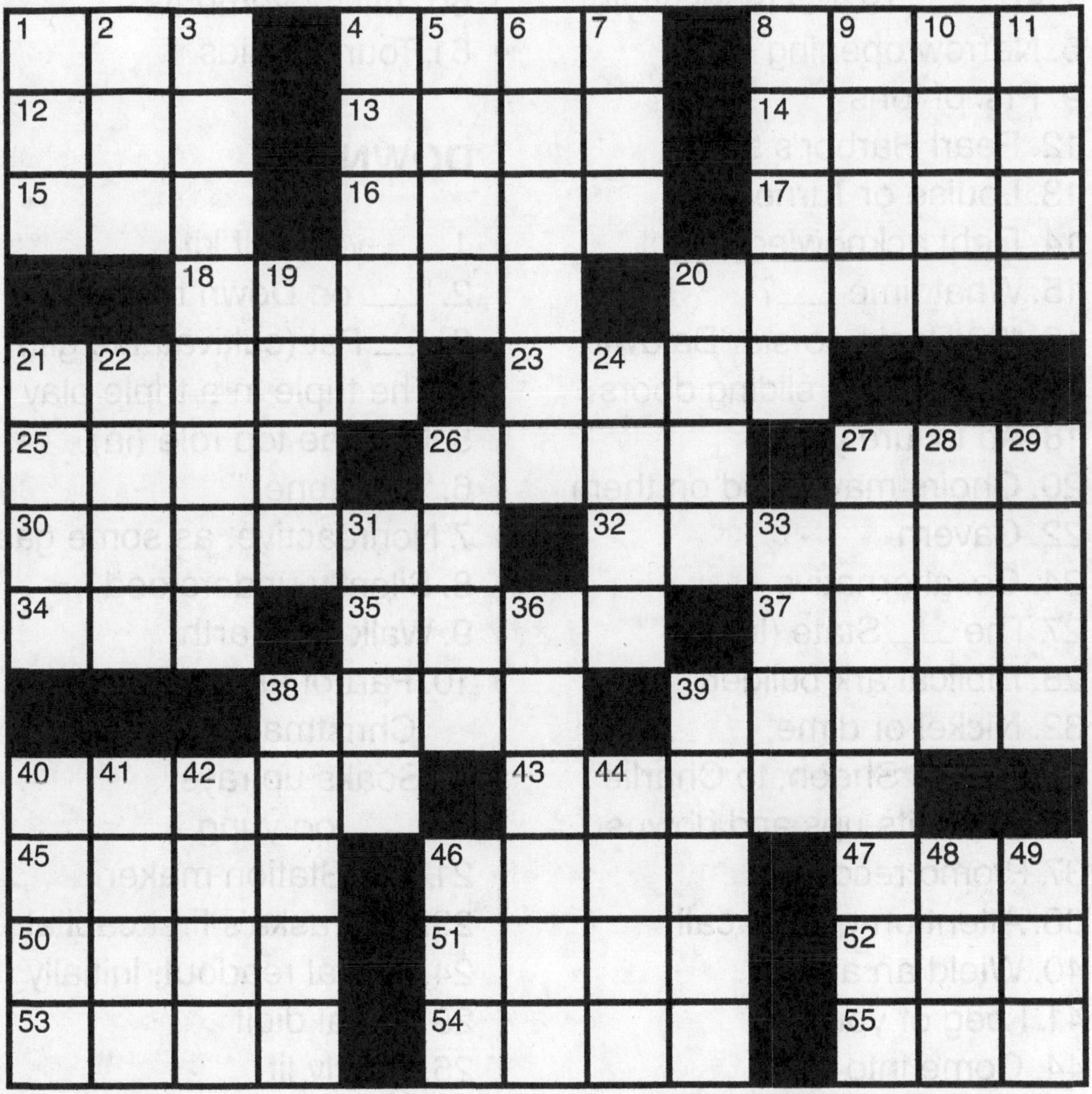

38. Toothpaste brand
39. Dutch bloom
40. Illegally off base
41. Italian farewell
42. I'm ___ your tricks!
44. Guthrie who sang "Alice's Restaurant"
46. Kit ___ : candy bar
48. Dizzy Gillespie's genre
49. Partner of outs

ACROSS

1. Art ___ (1920s-1930s style)
5. Narrow opening
9. Pts. of tons
12. Pearl Harbor's site
13. Louise or Turner
14. Debt acknowledgment
15. What time ___?
16. "30 Rock" co-star Baldwin
17. Vehicle with sliding doors
18. Ad to lure you in
20. Choirs may stand on them
22. Cavern
24. Co. alternative
27. The ___ State (Idaho)
28. Biblical ark builder
32. Nickel or dime
34. Martin Sheen, to Charlie
36. It has its ups and downs
37. Promo recording
38. Attention-getting call
40. Wield an ax
41. I beg of you
44. Come into view
47. In one piece
52. "The Bell ___" (Sylvia Plath book)
53. Pinocchio, at times
55. Prefix meaning "same"
56. From ___ Z
57. Skin woe
58. Bit of chicanery
59. Crosses (out)
60. Tail movements
61. Tourists' aids

DOWN

1. ___-yourself kit
2. "___ on Down the Road"
3. ___ Pet (cultivatable gift)
4. The triple in a triple play
5. Had the top role (in)
6. "___ Abner"
7. Nonreactive, as some gases
8. Silently understood
9. Walk the Earth
10. Part of an old English Christmas feast
11. Soaks up rays
19. ___ foo yung
21. PlayStation maker
23. Nebraska's first capital
24. Digital readout, initially
25. Pedal digit
26. Poorly lit
29. Amazed audience utterance
30. Sailor's "yes"
31. ___ do you do?
33. Slangy denial
35. Wishes
39. Tokyo dough
42. Bochco TV drama

Puzzle 81

Solution on Page 334

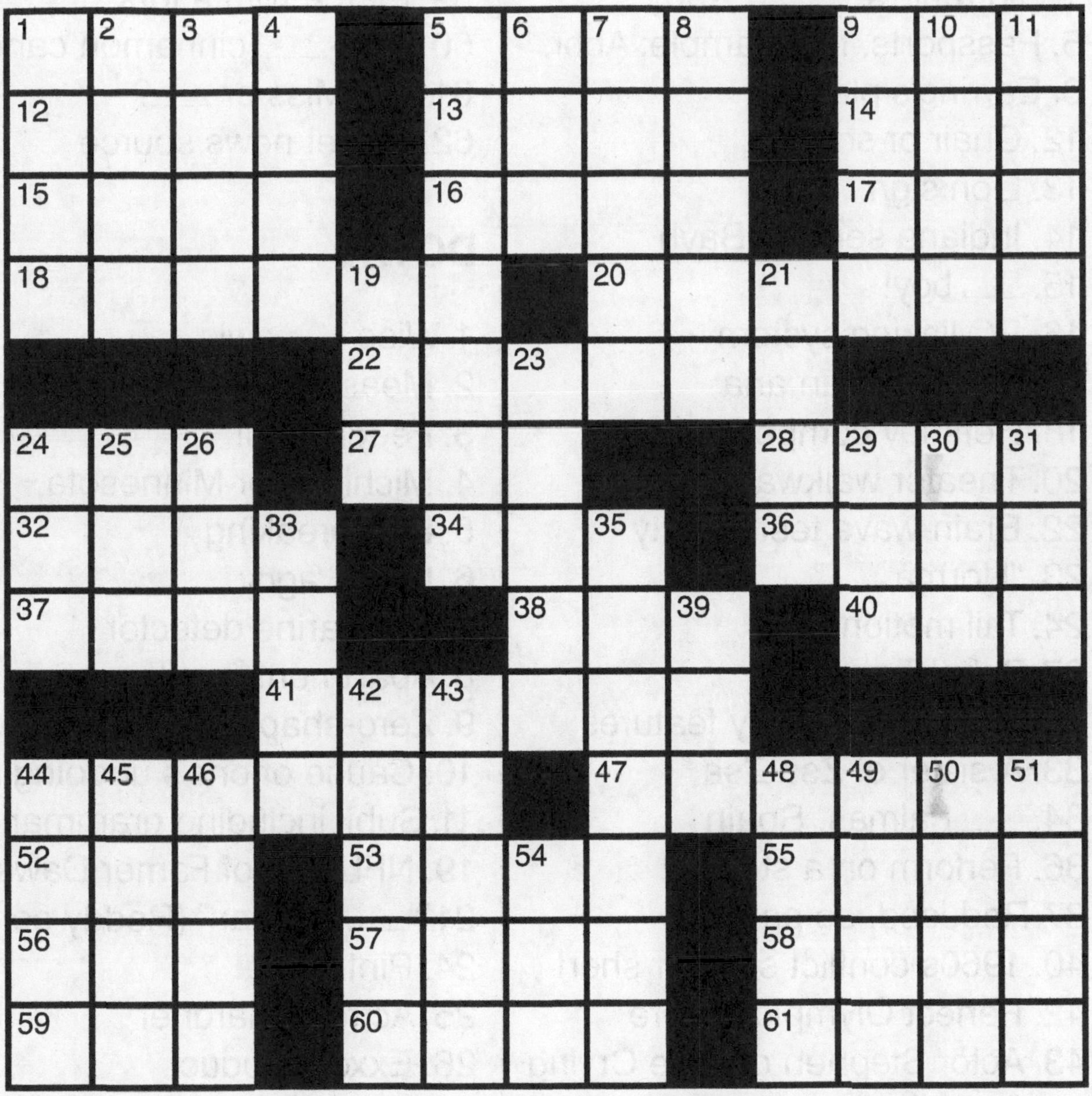

43. "Fear of Fifty" writer Jong
44. Stronger than dirt sloganeer
45. Hors d'ouevre spread
46. Major leaguers
48. Semester
49. Light greenish-blue
50. Cutting edge
51. Knots
54. "The Ice Storm" director ___ Lee

ACROSS

1. Old radio's "___ 'n' Andy"
5. Passports, for example: Abbr.
8. Earring's place
12. Chair or sofa
13. Lion sign
14. Indiana senator Bayh
15. ___ boy!
16. PC linking system
17. Performed an aria
18. Hershey competitor
20. Theater walkway
22. Brain-wave test, briefly
23. "Norma ___"
24. Tail motion
27. Rebel Turner
29. Monument Valley features
33. A sister of Zsa Zsa
34. ___ Palmas, Spain
36. Perform on a stage
37. Reduced, as pain
40. 1960s conflict site, for short
42. Perfect Olympics score
43. Actor Stephen of "The Crying Game"
45. Half an umlaut
47. Suddenly stop, as an engine
49. Hangmen's ropes
53. "___ a Lady" (Tom Jones hit)
54. Honest president
56. Aviation-related prefix
57. Sharpen, as a knife
58. Univ. dorm supervisors
59. Pierce with a fork
60. Red-___ (cinnamon candies)
61. Is it Miss or ___?
62. Soviet news source

DOWN

1. Wise ___ owl
2. Measure (out)
3. Feedbag fill
4. Michigan or Minnesota
5. Law-breaking
6. Narcs' agcy.
7. Submarine detector
8. Apartment dweller
9. Zero-shaped
10. Cause of one's undoing
11. Subj. including grammar
19. NFL Hall of Famer Dawson
21. "___ Woman" (Reddy song)
24. Pint-size
25. Actress Gardner
26. Exxon product
28. Catch some rays
30. Fri. follower
31. Perfect tennis serve
32. Train depot: abbr.
35. Blue feeling
38. Cleans the blackboard
39. ___ Monte (food giant)

Puzzle 82

Solution on Page 334

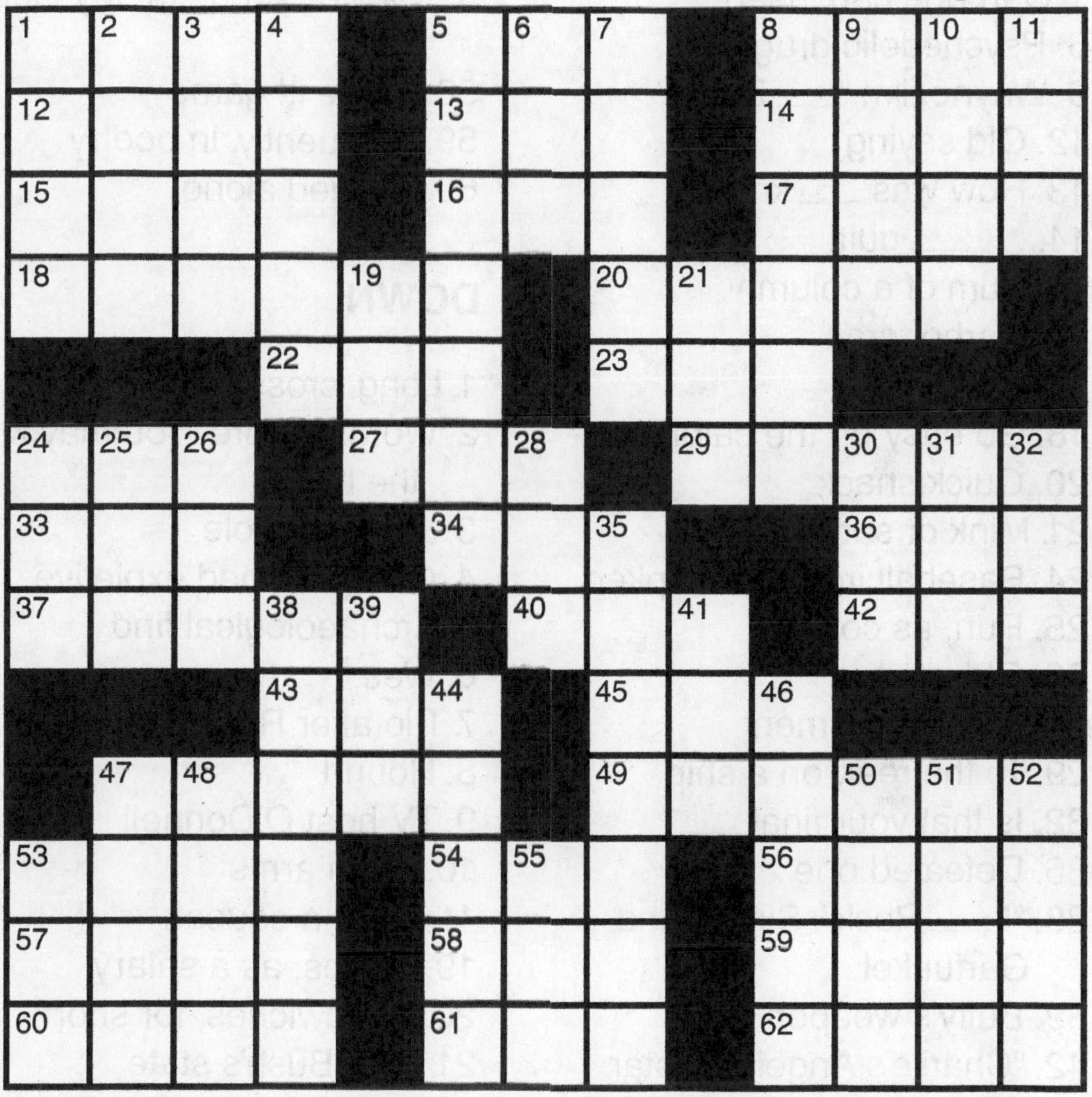

41. Cow word
44. Security feature
46. Raise a glass to
47. Get lost, fly!
48. Camper's shelter
50. ___ good example
51. Time periods
52. Blubbers
53. Quiet down!
55. High-jumper's hurdle

ACROSS

1. Garbage can insert
6. Psychedelic drug
9. Wayne film "___ Bravo"
12. Old saying
13. How was ___ know?
14. . . . ___ quit!
15. Sum of a column
16. Harbor craft
17. Actor Mineo
18. Go easy on the calories
20. Quick snack
21. Mink or sable
24. Baseball iron man Ripken
25. Run, as colors
26. Old vinyl
27. Send in payment
29. To the rear, on a ship
32. Is that your final ___?
36. Defeated one
38. "I ___ Rock": Simon and Garfunkel
39. Buffy's weapon
42. "Charlie's Angels" costar Lucy
44. Affectionate greeting
45. Witty sorts
46. Small amounts, as of cream
48. Pharmaceutical giant ___ Lilly
49. Enemy
51. Perform better than
55. One, to Fritz
56. "Leaving ___ Vegas"
57. Stevie Wonder's "My Cherie ___"
58. You're it! game
59. Frequently, in poetry
60. Lugged along

DOWN

1. Long. crosser
2. Words before "You may kiss the bride"
3. ___ King Cole
4. Old-fashioned expletive
5. Archaeological find
6. Wee
7. Trio after R
8. Hound
9. TV host O'Donnell
10. Up in arms
11. Fixed a squeak
19. Makes, as a salary
20. Sandwiches, for short
21. Gov. Bush's state
22. Downs' partner
23. String after Q
25. Big box
28. Soprano Callas
30. Moose cousins
31. Precious eggs
33. Crib cry
34. Cousin of an ostrich

Puzzle 83

Solution on Page 334

35. Maid's cloth
37. Firstborn sibling
39. Sugary
40. Actress Shire of "Rocky"
41. Growing older
43. WWII vessel
47. Japanese wrestling
49. Sitcom diner waitress
50. Dunderpate
52. Highchair user
53. Like library books, eventually
54. Old California fort

ACROSS

1. On the peak of
5. Part of ETA
8. "Little ___ of Horrors"
12. Shoe bottom
13. Bambi's mother, for one
14. It may be spun around a campfire
15. Half of a famous split personality
16. Physicians, for short
17. Heady brews
18. Tear away (from)
20. Disoriented
21. Drive-in feature
24. 11-pointer, in blackjack
26. Fuss over oneself
27. Utmost in degree
28. Wide of the mark
31. Massachusetts' Cape ___
32. Waves of grain color
34. It's north of Calif.
35. G.I.'s mail drop
36. Lamb's cry
37. Expressed wonder
39. Got together
40. Tickles the fancy
41. Eric of Monty Python
44. It might have a single coconut tree
46. Beans used for tofu
47. Holiday quaff
48. Peru's capital
52. Travelers' lodgings
53. 180 degrees from WNW
54. Supply-and-demand sci.
55. Like Playboy models
56. Lobe locale
57. And ___ what happened?

DOWN

1. Wood stove residue
2. Item in a playpen
3. Elderly
4. Nickname for a little guy
5. Madison Avenue types
6. Fishing poles
7. Say another way
8. No longer fresh
9. Saintly glow
10. Bullfight cheers
11. Annoyer
19. Give a new title to
21. Pet protection org.
22. Farm output
23. Perform again
25. Bumper coating
27. Michael Jordan's org.
28. Partners of aahs
29. At no charge
30. Government agents
33. Afternoon show

Puzzle 84

Solution on Page 334

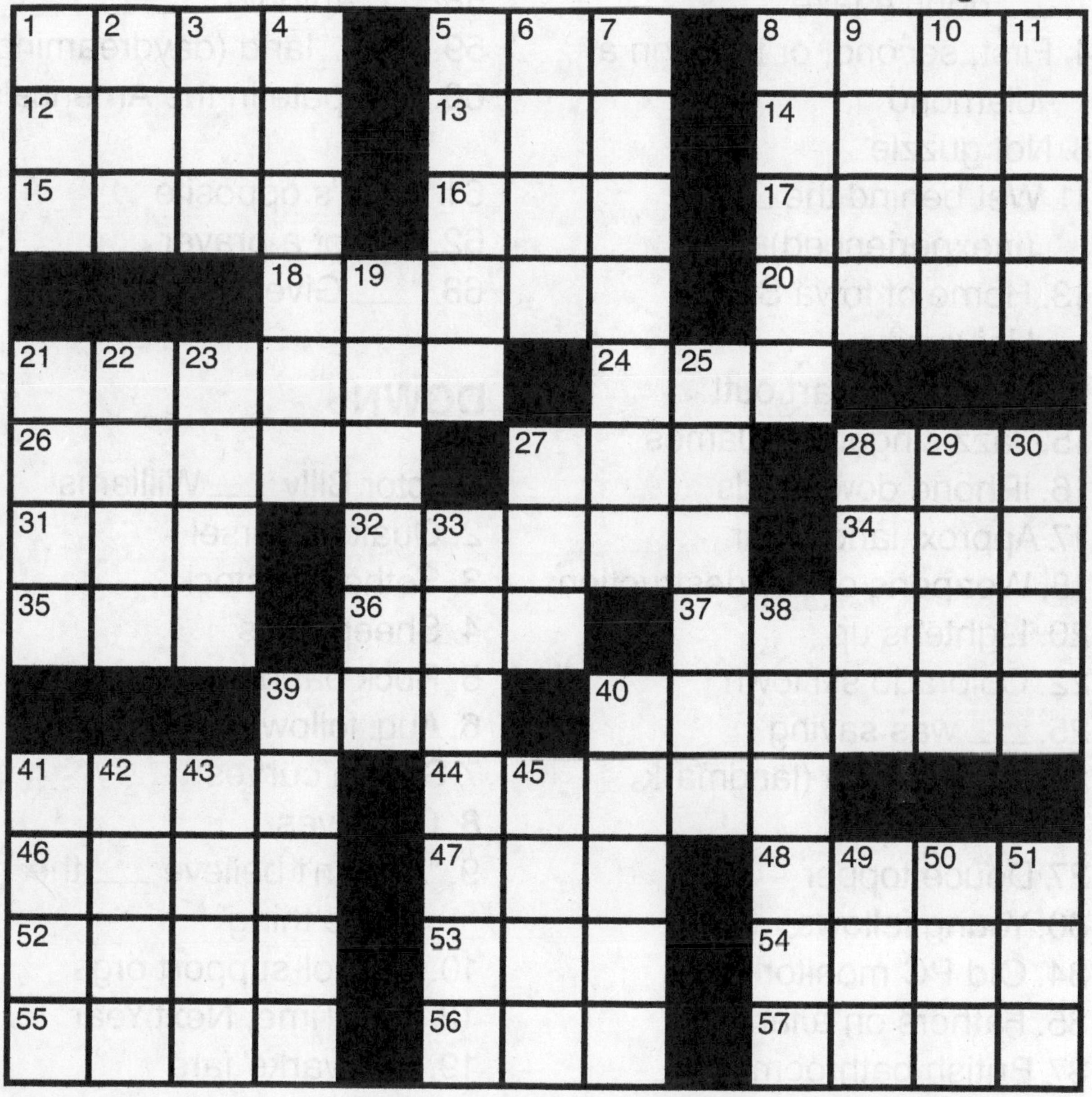

38. Factory store
39. Sloppy
40. "Ragged Dick" writer Horatio
41. Egyptian fertility goddess
42. Completed
43. Short-tailed wildcat
45. Cubs slugger Sammy ___
49. ___ liebe dich
50. Brother of Curly and Shemp
51. Political commentator Coulter

ACROSS

1. ___ double take
4. First, second, or third, on a diamond
8. Not guzzle
11. Wet behind the ___ (inexperienced)
13. Home of Iowa State University
14. ___ your heart out!
15. Jazz singer ___ James
16. iPhone downloads
17. Approx. landing hr.
18. Weapons of ___ destruction
20. Lightens up
22. Colorado ski town
25. ___ was saying
26. ___ v. Wade (landmark decision)
27. Deuce topper
30. Young fellows
34. Old PC monitor type
35. Fathers on a farm
37. British bathroom
38. Crystal ball gazer
40. ___, but not least . . .
41. Modern composer Brian
42. "It must have been something I ___!"
44. Liability's opposite
46. No longer fashionable
49. Eye irritation
51. Words before carte
52. Former Iranian leader
54. Soviet news service
58. ___ Antonio
59. In ___ land (daydreaming)
60. Compete in the America's Cup
61. NNW's opposite
62. End of a prayer
63. "___ Given Sunday"

DOWN

1. Actor Billy ___ Williams
2. Quaker morsel
3. Sotheby's stock
4. Sheep cries
5. Rock band boosters
6. Aug. follower
7. Slalom curves
8. Observes
9. ". . . can't believe ___ the whole thing"
10. School-support orgs.
12. "___ Time, Next Year"
19. Aardvarks' fare
21. Feel feverish
22. Circular segments
23. Achy after a workout
24. Sampras or Rose
25. Affirmative votes
28. Ruffle one's feathers
29. Noteworthy period
31. Saloon orders
32. All finished

Puzzle 85

Solution on Page 335

33. Chimney grime
36. Don't leave!
39. Univ. dorm overseers
43. Croatian-born physicist Nikola
45. Movie locations
46. Football throw
47. What a shame
48. Not crazy
49. Store window word
50. Larger ___ life
53. Meat with eggs
55. Small battery
56. Commandment violation
57. ___ as a fox

ACROSS

1. Floppy rabbit feature
4. Separate, as flour
8. Bubbly beverage
12. Seoul-based automaker
13. Pepsi-___
14. Alda or Arkin
15. Ltr. container
16. Author unknown, for short
17. Suffix with Oktober
18. Rustle, as cattle
20. Test for college srs.
22. Taxis
25. Caribbean resort island
29. New York theater award
32. Theater chain founder Marcus
34. Maple product
35. "I haven't a thing to ___!"
36. Large coffee maker
37. Bouncy
38. Cole who was "King"
39. Hunted animal
40. ___ of March
41. Napped leather
43. Ballgame spoiler
45. 12-mo. periods
47. University officials
51. Golfer's cry
54. Bluish green
57. Mammal that sleeps upside-down
58. Not quite closed
59. Fashion magazine founded in France
60. Numbers cruncher
61. Vile Nile creatures
62. Fail to hit
63. Plunked oneself down

DOWN

1. ___ out: makes do
2. "___ That a Shame"
3. Rant's partner
4. Milan opera house La ___
5. Lithium-___ battery
6. Waitress at Mel's Diner
7. Astronaut's beverage
8. More secure
9. Cheer for a torero
10. Prosecutors, briefly
11. Picnic scurrier
19. Great server on the court
21. Like sushi
23. Become hazy
24. More achy
26. Not new
27. Denuded
28. Condo units: Abbr.
29. Holds the title to
30. Gal's sweetheart
31. "Must've been something ___"
33. One-named singer with the hit "Orinoco Flow"

Puzzle 86

Solution on Page 335

37. Tree with cones
39. Pay-___-view
42. Hair colorists
44. Sits in neutral
46. From ___ to stern
48. "Sesame Street" skills
49. California wine county
50. Number on a baseball card
51. Air agcy.
52. Breakfast drinks, briefly
53. Emulate Eminem
55. Gin-maker Whitney
56. Gore and Roker

ACROSS

1. Word that modifies a noun (Abbr.)
4. Cease and desist
8. Trucker who broadcasts
12. Thompson of "Back to the Future"
13. TV's Donahue
14. Nays' opposites
15. PC linking acronym
16. Moon over Milano
17. Get together
18. U.S. disaster relief org.
20. Deep ___ bend
22. Belief: Suff.
24. Job to be run
28. Squirrels away
32. 3:1 or 7:2, e.g.
33. Commitment to pay
34. Late columnist Landers
36. Special ___: military force
37. Synagogue scroll
40. Driver's ID
43. ___ of Liberty
45. Evil spell
46. Like a wafer
48. Prefix with -nautics
51. Auto brand
54. Anything ___
56. Resistor unit
58. Currier's companion
59. Golfer's target
60. Dear ___ or Madam
61. Mannerly guy
62. Ring decisions
63. Boozer

DOWN

1. Nothing's opposite
2. Unhearing
3. Tarzan's love
4. Daryl Hannah comedy of 1984
5. Fri. preceder
6. Cry from a sty
7. 747, e.g.
8. Picture taker
9. Catch ya later!
10. Wide shoe specification
11. Q-U connectors
19. Lead-in to hap or hear
21. To ___ is human
23. Are you calling ___ liar?
25. . . . hit me like ___ of bricks
26. Pup's bites
27. Medicine quantity
28. Uses a stool
29. Horn sound
30. Saintly radiance
31. Weekend NBC hit, for short
35. Fed. biomedical research agcy.
38. Declare to be true
39. "What'd you say?"
41. Puts an end to

Puzzle 87

Solution on Page 335

42. Program file extension
44. Two cubed
47. Secluded corner
49. Flagmaker Betsy
50. Dayton's state
51. Russian plane
52. St. crosser
53. Barbie's beau
55. Strange Magic grp.
57. Lawrence Tero, professionally

ACROSS

1. Desert largely in Mongolia
5. Turkish topper
8. Milk choice
12. Computer image
13. Half of dos
14. Prefix meaning "against"
15. Classic muscle cars
16. Freud subject
17. Soft throws
18. ___ do ("That's fine")
20. Student's jottings
21. ___ and joy
24. In that case . . .
26. Gave an appraisal
27. No-goodnik
31. Over's partner
32. Most common English word
33. Gas pump spec.
34. Jetsam's partner
37. Kind of circle or tube
39. Pasta sauce maker
40. Blackmore's "Lorna ___"
41. "Time is ___" (Benjamin Franklin aphorism)
44. Off-key
46. Moby Dick chaser
47. Roswell sighting
48. Pager sound
52. Worldwide: Abbr.
53. Fix, as a fight
54. Thomas Edison's middle name
55. Amount of medicine
56. One-eighty from SSW
57. Don't touch that ___!

DOWN

1. Jazz job
2. Columbus Day's mo.
3. Ghostly greeting
4. Not outdoors
5. Energy source for engines
6. Danish alternative
7. Animal housing
8. Western pub
9. Half hitch or bowline
10. The Everly Brothers' "Let ___ Me"
11. ___ America
19. Baseball legend Williams
20. Govt. code breakers
21. Grad student's mentor
22. Julia of "The Addams Family"
23. "Leave ___ Beaver"
25. Opponent
28. Ian Fleming villain
29. . . . as ___ on TV
30. Fairy-tale meanie
32. Schoolyard game
35. ___ clef
36. Put into words
37. Boise's st.

Puzzle 88

Solution on Page 335

38. Pretty good!
41. Housekeeper
42. ___ you don't!
43. Turner and Cole
45. Seating section
47. Big coffee holder
49. ___ Lilly and Company
50. "Green Acres" star Gabor
51. Good bud

ACROSS

1. Recipe amount: Abbr.
5. Number-crunching pro
8. Some early PCs
12. Lion's sound
13. Sharpshooter's asset
14. Nair competitor
15. What am I getting myself ___?
16. A/C meas.
17. Moist, as morning grass
18. Neighbor of Croatia
20. Twirls
22. Dog's warning
23. Brain scan, briefly
24. One way, on a swing
27. Frat party container
29. Score unit
33. Sound in a bar
34. Capote, to friends
36. Not near
37. Chipped in chips
40. And others: Abbr.
42. Diffident
43. Speak ill of, in slang
45. Emergency PC key
47. Sales pitch
49. Sisters' daughters
53. Gambler's marker
54. Photo ___ (P.R. events)
56. Alaskan city near the Arctic Circle
57. Give (out) sparingly
58. CAT scan alternative
59. Hefty volume
60. Auctioneer's closing word
61. Popeye's Olive ___
62. Constellation component

DOWN

1. Chi-town paper, with "the"
2. Sonny of Sonny and Cher
3. Tests for srs.
4. Fork feature
5. Club with a floor show
6. Center of a peach
7. Make smile
8. Rainbow color
9. Has-___
10. Kitten cries
11. Hog's place
19. Drive up the wall
21. Kind of rally
24. Govt. mortgage provider
25. ___ Tin Tin (heroic dog of 1950's TV)
26. Sept. follower
28. Coll. seniors' test
30. No ___, ands, or buts!
31. Yeah's opposite
32. Attempt
35. Knife or fork
38. Prepared for printing
39. Conk out, as an engine

Puzzle 89

Solution on Page 336

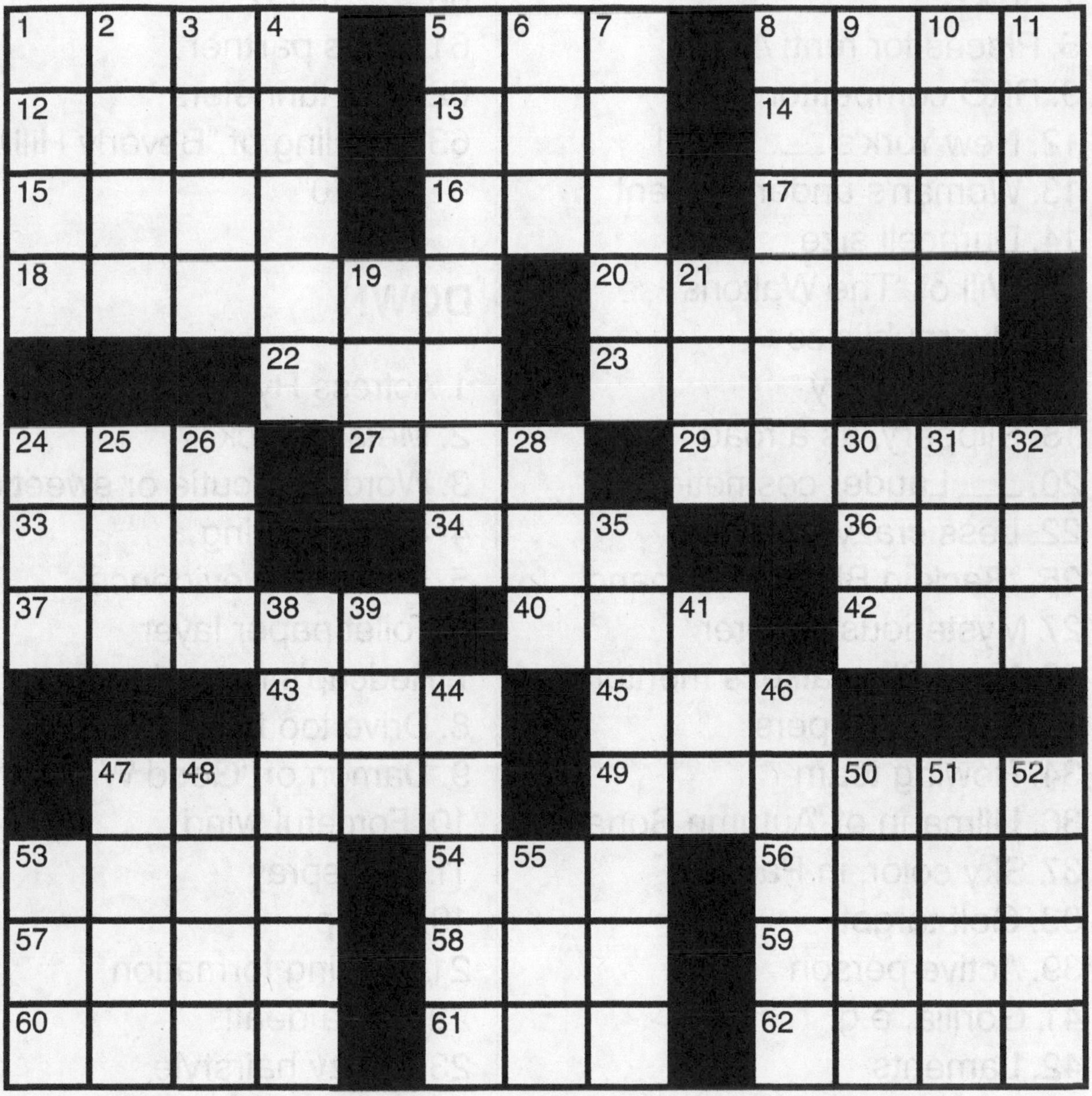

41. "___: Miami" (David Caruso series)
44. Sports replay technique
46. Pennies
47. Chase away
48. Aspirin unit
50. Old geezer
51. Jane Austen heroine
52. Crystal ball user
53. LPs' successors
55. Be nosy

ACROSS

1. Sulk
5. Places for rent: Abbr.
9. RKO competitor
12. New York's ___ Canal
13. Woman's undergarment
14. Duracell size
15. Will of "The Waltons"
16. Overpublicize
17. RN specialty
18. Slippery, as a road
20. ___ Lauder cosmetics
22. Less crazy
25. "Back in Black" rock band
27. Mysterious hoverer
28. Luke Skywalker's mentor
30. Egyptian vipers
34. Rowing team
36. Ullmann of "Autumn Sonata"
37. Sky color, in Paris
38. Golf target
39. Active person
41. Gorilla, e.g.
42. Laments
44. Roof overhangs
46. Wilderness photographer Adams
49. Clock-setting std.
50. Melancholy
51. Printing goof
54. Mrs. Truman
58. Single: Prefix
59. Flower given on Valentine's Day
60. ___ reflux
61. Pop's partner
62. Tiny tunnelers
63. Spelling of "Beverly Hills, 90210"

DOWN

1. Actress Ryan
2. Metallic rock
3. Word with cutie or sweetie
4. Spine-chilling
5. Like arson evidence
6. Toilet paper layer
7. Redcap's reward
8. Drive too fast
9. Damon of "Good Will Hunting"
10. Forceful wind
11. Riot spray
19. Weep
21. Healing formation
22. ___ a deal!
23. Frizzy hairstyle
24. Christmas song
25. Hasta la vista!
26. Grotto
29. "Ye ___ Curiosity Shoppe"
31. Many a Balkan
32. ___ Le Pew
33. Litigates
35. ___ number one!

Puzzle 90

Solution on Page 336

40. Dream letters
43. The "U" of UHF
45. In the box and ready to hit
46. Homecoming attendee, for short
47. Naughty deed
48. Sink's alternative
49. Travels
52. Hither's opposite
53. Calif. clock setting
55. Environmentalist's prefix
56. What to call an officer
57. Reagan's "Star Wars" prog.

ACROSS

1. Little lies
5. PC monitor
8. Bout enders, for short
12. Trim, as text
13. "Curb Your Enthusiasm" network
14. St. ___'s fire
15. Extinct flightless bird
16. Order between "ready" and "fire"
17. Salacious glance
18. Tin-tin lead-in
20. Period of fasting
21. Regret deeply
24. Put down, slangily
26. Notre Dame's Fighting ___
27. Tue. preceder
28. ___ Constitution
31. CPR administrant
32. Congregational cries
34. Sound of a lightning bolt
35. Comedian Louis
36. ___ nut (wheel fastener)
37. ___ and kicking
39. Bon Jovi's "___ of Roses"
40. I'll be right there!
41. Go on the lam
44. Dem.'s foe
45. Temperamental performer
46. Co. bigwig
48. Comical playlet
52. Currier's partner in lithography
53. Have title to
54. One, to Hans
55. Euro part
56. Craven of horror
57. Cold and damp, as a basement

DOWN

1. Gave a meal to
2. If ___ say so myself
3. Bridge action
4. Mall units
5. Gregorian music style
6. Clean-up hitter's stat
7. Mix or Cruise
8. Spills the beans
9. Swiss painter Paul
10. Writing on the wall
11. Arrange logically
19. Take a breath
21. Property claim
22. Military organization
23. Tiny biter
24. Put on, as clothes
25. Out of one's mind
27. Ryan of "When Harry Met Sally"
28. Israeli submachine guns
29. Put money in the bank
30. On ___ (without a buyer)

Puzzle 91

Solution on Page 336

33. Really bad coffee
38. Ended, as a subscription
39. Beauty's counterpart
40. Oscar winner Jeremy ___
41. Bank acct. guarantor
42. Opposite of taped
43. ___-steven
46. Moo maker
47. Female sheep
49. Rio automaker
50. Traveler's stopover
51. Sound of disapproval

ACROSS

1. Ask too many questions
4. ___ Romeo (sports car)
8. Trucker's rig
12. Hollywood Squares win
13. Tilt like Pisa's tower
14. Relative of a gator
15. ___ favor, senor!
16. Actor Grant
17. Capitol Hill helper
18. Dictation takers
20. Painful stomach problem
21. Sound of relief
22. AOL, e.g.: Abbr.
23. Barbershop touch-up
26. Ballpark official
27. You, there!
30. It's part of growing up
34. Young ___ (kids)
35. Phone bk. info
36. Korbut of the 1972 Olympics
37. Expected in
38. Fast jet, for short
40. Hollywood Walk of Fame sights
43. Angel hair and penne
47. Heavy book
48. Starting on
50. Outspoken boxer
51. Canine comments
52. Stable mom
53. Stimpy's cartoon pal
54. What swish shots miss
55. Middle of March
56. Sound uttered while shaking the head

DOWN

1. Boston ___ Orchestra
2. Underlying cause
3. Days of ___ (ancient times)
4. Reynolds Wrap maker
5. Dog strap
6. "___ from the Madding Crowd"
7. Ronnie Milsap's "___ Day Now"
8. Where hair roots grow
9. Idle of Monty Python
10. À la ___ (with ice cream)
11. Cake finisher
19. "What's in a ___?" (Juliet)
20. Letter carriers' org.
22. "___ Believer" (Monkees tune)
23. Capote, familiarly
24. "___ Tin Tin"
25. For what ___ worth
26. Raises, as the ante
27. Linden of "Barney Miller"
28. Easter basket item
29. Vote of support
31. Burden of proof
32. Friend or ___?
33. Boozehounds
37. Woman's apparel

Puzzle 92

Solution on Page 336

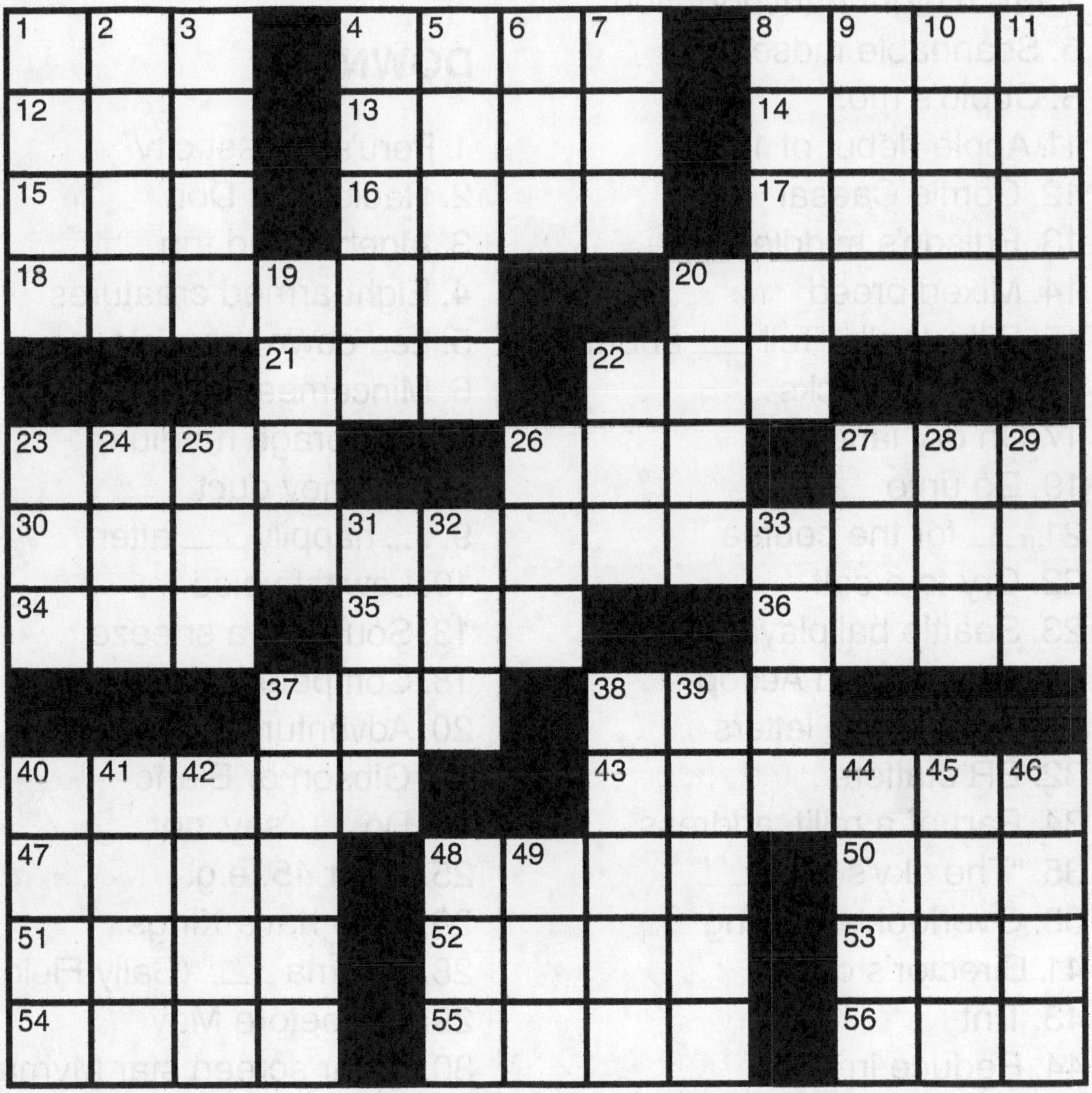

38. Mold's origin
39. What some crooks crack
40. Night twinkler
41. Pop singer Amos
42. Letters on a radio switch
44. Pucker-inducing
45. Pub draughts
46. Plummet
48. "What Kind of Fool ___?"
49. In a funk

ACROSS

1. Prom night transportation
5. Scannable mdse. bars
8. Cupid's mo.
11. Apple debut of 1998
12. Comic Caesar
13. Edison's middle name
14. Mixed breed
15. Billy Joel's "Tell ___ about It"
16. Billiards sticks
17. On dry land
19. Do unto ___ . . .
21. ___ for the course
22. Cry to a calf
23. Seattle ballplayer
27. Lesson from Aesop
31. Sixth sense letters
32. ER staffers
34. Part of a milit. address
35. "The sky's the ___!"
38. Overlook's offering
41. Director's call
43. Tint
44. Reduce in rank
47. Speechified
51. Victor's cry
52. Eagles' org.
54. Prefix meaning trillion
55. Catholic ritual
56. ___-la-la
57. Deposited
58. ___-Caps (Nestlé candy)
59. Not vert.
60. 1978 Village People hit

DOWN

1. Peru's largest city
2. Radio host Don
3. Algebra and trig
4. Eight-armed creatures
5. Led down the aisle
6. Mincemeat dessert
7. PC storage medium
8. Chimney duct
9. . . . happily ___ after
10. Lowest voice
13. Sound of a sneeze
18. Competed politically
20. Adventure hero Swift
23. Gibson or Blanc
24. Do ___ say, not . . .
25. 33 or 45, e.g.
26. They have Xings
28. "Norma ___" (Sally Field film)
29. Mo. before May
30. Silver screen star Myrna
33. Learned one
36. Desktop pictures
37. Egypt's King ___
39. Where Switz. is
40. With every hair in place
42. Sophomore's grade
44. Lowers, as a light
45. McGregor of "Moulin Rouge!"

Puzzle 93

Solution on Page 337

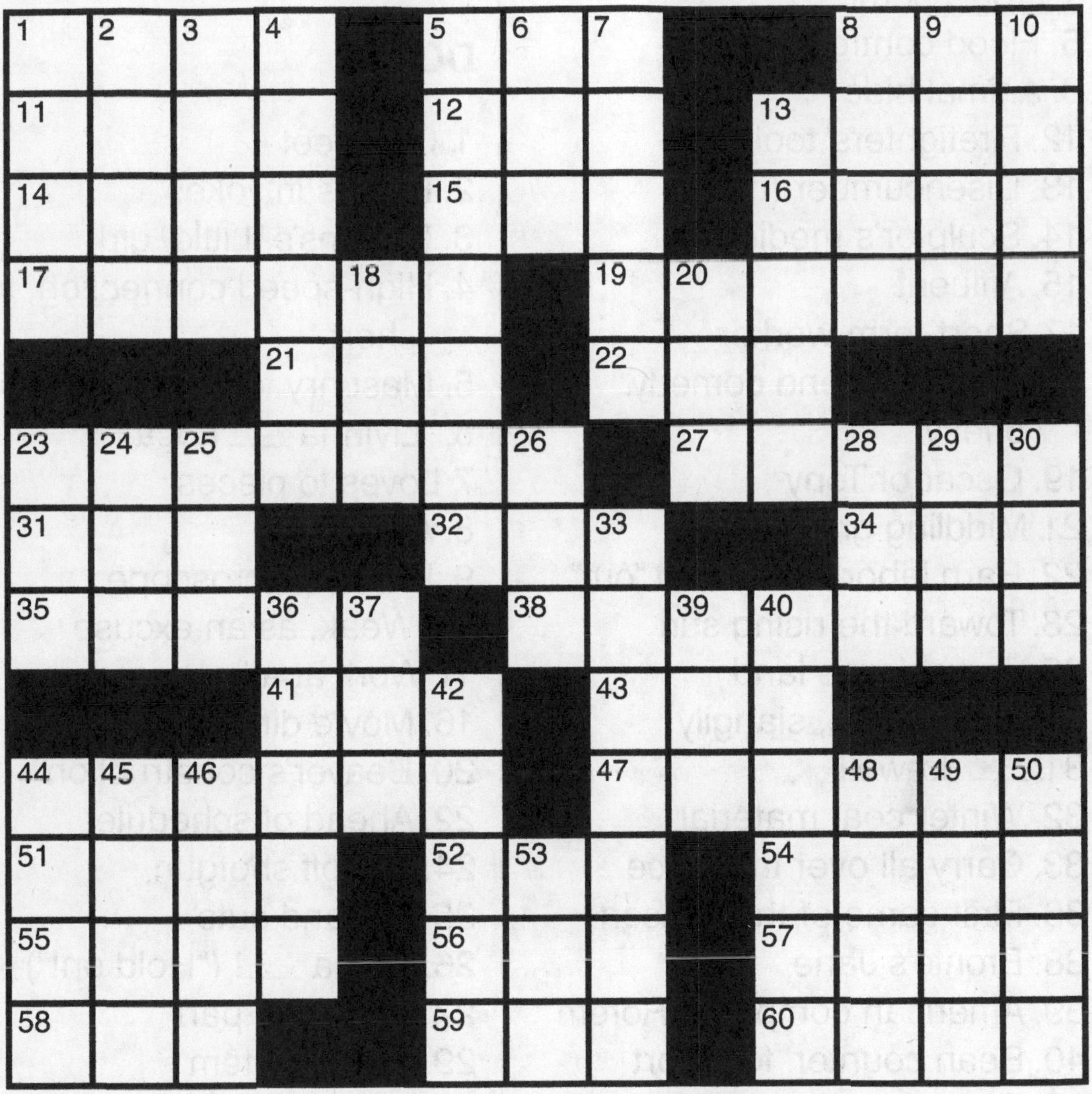

46. Soup with sushi
48. Go, ___!
49. Hockey star Lindros
50. Absurdist art movement
53. To's reverse

ACROSS

1. Frog's home
5. Flood control proj.
8. Animal hide
12. Firefighters' tools
13. Disencumber (of)
14. Sculptor's medium
15. Affluent
17. Short-term worker
18. NBC weekend comedy, briefly
19. Oscar or Tony
21. Middling grade
22. Earn laboriously, with "out"
23. Toward the rising sun
25. Jerusalem's land
28. Intelligence, slangily
31. ___ do-well
32. Winter coat material
33. Carry all over the place
36. First game of the season
38. Brontë's Jane
39. American composer Rorem
40. Bean counter, for short
42. Extend, as a subscription
44. For shame!
47. Wyatt of the Wild West
49. "Daily Planet" reporter
51. Bart Simpson's sister
52. Subj. for some immigrants
53. Like ___ of bricks
54. Snow transport
55. Aunt or uncle: Abbr.
56. Chews the fat

DOWN

1. Cat's feet
2. Beasts in yokes
3. Dickens's "Little" girl
4. High-speed connection, for short
5. Masonry tool
6. "Livin' la ___ Loca"
7. Loves to pieces
8. Agt.'s take
9. Kind of microscope
10. Weak, as an excuse
11. Work at a keyboard
16. Movie director's unit
20. Beaver's construction
22. Ahead of schedule
24. ___-off shotgun
25. ___ and outs
26. Just a ___! ("Hold on!")
27. Practice a part
29. Stubbed item
30. Popular camera type, for short
34. Make a goof
35. Spud preparer's tool
36. "The Iceman Cometh" playwright Eugene
37. Church seating
40. Disney collectibles

Puzzle 94

Solution on Page 337

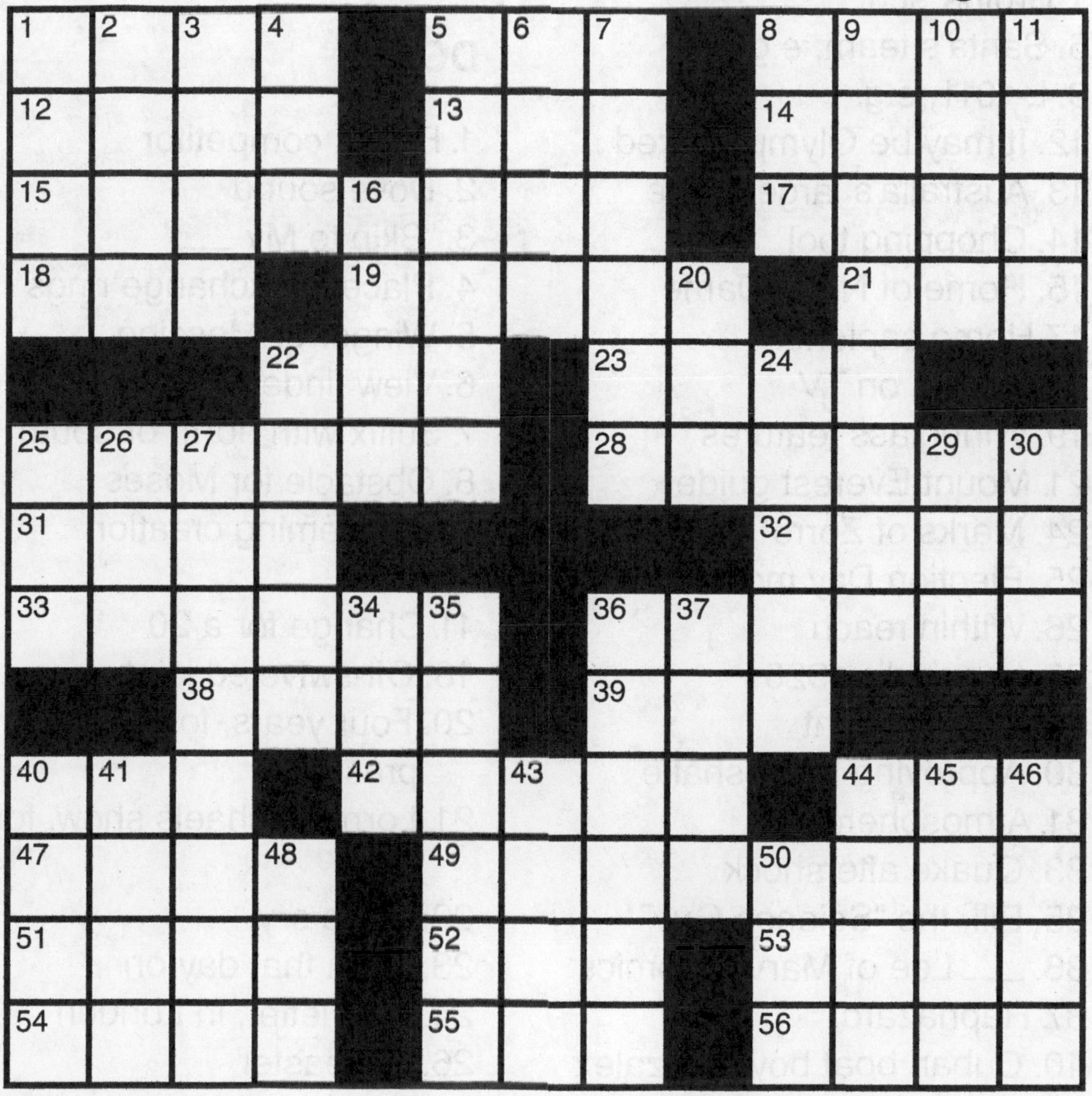

41. Mop's companion
43. Bloodhound's asset
44. Bye-bye, in Brighton
45. Snooty person
46. Ranges of knowledge
48. Shoulder enhancer
50. Word after jet or time

ACROSS

1. Bruins' sch.
5. Santa's team, e.g.
9. L-1011, e.g.
12. It may be Olympic-sized
13. Australia's largest lake
14. Chopping tool
15. Home of Notre Dame
17. Homo sapiens
18. Shows on TV
19. Wineglass features
21. Mount Everest guide
24. Marks of Zorro
25. Election Day mo.
26. Within reach
28. Leopold's 1920s co-defendant
30. Approving head shake
31. Atmosphere
33. Quake aftershock
35. Bill, the "Science Guy"
36. ___ Lee of Marvel Comics
37. Haphazard
40. Cuban boat boy Gonzalez
42. Spanish Surrealist Joan
43. Revolver
44. The same
49. Alphabet openers
50. January 1 title word
51. Chimney buildup
52. Lousy grade
53. Camp beds
54. Fraternal members

DOWN

1. FedEx competitor
2. Dove sound
3. "Skip to My ___"
4. Place to exchange rings
5. Winger or Messing
6. View finders?
7. Suffix with north or south
8. Obstacle for Moses
9. Ian Fleming creation
10. Test
11. Change for a 20
16. Oft-swiveled joint
20. Four years, for a U.S. president
21. Lorne Michaels show, for short
22. Owl's cry
23. From that day on
24. Last letter, in London
26. ___'easter
27. Toy on a string
29. Phi ___ Kappa
30. The "N" in NCO
32. Not Rep. or Ind.
34. Lunatic
37. Orange covers
38. Paintings and such

Puzzle 95

Solution on Page 337

39. Let's make some ___!
40. Cry of shock
41. Oil change go-with
42. Go soft, as butter
45. Batman and Robin, e.g.
46. Rank above maj.
47. Thumbs up
48. Some USN officers

ACROSS

1. Raw metals
5. High card
8. Reggae relative
11. Bump on the skin
12. Tach letters
13. James Brown's genre
14. Tech. college major
15. Classroom replacement
16. Peevish complaint
17. Moe, Curly, or Larry
19. Puts forth, as effort
21. ___ of iniquity
22. Toon pal of Stimpy
23. Gridiron pitchout
27. Take everything off
31. Where did ___ wrong?
32. Dawson or Dykstra
34. Shiverer's sound
35. Having melody and harmony
38. Listlessness
41. ___ tai
43. Meth. or Cath.
44. Give, as homework
47. Androids
51. Desserts with crusts
52. Surgeons' org.
54. Prepare for publication
55. Top exec.
56. Louse-to-be
57. Hitchhiker's quest
58. Chairman pro ___
59. U-turn from WNW
60. One twixt 12 and 20

DOWN

1. Is in arrears
2. Diatribe
3. Logician's "therefore"
4. Walked with a purpose
5. Weapons stash
6. PC "brain"
7. Hot coal
8. Take to the sky
9. Composer Weill
10. "The Sound of Music" backdrop
13. What Fido follows
18. Deutschland: Abbr.
20. Deletes, with "out"
23. English ___ (coll. course)
24. George Harrison's "All Those Years ___"
25. Coal unit
26. Moon vehicle, for short
28. Slugger's stat
29. Tax org.
30. Before: Prefix
33. Do a voice-over, perhaps
36. Out of kilter
37. Jet ___ (traveler's woe)
39. Tolstoy or Buscaglia
40. Physicist Einstein
42. Asinine

Puzzle 96

Solution on Page 337

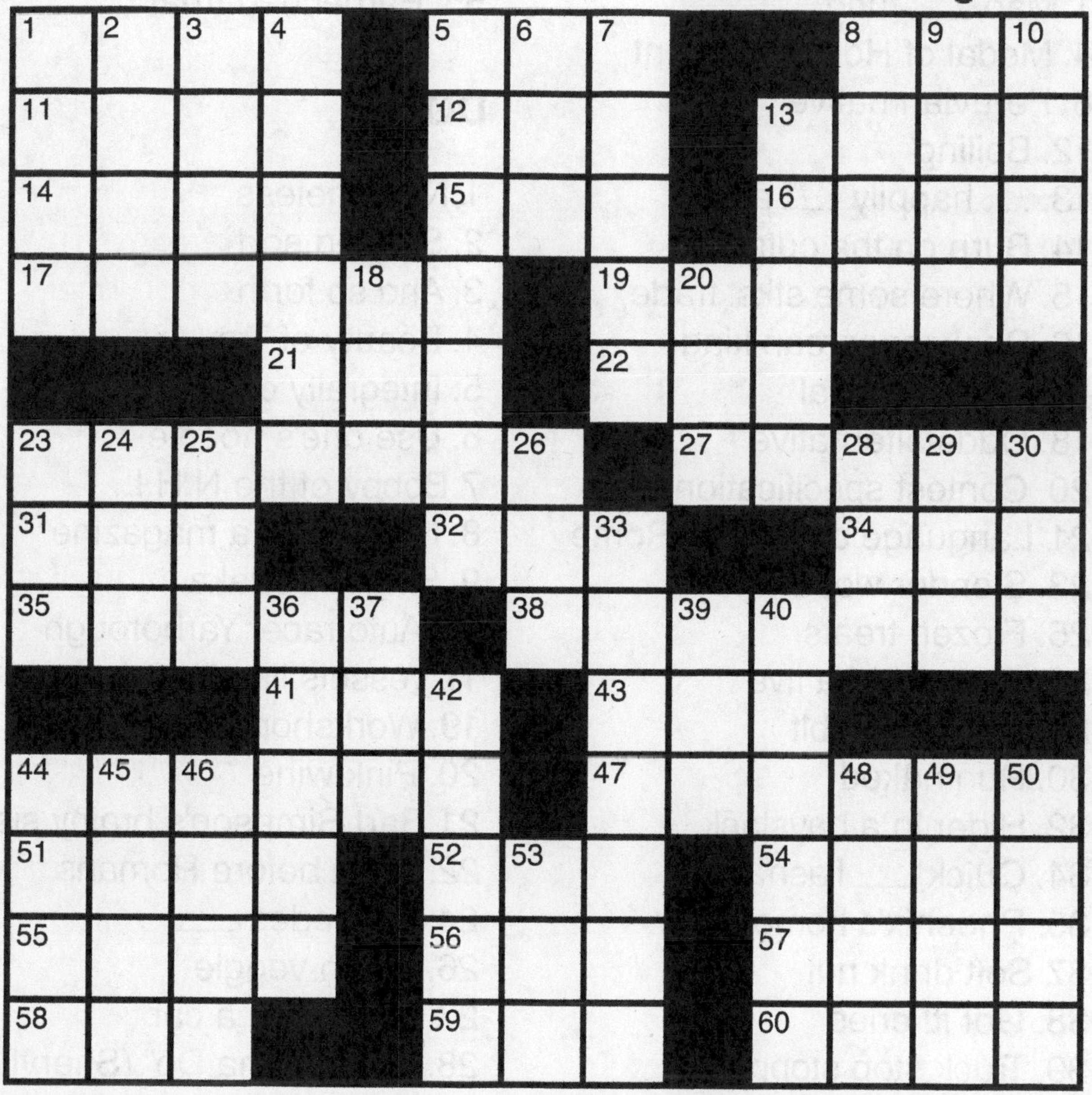

44. Scheduled mtg.
45. Foal's father
46. Give the appearance of
48. Dog tormented by Garfield
49. Alabama's Crimson ___
50. British submachine gun
53. Wrong: Pref.

ACROSS

1. Mao ___-tung
4. Medal of Honor recipient
8. Peruvian native
12. Boiling
13. . . . happily ___ after
14. Burn on the outside
15. Where some stks. trade
16. Shakespearean king
17. Scarf material
18. Odds alternative
20. Contest specifications
21. Language of ancient Rome
23. Slender woodwind
25. Frozen treats
26. Change of a five
27. Feedbag tidbit
30. Run naked
32. Hider in a haystack
34. Quick ___ flash
35. Phoenix's home: Abbr.
37. Soft drink nut
38. Got it! cries
39. Truck stop stoppers
40. Knife wounds
43. All kidding ___ . . .
45. Suffix with million
46. Favoritism or discrimination
47. Bath site
50. Windsor or sheepshank
51. Slips behind
52. Prefix with center
53. ___-serif
54. ___ went thataway!
55. Barbecued treat

DOWN

1. Ne'ertheless
2. Soused sort
3. And so forth
4. Beauty of Troy
5. Integrally divisible by two
6. Use one's noodle
7. Bobby of the N.H.L.
8. Number of a magazine
9. Singer Sedaka
10. Auto racer Yarborough
11. Vessels like Noah's
19. Workshop gripper
20. Pink wine
21. Bart Simpson's brainy sister
22. Book before Romans
24. Mercedes ___
26. Cajun veggie
27. Counter in a car
28. "___ Wanna Do" (Sheryl Crow tune)
29. Darjeeling and oolong
31. Satisfied sounds
33. ___ out (barely made)
36. Book after Song of Solomon
38. Aids and ___
39. Spacek of "Coal Miner's Daughter"

Puzzle 97

Solution on Page 338

40. Fifth Avenue landmark
41. R&B singer Turner
42. Elvis ___ Presley
44. Like some advice
46. Sandwich on toast
48. News agcy.
49. Highchair attire

ACROSS

1. Roadies carry them
5. Nonstick cooking spray
8. Old space station
11. NASCAR's Yarborough
12. Thurman of "The Avengers"
13. Surrender, as land
14. "___ Fire": Springsteen hit
15. Letters between K and O
16. Like deserts
17. Spiderlike bug
20. Plopped (down)
21. Home of the Braves: Abbr.
22. Pal in Paris
25. 1960s Chinese chairman
27. Bother persistently
31. New Balance competitor
33. Gosh, it's cold!
35. Very long story
36. Actress Close
38. Slangy wonderful
40. Corn holder
41. New England fish
43. No ___ (Chinese menu phrase)
45. Exotic destinations
52. Barbecue offerings
53. New Deal agcy.
54. Cheesy fiction
55. Lake near Niagara Falls
56. Children's game
57. Wry Bombeck
58. ___ Moines
59. Steady as ___ goes
60. Piggy bank opening

DOWN

1. Citric ___
2. Bear with cold porridge
3. Trudge (along)
4. Puts in the mail
5. Soda can feature
6. Bullets and such
7. Food from heaven
8. A ___ pittance
9. Got it, man
10. Johnny Bench's team
13. Maria of the Met
18. Sweet potato cousin
19. Communications conglomerate
22. Hulk director Lee
23. $1,000,000, for short
24. Prez after Harry
26. Hockey Hall of Famer Bobby
28. Tic-toe connection
29. "Long, Long ___"
30. Bill at the bar
32. Crate up
34. Rioting
37. Presently
39. Hi-speed connection
42. Pub projectiles
44. Stares open-mouthed

Puzzle 98

Solution on Page 338

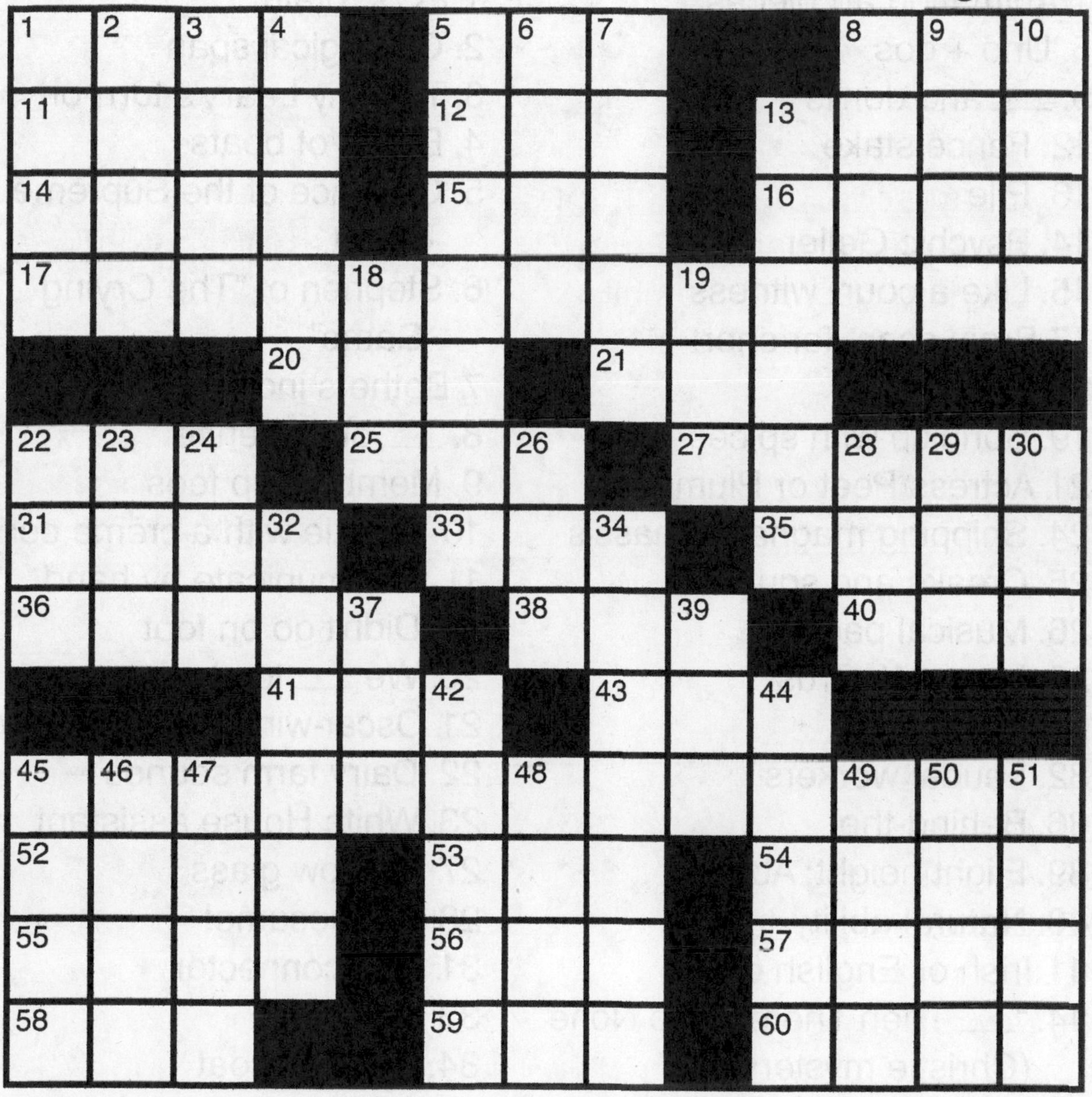

45. Flintstone fellow
46. Million or billion suffix
47. Stats for sluggers
48. Right on!
49. Barbell rep
50. Tickle me ___
51. Falling-out

ACROSS

1. Animation art pieces
5. Uno + dos
9. ___ and don'ts
12. Fence stake
13. Pile
14. Psychic Geller
15. Like a court witness
17. Brain scan, for short
18. CD-___
19. Sprinkle with spices
21. Actress Peet or Plummer
24. Shipping magnate Onassis
25. Creaks and squeaks
26. Musical pace
29. In ___ We Trust
30. Tax mo.
32. Feudal workers
36. Behind-the-___
39. Flight height: Abbr.
40. Natural ability
41. Irish or English dog
44. "___ Then There Were None" (Christie mystery)
45. Submachine gun
46. Very observant
51. Hot temper
52. Computer keyboard key
53. Brand of spaghetti sauce
54. Tiny bit
55. Listening organs
56. Urban air problem

DOWN

1. PC's "brain"
2. Geological span
3. Timothy Leary's turn-on
4. Backs of boats
5. Clarence of the Supreme Court
6. Stephen of "The Crying Game"
7. Bothers incessantly
8. ___ of influence
9. Membership fees
10. Cookie with a crème center
11. Communicate by hand
16. Didn't go on foot
20. We ___ to please
21. Oscar-winning director Lee
22. Dairy farm sounds
23. White House assistant
27. Window glass
28. ___ sesame!
31. Q-U connector
33. Squealer
34. Sheep's coat
35. Rock layers
36. Plays for time
37. Mr. Peanut prop
38. Tribal advisers, typically
41. Clubs or hearts
42. Pound of literature
43. Laced up
47. Watchdog's warning

Puzzle 99

Solution on Page 338

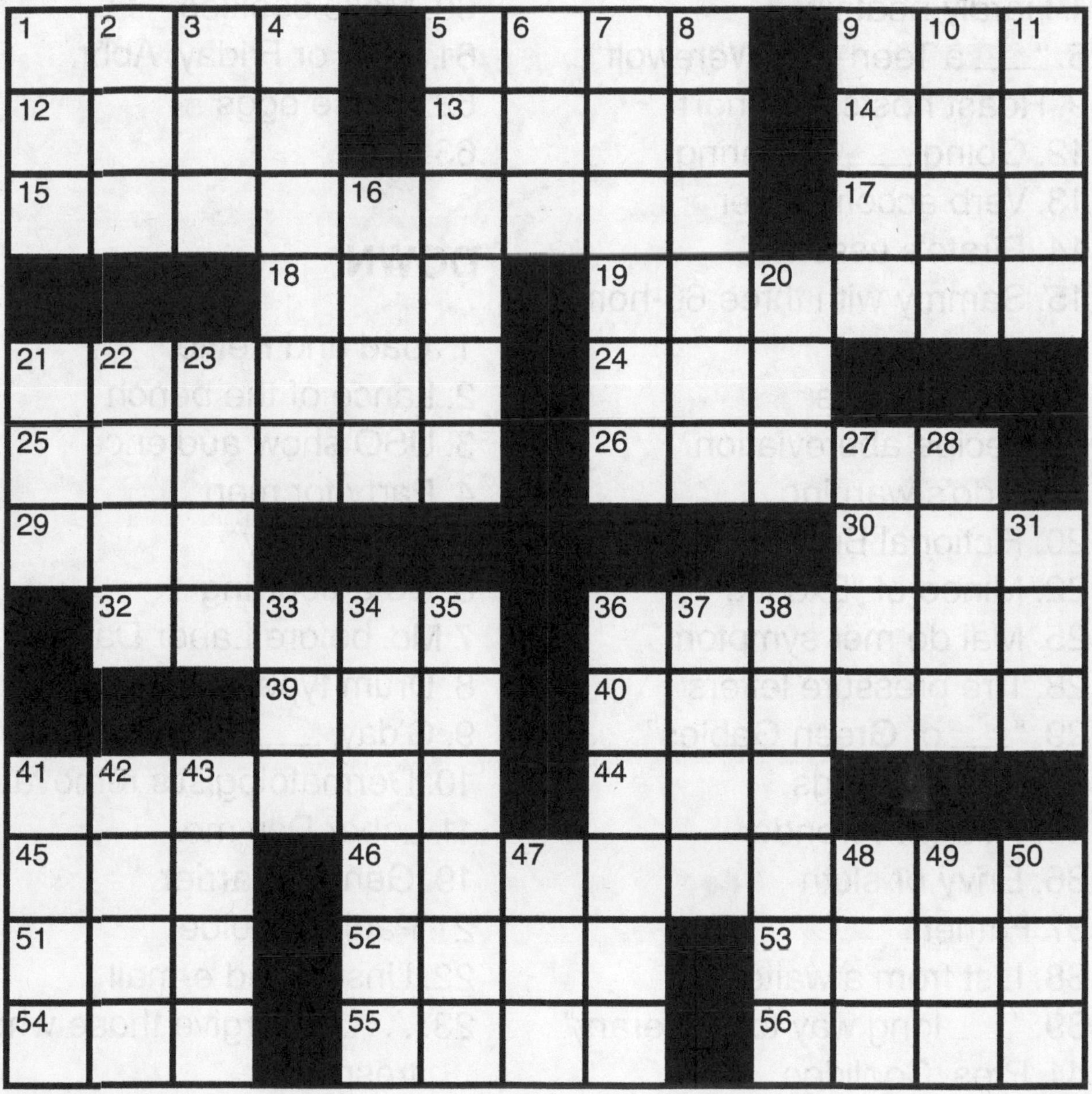

48. Thanksgiving tuber
49. It may be puffed up
50. Excavated

ACROSS

1. Hardly neatniks
5. "___ a Teen-age Werewolf"
9. Roast hosts, for short
12. Going ___ (bickering)
13. Verb accompanier
14. Pirate's assent
15. Sammy with three 60-homer seasons
16. Roman robe
17. Recipe abbreviation
18. Fido's warning
20. Fictional Butler
22. Mineo of "Exodus"
25. Mal de mer symptom
28. Tire pressure letters
29. "___ of Green Gables"
30. Feed, as pigs
34. Fills with wonder
36. Envy or sloth
37. Father
38. List from a waiter
39. "___ long way to Tipperary"
41. Pres. Coolidge
42. Self-___ (pride)
44. Carrier to Amsterdam
45. Tongue's sense
48. Caustic substance
50. ___ thumbs: clumsy
51. Yahtzee pieces
54. Springsteen's nickname, with "the"
58. Architect I. M. ___
59. Puts on TV
60. Make cookies
61. Bilko or Friday: Abbr.
62. Louse eggs
63. Omit

DOWN

1. Joad and Kettle
2. Lance of the bench
3. USO show audience
4. Party for men
5. On the way
6. Go a-courting
7. Mo. before Labor Day
8. Drum type
9. G'day, ___!
10. Dermatologist's removal
11. Labor Day mo.
19. Genetic carrier
21. Padlock holder
22. Unsolicited e-mail
23. . . . ___ forgive those who trespass . . .
24. Bank's property claim
26. Join forces
27. Lacking meaning
31. Be deficient in
32. Down Under gemstone
33. Tree in Miami
35. Bird-feeder block
40. TV's "Judging ___"

Puzzle 100

Solution on Page 338

43. Alternative to a station wagon or convertible
45. Spigots
46. Break ___!
47. Thin cut
49. Recedes, as the tide
52. Caesar's three
53. Old PC component
55. Acorn maker
56. Hit the slopes
57. Autumn mo.

ACROSS

1. Agrees to
4. Mac alternatives
7. Volcanic rock material
12. Butter slice
13. Held first place
14. Don't get any funny ___!
15. End of an ___
16. Estranges
18. Make a connection (to)
20. Let 'er ___!
21. All over again
22. Prohibit
24. It may be rolled out in the rain
28. Brooks or Gibson
30. El ___ (Spanish hero)
32. High, arcing shot
33. When doubled, a dance
35. Buying binge
37. Mantra syllables
38. Butterfly catcher's need
39. Tool and ___
40. RR depot
42. ___-do-well
44. ___ Wednesday (Lent starter)
46. Look at lasciviously
49. Writer Fleming
51. Mistake remover
53. Pupil of Plato
57. One ___ million
58. Zellweger of "Bridget Jones's Diary"
59. In poor health
60. Talk smack about
61. Group of key officers
62. Tofu source
63. Opposite of WSW

DOWN

1. Pavarotti genre
2. Grammy winner Carpenter
3. Standoff
4. Builder's map
5. Paparazzi target
6. "Star Wars" program, for short
7. Above-the-knee skirt
8. Change with the times
9. ___ a life!
10. Daisy or Fannie
11. Beast of burden
17. Bert's Muppet buddy
19. Great respect
23. Farm measures
25. Next to
26. CD-___ (computer insert)
27. Frontline airer
29. Dropped drug
31. ___ Plaines, Illinois
33. Larry King's channel
34. Haw lead-in
36. Baby grand, e.g.
41. Burnt ___ crisp

Puzzle 101

Solution on Page 339

43. Choir platform
45. Welcoming word
47. Stalin's predecessor
48. Rub out with rubber
50. To ___: perfectly
52. Depend (on)
53. Pop fly's path
54. Stephen of "Michael Collins"
55. Like Perot's party: Abbr.
56. My country ___ of thee . . .

ACROSS

1. Pairs
5. Half a devious laugh
8. Pudding fruit
12. Fissure
13. It climbs the walls
14. Hoarseness
15. Facts, briefly
16. A-one
18. Cozumel cash
19. Omaha's home: Abbr.
20. Low in spirits
23. Overhead storage spot
28. Attila follower
31. Obey
33. Like Santa's cheeks
34. WWII cipher machine
36. Big lizard
38. Big trucks
39. Let us know, on an invitation
41. Singer McLean
42. Patriot Allen
44. Mole, to a gardener
46. Sci-fi saucer
48. Muddy up
52. Adversary
57. SeaWorld whale
58. ___ to say (implying)
59. Ick!
60. Admonishing sounds
61. Authoritative decree
62. Actress Susan
63. Salty sauces

DOWN

1. Cause to stumble
2. Chianti or chablis
3. Slays, mob-style
4. Got to one's feet
5. Strike
6. Tennis champ Goolagong
7. Publicist's job
8. Tennis instructor
9. Opposite of long.
10. Pac-10 sch.
11. Radar gun meas.
17. Lakers' org.
21. Unit of electrical resistance
22. Become threadbare
24. 1990 one-man Broadway show
25. Frog's relative
26. But there ___ joy in Mudville . . .
27. Blue-green
28. Help yourself
29. Liter or meter
30. Close by, in poetry
32. Enter the water headfirst
35. Youth gp.
37. Nav. system
40. Water absorber

Puzzle 102

Solution on Page 339

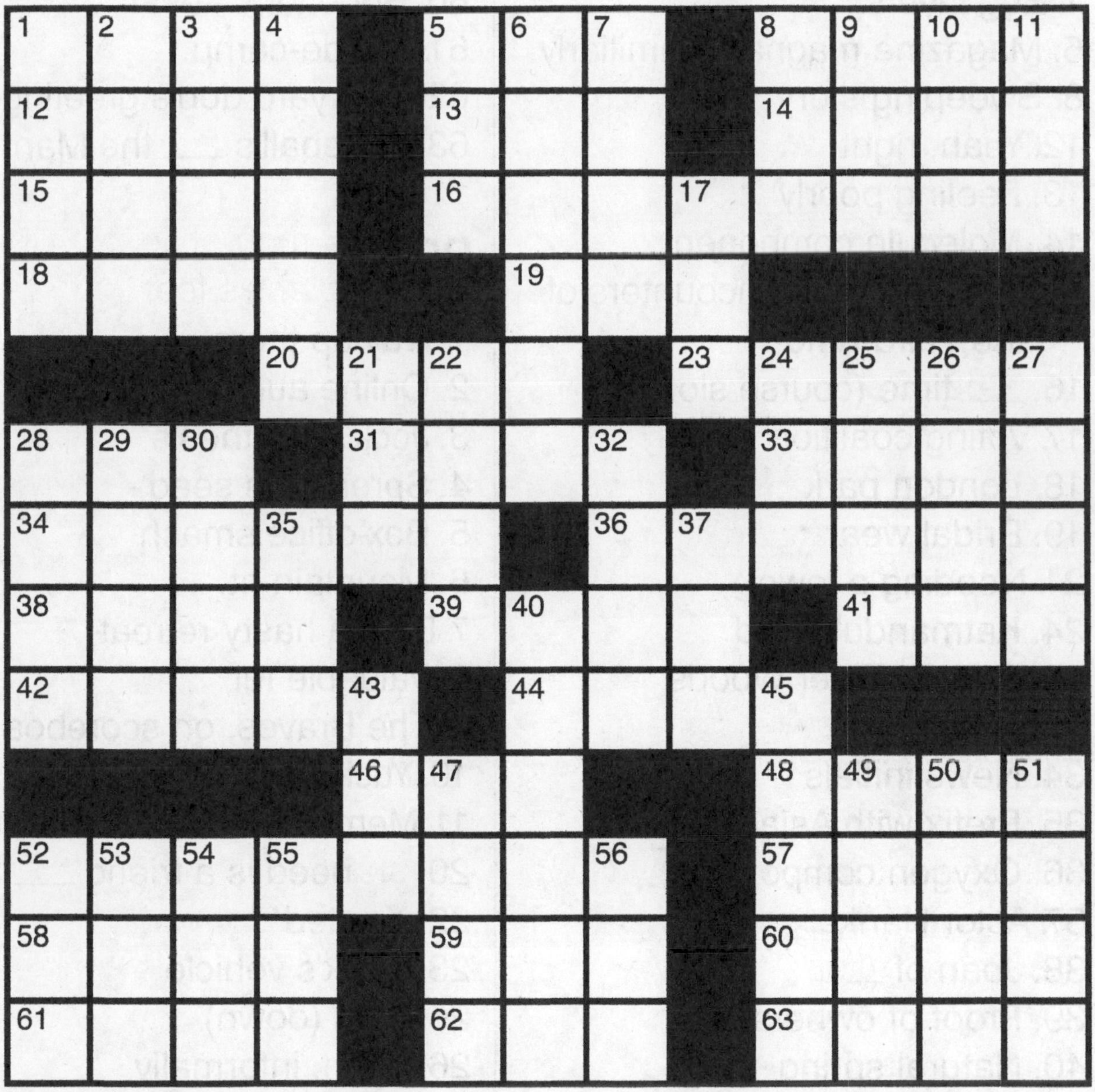

43. Habit wearer
45. Runs easily
47. Hatfield/McCoy affair
49. . . . ___ they say
50. Totally gross
51. Lad's mate
52. Clumsy sort
53. Trident-shaped Greek letter
54. Singer/actress Zadora
55. Frequently, to a bard
56. "Love ___ neighbor"

ACROSS

1. Egg layers
5. Magazine magnate, familiarly
8. Sweeping story
12. Yeah, right
13. Feeling poorly
14. Molecule component
15. Teri of "Close Encounters of the Third Kind"
16. ___ time (course slot)
17. Voting coalition
18. London park
19. Bridal wear
21. Needing a towel
24. Katmandu's land
28. Org. for Tiger Woods
31. Swift
34. News initials
35. Prefix with Asian
36. Oxygen compound
37. Actor Hanks
38. Joan of ___
39. Proof of ownership
40. Natural spring
41. Japanese restaurant fare
43. Football distances: Abbr.
45. Mil. weapon that can cross an ocean
48. Swamp snapper
52. "The ___ Man"
55. Confederate soldier, for short
57. Greasy
58. Summoned Jeeves
59. Tire fill
60. Robe for Caesar
61. ___-de-camp
62. Junkyard dog's greeting
63. Baseball's ___ the Man

DOWN

1. Way up there
2. Online auction house
3. Jock's antithesis
4. Spread, as seed
5. Box-office smash
6. Mountain ht.
7. Beat a hasty retreat
8. Valuable fur
9. The Braves, on scoreboards
10. Yucky stuff
11. Memorable films cable sta.
20. . . . need is a friend ___
22. X-rated
23. Hack's vehicle
25. Sets (down)
26. Each, informally
27. Peruvian capital
28. Pod contents
29. Spiritual adviser
30. Rainbow shapes
32. Peach center
33. Sit ___ by (do nothing)
42. Door swinger
44. Glasgow residents

Puzzle 103

Solution on Page 339

46. Be boastful
47. Golda of Israel
49. Unruly event
50. Gold-medal gymnast Korbut
51. Greenish-blue
52. ___ la la
53. "Bali ___"
54. Not Dem. or Rep.
56. Man, it's cold!

ACROSS

1. "Hannah and ___ Sisters"
4. Dir. opposite NNE
7. Unmannered fellow
11. St. crossing
12. Physician, ___ thyself
14. German auto
15. Shrink
17. Duo plus one
18. Co. known as "Big Blue"
19. Skeleton's place?
21. Diver's gear
24. Cause of a game delay
25. Baseball hats
26. Spray can emission
29. Patient care grp.
30. Violinist Isaac
31. ___ and tuck
33. Give the right, as to privileges
35. Golfers' supports
36. The ___ of March
37. Dumbwaiter, essentially
38. Like the season before Easter
41. Moon vehicle
42. October birthstone
43. Fiasco
48. TV's Nick at ___
49. Old wound mark
50. Encouragement at the bullring
51. Frosts, as a cake
52. Since Jan. 1, in financials
53. Ring decision, briefly

DOWN

1. "If I ___ a Hammer"
2. First lady?
3. DVR button
4. Biblical land with a queen
5. Line of stitches
6. ___ it something I said?
7. Conductors' sticks
8. Not theirs
9. Garfield dog
10. Urban unrest
13. Spy novelist John
16. Barbecue entrée
20. Simba, for one
21. Coll. or univ.
22. I ___, I saw, I conquered
23. Once ___ a time . . .
24. Film vault collection
26. Waits upon
27. "Dedicated to the ___ Love"
28. Big fibs
30. "West ___ Story"
32. Winter clock setting in S.F.
34. Bestseller list entries
35. "Uncle ___ Cabin"
37. Listened to
38. Anderson of "WKRP in Cincinnati"

Puzzle 104

Solution on Page 339

1	2	3		4	5	6			7	8	9	10
11				12			13		14			
15			16						17			
			18				19	20				
21	22	23				24						
25					26					27	28	
29				30					31			32
	33		34					35				
			36					37				
38	39	40				41						
42				43	44				45	46	47	
48				49					50			
51					52				53			

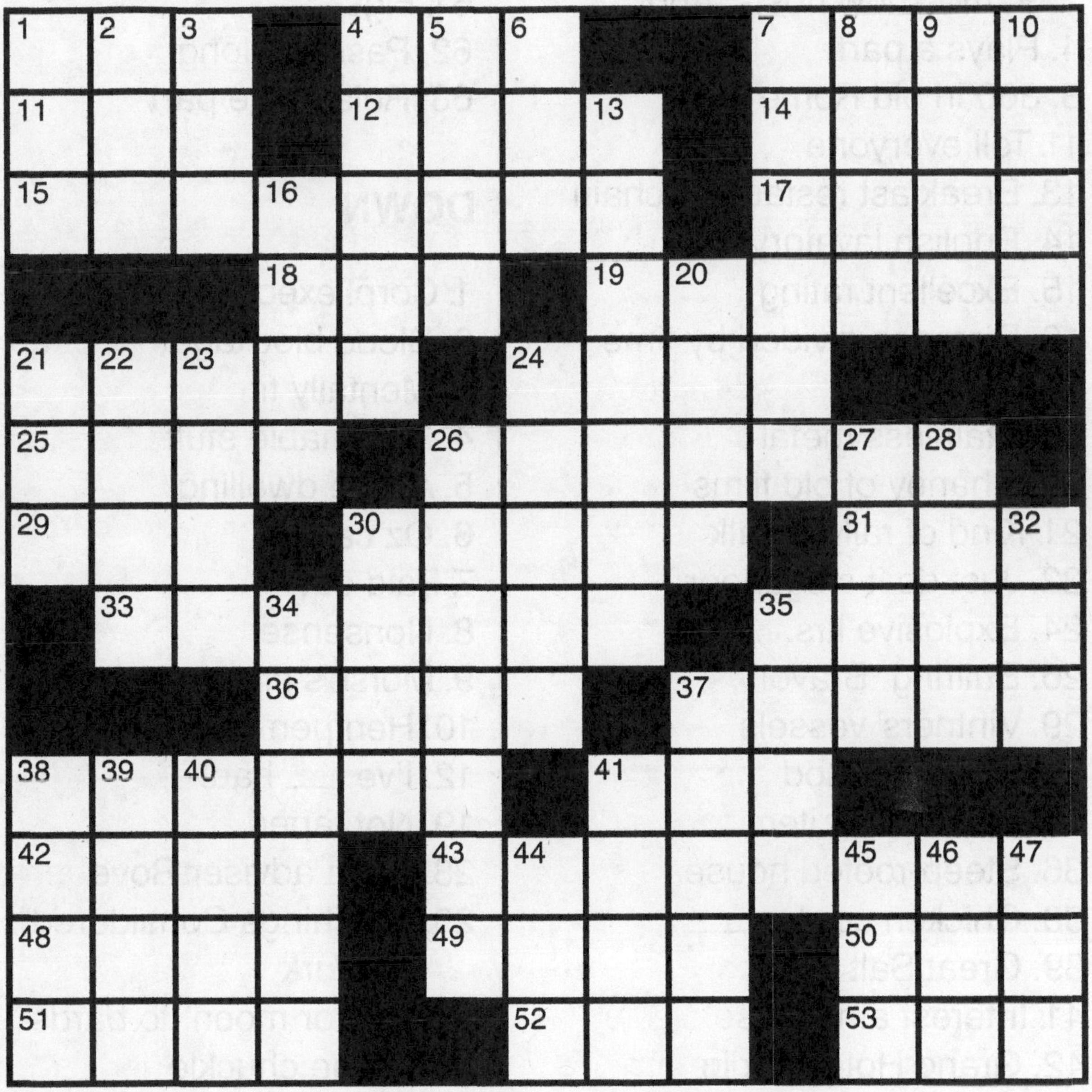

39. Ben-Hur, for one
40. Basketball great Archibald
41. Exam for a wannabe atty.
44. Slippery, as winter sidewalks
45. Kiddie
46. Antlered critter
47. Old Olds car

ACROSS

1. Game-show hosts: Abbr.
4. Plays a part
8. 300 in old Rome
11. Tell everyone
13. Breakfast restaurant chain
14. English lavatory
15. Excellent rating
16. Distance divided by time
17. Big fuss
18. Stainless metal
20. Chaney of old films
21. Kind of rally or talk
22. Just do it sloganeer
24. Explosive ltrs.
26. Bullring "Bravo!"
29. Vintners' vessels
31. Appeal to God
34. Hair-setting item
36. Steep-roofed house
38. Chicken cordon ___
39. Great Salt ___
41. Interest amt.
42. Grand Hotel studio
44. Not a ___ out of you!: "Shh!"
46. Top flier
48. Rink surface
50. Arranges by type
54. Panel truck
55. Not wild
57. Hammer or saw
58. Say no, with "out"
59. Overhead transportation
60. Chinese: Prefix
61. Figs.
62. Passed along
63. Relay race part

DOWN

1. Corp. execs' degrees
2. Blood blockage
3. Mentally fit
4. Breathable stuff
5. Alpine dwelling
6. Oz canine
7. Paid out
8. Nonsense
9. Morse's creation
10. Hen pen
12. I've ___ had!
19. Not taped
23. Bush adviser Rove
25. "All Things Considered" network
26. Sun or moon, to bards
27. Online chuckle
28. Tungsten and tellurium
30. For goodness ___!
32. Rambler mfr.
33. You ain't seen nothin' ___!
35. Big galoot
37. Doctors' charges
40. Tarzan, for one
43. Catchers' gloves

Puzzle 105

Solution on Page 340

45. Stew holders
46. Bell-ringing cosmetics company
47. Crime chief
49. Give a darn
51. Agitate
52. Dial sound
53. Wade through mud
56. Ambulance worker, for short

ACROSS

1. Make a pick
4. Quickly, in the I.C.U.
8. Toronto's prov.
11. Helps out
13. Reduce, as expenses
14. Beavis and Butt-head laugh
15. The "T" of S.A.T.
16. Gets older
17. ___ tai (cocktail)
18. Photo ___ (media events)
20. Midterms, e.g.
22. Listerine alternative
25. They're soaked up at the beach
27. Roll of bills
28. Untruths
30. Mary's fleecy follower
34. Who ___ to argue?
35. ___ Park, CO
37. Sheep's plaint
38. High schooler, probably
40. Wingless parasites
41. B&O and Amtrak
42. Not tied down
44. Stock up on
46. Weighing site
49. Crime lab evidence, briefly
50. Civil ___
51. Shells and bullets
54. Cook's amts.
58. Genesis vessel
59. James of TV's "Las Vegas"
60. Terra firma
61. Some undergrad degs.
62. Hula hoops and yo-yos
63. Start for Paulo or Luis

DOWN

1. Feedbag grain
2. Little Jack Horner's dessert
3. NFL six-pointers
4. Resorts with springs
5. ___, you're it!
6. ___ you ready?
7. Short-tempered
8. Units of resistance
9. ___ as a pin
10. Get a load of ___!
12. Freeze!
19. Brazilian soccer star
21. Immigrant's subj.
22. Swing at a fly
23. And it ___ to pass . . .
24. Garfield canine
25. Fix a shoelace
26. Hold on ___!
29. The Emerald ___ (Ireland)
31. Cadabra preceder
32. Red planet
33. Low voice
36. Connery of 007 fame
39. Packers' org.
43. Don't just stand there

Puzzle 106

Solution on Page 340

45. Wrestling surfaces
46. Clean the deck
47. Actress Irene of “Fame”
48. Boats like Noah’s
49. Mafia bigwigs
52. Great Leap Forward leader
53. Merry month
55. Distress call letters
56. Zadora
57. ___-Blo fuses

ACROSS

1. Sheet of glass
5. Holds close
9. Punk rocker Vicious
12. Transport on rails
13. Straight ___ arrow
14. Sense of self-importance
15. German automaker
16. Sha ___ (doo-wop group)
17. Become compost
18. ___ quo
20. Says hello to
22. Some boxing wins, for short
24. K-O filler
25. "Delta of Venus" author Anaïs
28. Slippery tree
29. SWM part
32. Openly declare
34. Rowboat mover
36. Big fusses
37. Hackman of Hollywood
38. B-ball official
40. More of the same: Abbr.
41. Home of the NFL's Rams
43. Tic ___ (mint)
44. ___ Peanut Butter Cups
47. Libra's symbol
52. Have the deed to
53. Voice above a tenor
55. ___ contendere (court plea)
56. Calendar pgs.
57. Before long
58. Golden ___ (senior)
59. Barely manage, with "out"
60. ___ company, three's a crowd
61. "___ Like It Hot"

DOWN

1. Elem. school groups
2. Stuck in ___
3. Nothing, in Mexico
4. Give forth
5. Harrison Ford's "Star Wars" role
6. Springsteen's "Born in the ___"
7. Crips or Bloods
8. Traffic tie-up
9. Play to the balcony?
10. Jim Croce's "___ a Name"
11. Connect the ___
19. Luau instrument, for short
21. Actress Thompson of "Howards End"
23. Like crossword solvers, naturally
25. Horse that's had it
26. ___ said it before . . .
27. Meaningless words
30. Stephen King's "Salem's ___"
31. PC bailout key
33. Dampens
35. Justifications
39. TV monitoring gp.
42. Fewest

Puzzle 107

Solution on Page 340

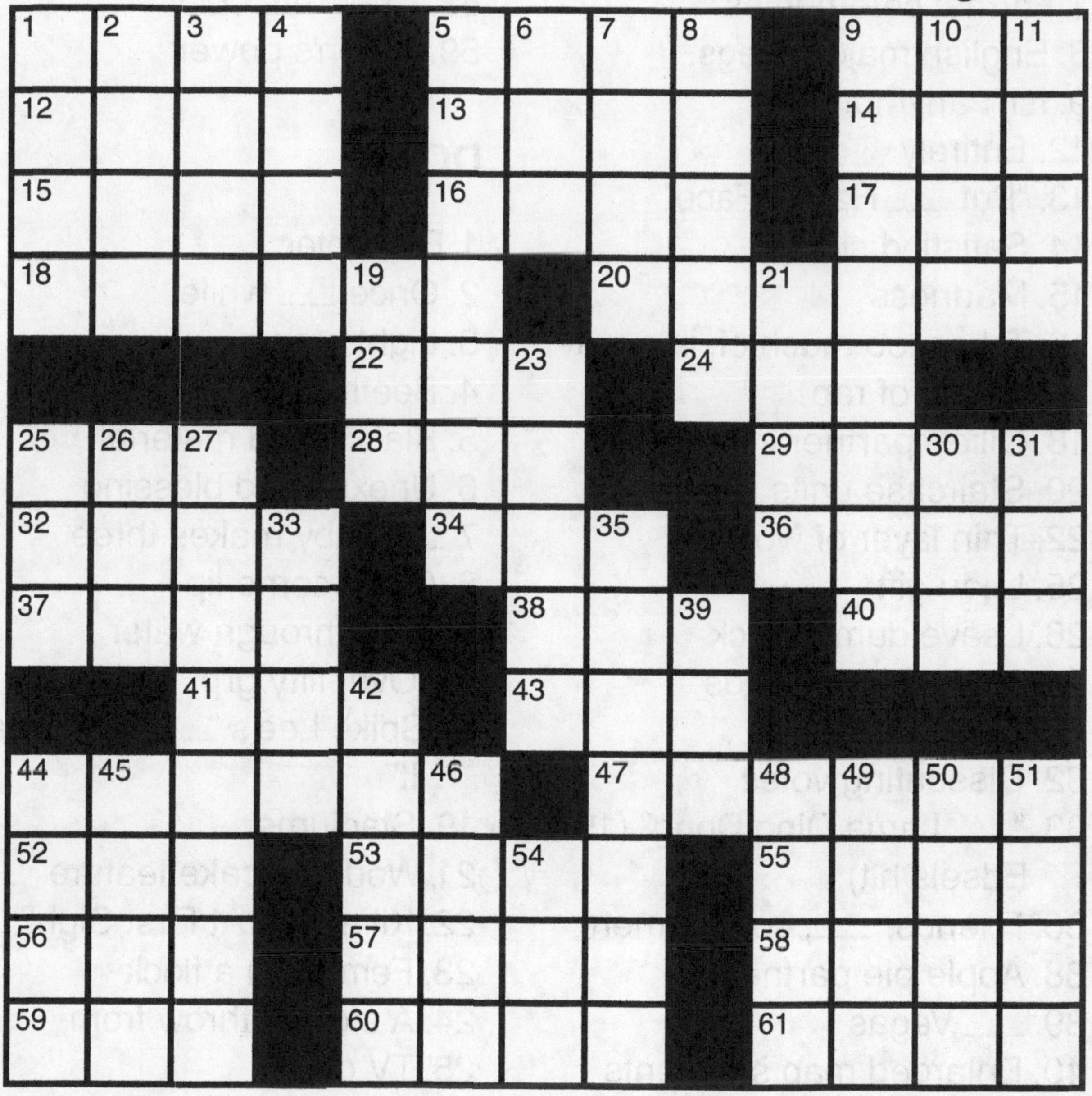

44. Capital of Italy
45. "Return of the Jedi" forest dweller
46. Glacial
48. Collections of reminiscences
49. Corporate symbol
50. Grades 1–6: Abbr.
51. Sensitive to the touch
54. "___ Legit to Quit"

ACROSS

1. Formal ceremonies
6. English majors' degs.
9. Isn't anymore
12. Entirely
13. "Put ___ Happy Face"
14. Satisfied sigh
15. Madness
16. Takes too much of, in a way
17. Doctor of rap
18. Ollie's partner in comedy
20. Staircase units
22. Thin layer of wood
25. Luau gift
26. Leave dumbstruck
27. Cleared the boards
30. Guide
32. Dissenting votes
33. "___ Lama Ding Dong" (1961 Edsels hit)
36. Friends, ___, countrymen
38. Apple pie partner?
39. ___ Vegas
40. Enlarged map segments
43. "The Canterbury ___"
46. Mosquito repellent ingredient
47. "___ to Joy"
48. Mai ___ (rum cocktail)
50. Soup go-with
54. Jaws sighting
55. December 24, e.g.
56. Overused, as an expression
57. Young-___ (kids)
58. Checkers color
59. Fulton's power

DOWN

1. Perimeter
2. Once ___ while
3. Light brown
4. Beethoven's "Für___"
5. Blackboard material
6. Unexpected blessing
7. ___ baby makes three
8. Gives some lip
9. Walk through water
10. Over-fifty grp.
11. Spike Lee's "___ Gotta Have It"
19. Stadiums
21. Wedding cake feature
22. Kilmer of "At First Sight"
23. Female in a flock
24. A stone's throw from
25. TV collie
28. "Apollo 13" director Howard
29. Notre ___
31. Ration (out)
34. Bon ___ (clever remark)
35. Pro-___ (certain tourneys)
37. Top chess player
41. Birds' homes

Puzzle 108

Solution on Page 340

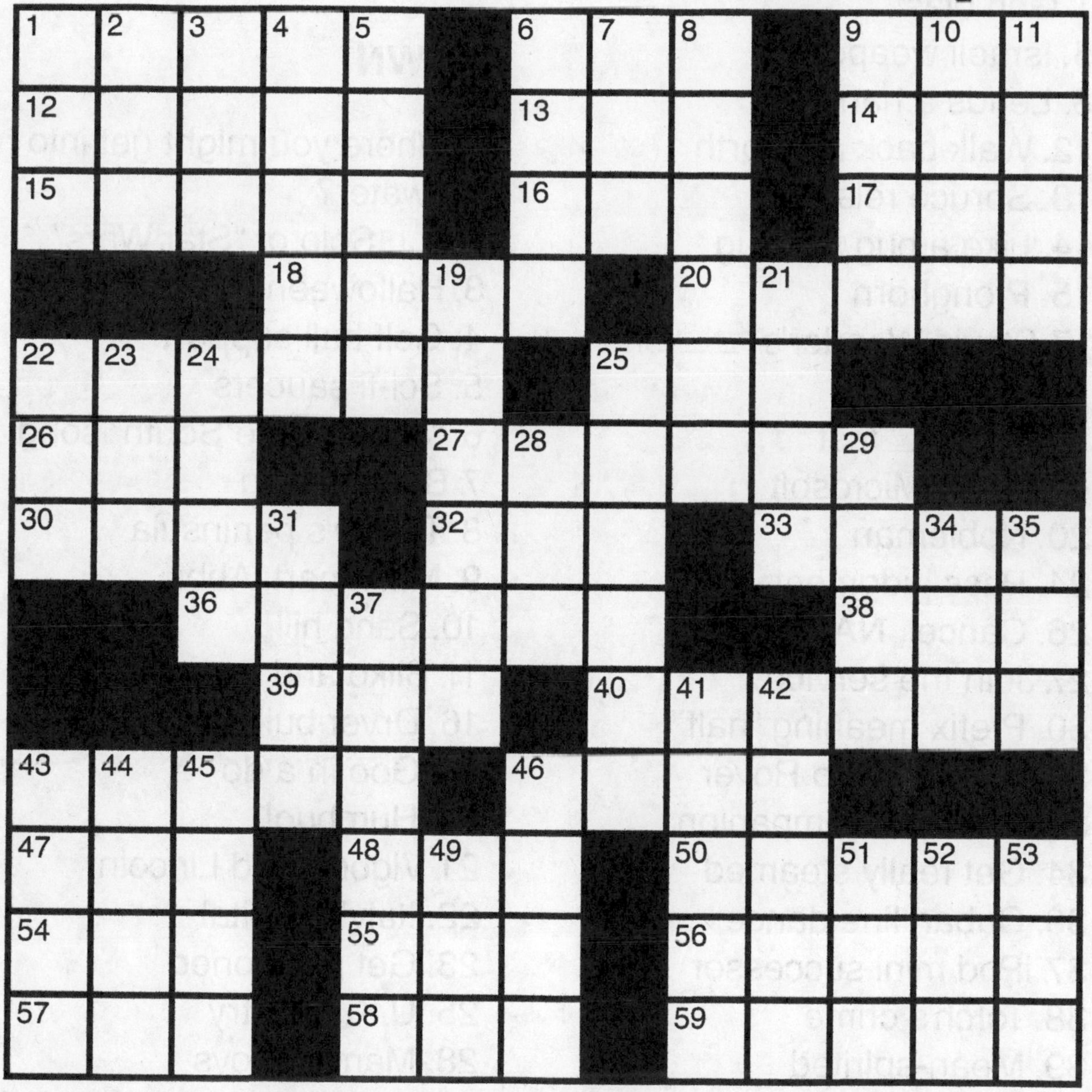

42. Get the ball rolling
43. Soybean product
44. Server's edge, in tennis
45. Telescope part
46. Went out, as a fire
49. Pennsylvania or Madison: Abbr.
51. Big fib
52. Words before glance or loss
53. Rep.'s rival

ACROSS

1. Gun blast
5. Israeli weapon
8. Lends a hand to
12. Walk back and forth
13. Spruce relative
14. Like a bug in a rug
15. Pronghorn
17. Stevie Wonder's "___ She Lovely"
18. This ___ test . . .
19. Bill of Microsoft
20. Nobleman
24. Pass judgment
26. Cancel, NASA-style
27. Join the service
30. Prefix meaning "half"
31. Command to Rover
32. Cranny's companion
34. Get really steamed
36. Cuban line dance
37. iPod mini successor
38. Torch's crime
39. Mean-spirited
42. Alley ___!
44. Construction site watchdog, for short
45. Follow, as a principle
50. Cut calories
51. Cooking spray brand
52. Had the answer
53. Marquis de ___
54. ___ kingdom come . . .
55. Racetrack shape

DOWN

1. Where you might get into hot water?
2. ___ Solo of "Star Wars"
3. Halloween mo.
4. Golf ball support
5. Sci-fi saucers
6. "Song of the South" song
7. Bitter feeling
8. Turkey's peninsula
9. M.I.T. part: Abbr.
10. Sand hill
11. Bilko and Pepper: Abbr.
16. Dryer buildup
19. Goo in a do
20. Humbug!
21. Vigoda and Lincoln
22. Italy's capital
23. Get positioned
25. U.K. country
28. Mama's boys
29. And miles ___ before I sleep
31. London's Big ___
33. It's north of Okla.
35. Drop of golden sun
36. Superman accessory
39. Agrees nonverbally
40. Most populous continent
41. Lose, as skin

Puzzle 109

Solution on Page 341

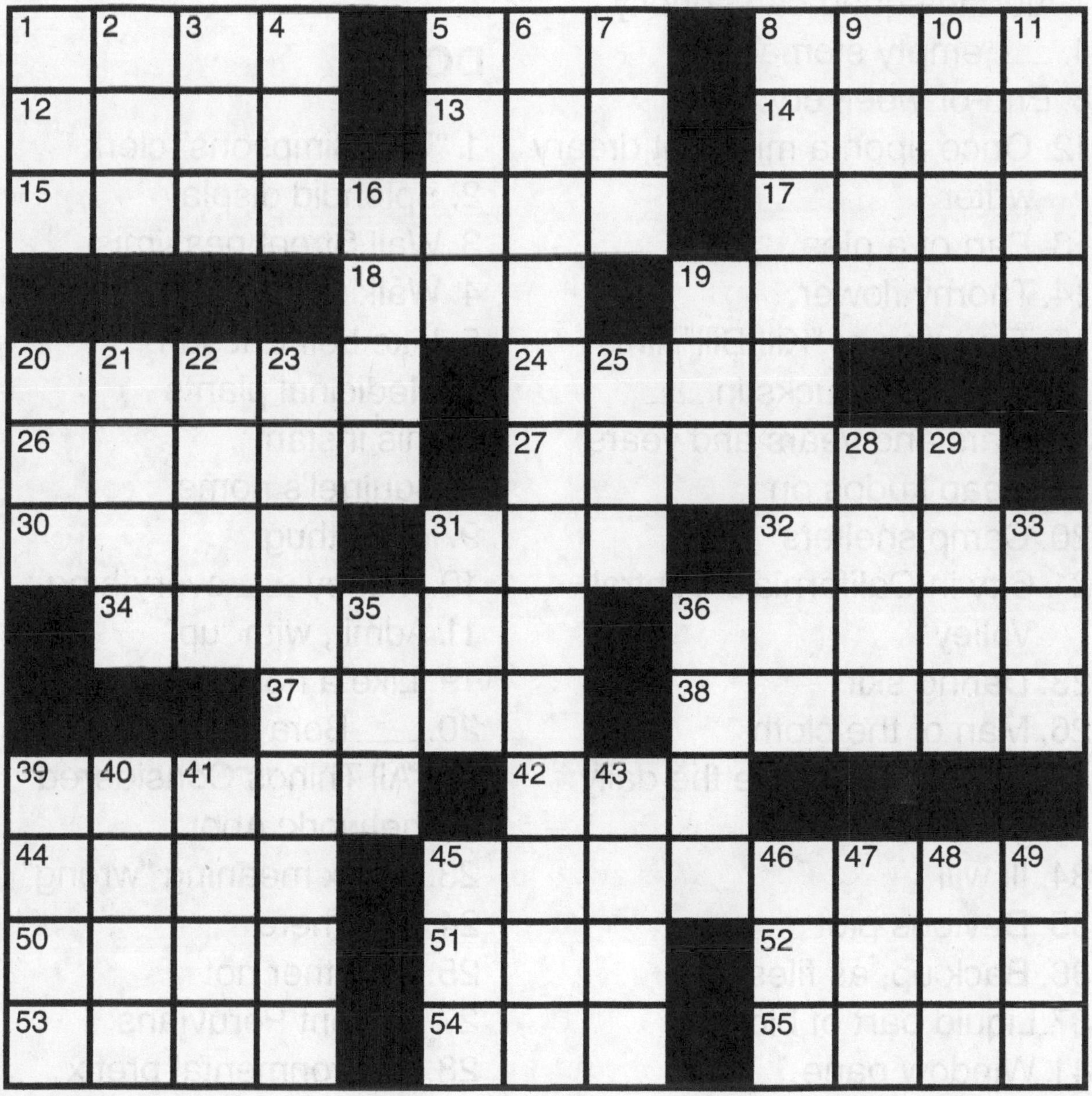

43. That's a surprise!
45. Likely
46. Early MGM rival
47. Letter holder: Abbr.
48. Lipton drink
49. Night bird

ACROSS

1. Alert to squad cars, briefly
4. ___ empty stomach
8. End-of-week cry
12. Once upon a midnight dreary writer
13. Part of a plea
14. Thorny flower
15. Thurman of "Kill Bill" films
16. Get one's ducks in ___
17. Years and years and years
18. Heap kudos on
20. Camp shelters
21. City in California's Central Valley
23. Daring skirt
26. Man of the cloth
31. Unable to escape the daily grind
34. Ill will
35. Devious plot
36. Back up, as files
37. Liquid part of blood
41. Window pane
45. Sweetened the pot
48. Han Solo's love
49. Animation units
50. Suffix with star or tsar
52. Travelers' havens
53. Apply macadam to
54. Sporty Pontiac
55. Belfry inhabitants
56. ___-friendly (easy to operate)
57. You betcha!

DOWN

1. "The Simpsons" clerk
2. Splendid display
3. Wall Street pessimist
4. Walking ___ (elated)
5. Like Leif Ericson
6. Medicinal plants
7. This instant
8. Squirrel's home
9. Hired thug
10. Money ___ everything
11. Admit, with "up"
19. Like a house ___
20. ___ Bora (Afghan region)
22. "All Things Considered" network: Abbr.
23. Prefix meaning "wrong"
24. Ltd., here
25. I'd rather not
27. Ancient Peruvians
28. Environmental prefix
29. Soak (up)
30. Gonna ___ with a little help from my friends
32. Baseball officials, for short
33. ___ Aviv, Israel
38. Neighborhoods
39. Burn balm
40. Tightwad

Puzzle 110

Solution on Page 341

41. Smooth-talking
42. Songstress Horne
43. "___ Too Proud to Beg" (1966 hit)
44. Mouth off to
46. Nervously irritable
47. Be overly fond
49. PC heart
51. Clean the floor

ACROSS

1. "A Nightmare on ___ Street"
4. Conclusion
7. Picket line crosser
11. ___ into (attacks)
13. Norma ___ (Sally Field role)
14. Drive-___ window
15. Breath freshener
16. Photo ___: publicity events
17. Sweet potatoes
18. Remained
20. Evening hour
22. Looked lecherously
24. Agt.'s share
27. Fibber of old radio
30. Surgeons' workplaces, for short
31. Road service org.
32. Football field measure
33. Wagon-wheel path
34. Speech impediment
35. Boxing ref's call
36. My dog ___ fleas
37. Rich pastry
38. Cut with an ax
39. Film director's cry
41. Be behind in payments
42. La Scala productions
46. Goat cheese
49. Six-pack component
51. Rollick or frolic
52. Horse's foot
53. So ___! ("Me, too!")
54. Kind of wrestling
55. Raggedy ___ (doll)
56. Major TV brand
57. Young child

DOWN

1. They line some old streets
2. Café additive
3. Mimicking bird
4. Wash away, as soil
5. Get a little shuteye
6. Baked Alaska, e.g.
7. Hellish river
8. When repeated, a Latin dance
9. Supply with weapons
10. School transport
12. Did salon work
19. Wide shoe designation
21. Bouncers' requests
23. Yank out of bed
24. Two of a kind
25. Throw, as dice
26. It's a race to break it
27. Legendary story
28. Wedding reception centerpiece
29. Flourish
33. Indy entry
34. Recluses
36. Hee ___
37. Shirt or blouse

Puzzle 111

Solution on Page 341

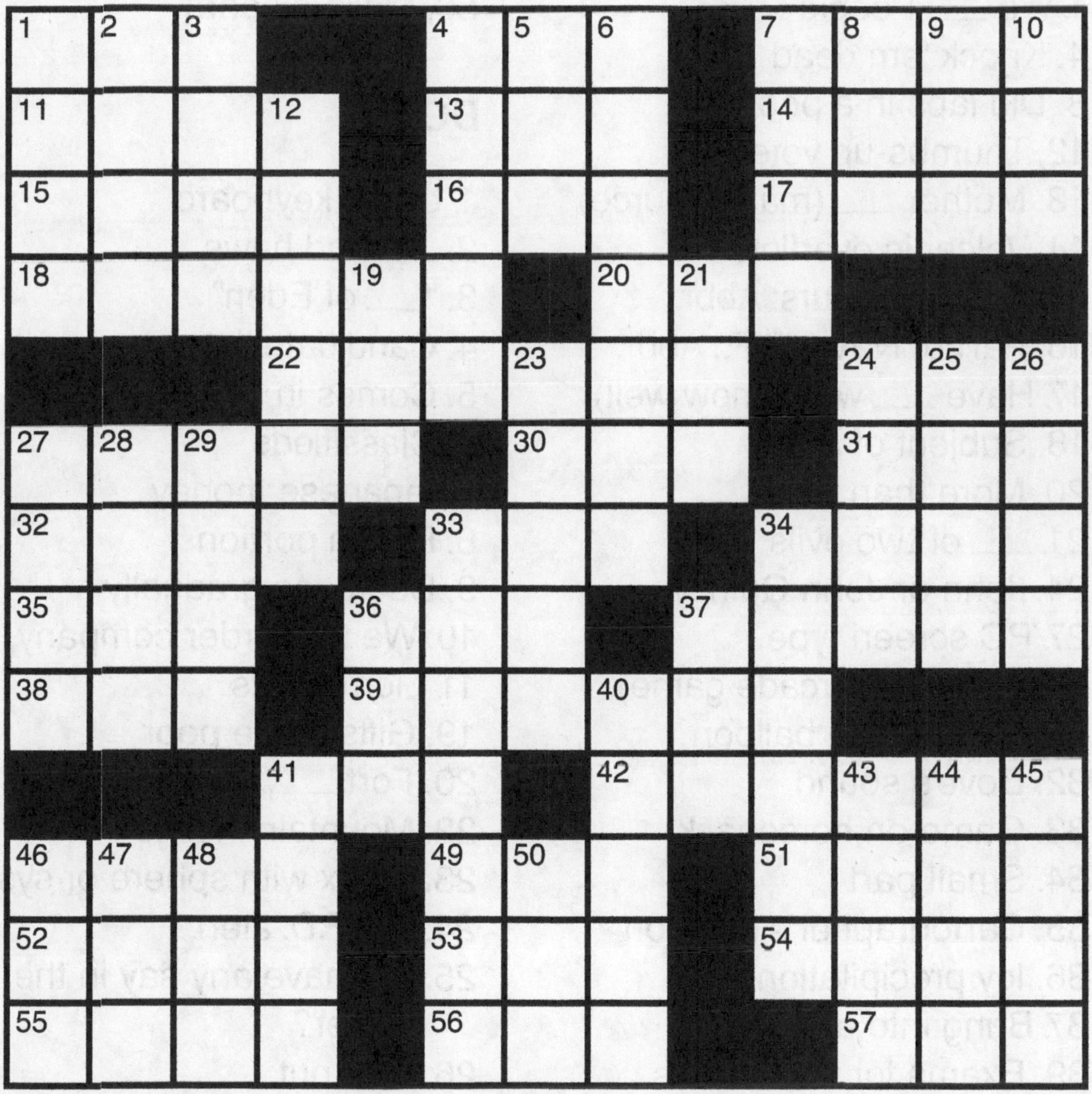

40. Part of ancient Asia Minor
41. Clodhoppers
43. Defeat decisively
44. Bullets and BBs
45. Primer dog
46. Home loan agcy.
47. Geological stretch
48. Won — soup
50. One-time Jeep mfr.

ACROSS

1. We ___ People . . .
4. Knock 'em dead
8. Did laps in a pool
12. Thumbs-up vote
13. Mother ___ (major source)
14. Volcanic overflow
15. Evening hours: Abbr.
16. Part of N.A.A.C.P.: Abbr.
17. Have ___ with (know well)
18. Subject of a will
20. More than fat
21. ___ of two evils
24. John or John Quincy
27. PC screen type
28. ___-Man (arcade game)
31. Bursts, as a balloon
32. Dove's sound
33. Game on horseback
34. Small part
35. Cartographer's creation
36. Icy precipitation
37. Bring into existence
39. Exams for future attys.
43. Gives a speech
47. Speed skater Apolo Anton ___
48. The ___ the merrier!
50. Caribou relative
51. ___ a good example
52. Learning by memorization
53. Six-sided game piece
54. Performed a glissade
55. "___ Girl" (TV show)
56. Make a seam

DOWN

1. Use a keyboard
2. ___ and haws
3. "___ of Eden"
4. Candidate lists
5. Comes in last
6. Classifieds
7. Japanese money
8. Bacon portion
9. Decrease gradually
10. We try harder company
11. Lion's locks
19. Gifts to the poor
20. Fort ___, Calif.
22. Mountain incline
23. Prefix with sphere or system
24. L.A.P.D. alert
25. ___ have any say in the matter?
26. Well put
28. "The Raven" writer
29. Drink with a head on it
30. Campsite bed
32. Garage contents
33. Not guilty, for one
35. TV hosts
36. Avenue
38. Major artery

Puzzle 112

Solution on Page 341

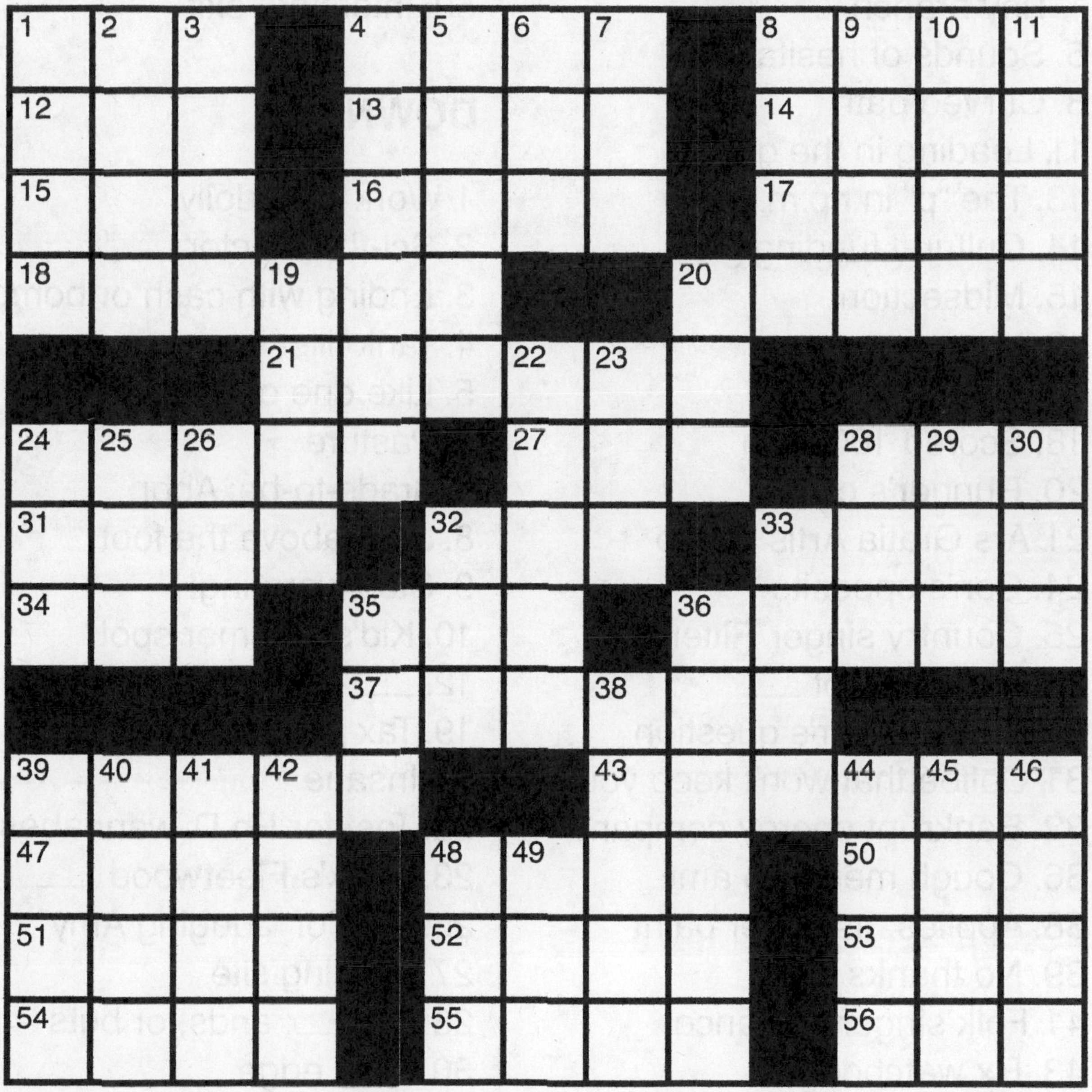

39. Profit's opposite
40. Writer-illustrator Silverstein
41. The "A" of ABM
42. Warty hopper
44. Turner and Danson
45. Romanian-born Wiesel
46. Slant unfairly
48. I pity the fool star
49. ___ la la!

ACROSS

1. Tiny branch
5. Sounds of hesitation
8. Curved path
11. Leading in the game
13. The "p" in r.p.m.
14. Cultural funding grp.
15. Midsection
16. Mas' mates
17. J–N connector
18. Scored 100% on
20. Runner's circuit
21. Ars Gratia Artis studio
24. Con's opposite
25. Country singer Ritter
26. Lawrence of ___
29. Philosopher's question
31. Coffee that won't keep you up
32. Bankrupt energy company
36. Cough medicine amt.
38. Applies, as finger paint
39. No thanks
41. Folk singer DiFranco
43. Rx watchdog
44. Grassy clump
45. Basic idea
47. Wine and dine
48. Not pro
49. Lion sounds
54. AOL or MSN: Abbr.
55. Modifying word: Abbr.
56. Popular Internet company
57. Retrieve
58. Ewe's plaint
59. Interstate exit

DOWN

1. Work on a doily
2. Sci-fi's "Doctor ___"
3. Ending with cash or bombard
4. Tank filler
5. Like one of the two jaws
6. Pasture
7. Grads-to-be: Abbr.
8. Joint above the foot
9. Stop worrying!
10. Kid's summer spot
12. ___ double-take
19. Tax preparer, for short
21. Insane
22. Test for Ph.D. wannabes
23. Rock's Fleetwood ___
25. Daly of "Judging Amy"
27. Soaking site
28. No ___, ands, or buts
30. Skirt edge
33. Brit. flying group
34. California's Fort ___
35. Govt. code crackers
37. Chinese temple
38. Female sib
39. Condemned's neckwear?
40. Take in, as a stray
42. Japanese fighter

Puzzle 113

Solution on Page 342

44. Big swallow
46. Hear, as a case
48. It's hailed in cities
50. Rower's need
51. Cry of discovery
52. CD-___
53. Absorb, with "up"

ACROSS

1. Horse-stopping exclamation
5. Test proctor's call
9. ___ Pérignon
12. Estate receiver
13. Dumb ___ ox
14. 1950s prez
15. Nobel Peace Prize city
16. Clark's crush on "Smallville"
17. I never ___ a man I didn't like
18. G.I. entertainers
20. Get in the way of
22. South Africa's Mandela
25. Crazy as a ___
26. 1986 sci-fi sequel
27. Intense passion
29. Small drink of liquor
30. Cauldron
32. Golfer Palmer, familiarly
36. Actress Lansbury
39. Work to get, as someone's trust
40. Beverage chest
41. Hullabaloo
43. Six-pointers, for short
44. This ___ better be good!
45. El ___ (Pacific phenomenon)
47. ___ Piper
51. Now ___ seen everything!
52. Pastry prettifier
53. Leggo my ___!
54. Train unit
55. Shelter beds
56. Stolen money

DOWN

1. A question of identity
2. For ___ a jolly . . .
3. Saudi export
4. Inspire, as curiosity
5. Eagle's claws
6. It ___ far, far better thing . . .
7. Capital of the Philippines
8. Amorously inflame
9. One-time paperback
10. Gave a thumbs-up
11. Apportion, with "out"
19. Prince, to a king
21. Pea container
22. Bert Bobbsey's twin sister
23. Kazan who directed "On the Waterfront"
24. One who can see what you're saying
28. Abnormal breathing sound
31. Road surface
33. Viet ___
34. Like many O. Henry stories
35. Singer Caruso
36. Cast members
37. Sign of approval
38. God's honest truth
41. In high style
42. Volcano's output

Puzzle 114

Solution on Page 342

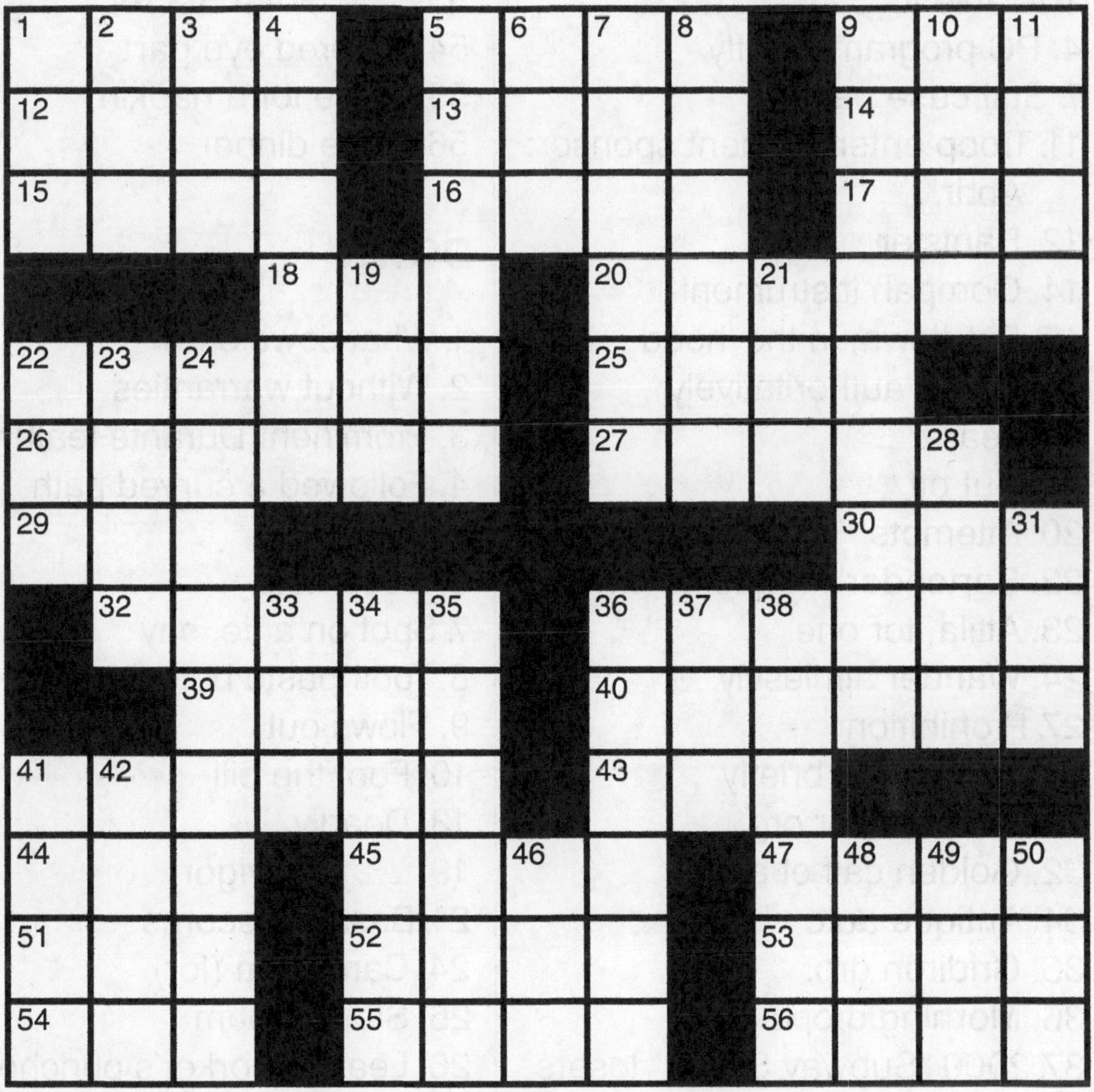

46. Volleyball court divider
48. May ___ now?
49. Id's counterpart
50. Period

ACROSS

1. Is able to
4. PC program, briefly
7. Staircase part
11. Troop entertainment sponsor: Abbr.
12. Banister
14. Oompah instrument
15. Put down, in the 'hood
16. Quote authoritatively
17. Dear ___
18. Cut off
20. Attempts
22. Bartender's requests, maybe
23. Attila, for one
24. Wander aimlessly
27. Prohibition
28. Nightwear, briefly
31. Detroit labor org.
32. Golden calf et al.
34. Antique auto
35. Gridiron grp.
36. Morning drops
37. 2000 "Subway Series" losers
38. Small child
39. Fed. purchasing group
41. Nonpoetic writing
43. Assumed name
46. Sound of distress
47. Amount between all and none
49. "Play It Again, ___"
51. Bush adviser Karl
52. It marches on
53. "___ Got a Secret"
54. Colored eye part
55. Place for a napkin
56. Gave dinner

DOWN

1. What cows chew
2. Without warranties
3. Prominent Durante feature
4. Followed a curved path
5. Twosomes
6. Deep hole
7. Spot on a tie, say
8. Toothpaste holder
9. Flows out
10. Foot the bill
13. Deadly
19. ___ and vigor
21. Baseball scores
24. Campaign (for)
25. Stumblebum
26. Leatherworker's puncher
27. Violist's need
28. Post- opposite
29. Boeing 747, e.g.
30. Shipwreck signal
32. They're exchanged at the altar
33. Dislike with a passion
37. Chiang ___ (Thai city)

Puzzle 115

Solution on Page 342

38. Musical sounds
39. Beta's follower
40. Insomniac's need
41. Impoverished
42. Sitar master Shankar
44. ___ I care!
45. Put away for a rainy day
46. Hosp. scan
48. Salad dressing ingredient
50. Club ___ resort

ACROSS

1. Thanksgiving, e.g.: Abbr.
4. Mouth bone
7. Crusty dessert
10. Toward the sunset
12. Lincoln, informally
13. Kind of pear
14. Tiny, as a town
16. Suspicious of
17. Tax-auditing org.
18. Supplementary feature
19. Cupcake covering
22. Measly
24. Table supports
25. Makes mad
28. Cousin of an onion
29. Gimme ___! (start of an Iowa State cheer)
30. Cairo's waterway
32. Suppress
34. Elmer's product
35. Astronaut Armstrong
36. Judge's assistant
37. Rise and ___!
40. It follows April in Paris
41. Ending with hard or soft
42. Traveling troupe's gig
47. Tiny bit
48. Sighing sounds
49. Hockey legend Gordie
50. Japanese currency
51. Intl. clock standard
52. GP's assistants

DOWN

1. ___ can play that game
2. Rooster's mate
3. Put to good ___
4. Cookie holders
5. Sit-up targets
6. Tiny
7. Duck's home
8. Colon's meaning, in analogies
9. Supply-and-demand subj.
11. Easily offended
13. Twists and turns in a bowling alley
15. Part of NOW: Abbr.
18. "Brokeback Mountain" director Lee
19. Ailing
20. So-so marks
21. "___ the Blues When It Rains"
22. Group of experts
23. Prefix with lateral
26. Get one's dander up
27. Disparaging remark
29. "___ Baba and the 40 Thieves"
31. A spider!
33. Service charge
36. Dishonorable one

Puzzle 116

Solution on Page 342

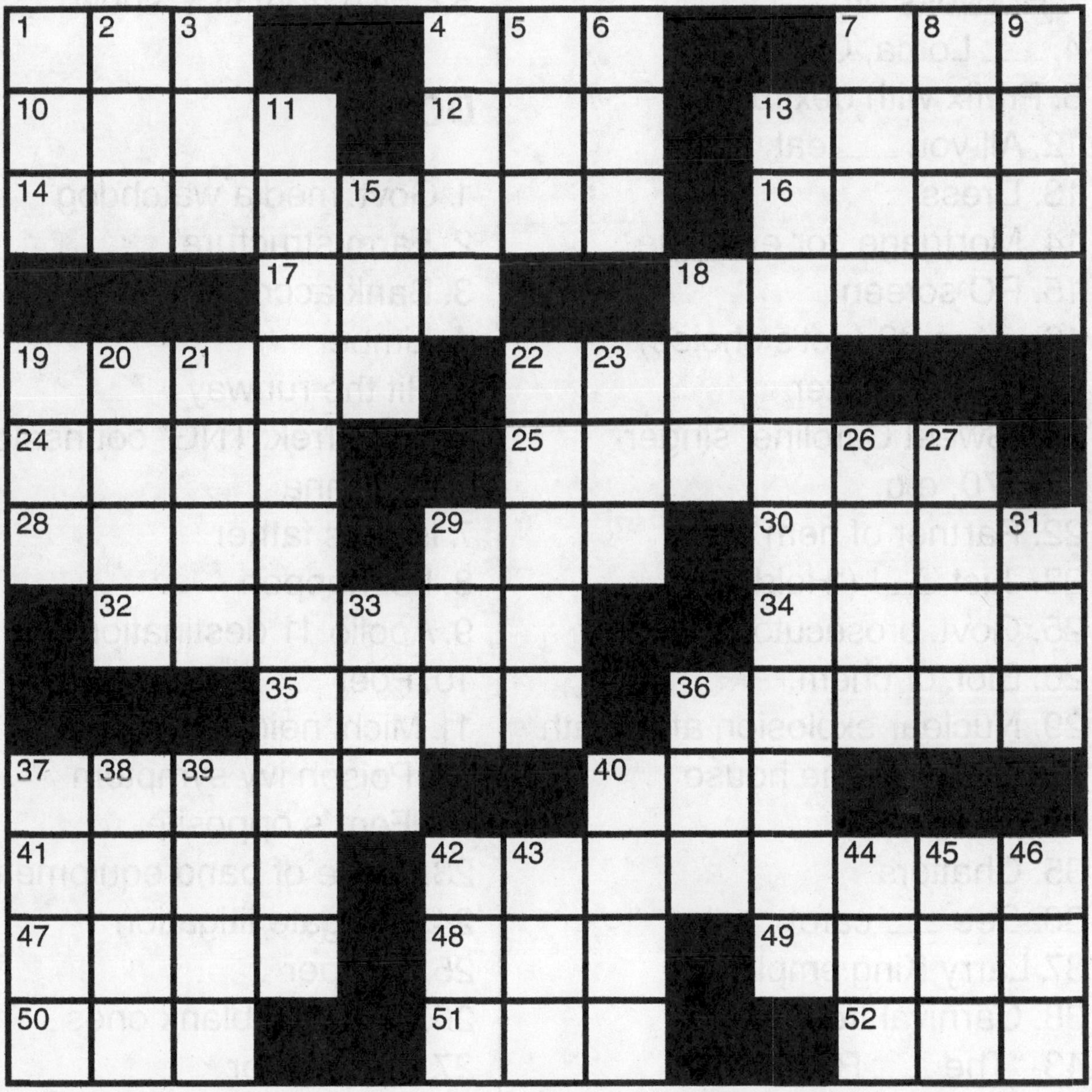

37. Move in the breeze
38. Love's opposite
39. Neighbor of Pakistan
40. Sail support
42. Old cloth
43. Electrical resistance unit
44. Opposite of vert.
45. Part of B.Y.O.B.
46. Filmmaker Craven

ACROSS

1. Hoover's org.
4. ___ Loma, Calif.
8. Prefix with dextrous
12. All you ___ eat
13. Dress
14. Mortgage, for example
15. PC screen
16. ___ out? (pet's choice)
17. Manor master
18. "Sweet Caroline" singer
21. I-70, e.g.
22. Partner of hem
23. Just ___! ("Hold on!")
25. Govt. prosecutors
26. Biol. or chem.
29. Nuclear explosion aftermath
33. Animal in the house
34. ___ deco
35. Chatters
36. See ___ care!
37. Larry King employer
38. Carnival treat
43. "The ___ Ranger"
44. Pants on fire person
45. Disconsolate
47. Oyster relative
48. Would you care for anything ___?
49. Where surgeons work: Abbr.
50. Cub scout groups
51. Straphanger's lack
52. Live from N.Y. show

DOWN

1. Govt. media watchdog
2. Farm structure
3. Bank accrual
4. Limber
5. Hit the runway
6. "Star Trek: TNG" counselor Deanna
7. Isaac's father
8. Let happen
9. Apollo 11 destination
10. Poet
11. Mich. neighbor
19. Poison ivy symptom
20. Fem.'s opposite
23. Piece of band equipment
24. Instigate litigation
25. j topper
26. Blankety-blank ones
27. Soup order
28. Co. photo badges, e.g.
30. Huck's craft
31. Baltimore nine
32. Nashville's Loretta
36. Agenda details
37. Insertion mark

Puzzle 117

Solution on Page 343

38. Old king of rhyme
39. Chestnuts roasting ___ open fire
40. Christie's "Death on the ___"
41. House in Spain
42. Kitten's plaything
43. Watch display, for short
46. Cable modem alternative, briefly

ACROSS

1. Glass container
4. Drs.' group
7. Take out of the freezer
11. Had some chow
12. Prepare for takeoff
14. Time gone by
15. Rapper ___ Def
16. Wee warbler
17. Easy win
18. Salad-bowl wood
20. Changes to fit
22. Nasty campaign tactic
24. 1982 Disney film starring Jeff Bridges
25. Capricorn's symbol
26. Blew, as a volcano
29. Show showers
30. Nonchalant
31. Culpa starter
33. Mascara site
35. Neeson of "Clash of the Titans"
36. Kid around
37. The ___ of time
38. Make a choice
41. Gold deposit
42. Business V.I.P.
43. TV's "American ___"
45. "Brave ___ World"
48. Fuel from a bog
49. Ice cream holder
50. ___-Magnon
51. Sounds of disapproval
52. Old what's-___-name
53. British rocker Brian

DOWN

1. Musical free-for-all
2. ___ Z (you name it)
3. Quit worrying
4. In armed conflict
5. ___ my words
6. Tree feller
7. Despot
8. Hula ___
9. In ___: stuck
10. Drenches
13. Hurrying
19. End a fast
21. Narc's seizure
22. Lt.'s subordinate
23. Change residences
24. Garbage
26. Stretchy, as a waistband
27. High rank
28. Wanted-poster option
30. Political coalition
32. Morning hrs.
34. Kicks out
35. Young man
37. They're always underfoot
38. Aug. follower
39. Divorcées

Puzzle 118

Solution on Page 343

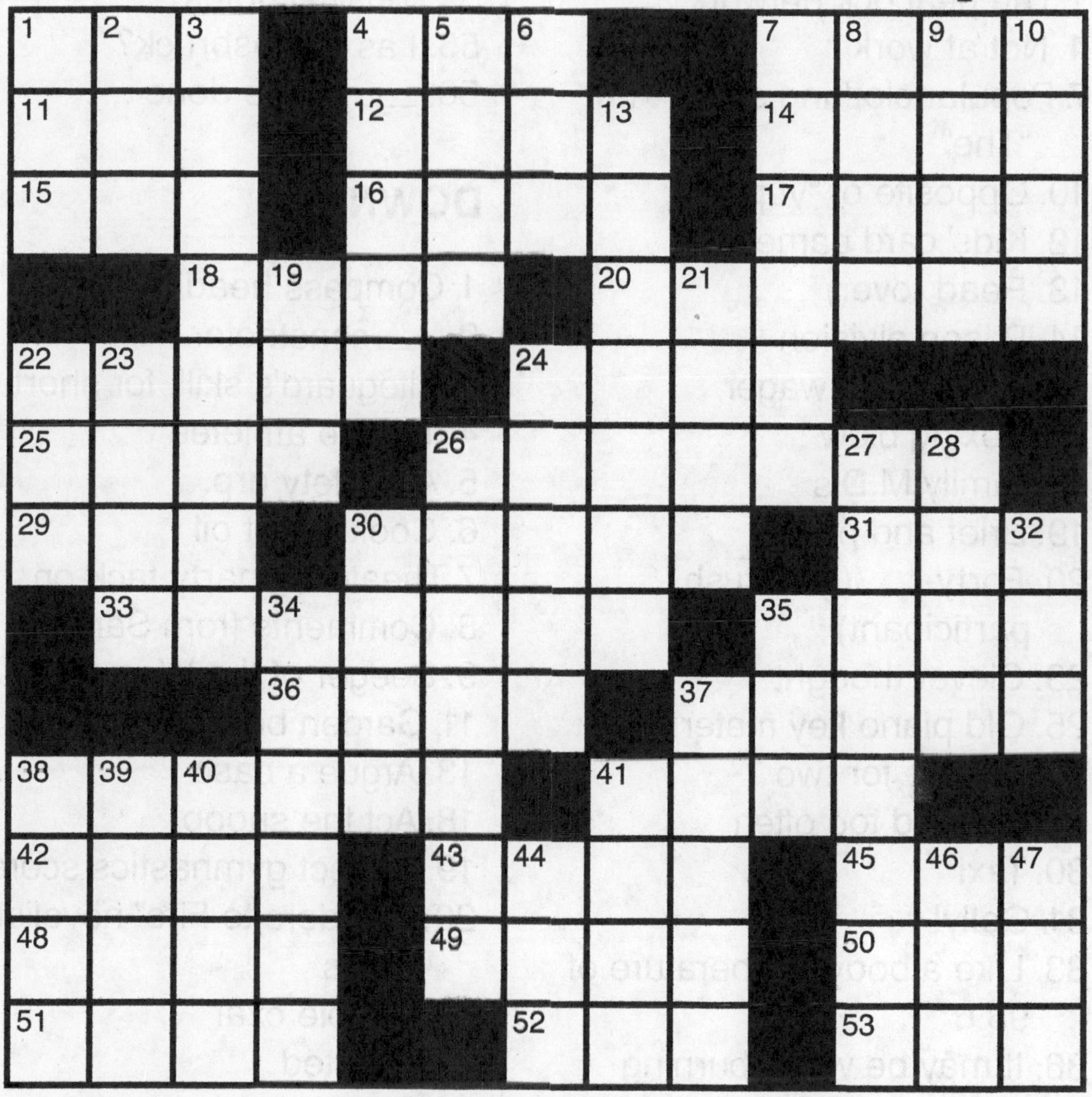

40. Plumbing problem
41. Actress Anderson
44. Homer Simpson exclamation
46. Suffix for southeast
47. Seek the affection of

ACROSS

1. The peacock network
4. Not at work
7. Popular clothing store, with "The"
10. Opposite of "yup"
12. Kids' card game
13. Read (over)
14. Prison division
15. Make, as a wager
16. Boxing blow
17. Family M.D.s
19. Brief and pithy
20. Forty-___ (gold rush participant)
23. Clever thought
25. Old piano key material
26. Bicycle for two
29. Remind too often
30. Taxi
31. Golly!
33. Like a body temperature of 98.6°
36. It may be wood-burning
38. Part of HRE
39. Bothered
40. Tom Sawyer author
43. 6, on a telephone
44. Heads ___, tails you lose
45. Loan org.
47. Holds title to
51. Oscar night transport
52. Disposable pen maker
53. Sandwich bread
54. Musical notes
55. I as in Innsbruck?
56. ___ will be done . . .

DOWN

1. Compass heading
2. ___ constrictor
3. Lifeguard's skill, for short
4. Temple athletes
5. Air safety grp.
6. Cook in hot oil
7. Theater or party tack-on
8. Comments from Sandy
9. Seeger of the Weavers
11. Garden border tool
13. Argue a case
18. Act the snoop
19. Perfect gymnastics score
20. "Ladders to Fire" novelist Anaïs
21. Terrible czar
22. Aborted
23. Milan's land
24. Mini-glob
27. Creature from the forest moon of Endor
28. Get out of my seat!
30. Iron Man Ripken
32. Unite in marriage

Puzzle 119

Solution on Page 343

34. Horned animal with thick skin
35. Tues. preceder
36. Envy or gluttony
37. Scout group
40. Pinball infraction
41. What V-J Day ended
42. Points at the target
43. Jet speed unit
45. "Without a Trace" org.
46. Latin adverb
48. Sense of humor
49. Ultimate in degree
50. Declare

ACROSS

1. Resistance units
5. Karaoke need, briefly
8. Sluggish
12. ___ the bill: pay
13. Hosp. area for acute conditions
14. Went fast
15. Festive celebration
16. Drano ingredient
17. Had misgivings about
18. Kilmer of "The Doors"
20. After-hours money sources, for short
21. Like a teetotaler
24. Joseph's wife
27. I like ___
28. Piece of garlic
30. Prof.'s degree
33. Orlando's state: Abbr.
34. Eagle's weapon
35. Mauna ___
36. Cigarette substance
37. Wonderstruck
38. Pick a card, ___ card
39. Cake decorator
40. Heredity units
42. Channel for armchair athletes
45. Abbr. at the end of a proof
46. How do you like ___!
47. Toward the back of a boat
49. Cosby show
53. Nat King ___
54. Batter's stat
55. Floor covering
56. Satan's domain
57. Tombstone inscription
58. Get off ___ free

DOWN

1. Popular insect repellent
2. Groundbreaking tool
3. Clever comment
4. Comedian Martin
5. Pepper grinder
6. Very cold
7. Billiard stick
8. Homeless animal
9. Ill-mannered sort
10. Fast-growing city near Provo
11. Ties the knot
19. Extremely cold
21. Prepare flour
22. Neighbor of Tex.
23. Stand
24. Back tooth
25. State openly
26. Go back on a promise
29. Lois of the "Daily Planet"
30. Course of action
31. Practice, as skills
32. Calendar units
39. Computer chip maker

Puzzle 120

Solution on Page 343

41. Revises, as text
42. ___-A-Sketch: drawing toy
43. Pump or clog
44. ___ Mall cigarettes
45. Cotton swab
47. Departure's opposite: Abbr.
48. J. Edgar Hoover's org.
50. Attack command to Fido
51. Arafat's grp.
52. Are we there ___?

ACROSS

1. Field's yield
5. Chat room guffaw
8. Jail unit
12. Syllables from Santa
13. ___ were you . . .
14. Puerto ___
15. Money for the poor
16. Take one's cuts
17. Rooney of "60 Minutes"
18. Bother
20. Tide type
22. First Lady before Michelle
24. Word with gender or generation
27. Bunch of bees
31. Capital of New Mexico
33. Toy with a tail
34. Wire diameter measure
35. Actress Meg
36. Certain triathlete
38. Stadium levels
39. Energy
40. Quarrel
42. Agt's. take
43. Fitted one within another
48. Petite or jumbo
51. Uganda's ___ Amin
53. Bees' home
54. . . . with a banjo on my ___
55. Ready or ___ . . .
56. I knew ___ instant . . .
57. Pull sharply
58. Sleet-covered
59. Confined, with "up"

DOWN

1. I say, old ___
2. Part in a play
3. Electrical units
4. Newsgroup message
5. Follower of Virgo
6. Son-gun filler
7. Without metaphor
8. Sea creature that moves sideways
9. Ich bin ___ Berliner: JFK
10. Watch readout, briefly
11. "The Thin Man" actress Myrna
19. Stately tree
21. Blackball
23. On, as medication
24. Marvin of Motown
25. From quite a distance
26. Ink dispensers
27. Uno card
28. Barbed ___
29. Perched on
30. Stimpy's cartoon buddy
32. One less than quadri-
34. Drink with an olive
37. PC alternative
38. Summer shirt
41. Like-mindedness

Puzzle 121

Solution on Page 344

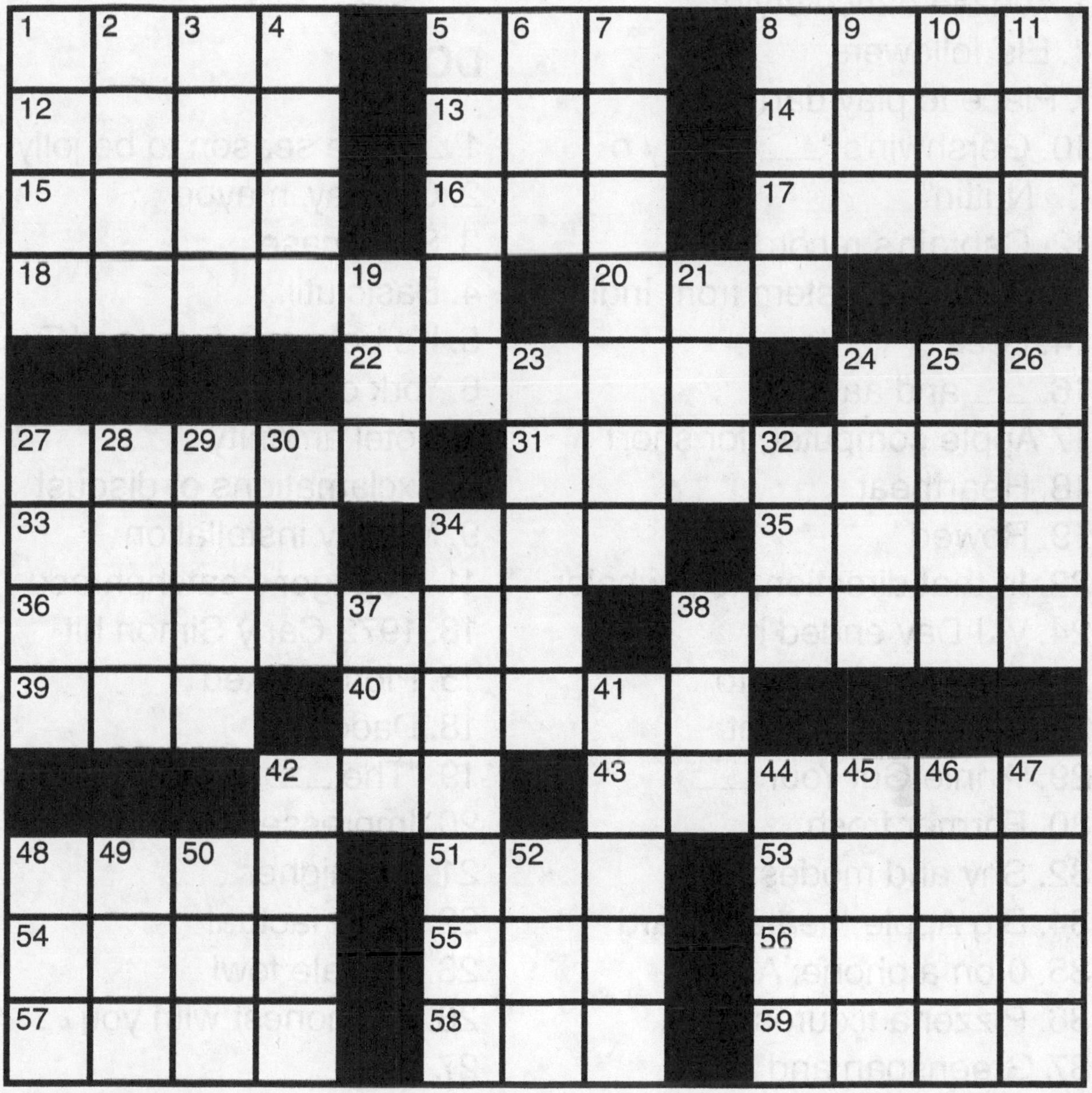

42. Sneak preview
44. Use FedEx, say
45. Fork prong
46. Sen. Bayh of Indiana
47. Fender flaw
48. Where a telescope is aimed
49. Once ___ lifetime
50. Chinese discipline
52. Med school grad

ACROSS

1. Audible dance style
4. Els' followers
7. Place to play darts
10. Gershwin's "___ Plenty o' Nuttin'"
12. Captain's record
13. Exercise system from India
14. Lees
16. ___ and aahs
17. Apple computer, for short
18. Heartbeat
19. Rowed
22. In that direction, to a whaler
24. V-J Day ended it
25. Turns back to zero
28. A smaller amount
29. "Annie Get Your ___"
30. Former frosh
32. Shy and modest
34. Big Apple theater award
35. 0 on a phone: Abbr.
36. Pizzeria fixtures
37. Greenspan and Arkin
40. Agcy. for homeowners
41. Bigger than big
42. Kitschy lawn figure
47. Follow, as orders
48. Touched a match to
49. Hair removal brand
50. ___, Virginia, there is a . . .
51. Gridiron divs.
52. Ryder Cup org.

DOWN

1. ___ the season to be jolly
2. Go gray, maybe
3. Seed case
4. Basic util.
5. It's between Sun. and Tue.
6. York or Bilko: Abbr.
7. Motel amenity
8. Exclamations of disgust
9. Military installation
11. Manager's catchphrase
13. 1972 Carly Simon hit
15. Plenty ticked
18. Daddies
19. "The ___ and the Pussycat"
20. Impressed
21. Get higher
22. More factual
23. Female fowl
26. ___ honest with you . . .
27. Whirl
29. Test for coll. seniors
31. "___ So Fine": 1963 #1 hit
33. Downs' opposite
36. Measure of resistance
37. Sailor's greeting
38. Grease job
39. "Rock of ___"

Puzzle 122

Solution on Page 344

40. Domino or Waller
42. Spider's prey
43. "Put a ___ on it!"
44. Short snooze
45. Band booking
46. Are you a man ___ mouse?

ACROSS

1. Medical insurance abbr.
4. PC panic button
7. ___ Rushmore
12. Forbid
13. Wine tasting?
14. Jazz great Shaw
15. Poor movie rating
17. When it ___, it pours
18. Garment bottom
19. Shoreline irregularity
20. Secret stash
23. Eggy drink
24. GI entertainment sponsor
25. Prefix with bytes or bucks
28. Jane Austen classic
32. Tavern
33. Holy one
35. What you breathe
36. Mimicked
38. Crossword hint
39. Paranormal showman Geller
40. Come again?
42. Wielded authority
44. Title colonel in a 1960s sitcom
47. Afternoons and evenings, briefly
48. Tennis champ Chris
49. Gets one's bearings
53. Physics Nobelist Enrico
54. Believe it or ___!
55. Just great
56. Courtroom event
57. Poem of tribute
58. No. on a transcript

DOWN

1. "Entourage" network
2. "A ___ for All Seasons"
3. Long-distance number starter
4. Holds in high regard
5. Thailand's former name
6. EMT's forte
7. Nintendo's Super ___ Bros.
8. Juice source
9. Elec. company
10. Number of Muses
11. Trial run
16. Quiet!
20. Havana's home
21. Quickly!, on an order
22. Apple leftover
23. Half of Mork's farewell
26. "Hurting ___ Other" (The Carpenters)
27. Baseball great Hodges
29. Badly claw
30. Oozy ground
31. Like a dust bowl
34. Orkin target
37. Greg's sitcom partner

Puzzle 123

Solution on Page 344

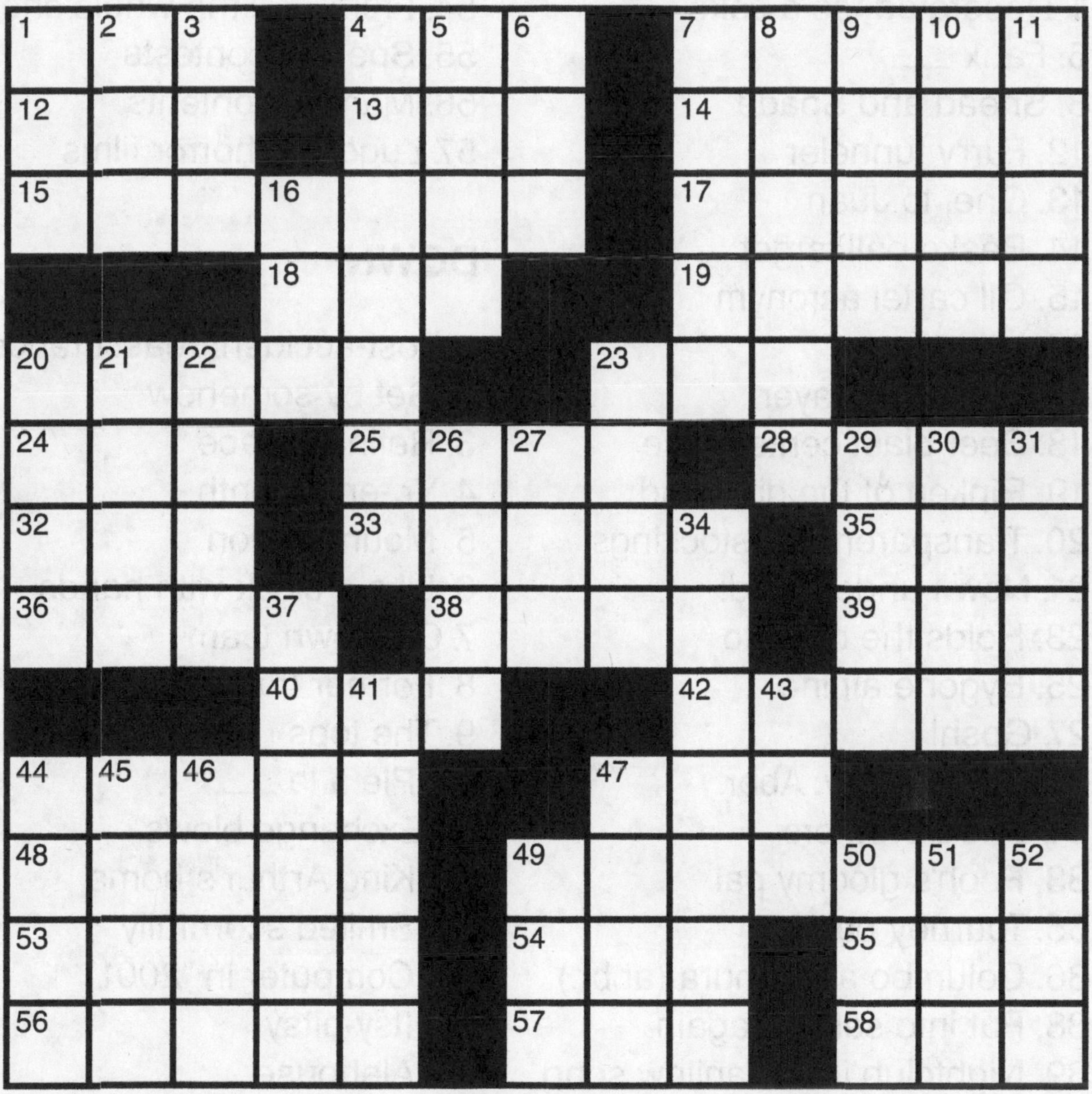

41. ___ we meet again
43. ___ it or lose it
44. Lift with effort
45. Partner of "done with"
46. Halliwell of the Spice Girls
47. Cow poke?
49. Lennon's widow Yoko
50. Racehorse, slangily
51. First-rate
52. Calypso cousin

ACROSS

1. Decorated, as a cake
5. Faux ___
8. Snead and Spade
12. Furry tunneler
13. One, to Juan
14. Basketball target
15. Oil cartel acronym
16. Nth degree
17. Wing ___ prayer
18. Beer blast centerpiece
19. Ripken of the diamond
20. Transparent, as stockings
21. Now I understand!
23. Holds the deed to
25. Bygone airline
27. Gosh!
28. Roget entry: Abbr.
31. Dad's brothers
33. Pooh's gloomy pal
35. Tourney pass
36. Columbo and Uhura (abbr.)
38. Put into service again
39. Nightclub in a Manilow song
40. Immigrant's course: Abbr.
41. Banana treat
44. Stashed away
46. Russian fighter jet
49. But ___, there's more!
50. ___-10 Conference
51. Nothing
52. Wile E. Coyote's supplier
53. Biblical transport
54. From ___: the whole shebang
55. Spelling contests
56. Manger contents
57. Lugosi of horror films

DOWN

1. Post-accident reassurance
2. Get by somehow
3. Refined grace
4. Yr.-end month
5. Mountain lion
6. Like a clock with hands
7. Chi-Town team
8. Former Iranian leaders
9. The tops
10. Pie à la ___
11. Exchange blows
19. King Arthur's home
20. Smiled scornfully
22. Computer in "2001"
24. Itsy-bitsy
25. Alehouse
26. Press ___ key to continue
28. Close companion
29. Many months: Abbr.
30. Jacqueline Kennedy ___ Bouvier
32. Gas-additive letters
34. Agreeable reply

Puzzle 124

Solution on Page 344

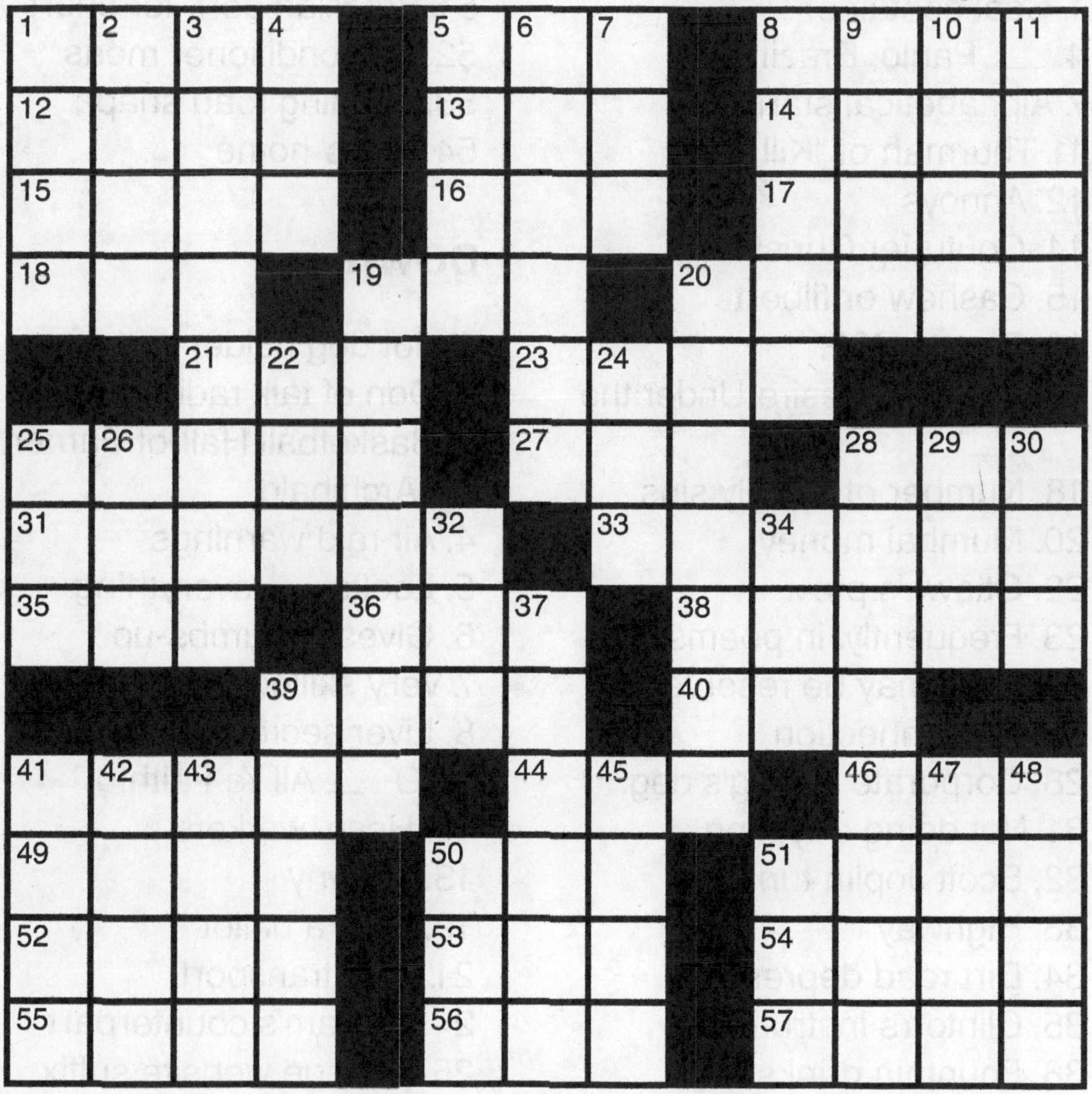

37. African desert
39. Uses as a reference
41. Sailor's mop
42. Walk nervously
43. Margarita fruit
45. Disgusting
47. Fox's "American ___"
48. Mideast's ___ Strip
50. Oom-___
51. Take into custody

ACROSS

1. Coal container
4. ___ Paulo, Brazil
7. Alphabetical start
11. Thurman of "Kill Bill"
12. Annoys
14. Couturier Christian
15. Cashew or filbert
16. Part of R&R
17. O'Neill's "Desire Under the ___"
18. Number of deadly sins
20. Mumbai money
22. Ottawa's prov.
23. Frequently, in poems
24. They may be reserved
27. L-P connection
28. Corporate bigwig's deg.
31. Not doing anything
32. Scott Joplin tune
33. Highway
34. Dirt road depression
35. Clinton's instrument
36. Fountain drinks
37. Play on the radio
38. From ___ Z (completely)
39. Cut off your nose to ___ your face
41. Rapids transits
44. Parroted
45. Leg part below the knee
47. Hole puncher
49. Tiny skin opening
50. ___ the line (obeyed)
51. Brazilian port, for short
52. Air conditioner meas.
53. Winding road shape
54. Hogs' home

DOWN

1. Hot dog holder
2. Don of talk radio
3. Basketball Hall-of-Famer Archibald
4. Air-raid warnings
5. Looks ___ everything
6. Gives a thumbs-up
7. Very skilled
8. Liver secretion
9. "O ___ All Ye Faithful"
10. Hosp. workers
13. Brawny
19. Cast a ballot
21. ET's transport
24. Madam's counterpart
25. College website suffix
26. Ctrl + ___ + Del
27. To the ___ (fully)
28. Hip, in the 1960s
29. Ram's cry
30. Madison Avenue products
32. Least cooked
33. Santa's landing spot
35. Create a lap

Puzzle 125

Solution on Page 345

36. Prepares for the anthem
37. Assistants
38. Sign before Taurus
39. You missed a ___!
40. Land of Lima and llamas
42. Old mariners
43. Houlihan portrayer
44. Police dept. alert
46. Gardening tool
48. Myrna of the movies

ACROSS

1. Sail holder
5. Goddess pictured in Egyptian tombs
9. Tanning lotion abbr.
12. "Little Man ___" (Foster film)
13. Rain forest feature
14. Pod resident
15. Tree juices
16. Ready and willing partner
17. &
18. Harbor boat
20. Opposed (to)
22. Electric current unit
25. Bite like a pup
26. Bits of wisdom?
27. Handed out cards
30. They may administer IVs
31. Are ___ for real?
33. March 17 honoree, for short
37. Surgical beams
40. Miner's discovery
41. Comes up in conversation
42. Egg hunt holiday
45. The Who's "I Can ___ for Miles"
46. Opposite of "Huh?"
47. Loch of lore
49. Read cursorily
53. Beam of light
54. Norway's capital
55. Dramatic entrance announcement
56. There are 2.2 in a kg.
57. New Mexico art community
58. Take ___ from me . . .

DOWN

1. Rushmore and Rainier (abbr.)
2. Roadside rescuers: Abbr.
3. Fuel additive
4. Sample bottle of perfume
5. Representations
6. Sis or bro
7. What no man is
8. Singer Nicks of Fleetwood Mac
9. Practice boxing
10. Writing implements
11. Lose luster
19. Web address, briefly
21. Fed. emissions watchdog
22. Follower of Mar.
23. ___wear department
24. The Ghost of Christmas ___
28. Caustic solutions
29. Drove like mad
32. Aircraft-carrier letters
34. Flower holder
35. Retort to "Am too!"
36. Humanitarian Mother ___
37. Rodeo ropes

Puzzle 126

Solution on Page 345

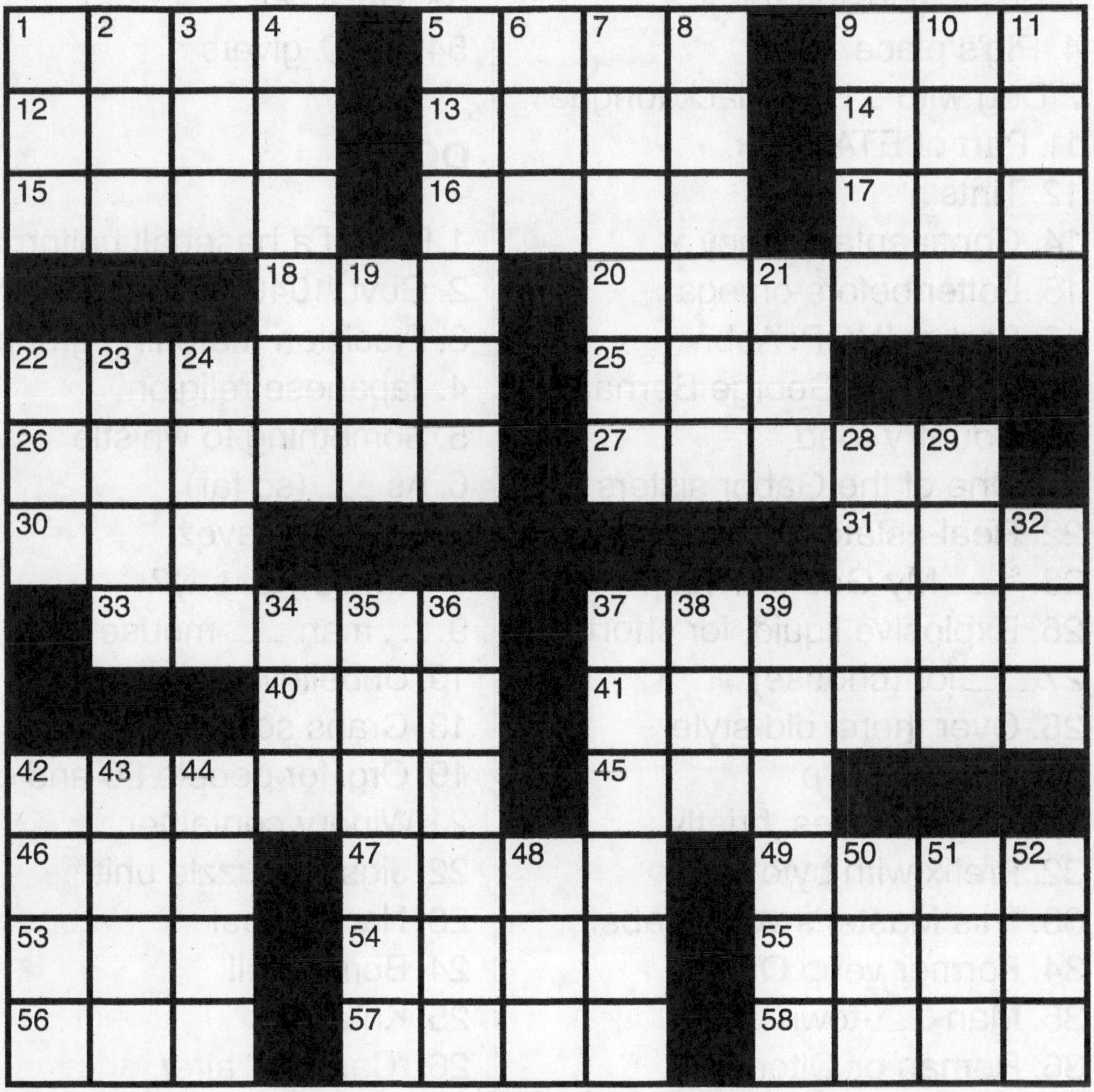

38. "Chances ___" (Johnny Mathis hit)
39. Nap in Oaxaca
42. Actor James ___ Jones
43. Captain with a whalebone leg
44. Simon ___
48. ___-mo replay
50. Krazy ___ of the comics
51. Exiled Amin
52. Atlas page

ACROSS

1. El ___ (Heston role)
4. Pig's place
7. Dog with a blue-black tongue
11. Part of ETA: Abbr.
12. Tints
14. Continental money
15. Letter before omega
16. Part of IHOP: Abbr.
17. Playwright George Bernard
18. Country road
20. One of the Gabor sisters
22. Real-estate map
23. "___ My God to Thee"
26. Explosive liquid, for short
27. ___ for (choose)
28. Over there, old-style
30. Chick's chirp
31. Ring victories, briefly
32. Prefix with byte
33. "His Master's Voice" label
34. Former veep Quayle
35. Man-___-town
36. Roman or Ottoman
38. 3M product
39. ___ & Perrins (sauce brand)
40. Sit for a picture
41. Chimney passage
44. Bugs Bunny, e.g.
46. Annual b-ball shootout
49. Minnelli of "Cabaret"
50. Perimeter
51. Card holder: Abbr.
52. Came to rest on a wire, e.g.
53. H-E-L-P!
54. T.L.C. givers

DOWN

1. Part of a baseball uniform
2. Govt. 1040 auditor
3. Precision marching group
4. Japanese religion
5. Something to whistle
6. As ___ (so far)
7. Activist Chavez
8. What'd you say?
9. . . . man ___ mouse?
10. Unbelievable!
13. Grabs some shuteye
19. Org. for people 50 and over
21. Winery container
22. Jigsaw puzzle unit
23. Nary a soul
24. Bombshell
25. Knave
26. "Car Talk" airer
29. ___ King Cole
31. Activity with chops and kicks
32. Wall St. degrees
34. Yahtzee cube
35. Does penance (for)
37. Cummerbund fold
40. ___ stick
41. Miami's state: Abbr.

Puzzle 127

Solution on Page 345

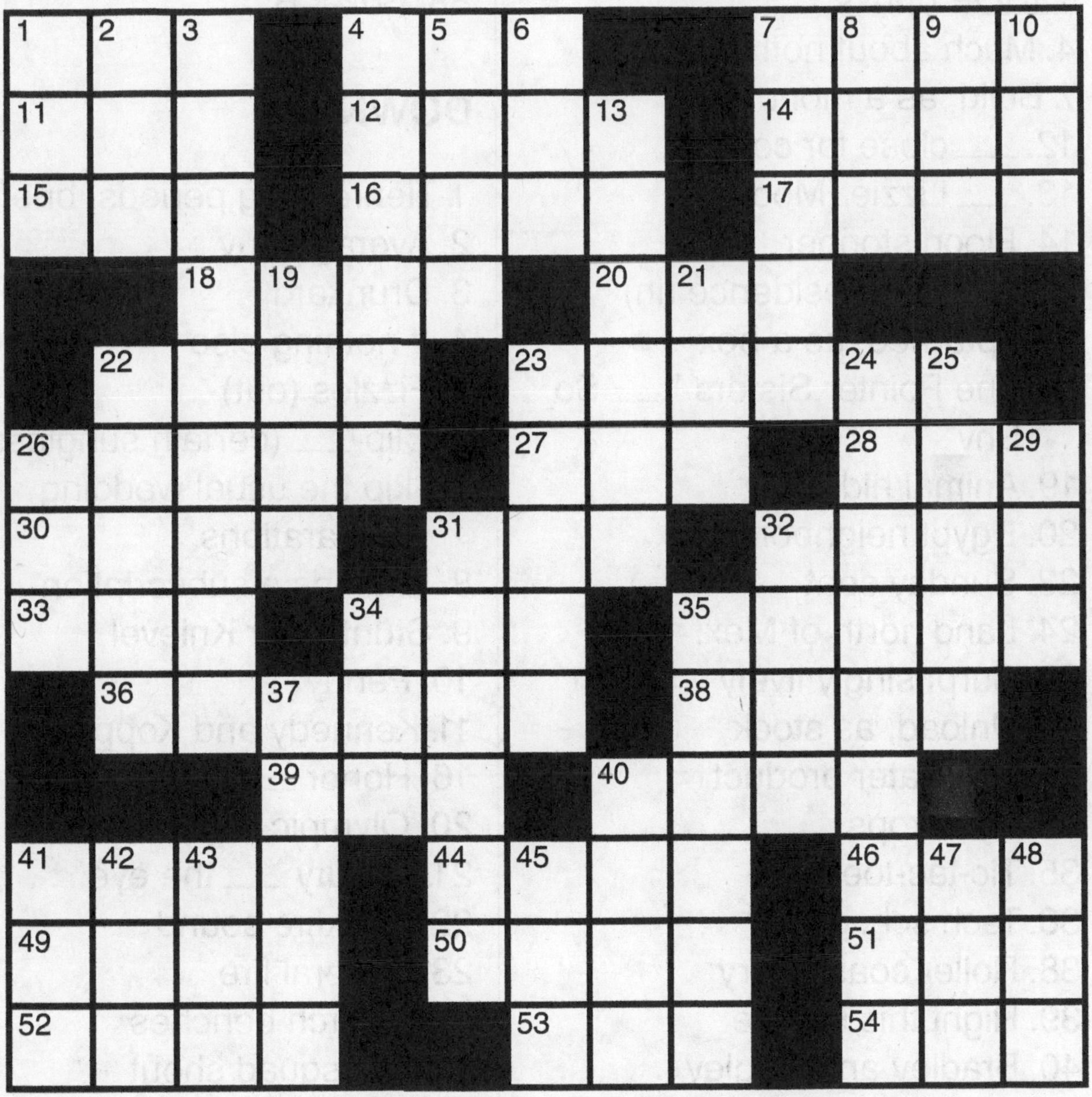

42. Capp's "___ Abner"
43. Israeli firearm
45. Takes too much, briefly
47. Cozy lodging
48. Den sets

ACROSS

1. IHOP drinks
4. Much about nothing
7. Build, as a monument
12. ___ close for comfort
13. ___ Lizzie (Model T)
14. Flood stopper
15. Takes up residence (in)
17. Upturned, as a box
18. The Pointer Sisters' "___ So Shy"
19. Animal hides
20. Egypt neighbor
23. Sunday seat
24. Land north of Mex.
25. Surprisingly lively
28. Unload, as stock
32. Beefeater product
33. Eye drops
35. Tic-tac-toe win
36. Tech sch. grad
38. Roller coaster cry
39. Right this minute
40. Bradley and Begley
42. Classroom furniture
44. Bead counters
47. Money roll
48. Taxi ticker
49. Chemical-free
53. Artfully escape
54. Phooey!
55. Luau instrument, informally
56. Winona of "Girl, Interrupted"
57. Capt.'s inferiors
58. Boxer Baer

DOWN

1. Tiebreaking periods, briefly
2. Average guy
3. Drunkard
4. If nothing else
5. Fizzles (out)
6. Clip-___ (certain sunglasses)
7. Skip the usual wedding preparations
8. Extends a subscription
9. Stunt biker Knievel
10. Penny
11. Kennedy and Koppel
16. Honor ___ father . . .
20. Olympic sled
21. Beauty ___ the eye . . .
22. Backfire sound
23. Funeral fire
26. Church benches
27. Pep squad shout
29. Geologic periods
30. Appearance
31. Temperature extremes
34. Calms
37. Inch back slowly, as a hairline
41. More grim
43. College Website letters
44. Part of U.S.A.

Puzzle 128

Solution on Page 345

45. Group of birds
46. Just slightly
47. Just a sec!
49. Gridiron gp.
50. Bacardi, e.g.
51. Letters before an alias
52. Superman foe Luthor

ACROSS

1. Clean air grp.
4. Certain computers
8. Like some stocks, for short
11. Take a siesta
13. Bubble, bubble, ___ and trouble . . .
14. ___ de Janeiro
15. "___ Man" (1984 Estevez film)
16. Pet advocacy org.
17. Later-yrs. nest egg
18. Franklin known as the Queen of Soul
20. Be pleasing (to)
22. Tightened
23. Minds, as a bar
24. Product pitches
25. Periscope piece
28. Suit to ___ (fit perfectly)
29. Trousers
31. Colorless
35. "Star Wars" princess
36. ___ tee (exactly)
39. Word with spitting or mirror
41. Sheets and pillowcases
43. Sharp comeback
45. Upper crusts
46. Ginger ___ (Canada Dry product)
47. What stainless steel doesn't do
49. Heading on a list of chores
50. Its symbol is Sn
51. I'm working ___
52. Civil or elec. expert
53. Take nourishment
54. Decorate anew
55. Filming site

DOWN

1. Printed mistakes
2. Looked intently
3. Colorado trees
4. Words with a handshake
5. ___ till you drop
6. Cats' prey
7. Writer's angle
8. The ___ Express
9. Angry outburst
10. Not fine-grained
12. Two-year-olds
19. Aid
21. Antidrug agcy.
26. Compass pt. opposite SSW
27. Heel style
30. Go to sea
31. Jolly Roger flier
32. Flyer Earhart
33. Present but not visible
34. Kind of trip for the conceited
36. "The Grand ___"
37. Nervous as a cat

Puzzle 129

Solution on Page 346

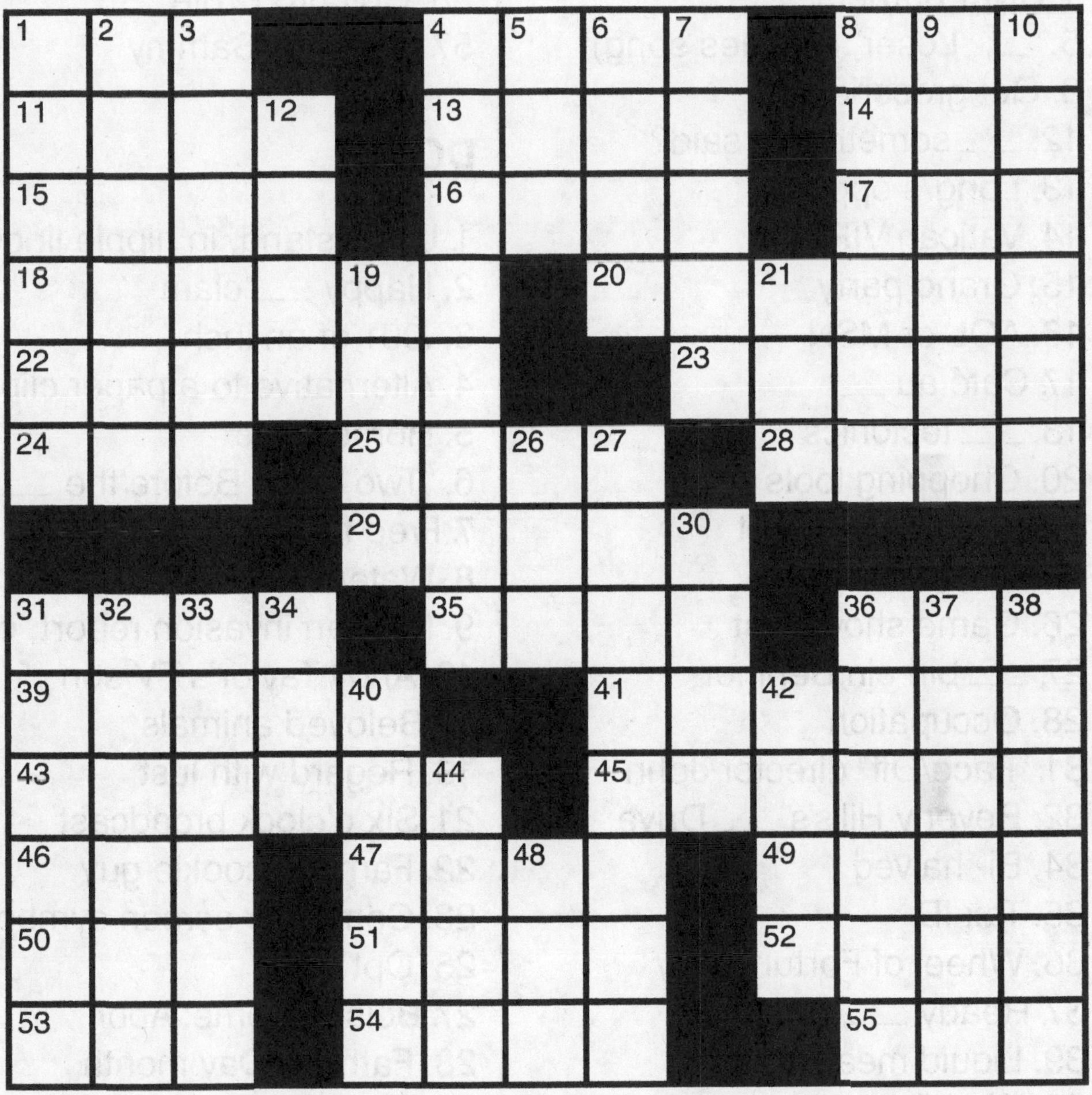

38. Distribute into categories
40. Proofreader's find
42. Nick at ___
44. Ditty
48. Vicious of the Sex Pistols

ACROSS

1. River barriers
5. "___ Loser" (Beatles song)
8. Get groceries
12. ___ something I said?
13. Long.'s opposite
14. Vatican VIP
15. Grand party
16. AOL or MSN
17. Café au ___
18. ___ tectonics
20. Chopping tools
21. Caught in the act
24. ___ your age!
26. Game show host
27. ___ bin ein Berliner
28. Occupation
31. "Face/Off" director John
32. Beverly Hills's ___ Drive
34. Bi- halved
35. Tax ID
36. Wheel of Fortune buy
37. Ready ___, here . . .
39. Liquid meas.
40. Wedding helpers
41. Broadway Auntie
44. Stooges count
46. Prima donnas have big ones
47. Mo. after July
48. Wander around the web
52. Iron corrosion
53. Test for M.A. hopefuls
54. Fed. food inspectors
55. Say no to, as a bill
56. Golf pro Ernie
57. Slugging Sammy

DOWN

1. Understand, in hippie lingo
2. Happy ___ clam
3. .001 of an inch
4. Alternative to a paper clip
5. Homer epic
6. "Two Years Before the ___"
7. Free from strife
8. Water-balloon impact sound
9. Martian invasion report, e.g.
10. Andy Taylor's TV son
11. Beloved animals
19. Regard with lust
21. Six o'clock broadcast
22. Famous cookie guy
23. Computer screen symbol
25. Opt for
27. Boise's home: Abbr.
28. Father's Day month
29. ___ about: approximately
30. Bridle parts
33. In the spotlight
38. Medical research monkey
39. Basil-and-pine-nuts sauce
40. Cravings
41. Griffin of game shows
42. Tropical fever

Puzzle 130

Solution on Page 346

43. Maximum
45. Throw
49. Mil. entertainment group
50. Streets: Abbr.
51. Air safety agcy.

ACROSS

1. "Three Men ___ Baby"
5. Walton of Walmart
8. Goatee's locale
12. Ketch or yawl
13. Prefix with gram or center
14. Uncle's partner
15. PC key below Shift
16. B&O and Union Pacific
17. Polish Nobelist Walesa
18. National park in Alaska
20. Santa's little helper
22. African adventure
24. Police alert, for short
27. "A Taste of ___"
30. Layered sandwich, briefly
31. Arthur or Lillie
32. Bush's "___ of evil"
33. Kind of sauce
34. Hollow-stemmed plant
35. Stimpy's partner
36. Basic version: Abbr.
37. Prettiest at the ball
38. L-P filler
39. In layers
41. First mo.
42. Forward flow
46. Cunning
49. Moo ___ gai pan
51. Rebounding sound
52. Ash containers
53. Tree popular in street names
54. Fake coin
55. Pub serving
56. Highways: Abbr.
57. Pre-coll. exams

DOWN

1. Start of an alphabet song
2. Post-it, e.g.
3. Mend, as socks
4. They'll show you the world
5. Letter flourish
6. Showery mo.
7. Scroogelike
8. Baby elephant
9. Color gradation
10. Business letter abbr.
11. To the ___ degree (extremely)
19. Now I ___ me down to sleep . . .
21. On, as a lamp
23. Humble place
24. Adam's second son
25. Banana part
26. Expressed, as farewell
27. Cause injury to
28. Field team
29. Boy, in Bogotá
33. Bee or wasp
34. Set right
36. The bus stops here: Abbr.

Puzzle 131

Solution on Page 346

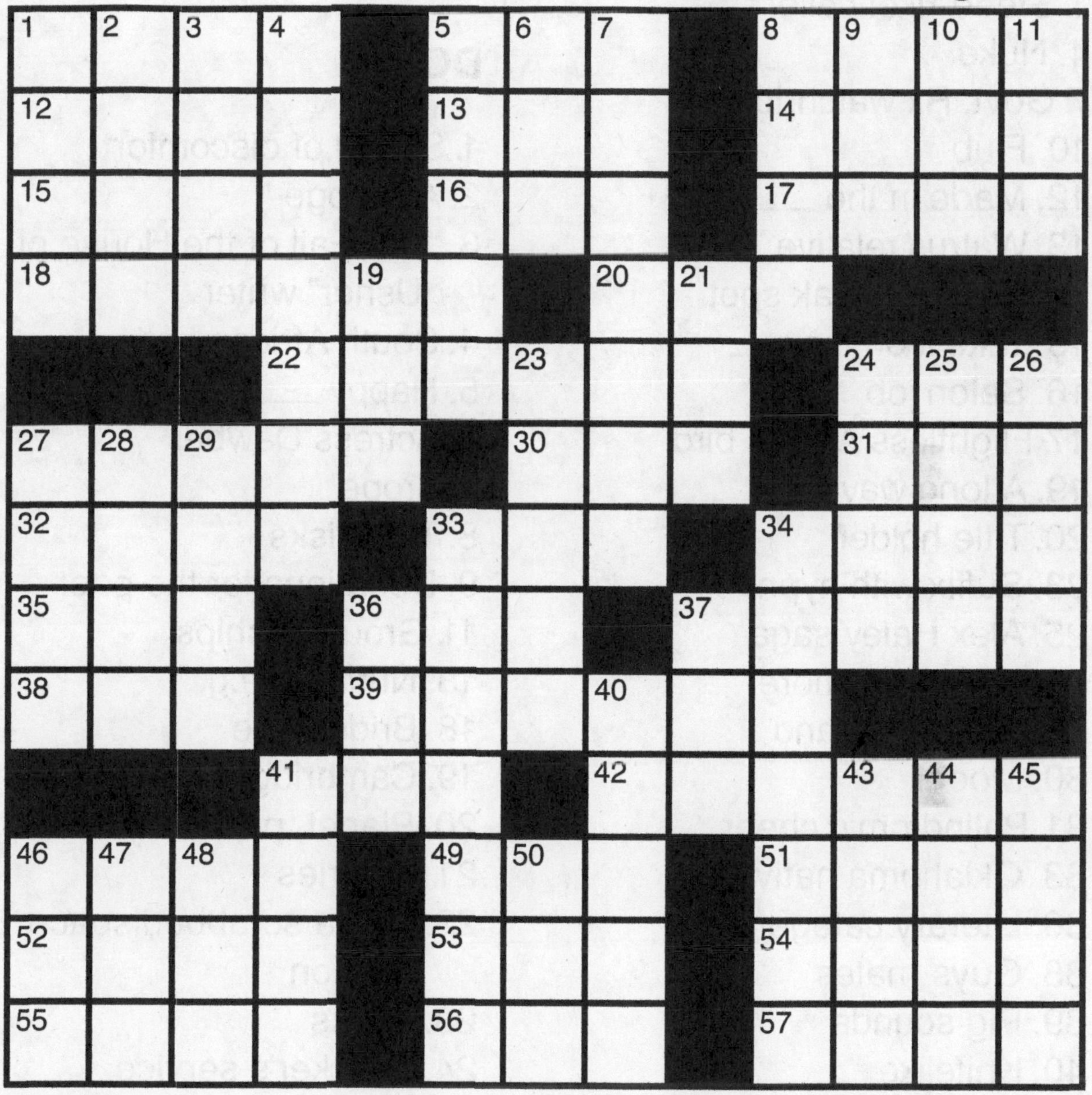

37. Actor Affleck
40. Hotel offerings
41. Surely you ___
43. Golden State coll.
44. Closed tight
45. Takes most of
46. Hole in the green
47. Spoonbender Geller
48. Country music network, once
50. The "O" in G.O.P.

ACROSS

1. Steee-rike! caller
4. Nuke
7. Govt. Rx watchdog
10. Flub
12. Made in the ___
13. Walrus relative
14. Achilles' weak spot
15. Take it on the ___
16. Salon job
17. Flightless Aussie bird
19. A long way
20. Title holder
23. Suffix with hypn-
25. Alex Haley saga
26. Let's hear more!
29. Dog command
30. Mooer
31. Palindromic cheer
33. Oklahoma native
36. Literary category
38. Guys' mates
39. Pig sounds
40. Knifelike
43. Former rival of AT&T
44. TV, slangily, with "the"
45. ___-Magnon man
47. Data, for short
51. Planets
52. Concealed
53. Like service station rags
54. Tire layer
55. Stomach muscles, briefly
56. Film producer Roach

DOWN

1. Sound of discomfort
2. A Stooge
3. "The Fall of the House of Usher" writer
4. South African native
5. Happy ___ lark
6. Actress Dawber
7. Grope
8. Take risks
9. Donations for the poor
11. Group of ships
13. Nutmeg, e.g.
18. Bride's title
19. Cambridge sch.
20. Planet, poetically
21. Miseries
22. Like a scrubbed space mission
23. Stinks
24. Wrecker's service
27. Country music's Loretta
28. Merry escapade
30. Cartoon collectible
32. Affirmative
34. Fairy tale monsters
35. Catch forty winks
36. "You've ___ Mail"
37. Refrain in "Old MacDonald"

Puzzle 132

Solution on Page 346

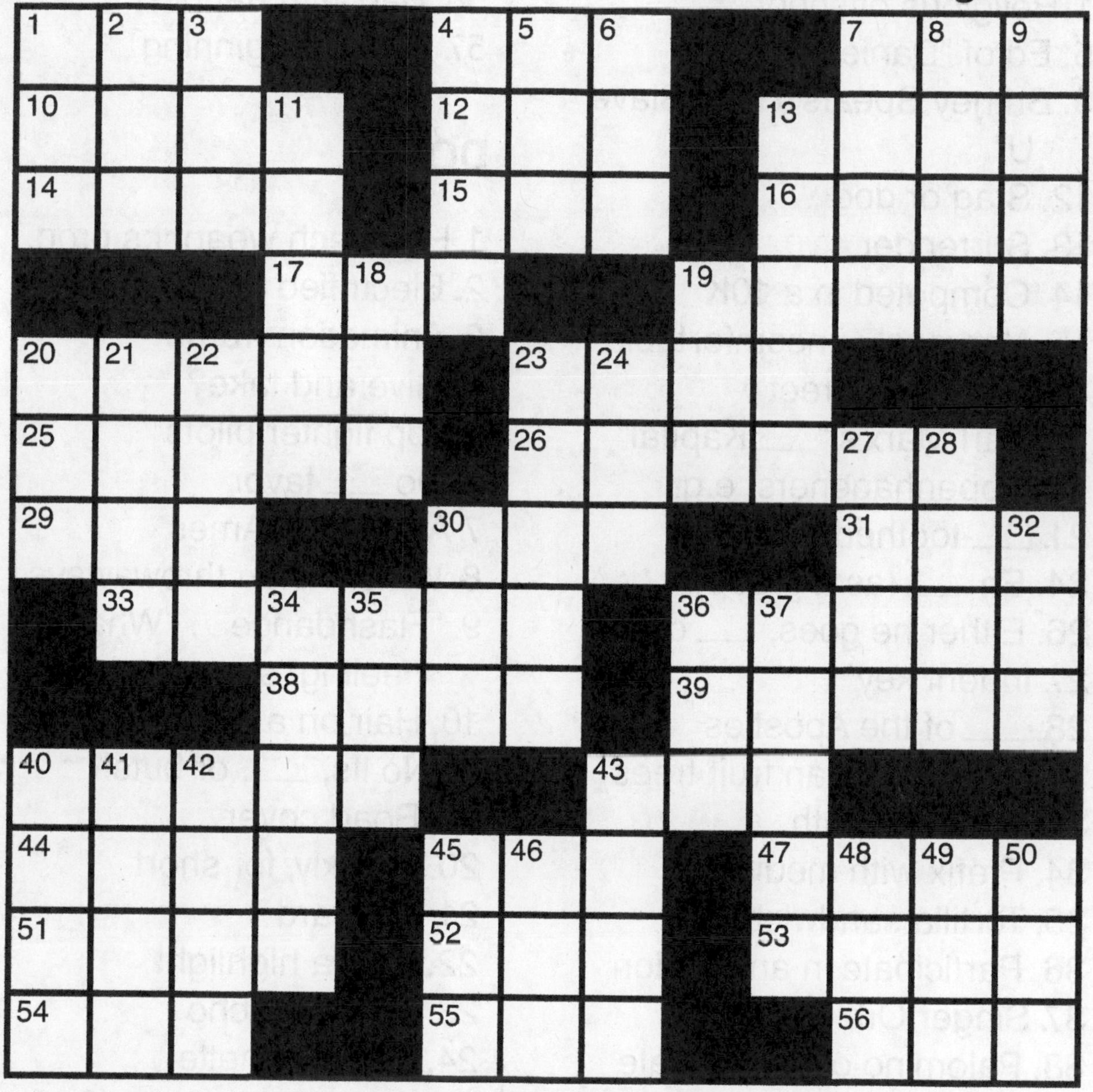

40. Go no further
41. Toss
42. Dear advice columnist
43. Mount Olympus dwellers
45. Half a dance's name
46. Adam's spare part
48. Biomedical research org.
49. It's south of Ga.
50. Animated Olive

ACROSS

1. Religious offshoot
5. Ed of "Daniel Boone"
9. Britney Spears's "___ Slave 4 U"
12. Stag or doe
13. Surrender
14. Competed in a 10K
15. Nervously uncomfortable
17. Dead-___ street
18. Karl Marx's "___ Kapital"
19. Copenhageners, e.g.
21. ___-toothed tiger
24. En ___ (as a group)
26. Either he goes, ___ do!
27. Indent key
28. ___ of the Apostles
31. Mediterranean fruit trees
33. Rainbow path
34. Prefix with medic
35. Tortilla sandwich
36. Participate in an auction
37. Singer Orbison
38. Palomino or Clydesdale
40. Baseball card data
42. Meeting transcriber
44. Fallen space station
45. Tiller's tool
46. Equipment
52. Come-___ (inducements)
53. Coin opening
54. Miniature plateau
55. Iris's place
56. Bag with handles
57. Plant's beginning

DOWN

1. High-tech weapons prog.
2. Electrified fish
3. Animation frame
4. Give and take?
5. Top fighter pilots
6. Do ___ favor
7. Asner and Ames
8. Watermelon throwaways
9. "Flashdance . . . What a Feeling" singer
10. Hair on a horse's neck
11. No ifs, ___, or buts!
16. Road cover
20. Quickly, for short
21. Not hard
22. Opera highlight
23. Head honcho
24. ___ Antoinette
25. Introductory letters?
27. Soda can features
29. Gait between walk and canter
30. Declares
32. In the near future
39. Celebrity skewering

Puzzle 133

Solution on Page 347

40. Madam's partner
41. Aerial railway cars
42. Loafer or moccasin
43. Cereal spokestiger
44. Chess ending
47. Arafat's org.
48. Stovetop item
49. Driving range peg
50. ___ as directed
51. Unhappy

ACROSS

1. Dog's treat
5. Bit of pond vegetation
9. Salk and Pepper: Abbr.
12. Figure skater's jump
13. Locomotive fuel
14. Extra-wide, at the shoe store
15. Judge's attire
16. Hoarse voice
17. Sedan or coupe
18. Kitchen VIP
20. Thermonuclear blast maker
22. Sticky stuff
25. Talk and talk and talk
26. To and ___
27. Get out of bed
30. Unconscious state
34. Detergent brand
35. Hardly enough
37. Soak up gravy
38. One of 16 in a cup: Abbr.
40. Whiz at tennis serves
41. Deadly cobra
42. Feb. preceder
44. Yawning gulf
46. Expire, as a subscription
49. Central American Indian
51. Yoko of "Double Fantasy"
52. Picket-line crosser
54. Lion's home
58. Bout stopper, for short
59. Leak slowly
60. King's address
61. My gal of song
62. Eliot or Frost
63. VISA alternative, briefly

DOWN

1. Happy hour locale
2. Losing tic-tac-toe line
3. Cornhusker St.
4. Vote into office
5. Farmland division
6. Goof off
7. Pedal next to the brake
8. Beta preceder
9. Art ___: geometric style
10. Quantity of paper
11. Many a Bosnian
19. His and ___
21. It's on the telly
22. Dismissive sound
23. United ___ Emirates
24. Cries convulsively
25. Hereditary carrier
28. ___ hardly wait!
29. Cul-de-___
31. "The Star-Spangled Banner" start
32. Rolling stone's lack
33. Computer programs, for short
36. Carhop's carrier
39. Bedwear, briefly

Puzzle 134

Solution on Page 347

43. Man with morals
45. Model builder's wood
46. Real estate parcels
47. Paul who sang "Diana"
48. Office wagering
49. Rat's challenge
50. Help illegally
53. Loving murmur
55. Point at a target
56. Intense anger
57. Harrison of "My Fair Lady"

ACROSS

1. Classic Pontiac muscle cars
5. Sized up visually
9. College transcript no.
12. Cry of anticipation
13. 1920s–1940s art style
14. Certain retriever, briefly
15. Use a wrecking ball on
16. From ___: completely
17. Poet's planet
18. Gives in
20. Room to maneuver
22. Connected to the Internet
24. Kind of symbol
27. Hair goo
28. Mary had a little one
32. Cat's cry
34. Coll. dorm VIPs
36. Fat used in candlemaking
37. Mama's partner
38. Mom's month
40. Homophone for new
41. Katmandu resident
44. John, Paul, George, or Ringo
47. Envelope enclosure
52. Treater's pickup
53. Shoestring
55. Maui feast
56. Internet address, briefly
57. Cast-___ stomach
58. Copier input: Abbr.
59. Stealthy
60. Mail-chute opening
61. Pantheon members

DOWN

1. Bloody
2. Southeast Asian cuisine
3. Trickle
4. Writer/illustrator Silverstein
5. Lou Grant portrayer
6. Are we having fun ___?
7. Food-poisoning bacteria
8. Egg carton count
9. Post-sunset effect
10. Prefix with legal
11. Dear advice-giver
19. Follow everywhere
21. Morays, e.g.
23. Peruvian beast
24. Ref's cousin
25. Unimpressive brain size
26. Badge wearer
29. Jul. follower
30. Fraternity members
31. Appliance meas.
33. Privation
35. Noteworthy
39. Yang's counterpart
42. ___ Island (immigrants' site)
43. Oyster's prize
44. A/C measures
45. "Duke of ___" (1962 hit)
46. With adroitness

Puzzle 135

Solution on Page 347

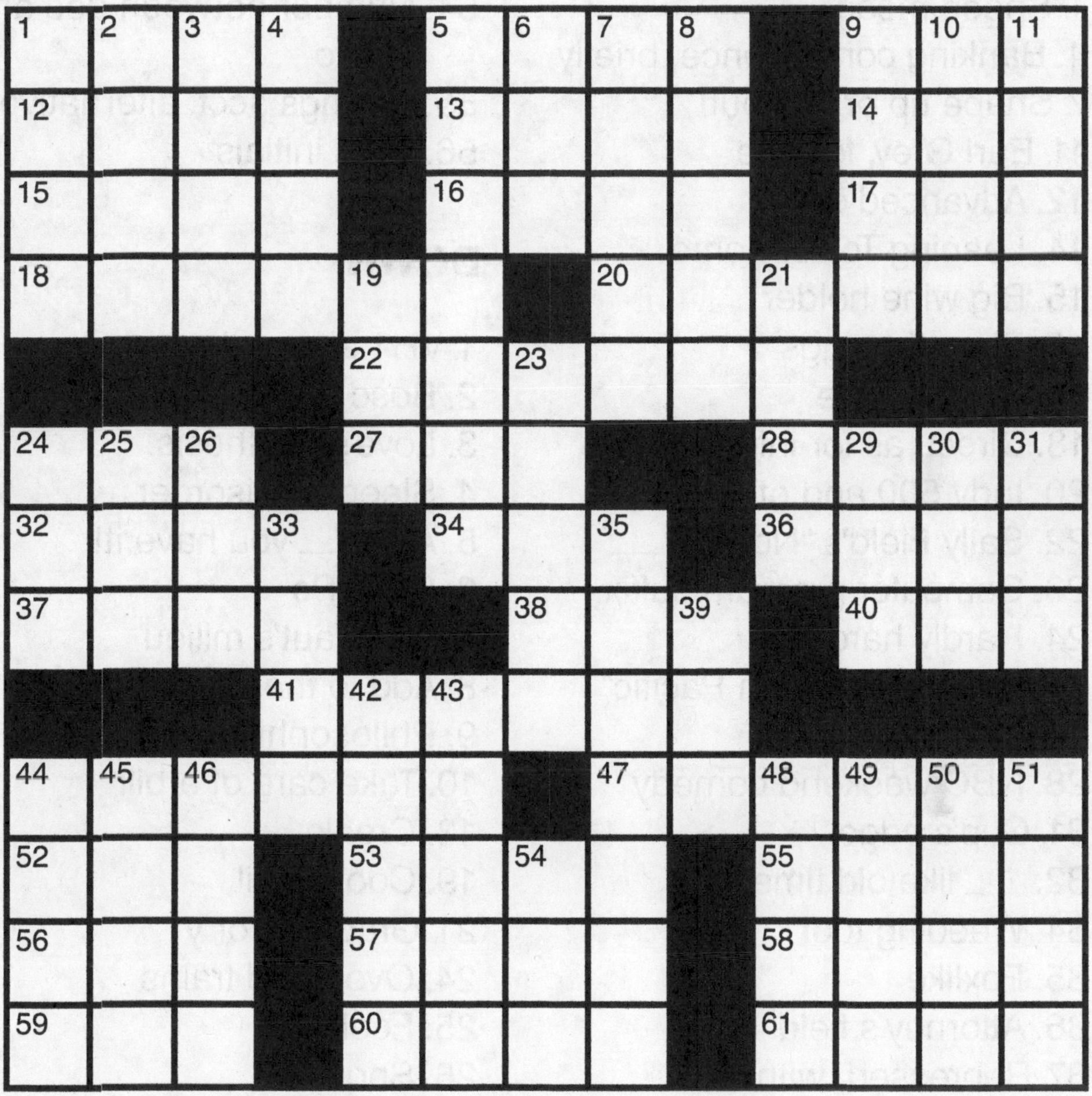

48. Trudge through the mire
49. Currency on the Continent
50. Police assault
51. Actions on heartstrings and pant legs
54. Dovish sound

ACROSS

1. Speed meas.
4. Banking convenience, briefly
7. Shape up or ___ out!
11. Earl Grey, for one
12. Advanced degs.
14. Leaning Tower home
15. Big wine holder
16. Place for eggs
17. Military force
18. Direct, as for info
20. Indy 500 and others
22. Sally Field's "Norma ___"
23. Computer program suffix
24. Hardly hard
27. "Bali ___" ("South Pacific" song)
28. NBC weekend comedy
31. Cup's edge
32. ___ like old times
34. Weeding tool
35. Foxlike
36. Attorney's field
37. Repressed, with "up"
38. "Morning ___ Broken"
39. High-speed Internet letters
41. Actors' surface
43. Parts of molecules
46. Barbecue rod
47. Enticement
49. Thumbs-up response
51. Without a doubt
52. Eject, as lava
53. ___ tai (drink)
54. Number between dos and cuatro
55. Savings acct. alternatives
56. Alias initials

DOWN

1. VH1 alternative
2. Bosc or Bartlett
3. Love's antithesis
4. Sleeping disorder
5. And ___ you have it!
6. ER VIPs
7. Astronaut's milieu
8. Add to the staff
9. Philosophies
10. Take care of a bill
13. Creek
19. Cook in oil
21. Graph's x or y
24. Overhead trains
25. Feel ill
26. Snoop
27. Cut down
28. That's all ___ wrote!
29. ___ sequitur
30. "Live and ___ Die"
32. Smelter's waste
33. Painting stands
37. Mideast grp.
38. Abominates

Puzzle 136

Solution on Page 347

39. Took a risk
40. One-pot dinners
41. Thing on a cowboy's boot
42. Radial, e.g.
44. Papa's mate
45. Relax in the tub
46. Concorde, notably: Abbr.
48. ___ symbol (bar code)
50. Korean automaker

ACROSS

1. Like most N.B.A. players
5. Strike with open hand
9. ___ the season to be jolly . . .
12. "The Andy Griffith Show" boy
13. Sagan or Sandburg
14. Muhammad ___
15. Crooked
16. Full of breezes
17. Cambridge univ.
18. Alimony receivers
19. Ike's initials
20. Bee ___ ("Stayin' Alive" singers)
21. Location identifier, for short
23. "___ Pepper's Lonely Hearts Club Band"
25. Tippy craft
28. Avenues
32. One, in Germany
33. Salary increase
35. Mai ___ (drink)
36. Periodic table listing
38. Romanov rulers
40. CBS forensic drama
41. Calf's call
42. Campaign funders, for short
45. Soccer Hall of Famer Hamm
47. Clarinetist Artie
51. 1950s prez
52. Impudent back talk
53. Like a carbon copy
54. Ascot
55. ___ extra cost to you
56. Stunt rider Knievel
57. Q and A part: Abbr.
58. Exodus author Uris
59. Fender ding

DOWN

1. Fit ___ tied
2. Mountaintop
3. Bit of poetry
4. Come on!
5. A whole slew
6. ___-back (relaxed)
7. Nabs
8. Perform diligently, as a trade
9. Change from wild to mild
10. Nastase of tennis
11. Uses a sofa
20. Former AT&T rival
22. Israel's Shimon
24. Screen siren Garbo
25. Grade between bee and dee
26. Feel bad
27. Opposite SSW
28. Use a chair
29. Approx. landing hour
30. Road goo
31. Bro's relative
34. Perk up

Puzzle 137

Solution on Page 348

37. Show hosts, for short
39. Spoke impudently to
41. Stoneworker
42. Bread for a gyro
43. Having the same properties
44. Average marks
46. That ___ excuse
48. "___ Gun Will Travel"
49. Grace finisher
50. Whip mark
52. Mineo of film

ACROSS

1. Lions and tigers
5. Bray starter
8. Pond scum component
12. Roof overhang
13. Olive in the comics
14. Crazy bird
15. Young woman
16. "Playboy" founder, familiarly
17. Agent 007
18. Peek add-on
20. Apportions, with "out"
21. SeaWorld whale
24. Golfer's shout
26. Cafeteria customer
27. ___-night doubleheader
28. Travel rtes.
31. Director's "Stop!"
32. Fighter with Fidel
33. You've Got Mail co.
34. On the ___ (furtively)
35. Bartender on "The Simpsons"
36. Shampoo step
38. Phoenix's NBA team
39. Threw in
40. Get to one's feet
43. Scholarly book
45. Head case?
46. Mauna ___ (Hawaiian volcano)
47. Start of a magician's cry
51. Elton John's "Don't Let the Sun Go Down ___"
52. Annoy
53. Neighbor of Cambodia
54. Kind of pressure
55. Speakers' hesitations
56. Went down like a stone

DOWN

1. Fantasia frame
2. Motorist's org.
3. Boob tubes
4. Big Bird's street
5. Cry from Santa
6. Inner calm
7. Keebler cookie maker
8. "The Zoo Story" playwright Edward
9. Stolen goods
10. Going, going, ___!
11. & & &
19. Prickly seed cover
20. Hosp. picture
21. Parts of a min.
22. Tow
23. Lawyer: Abbr.
25. Have a payment due
28. Author Ayn
29. Prescription quantity
30. Snow glider
32. Pro and ___
35. Wet dirt

Puzzle 138

Solution on Page 348

36. It's used for battering
37. Things to live up to
38. Lip-curling smile
40. Sty food
41. Prong of a fork
42. Pinnacle
44. Hardwood trees
46. Lucy of "Charlie's Angels," 2000
48. Sheep sound
49. Nancy Reagan's son
50. Thought you'd never ___

ACROSS

1. Sloppy Joe holder
4. Shane star
8. Jack Horner's find
12. Sort of: suffix
13. Crème cookie
14. Small, medium, or large
15. Poe story, "The ___ Heart"
17. Cole Porter's "I ___ Love"
18. The Beatles' "Let ___"
19. Lip application
20. Liquid-Plumr rival
23. How do you like ___ apples?
25. Dressing gown
26. Phobia
27. Secret govt. group
30. Immediately
32. Take offense at
34. You-know-___
35. Fermented honey drink
37. Group of athletes
38. Campaign pros
39. Botanical fence
40. Yellowstone animal
43. Spicy Asian cuisine
45. Even ___ speak . . .
46. Lumberjack's tool
50. Shut loudly
51. Fail to include
52. Mean Amin
53. Some male dolls
54. "___ Ha'i": "South Pacific" song
55. Banned insecticide

DOWN

1. Went for
2. Put into service
3. Stanley Cup gp.
4. Quick pick game
5. ___-Israeli relations
6. X out
7. Female deer
8. Biblical hymn
9. Long car, for short
10. Submachine guns
11. Macy's department
16. Sheets, pillowcases, etc.
19. Chicago star Richard
20. Take a card
21. Rocker David Lee
22. Peek or bug ending
24. Rocklike
26. Touch
27. On a ___-to-know basis
28. Hangup
29. "Ma! He's Making Eyes ___"
31. Don't gimme that!
33. Beer holder
36. Respiratory problem
38. Wordsworth works
39. West Indies republic

Puzzle 139

Solution on Page 348

40. Enjoy the sun
41. Man or Wight
42. Graceful swimmer
44. Signal, as a cab
46. Kernel holder
47. Caesar of comedy
48. Put two and two together
49. Knack for comebacks

ACROSS

1. Avenue crossers: Abbr.
4. Prescription writers: Abbr.
7. Film director Frank
12. Munch
13. Waiter's payoff
14. Light bulb gas
15. Greek letter X
16. Neckline style
17. Reads, as a bar code
18. Truck weight unit
19. Pepper's partner
21. Big video game maker
23. Hospital trauma ctrs.
24. Fleeting fashion
27. Mighty Ducks' org.
29. Hanker for
32. Juicy steak
35. Singer Midler
36. Take into custody
38. Pres. Lincoln
39. Rotten
40. Sounds of relief
42. Chocolate candy
46. Lumberjacks' tools
47. Have an evening meal
48. Detox locale
52. Novelist Fleming
54. Untruth
55. ___ and desist
56. Bro or sis
57. U.S./U.K. divider
58. Elite invitee roster
59. Doting letters
60. Brooks of comedy

DOWN

1. Religious splinter groups
2. Nevada resort
3. Police trap
4. "Total Request Live" network
5. Fuel for big rigs
6. Thrown weapon
7. Players in a play
8. Rainbow's shape
9. Mickelson's org.
10. Politico ___ Paul
11. The A of Q&A (abbr.)
20. 1960s hallucinogen
22. "The Diary of ___ Frank"
24. ___ to be tied (angry)
25. The "A" in MoMA
26. Fiddle-de-___
28. For ___ a jolly good fellow
30. Flow back
31. Hide-and-___
32. File folder feature
33. Uplifting undergarment
34. City reg.
37. Tariff
38. Lay into
41. Bank robber's job
43. Muhammad's religion
44. High-end hotel option

Puzzle 140

Solution on Page 348

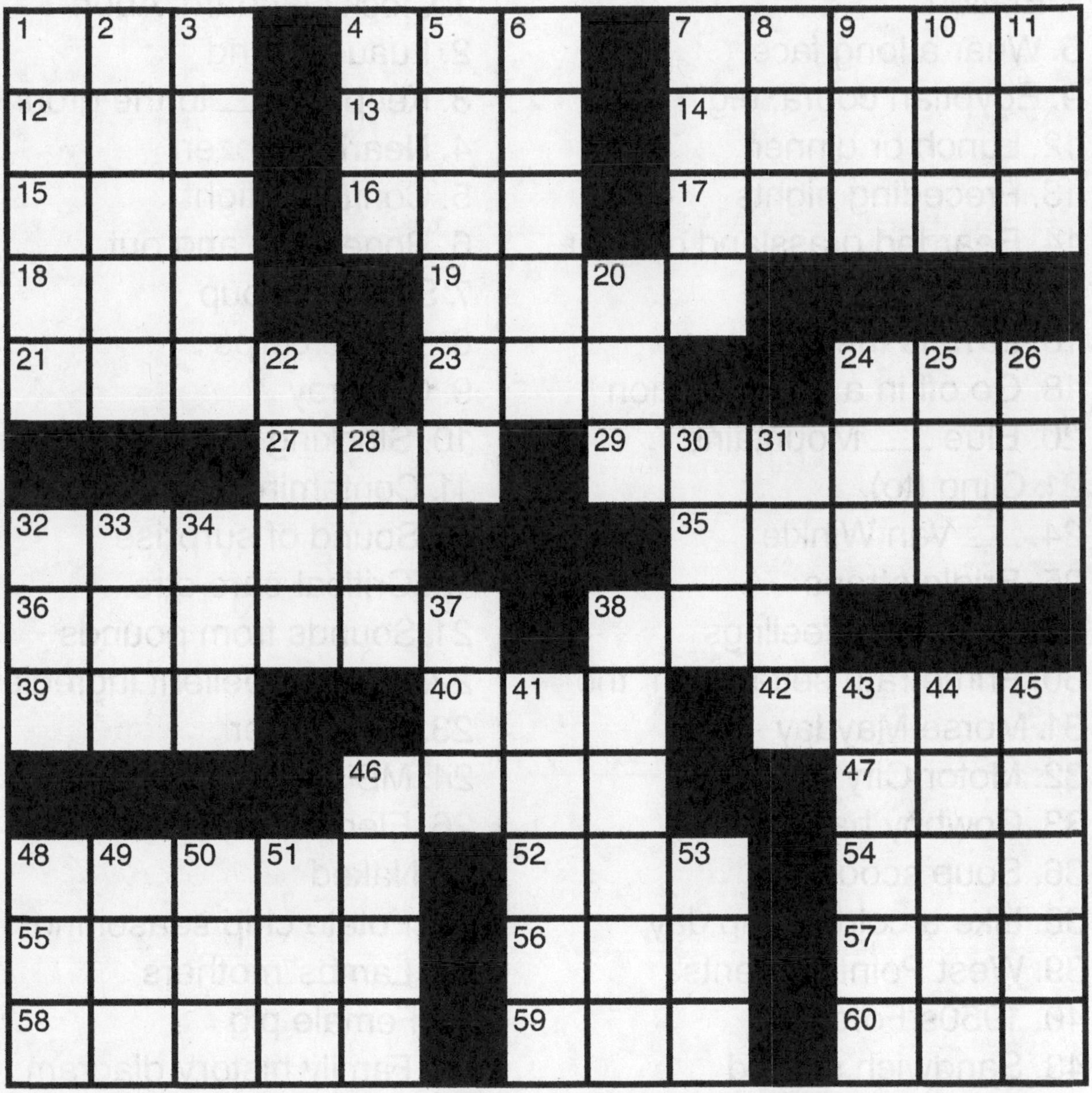

45. Participate in a bee
46. Encourage in crime
48. "His Master's Voice" co.
49. Electric fish
50. "Bali ___"
51. Donkey's cousin
53. "30 Rock" network

ACROSS

1. Elation
5. Wear a long face
9. Egyptian cobra, e.g.
12. Lunch or dinner
13. Preceding nights
14. Bearded grassland dweller
15. Become bushed
16. 2012 is the next one
18. Go off in a new direction
20. Blue ___ Mountains
21. Cling (to)
24. ___ Van Winkle
25. Bridle straps
26. Strong, as feelings
30. Prime rate setter, with "the"
31. Morse Mayday
32. Motor City labor org.
33. Cowboy hat
36. Soup scooper
38. Like a cold, damp day
39. West Point students
40. 1950s Ford flop
43. Sandwich spread
44. Set free
46. Excellent, in modern slang
50. Transcript stat.
51. Lawn burrower
52. Mall carryall
53. ___-out clause
54. Part of M.I.T.: Abbr.
55. Wing measurement

DOWN

1. Clock standard: Abbr.
2. Luau garland
3. Keep an ___ to the ground
4. Nearly a dozen
5. Confused fight
6. Roger, ___ and out
7. Split-___ soup
8. ___ de corps
9. Got gray
10. Stocking ruiner
11. Contaminant-free
17. Sound of surprise
19. Critical-care ctrs.
21. Sounds from pounds
22. Insect repellent ingredient
23. Take cover
24. MD's helpers
26. Elementary particle
27. Naked
28. Potato chip seasoning
29. Lambs' mothers
31. Female pig
34. Family history diagram
35. Deli meat
36. Deposit, as an egg
37. Takes as one's own
39. West Pointer, e.g.
40. It follows that
41. Johnny of "Pirates of the Caribbean"

Puzzle 141

Solution on Page 349

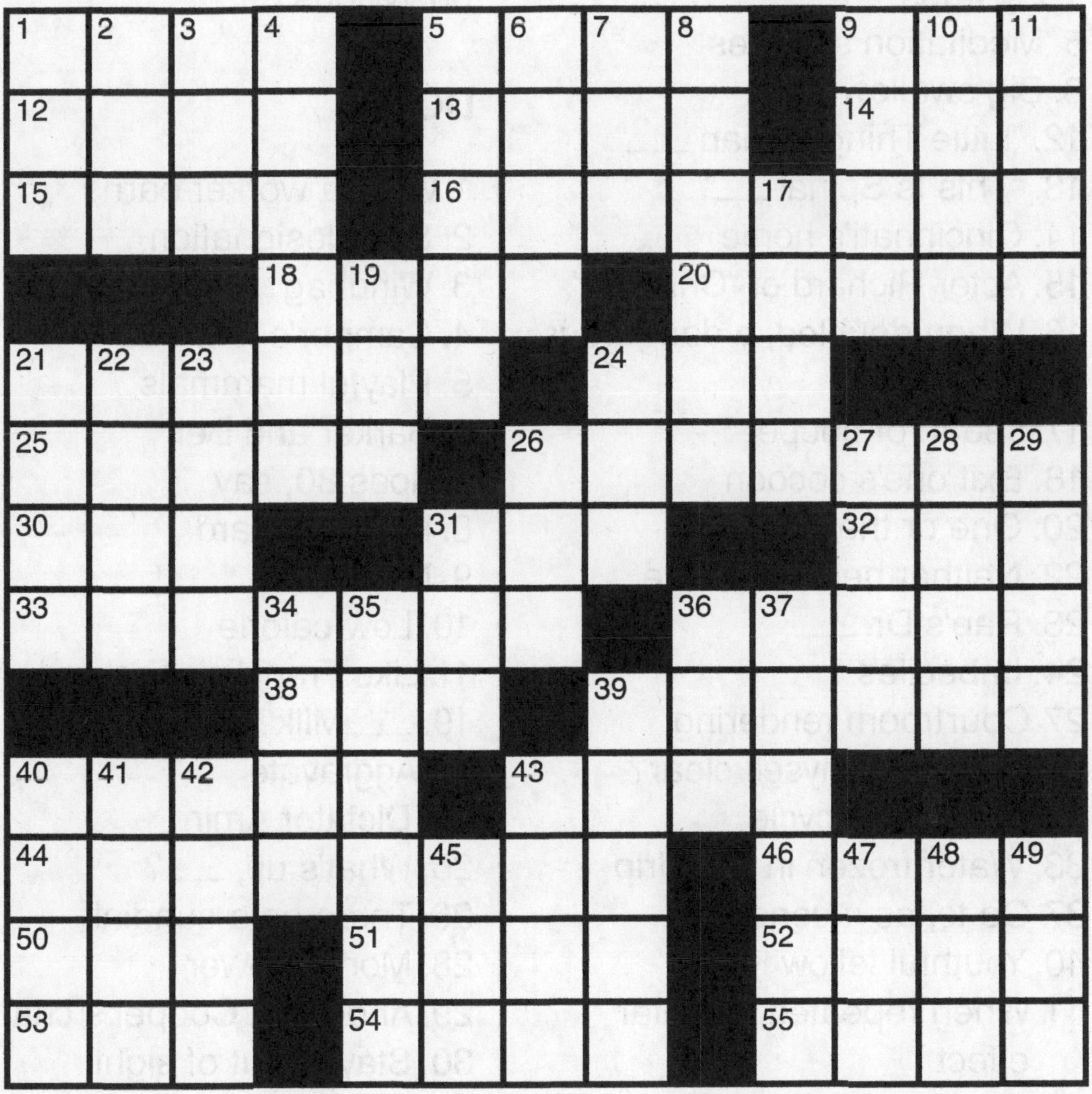

42. Wood strip used as a bed support
43. Kiss my grits TV diner
45. Dad, to Grandpa
47. Jump on one foot
48. One step ___ time
49. Perfect score in gymnastics

ACROSS

1. Fly traps
5. Meditation syllables
8. Big swallow
12. "Little Things Mean ___"
13. "This Is Spinal ___"
14. Cincinnati's home
15. Actor Richard of "Chicago"
16. When doubled, a dangerous fly
17. Sedan or coupe
18. Exit one's cocoon
20. One or the other
22. Neither here ___ there
23. Rap's Dr. ___
24. Imbeciles
27. Courtroom rendering
31. ___ make myself clear?
32. Prefix with cycle
33. Water frozen in mid-drip
37. Go to, as a concert
40. Youthful fellow
41. When repeated, a guitar effect
42. Fashion designer Giorgio
45. Shook hands (on)
49. Corp. heads
50. I'm freezing!
52. Gluck of opera
53. Cozy hideaways
54. Took the reins
55. Dirty literature
56. Potter's medium
57. Koch and Asner
58. Nylons

DOWN

1. What a worker earns
2. Sch. designation
3. Windbag
4. Camper's fuel
5. Playful mammals
6. Barker and Bell
7. Goes 80, say
8. Pointed beard
9. No way!
10. Low-calorie
11. Like Franklin's Richard
19. ___ Milk?
21. Aggravate
24. Dictator Amin
25. What's up, ___?
26. Three on a sundial
28. Mon. follower
29. Anderson Cooper's channel
30. Stayed out of sight
34. Chic
35. PC grouping
36. Fit for consumption
37. Grammys, e.g.
38. Baseball put-out
39. Defeat soundly
42. "Highway to Hell" band
43. Movie unit

Puzzle 142

Solution on Page 349

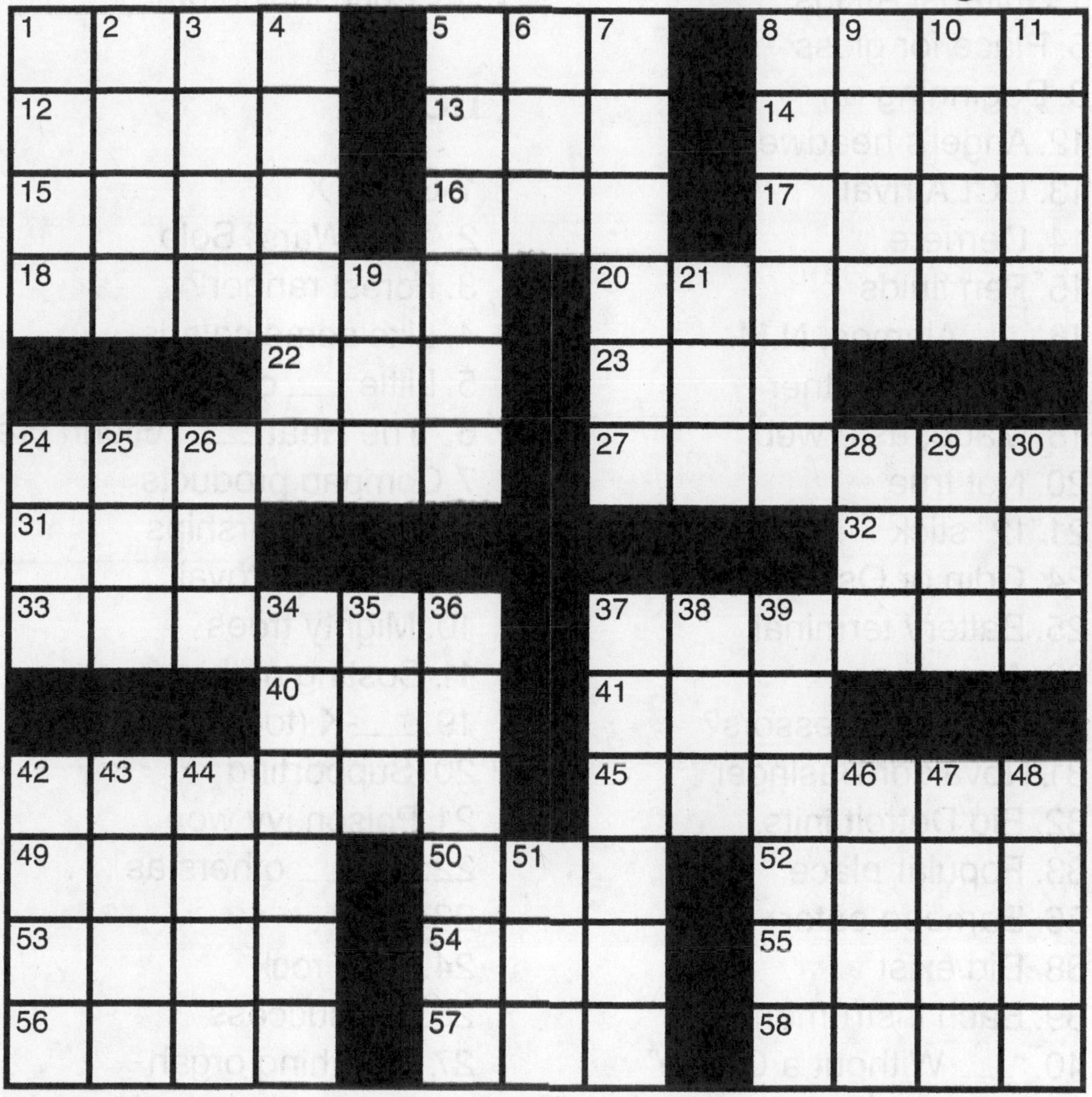

44. Ms. Lisa
46. Googly-eyed Muppet
47. Big Aussie birds
48. Prom partner
51. Stoplight color

ACROSS

1. Guitarist Atkins
5. Place for gloss
8. Beginning on
12. Angel's headwear
13. UCLA rival
14. Derriere
15. Pen fluids
16. ___ Alamos, N.M.
17. Model's partner
18. Made, as a web
20. Not true
21. 12" stick
24. Odin or Osiris
25. Battery terminal
26. Announces
30. VW predecessors?
31. Novak or Basinger
32. Big Detroit inits.
33. Popular place
36. Bamboo eater
38. Did exist
39. Bach instrument
40. "___ Without a Cause"
43. Lascivious
45. Chopped down
46. Mournful
47. Singer Arnold
51. Brazilian soccer legend
52. Overeat, with "out"
53. Pinot ___ (wine)
54. CAT ___
55. Get the chair
56. Price indicators

DOWN

1. Greek X
2. "Star Wars" Solo
3. Forest ranger?
4. Like some salads
5. Little ___ of the comics
6. "The Heat ___": Glenn Frey hit
7. Compaq products
8. Fleet of warships
9. ___ of approval
10. Mighty trees
11. Costing nothing
19. ___-K (toddlers' school)
20. Supporting
21. Poison ivy woe
22. Do ___ others as . . .
23. Boor
24. Ring rock
26. Big success
27. Breathing organ
28. Baby's first word, maybe
29. Ugly duckling, in time
31. WBA stats
34. Bjorn Borg's homeland
35. Buddy
36. Impact sound
37. Burning with passion

Puzzle 143

Solution on Page 349

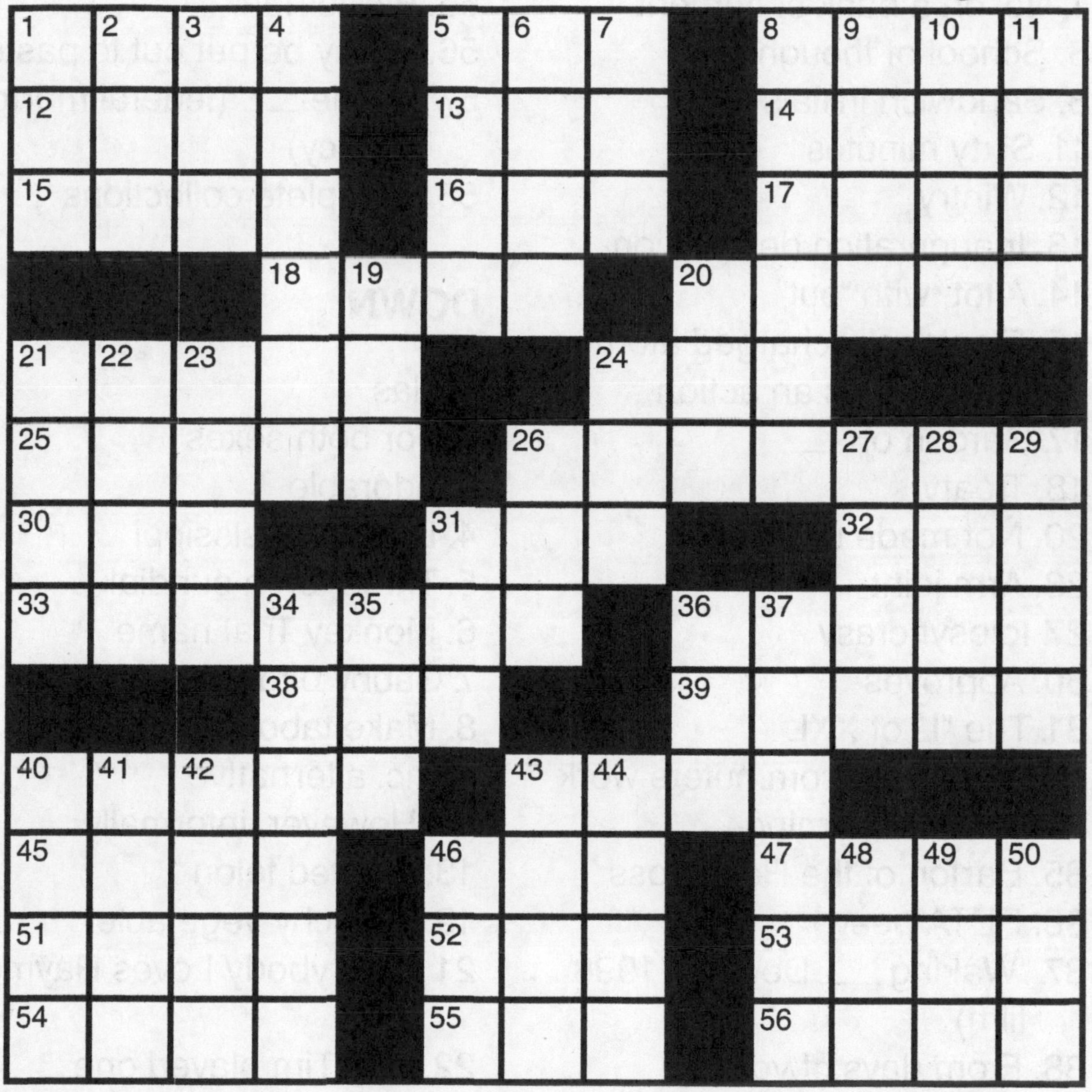

40. Emulates Eminem
41. Prez or veep
42. Actor Lugosi
43. Hibernation location
44. On pins and needles
46. Letters on a Coppertone bottle
48. 1949 film noir classic
49. Archaeological operation
50. Twelve-mo. spans

ACROSS

1. No. on a bank statement
5. School of thought
8. Sandwich initials
11. Sixty minutes
12. Wintry
13. Inauguration declaration
14. Allot, with "out"
15. Electrically charged atom
16. Reverse, as an action
17. Garden of ___
18. Treaty
20. Not made up
23. Arm joint
27. Idiosyncrasy
30. Approves
31. The "L" of XXL
32. Where telecommuters work
34. Word of warning
35. Barton of the Red Cross
36. PETA peeve
37. "Waking ___ Devine" (1998 film)
38. From days of yore
39. One-named New Age vocalist
41. Egg on
43. Give at no charge, as a hotel room
47. Sushi bar soup
50. Rioting group
52. Swedish furniture retailer
53. "Go Tell ___ the Mountain"
54. Cook, as bacon
55. Pickle herb
56. It may be put out to pasture
57. Fannie ___ (federal mortgage agency)
58. Complete collections

DOWN

1. Alas
2. For both sexes
3. Adorable
4. Lott of Mississippi
5. Three, on a sundial
6. Monkey Trial name
7. Gabby bird
8. Make taboo
9. Inc. alternative
10. However, informally
13. Wanted felon
19. Crunchy vegetable
21. "Everybody Loves Raymond" star
22. Tiny Tim played one
24. Raisin ___ (cereal)
25. Folklore meanie
26. Unwanted lawn growth
27. Stuffed tortilla
28. ___ be a cold day in . . .
29. Punched-out part of a paper ballot
33. Eugene's state

Puzzle 144

Solution on Page 349

34. Burger roll
36. Bogart's hat
40. Corrosive liquids
42. Car radio button
44. 1930s migrant
45. Liquefy
46. Best buds
47. What an MC wears
48. Who am ___ judge?
49. Miss Piggy, e.g.
51. See ya

ACROSS

1. Life stories, for short
5. Israeli submachine gun
8. Like omelets
12. Crotchety oldster
13. Dorm figures, for short
14. Pole or Czech
15. Fool
16. Buy a pig ___ poke
17. ___ as a button
18. Deception
20. ___ Motel ("Psycho" setting)
21. Has a bawl
24. Use a microwave
25. Coupes and convertibles
26. Carryall
30. ___-Pitch softball
31. Rapper ___ Rida
32. Big name in kitchen gadgets
33. Religious dissenter
36. Positive thinker Norman Vincent ___
38. The "A" in E.T.A.: Abbr.
39. Prefix with com or change
40. Every picture tells one
43. Steals, with "off"
45. Its symbol is Fe
46. Away from home
47. Term referring to a prev. citation
51. Nod off
52. Banners on the Internet
53. Civil War color
54. Got a good look at
55. Lock opener
56. Title

DOWN

1. A-E link
2. Paper in lieu of payment
3. Alley-___ (basketball maneuver)
4. Home music system
5. Literary Leon
6. Western writer Grey
7. This ___ test
8. Break out of jail
9. Market oversaturation
10. Entryway
11. Saint Laurent of fashion
19. Capt. Kirk's ___ Enterprise
20. Step to the plate
21. Money on hand
22. Run the country
23. Take ___ leave it
24. Animal house
26. Special treatment, for short
27. Gravy vessel
28. Auto shaft
29. Ending for "theater" or "church"
31. Tree with cones
34. Brought in, as a salary
35. Give it a whirl

Puzzle 145

Solution on Page 350

36. Dot on a die
37. Junior naval officer
40. Lateral part
41. Helen of ___
42. Move like molasses
43. Intentionally impolite
44. Teeny, informally
46. Acorn's source
48. Push-up lingerie item
49. "___ the Walrus"
50. Easter egg coloring

ACROSS

1. Fore's opposite
4. High or elementary (Abbr.)
7. Beach composition
11. Tell whoppers
12. Drawn tight
14. Like a 4-4 score
15. Wayside stopover
16. Long-distance callers' needs
18. Professor's job security
20. Jogged
21. Barely gets by, with "out"
22. Frozen potato brand
26. Estimate the value of
28. Mortarboard attachment
29. Dads
30. Baby docs, briefly
31. Prefix with intellectual
35. Takes care of
38. Teeter-totter
39. Gator relative
40. Thanks, but I already ___
41. Author Hemingway
44. Best of the bunch?
48. R and B singer Rawls
49. ___ Mountains (Asia/Europe separator)
50. ___ the bottle
51. To ___ is human . . .
52. Bundle of hay
53. World Series mo.
54. Train stop: abbr.

DOWN

1. Came down to Earth
2. Speeder's penalty
3. Volunteer State
4. Gazes steadily
5. Stroke gently
6. Palette selection
7. Jagger and the gang
8. Lend a hand to
9. Word before a dropped maiden name
10. Cavity filler: Abbr.
13. Diviner's deck
17. Irene of "Fame" fame
19. Don Ho's plunker
23. Kind of triangle
24. Borrower's burden
25. "The Sun ___ Rises"
26. PC programs
27. Encl. with a manuscript
32. In functioning condition
33. Computer info
34. Country singer Buck
35. Like the Grand Canyon
36. Off the mark
37. An eternity
42. Alphabetize, e.g.
43. Go left or right
44. Bathroom fixture
45. Is it a boy ___ girl?
46. Good friend
47. G.I.'s address

Puzzle 146

Solution on Page 350

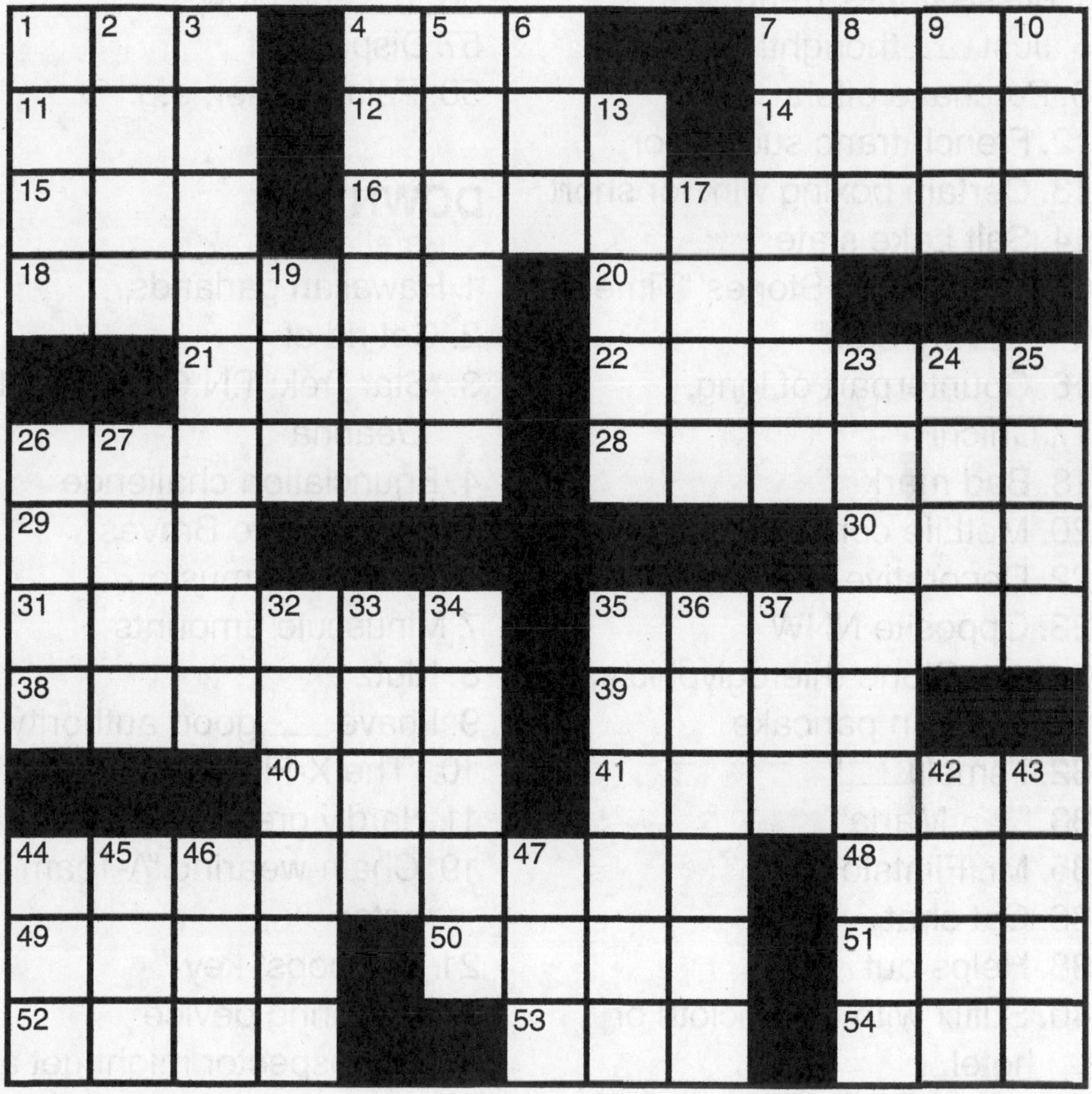

ACROSS

1. Mississippi's Trent
5. Just ___ thought!
8. Purchase offers
12. French franc successor
13. Certain boxing win, for short
14. Salt Lake state
15. The Rolling Stones' "Time ___ My Side"
16. Counterpart of long.
17. Chichi
18. Bad mark
20. MetLife competitor
22. Decorative vessel
23. Opposite NNW
24. ___ Stone (hieroglyphic key)
28. Parisian pancake
32. I smell ___!
33. "___ Maria"
35. Mr. Flintstone
36. Cat chat
38. Helps out
40. Suffix with cash, cloth or hotel
42. ___ Francisco
43. Carbo-loader's fare
45. 2000 candidate
49. Surprise "from the blue"
50. 24 hours
52. Online marketplace
53. Zero, on a court
54. Who ___ we kidding?
55. Actor's part
56. ___ she blows!
57. Dispose of
58. Palm reader, e.g.

DOWN

1. Hawaiian garlands
2. Get rid of
3. "Star Trek: T.N.G." counselor Deanna
4. Enunciation challenge
5. Home of the Braves
6. Caribbean music
7. Minuscule amounts
8. Klutz
9. I have ___ good authority
10. "The X-Files" agent Scully
11. Hardly gregarious
19. Chain-wearing "A-Team" actor
21. PC "oops" key
24. Battering device
25. A prospector might get a lode of it
26. ___ Tomé and Príncipe
27. Gardner of film
29. Often-hectic hosp. areas
30. Teacher's fave
31. Asner and Wynn
34. Made an attempt

Puzzle 147

Solution on Page 350

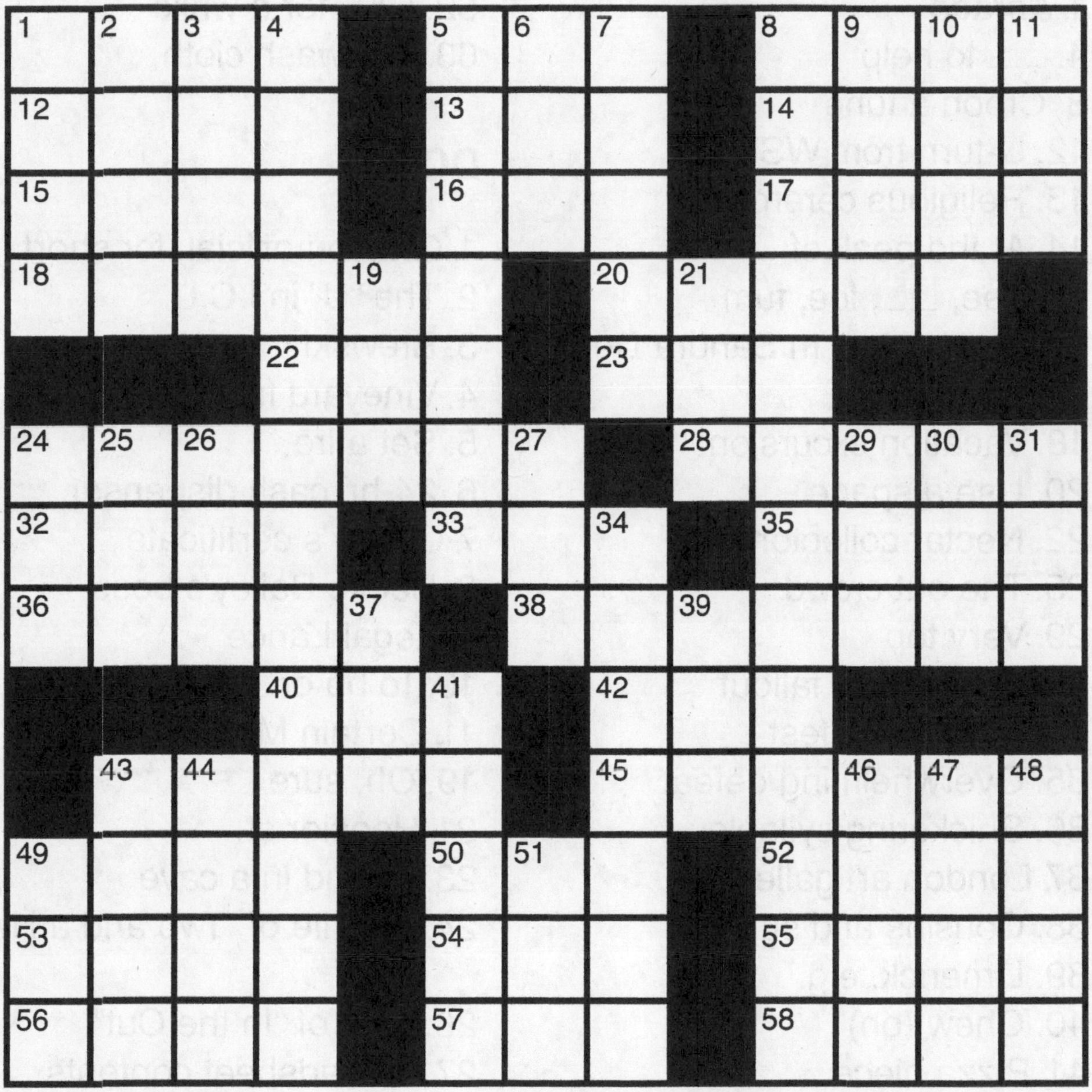

37. Movie backdrop
39. "My Gal ___"
41. Speeder spotter
43. Winnie the ___
44. Thomas ___ Edison
46. A woodwind
47. Breathing rattle
48. One taking a gander
49. Sandwich letters
51. Bush spokesman Fleischer

ACROSS

1. Abrade
4. ___ to help
8. Croon a tune
12. U-turn from WSW
13. Religious ceremony
14. At the peak of
15. Fee, ___, foe, fum
16. "Look ___, I'm Sandra Dee"
17. Goes bad
18. Vacation excursion
20. Use a spade
22. Nectar collectors
25. The out crowd
29. Very top
32. Punch card fallout
34. Have a gabfest
35. Overwhelming defeat
36. Snickering syllable
37. London art gallery
38. Cousins and such
39. Limerick, e.g.
40. Chew (on)
41. Pizza piece
43. Classic soda pop
45. Yuck!
47. Should that be true . . .
50. Actress Roseanne
53. Not an abstainer
56. Approves, briefly
58. Singer Burl
59. Entice
60. Cotton State: Abbr.
61. Stalagmite site
62. Give for a while
63. Car-wash cloth

DOWN

1. Gridiron official, for short
2. The "U" in I.C.U.
3. Brewski
4. Vineyard fruit
5. Set afire
6. 24-hr. cash dispenser
7. Owner's certificate
8. Beetle Bailey's boss
9. Legal Lance
10. To be or ___ to be
11. Certain MDs
19. Oh, sure
21. Hoosier st.
23. Sound in a cave
24. Charlie of "Two and a Half Men"
26. Meg of "In the Cut"
27. Spreadsheet contents
28. Distort, as data
29. Clumsy boats
30. Slinky's shape
31. City bond, for short
33. Weary comment
37. End-of-the-week cry
39. Pin for hanging
42. Put a hex on

Puzzle 148

Solution on Page 350

44. Employed
46. Bottom of a boat
48. Fly like an eagle
49. Tulsa's state: Abbr.
50. Lighter and pen maker
51. Gardner of "On the Beach"
52. Race, as an engine
54. Sic a lawyer on
55. Suffix with west
57. ___ Harbor, Long Island

ACROSS

1. Delivery room doctors, for short
4. Lose firmness
7. Avoid deliberately
11. Long. opposite
12. Santa ___: West Coast winds
14. Sweater Girl Turner
15. Easter egg application
16. Laze about
17. This must weigh ___!
18. Unskilled worker
20. Frequently, to bards
22. Lowly chess piece
23. Tennis great Andre
26. Red Sea parter
27. Squeal (on)
28. Code-breaking org.
30. Exodus author Leon
31. . . . ___ one for the Gipper
32. Shopping ___
33. Pre-___ student
34. ___ whiz!
35. Rice wines
36. Story that's "to be continued"
38. Mined rocks
39. Last word in the Pledge of Allegiance
40. ___ upon a time . . .
41. Darn!
44. Small-size bed
46. Word of assent
49. Unappealing skin condition
50. One of 18 on a golf course
51. Letters before ems
52. Large coves
53. NY time
54. Sty mother

DOWN

1. Like centenarians
2. San Francisco/Oakland separator
3. Get out of the way
4. Beauty parlors
5. Ever and ___
6. Four qts.
7. Venetian blind parts
8. Beanie or beret
9. First numero
10. Palindromic Bobbsey twin
13. Advertising catchphrase
19. She sheep
21. ___ Tuesday (Mardi Gras)
22. Skin openings
23. Disney's "Little Mermaid"
24. Dice Throw
25. The British ___
26. ___'s the word
29. Gore and Sharpton
31. Riches
32. Singer ___ Anthony
34. ___ Gerard (Buck Rogers portrayer)

Puzzle 149

Solution on Page 351

35. Shakespearean verse
37. Lenders' charges
40. Alternative to watercolors
41. Perfume amount
42. Sony rival
43. ___ number can play
45. Grief
47. "Evil Woman" rock group
48. Opposite of NNE

ACROSS

1. Current rage
4. Wed. follower
7. Musical staff insignia
11. Computer file name extension
12. Chaney of film
13. Dinero
14. Nothing
15. Collapsible bed
16. Batman's sidekick
17. Homer Simpson expletive
18. Sty residents
20. Blend
22. Moon-roving vehicle
23. Mins. and mins.
26. Deg. from Wharton
28. Holy Ohio city?
31. Of the Arctic or Antarctic
34. What's the ___ that can happen?
35. "Julius ___" (Shakespeare play)
37. Up there in years
38. Precursor of reggae
39. Barbie's guy
41. Brain-scan letters
44. Tricks
45. Hanukkah's mo.
47. Major mix-up
51. Prosecutors, for short
53. Hairstyling goop
54. Sister's attire
55. Fraternal lodge member
56. Just ___ suspected!
57. Beholder
58. Susan of "L.A. Law"
59. Account exec

DOWN

1. ___ for oneself
2. Self-evident truth
3. New ___, India
4. Motherly ministering, for short
5. Fanfare
6. Loosen, as a knot
7. Pigeon's sound
8. High tennis shot
9. Peyton Manning's younger brother
10. Ceiling spinner
13. ___ Butterworth's
19. London hrs.
21. Dec. 25
23. Not him
24. Country rtes.
25. Pub crawler
27. Maidenform product
29. Bird that hoots
30. Valuable vein
31. Dell products
32. Acorn producer
33. Actress Thompson of "Back to the Future"

Puzzle 150

Solution on Page 351

36. Studio once controlled by Howard Hughes
37. Bargain-hunter's favorite words
40. Came to a close
42. ___ Allan Poe
43. Birds in a gaggle
44. Stop the cameras!
46. Cut out, as coupons
47. ___ sells seashells . . .
48. Aye canceler
49. President Lincoln
50. Certain evergreen
52. Cloud locale

Answers

T	S	P		C	H	A	T			P	I	G
W	O	E		A	B	L	Y		U	R	S	A
O	U	R		R	O	S	S		P	O	M	P
	R	U	T	H		O	O	H	S			
			W	O	K		N	E	E	D	Y	
E	S	C	A	P	E	D		S	T	O	O	L
D	U	O			Y	O	U			T	R	I
U	R	B	A	N		A	M	A	S	S	E	D
	E	B	B	E	D		S	T	P			
			H	E	E	D		H	Y	M	N	
C	O	M	O		C	A	F	E		A	I	M
I	N	O	R		O	L	I	N		S	C	I
D	A	D			R	Y	E	S		H	E	X

Puzzle 1

R	O	W		M	A	S			S	N	U	B
E	P	I		T	R	U		B	O	O	N	E
U	R	L		S	A	P		I	N	G	O	T
P	A	D			F	E	R	N				
	H	E	H		A	R	K			C	P	U
			A	F	T		O	R	D	A	I	N
C	R	A	N	E				B	A	R	N	S
B	A	S	S	E	T		D	I	M			
S	H	H			W	O	E		P	B	S	
				Z	O	O	S			A	H	S
A	L	I	C	E		Z	E	D		T	O	O
M	O	O	R	E		E	R	R		O	O	P
P	U	N	Y			S	T	Y		N	T	H

Puzzle 2

P	I	T	S		D	I	T		A	S	H	E
A	T	O	M		D	O	E		S	H	A	M
T	E	R	A		T	N	N		T	O	T	S
S	M	E	L	L		S	E	R	I	E	S	
			L	T	D		T	N	T			
E	L	A	P	S	E	S		S	C	R	A	P
K	I	L	O		S	H	A		H	O	M	E
E	L	A	T	E		E	A	S	I	E	S	T
			A	U	G		H	E	N			
	A	S	T	R	O	S		A	T	L	A	S
A	U	T	O		O	T	S		I	S	T	O
T	R	U	E		S	A	Y		M	A	I	L
L	A	B	S		E	R	N		E	T	T	E

Puzzle 3

C	A	N		A	D	A	M		G	E	R	E
A	R	E		L	E	I	A		A	M	E	R
S	T	E	E	L	E	R	S		L	O	A	N
A	S	T	A	I	R	E		R	A	T	S	
			T	E	E		D	E	S	I	S	T
A	S	H	E	S		S	O	N		C	U	E
S	W	A	N		S	O	S		L	O	R	E
K	E	N		S	E	T		L	A	N	E	S
S	E	D	A	T	E		S	A	M			
	T	I	P	S		T	E	N	A	N	T	S
S	P	C	A		C	O	N	C	R	E	T	E
L	E	A	R		E	L	S	E		L	O	W
R	A	P	T		O	L	E	S		L	P	S

Puzzle 4

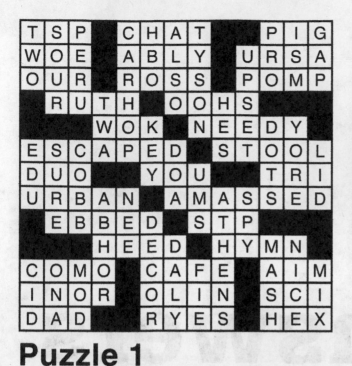

L	A	B	S		A	L	O	E		T	V	S
O	B	O	E		T	E	A	M		I	I	I
E	L	S	E		I	N	K	S		R	E	G
W	E	S	T		L	O	T		S	E	W	N
			H	A	T		R	S	T			
E	R	I	E	S		D	E	C	L	A	R	E
K	I	T		N	A	D	E	R		R	U	N
E	N	A	M	E	L	S		A	I	M	E	D
			T	R	A		P	M	S			
H	D	T	V		B	E	E		A	H	A	S
I	D	O		D	A	M	E		A	U	D	I
S	A	W		E	M	I	R		C	L	A	N
S	Y	N		M	A	T	S		S	A	M	E

Puzzle 5

B	R	A	D		P	A	R		H	M	O	S
R	O	L	E		T	I	E		A	U	N	T
A	T	T	A		A	M	S		S	L	E	D
S	C	A	R	F		S	E	N	S	E	S	
			M	A	C		T	E	L			
A	R	R	E	A	R	S		D	E	N	I	M
H	U	T			O	U	R			O	F	A
A	N	E	A	R		P	O	L	A	R	I	S
			C	A	P		B	O	N			
	N	A	C	H	O	S		L	I	S	P	S
M	O	R	E		S	H	A		M	O	A	T
E	A	T	S		T	I	M		A	L	L	Y
W	H	Y	S		S	P	A		L	O	S	E

Puzzle 6

O	P	T	S			H	R	S		F	L	A
G	L	E	E		P	E	E	N		R	O	D
L	I	N	E		A	F	R	O		A	N	D
E	E	N	Y		S	T	U		S	U	E	S
			A	C	T		N	A	P			
L	A	P		H	O	R		L	A	S	S	O
A	L	I		O	R	A	T	E		K	A	N
B	E	T	A	S		H	E	R		I	P	O
			G	E	L		A	T	O			
C	A	S	E		A	B	S		A	L	D	A
A	G	O		M	I	L	E		S	O	U	R
S	E	W		A	R	T	S		I	S	E	E
S	R	S		A	S	S			S	E	T	A

Puzzle 7

I	O	N			M	A	A			O	D	S
A	O	N	E		A	M	P		A	R	I	A
N	O	E	S		T	O	P		B	E	N	T
			T	I	E	S		S	A	L	E	S
E	N	T	E	R	S		B	U	S			
S	E	A	R	S		S	A	N	E	S	T	
P	S	T			T	U	T			T	O	O
	S	E	R	E	N	E		A	L	I	E	N
			E	M	T		S	P	A	R	S	E
B	A	S	E	S		S	I	R	S			
A	B	E	S		S	A	G		T	S	A	R
T	O	N	E		E	I	N		S	O	N	S
S	O	D			A	D	S			B	I	T

Puzzle 8

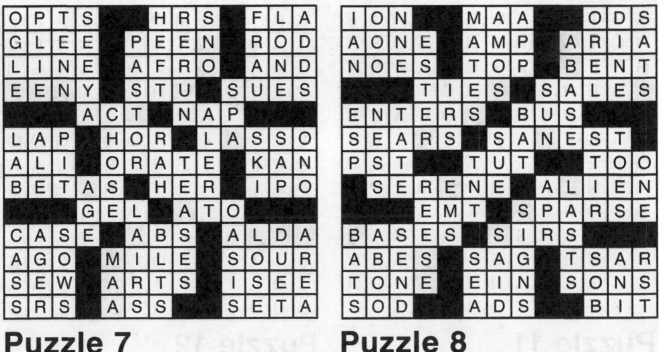

O	A	F			S	M	U	T		H	B	O
O	R	I	G		G	A	S	H		Y	E	A
O	M	E	N		T	A	C	O		P	A	R
			A	S	S	N		R	E	E	D	S
A	B	A	T	E		D	O	N	T			
G	A	S		E	S	P	N		C	O	N	N
O	M	S		S	T	A	M	P		M	O	O
G	A	T	E		I	K	E	A		N	U	N
			M	E	R	E		R	H	I	N	E
S	T	R	U	T		T	O	T	O			
P	O	E		H	T	T	P		S	C	A	M
A	D	D		Y	A	L	E		S	O	F	A
T	D	S		L	I	E	D			M	T	S

Puzzle 9

A	R	M	S		S	L	I	P		M	E	W
B	A	B	E		C	O	L	T		A	G	E
B	R	A	N		O	W	L	S		M	O	B
R	E	S	I	D	U	E			F	E	S	S
			O	R	R		C	A	D			
O	H	A	R	E		E	N	G	A	R	D	E
B	A	Y		S	H	O	N	E		E	Y	E
S	T	E	P	S	O	N		N	A	V	E	L
			L	Y	E		L	T	S			
P	L	A	Y			B	A	S	S	E	T	S
L	O	T		M	O	O	T		I	L	I	E
E	A	T		G	R	I	T		S	L	E	W
A	M	Y		M	I	L	E		T	A	R	S

Puzzle 10

A	H	A		S	I	P	S		S	W	A	P
N	O	T		A	R	C	H		T	O	R	A
G	E	E		G	A	T	E		A	W	R	Y
	S	E	R	A			S	C	I			
			U	S	E	S		O	R	A	L	S
T	A	L	E		L	E	T	S		L	E	A
O	L	E		C	L	E	A	T		T	A	P
M	O	N		H	A	R	T		M	A	P	S
S	T	O	R	E		S	A	A	B			
			O	R	S			N	A	S	T	
B	Y	E	S		P	S	A	T		I	A	M
E	A	S	E		A	N	N	E		N	R	A
E	Y	E	S		T	O	N	S		G	A	Y

Puzzle 11

K	R	I	S		M	O	W		B	A	R	S
I	A	M	A		T	A	I		A	S	E	C
E	V	E	S		S	T	D		S	I	G	H
V	E	T	S			H	E	A	T			
			Y	A	P			S	E	A	L	S
L	M	N		L	E	A	D	S		G	O	O
E	E	E		T	E	P	E	E		U	A	W
F	R	I		A	L	T	E	R		E	D	S
T	E	N	O	R			P	T	S			
			U	S	S	R			P	F	F	T
B	I	T	S		P	O	W		A	L	I	E
C	O	A	T		E	A	R		S	E	R	A
D	U	D	S		D	R	Y		M	E	S	S

Puzzle 12

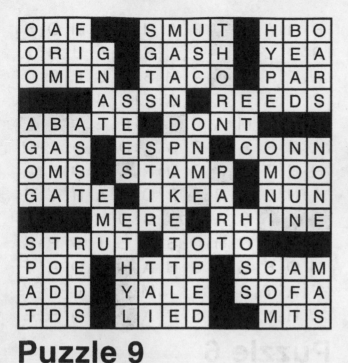

S	U	B		A	L	L			A	V	O	W
A	T	E		B	O	A	T		P	A	G	E
K	I	T		U	R	G	E		H	I	L	T
E	L	A	P	S	E		A	L	I	N	E	S
			H	E	N		P	A	D			
C	A	R	D			M	O	D		Z	O	O
O	P	U	S		B	U	T		G	E	A	R
P	E	G		N	O	D			R	E	F	S
			L	O	S		R	N	A			
A	S	I	A	N	S		O	O	D	L	E	S
R	A	N	T		E	Q	U	I		I	M	A
L	I	F	E		S	E	T	S		O	M	S
O	D	O	R			D	E	Y		N	Y	E

Puzzle 13

O	S	H	A		A	D	I	N		G	A	L
D	E	E	S		M	A	C	A	R	O	N	I
D	E	S	I		I	T	E	R	A	T	E	D
		I	N	O	N	E		R	I	O	T	S
L	A	T	I	N	O		P	O	D			
E	V	A	N	S		M	O	W		P	I	N
G	O	N	E		F	E	W		R	A	T	E
O	N	T		D	E	W		D	E	N	S	E
			R	E	B		R	E	L	O	A	D
D	R	A	I	N		T	O	N	E	R		
R	E	S	P	I	T	E	S		A	A	R	P
E	A	T	E	R	I	E	S		S	M	U	G
I	D	O		O	M	N	I		E	A	T	A

Puzzle 14

F	L	Y		B	L	A	B		U	S	D	A
D	I	E		L	O	V	E		N	O	U	N
A	P	P	E	A	R	E	D		L	O	C	K
			X	M	E	N		P	I	N	T	A
S	K	A	T	E		G	I	L	T			
H	E	I	R		R	E	B	A		G	L	O
E	N	R	A	G	E		I	T	A	L	I	C
L	O	Y		R	E	D	D		M	E	E	T
			W	A	K	E		C	A	N	D	O
I	T	C	H	Y		A	R	I	Z			
D	O	M	E		P	R	O	T	E	C	T	S
I	G	O	R		H	I	V	E		C	H	I
G	O	N	E		D	E	E	D		C	U	P

Puzzle 15

W	A	D	S		D	A	N		S	E	C	S
A	C	R	E		A	T	A		T	E	A	R
R	E	A	L		M	E	T		P	E	T	S
E	D	G	E			A	L	I	E			
			S	A	W	S		S	T	R	A	P
T	O	M		L	E	E		S	E	O	U	L
E	R	O	D	E	S		T	U	R	T	L	E
N	E	V	E	R		B	E	E		O	D	D
S	M	E	L	T		A	L	S	O			
			E	S	P	N			P	A	V	E
A	S	S	T		E	A	R		A	R	I	D
S	A	S	E		R	N	A		L	A	N	E
A	P	E	S		M	A	D		S	T	E	N

Puzzle 16

S	S	E		A	V	A			T	O	A	D
E	L	S		L	A	S	H		O	N	T	O
L	O	T		A	L	P	O		T	I	N	T
F	B	I		M	I	S	T	L	E	T	O	E
		M	O	O	D		T	I	M			
C	L	A	D			H	U	E		E	S	P
B	I	T	E	T	H	E	B	U	L	L	E	T
S	U	E		W	A	X			P	A	C	S
			M	I	R		T	O	S	S		
A	N	A	S	T	A	S	I	A		T	I	P
L	A	R	D		S	C	A	T		I	G	O
I	N	T	O		S	U	R	E		C	O	L
T	O	Y	S			D	A	S		S	T	L

Puzzle 17

A	B	C		O	C	T			F	I	T	S
B	O	O		C	E	E	S		A	C	E	S
C	O	M		U	S	M	C		T	H	A	N
S	T	E	E	L	S		O	T	C			
		A	L	A	N		T	O	A	S	T	S
A	N	G	O	R	A		T	A	T	T	O	O
B	O	A								R	U	T
U	N	I	T	E	S		S	N	E	E	R	S
T	E	N	A	N	T		P	E	P	E		
			R	O	E		A	G	A	T	H	A
T	R	I	G		E	Z	R	A		C	O	G
H	I	D	E		P	O	E	T		A	B	E
O	M	I	T			O	D	E		R	O	D

Puzzle 18

N	H	L		H	U	B			A	B	B	R
B	O	O		O	N	U	S		G	O	R	E
C	O	L		G	I	R	L		L	O	A	F
	P	L	U	T	O		A	M	O	N	G	
			P	I	N		L	O	W			
E	L	L	I	E		T	O	P		S	P	F
L	E	A	N		G	U	M		D	I	A	L
F	E	B		D	A	B		H	I	N	D	U
			F	E	Z		C	E	E			
	P	H	A	S	E		O	R	D	E	R	
B	L	O	C		B	A	B	E		L	O	P
C	O	S	T		O	U	R	S		M	B	A
D	Y	E	S			G	A	Y		S	S	W

Puzzle 19

C	R	A	M		P	U	B		A	L	U	M
S	I	R	E		E	S	E		R	A	Z	E
I	D	E	N	T	I	C	A	L	T	W	I	N
	S	A	S	H			M	I	L			
			A	U	L	D		L	E	E	R	S
B	O	O		D	A	R	T		S	L	A	W
R	U	N	S		Y	E	S		S	E	G	A
A	C	C	T		S	A	A	B		V	E	T
S	H	E	A	F		M	R	E	D			
			T	O	M			T	O	U	T	
E	P	L	U	R	I	B	U	S	U	N	U	M
L	E	A	R		N	A	M		S	I	N	O
F	A	M	E		E	S	S		E	X	A	M

Puzzle 20

B	Y	T	E		E	B	B		O	D	D	S
A	U	R	A		N	E	A		T	O	O	T
H	M	O	S		T	A	B		T	O	L	L
S	A	T	I	R	E		A	W	A	R	E	
			E	U	R		R	O	W			
S	T	A	R	T	E	R		E	A	S	E	L
I	S	H			D	I	P			R	Y	E
P	E	S	O	S		B	L	E	S	S	E	D
			C	I	A		E	S	T			
	S	T	A	R	R		A	C	R	O	S	S
L	E	I	S		N	O	S		O	H	O	H
E	A	V	E		A	W	E		L	I	S	A
T	R	O	Y		Z	E	D		L	O	O	M

Puzzle 21

C	P	A	S		L	A	L	A		L	I	V
P	U	L	P		O	N	E	B	Y	O	N	E
U	T	A	H		A	N	I	S	E	T	T	E
		N	E	E	D	S		O	N	T	O	P
L	E	A	R	N	S		H	R	S			
I	D	L	E	D		H	U	B		P	E	W
K	I	D	S		R	I	G		T	I	V	O
E	T	A		L	O	P		O	S	C	A	R
			M	A	T		C	R	E	A	S	E
H	O	M	E	R		P	A	R	T	Y		
O	N	E	L	I	N	E	R		S	U	E	S
R	E	S	T	A	R	E	A		E	N	V	Y
N	I	H		T	A	R	T		S	E	E	N

Puzzle 22

R	I	M	S		A	T	M		A	F	R	O
I	M	O	K		C	H	E		S	L	A	W
D	U	N	E		R	E	D		S	A	N	E
E	S	K	I	M	O		A	M	E	N	D	S
			N	A	B		L	E	N			
B	R	A		J	A	B		A	T	P	A	R
Y	O	K	E		T	U	E		S	E	M	I
E	N	A	C	T		N	A	G		R	P	M
			L	O	S		S	T	U			
C	A	S	I	N	O		T	O	N	S	I	L
A	S	A	P		N	N	E		A	T	N	O
A	T	M	S		G	E	R		R	U	N	G
N	O	S	E		S	A	N		M	D	S	E

Puzzle 23

I	G	O	R		C	H	E			F	H	A
T	O	B	E		R	E	V		C	L	A	D
T	O	I	L		T	W	I		H	E	L	D
O	P	T	I	C			C	L	E	A	T	S
			S	E	P		T	I	E			
I	D	A	H	O	A	N		T	R	Y	S	T
B	E	D			H	U	B			O	O	H
M	A	J	O	R		N	O	C	A	N	D	O
			V	E	T		P	O	T			
I	T	H	A	C	A			M	O	R	S	E
P	H	I	L		R	K	O		M	I	L	E
O	U	T	S		R	I	B		I	C	A	N
D	D	S			Y	D	S		C	O	P	Y

Puzzle 24

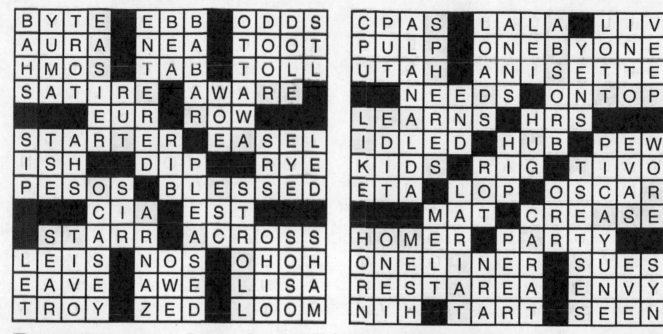

P	L	U	G		C	A	B	S		I	C	H
H	O	M	E		R	I	O	T		F	L	O
D	U	S	T		E	R	G	O		S	A	W
			S	W	A	Y		P	H	O	N	E
S	C	R	E	A	M		K	I	A			
S	L	O	T	H		P	E	T	I	T	E	
W	A	D			D	A	Y			R	P	M
	M	E	T	R	I	C		L	O	U	I	E
			H	O	P		D	E	T	E	C	T
A	P	L	U	S		N	A	T	O			
L	E	A		A	J	A	R		O	B	E	Y
E	E	G		R	O	P	E		L	U	N	A
G	P	S		Y	E	A	S		E	N	V	Y

Puzzle 25

S	G	T	S		L	A	D	S		L	O	P
A	L	E	C		A	B	E	L		A	T	A
N	O	D	E		U	C	L	A		T	I	N
			N	O	D			B	L	E	S	S
T	A	P	E	R		O	R	S	O			
I	N	A		B	A	B	A		R	E	B	A
D	E	N	Y		N	O	V		D	A	R	N
E	T	T	E		D	E	E	S		R	I	D
			L	E	I	S		A	G	N	E	S
R	A	S	P	S			E	M	U			
A	L	E		S	I	A	M		E	V	A	S
P	E	N		A	C	L	U		S	O	D	A
S	G	T		Y	E	A	S		S	L	O	W

Puzzle 26

M	A	T		O	F	F	S		S	T	E	P
R	Y	E		B	A	L	I		P	A	A	R
T	E	M	P	E	R	A	S		A	L	T	O
			E	Y	E	S		P	R	E	S	S
M	A	S	T	S		H	A	R	E			
I	A	T	E		S	I	N	E		N	R	A
S	H	O	R	T	A	N	D	S	W	E	E	T
S	S	W		O	C	T	A		A	M	F	M
			R	U	S	H		C	L	O	S	E
L	A	S	E	R		E	G	A	D			
A	N	N	S		E	P	I	S	O	D	E	S
S	K	I	T		P	A	S	T		R	E	P
S	A	P	S		A	N	T	E		S	K	Y

Puzzle 27

R	A	P		A	B	C	S		T	E	D	S
A	N	A		C	O	P	A		A	L	O	E
F	E	A	S	T	O	R	F	A	M	I	N	E
	T	R	I	O			E	S	P			
			D	R	O	P		H	A	S	T	E
I	T	B	E		G	I	V	E		L	E	E
T	H	E	B	E	R	L	I	N	W	A	L	L
L	A	D		N	E	O	N		A	W	L	S
L	I	S	T	S		T	E	A	S			
			O	U	T			C	T	R	L	
S	T	A	T	E	O	F	T	H	E	A	R	T
H	O	S	E		R	A	R	E		C	O	W
Y	A	P	S		N	A	Y	S		E	N	O

Puzzle 28

B	I	D	E		N	E	R	O		F	A	R
E	V	I	L		O	V	E	R	T	O	N	E
N	Y	S	E		S	E	P	A	R	A	T	E
		R	A	G	E	S		T	I	M	I	D
S	T	O	N	E	D		S	O	X			
A	R	B	O	R		B	A	R		T	L	C
G	O	E	R		J	O	G		S	O	I	L
S	I	D		L	A	W		H	Y	E	N	A
			V	O	W		R	E	S	T	E	D
F	L	O	A	T		P	I	N	T	O		
L	O	P	S	I	D	E	D		E	T	C	H
O	N	E	T	O	O	N	E		M	O	P	E
P	E	R		N	I	T	S		S	E	A	M

Puzzle 29

T	O	U	T		I	S	M		R	B	I	S
R	A	S	H		N	P	R		E	A	S	E
I	T	O	R		K	I	T		G	L	E	E
			E	A	S	T		O	G	L	E	S
B	E	S	E	T		T	E	R	I			
E	L	U	D	E		I	C	I	E	S	T	
N	I	N	O		O	N	O		J	A	I	L
	E	G	G	N	O	G		E	A	R	L	S
			N	E	H	I		S	C	A	L	D
A	D	M	I	T		M	A	S	K			
T	R	I	G		V	A	L		S	E	N	D
I	N	C	H		E	G	G		O	W	E	D
P	O	E	T		T	E	A		N	E	W	T

Puzzle 30

A	C	T	E	D		U	P	S		S	H	E
C	R	A	V	E		S	I	T		T	A	N
T	O	P	I	C		P	A	R		E	T	C
			T	A	S	S		I	M	P	E	L
C	A	B	A	L	A		T	V	A			
O	I	L			C	R	I	E	R	S		
P	L	E	D		R	I	D		T	E	S	H
		D	O	R	E	M	I			M	I	A
			P	H	D		E	T	H	I	C	S
M	I	N	E	O		B	R	I	E			
E	M	U		N	B	A		R	A	B	B	I
N	O	N		D	O	W		E	V	I	A	N
U	N	S		A	W	L		D	E	N	T	S

Puzzle 31

A	L	A	N		W	H	O		M	E	N	U
D	E	M	I		H	I	T		I	R	A	S
D	I	S	C		E	T	C		N	A	P	S
			K	E	N	T		U	N	S	E	R
L	I	F	E	R		H	O	P	E			
E	N	O	L	A		E	X	I	S	T	S	
O	K	R	A		E	C	O		O	R	A	L
	Y	A	N	K	E	E		S	T	O	L	E
			D	E	L	I		H	A	T	E	D
S	E	E	D	Y		L	E	A	F			
T	A	X	I		B	I	D		A	B	B	R
I	T	E	M		E	N	G		T	U	T	U
R	A	C	E		A	G	E		S	T	U	B

Puzzle 32

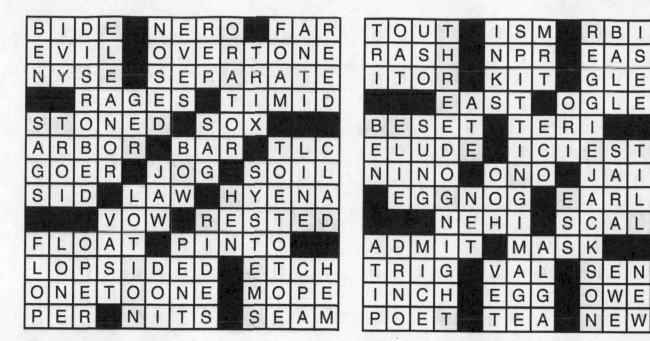

D	U	D			O	A	R	S		S	U	N
O	H	O	H		F	R	E	T		A	P	U
C	O	V	E		T	A	D	A		Y	O	N
S	H	E	A	R		B	O	G		O	N	S
			D	I	A	L		S	Y	N		
C	H	I		F	L	E	W		T	A	C	T
O	R	N	A	T	E		A	N	D	R	E	A
P	S	A	T		X	E	N	A		A	L	T
		S	A	C		L	E	G	S			
C	H	E		O	W	N		S	T	A	S	H
H	A	N		S	A	I	D		A	X	E	D
A	N	S		T	I	N	A		B	E	R	T
D	D	E		S	L	O	B			L	A	V

Puzzle 33

C	O	N			G	A	P	S		A	L	L
O	R	E	S		I	R	O	N		T	O	A
T	E	R	N		N	I	L	E		L	I	D
S	O	F	A	S		S	E	A	B	A	S	S
			P	U	N	T		D	E	N		
P	O	P		D	E	A	L		S	T	U	D
M	O	R	O	S	E		A	T	T	I	R	E
S	H	E	D		D	O	C	K		S	I	C
		S	D	I		C	E	O	S			
E	Y	E	S	O	R	E		S	L	A	S	H
T	E	N		W	E	A	N		A	W	A	Y
C	A	T		A	N	N	A		M	E	N	D
H	R	S		N	O	S	Y			D	D	E

Puzzle 34

B	R	A	Y		S	T	S		M	E	A	T
R	O	M	E		T	W	A		A	L	P	S
A	M	Y	S		O	I	L		D	E	P	P
			S	S	N		T	R	A	C	T	S
S	A	L	I	N	E		I	A	M			
A	D	O	R	E		O	N	T		C	S	I
F	I	N		A	D	D	E	R		O	T	S
E	N	G		K	I	D		A	T	E	A	M
			T	E	L		S	C	E	N	T	S
A	S	P	I	R	E		P	E	N			
C	L	A	M		M	N	O		S	U	I	T
L	U	T	E		M	E	T		E	G	G	O
U	G	H	S		A	B	S		S	H	O	W

Puzzle 35

O	K	E	D		I	S	M		S	L	A	M
S	I	Z	E		S	K	I		T	O	R	I
H	E	R	R		H	I	D		R	U	T	S
A	V	A	I	L		S	A	N	I	T	Y	
			D	E	N		S	U	P			
E	G	G	E	D	O	N		T	E	R	M	S
L	E	T			N	O	G			O	A	K
F	R	E	S	H		V	E	R	A	N	D	A
			E	B	B		L	A	V			
	I	G	N	O	R	E		M	E	C	C	A
O	K	L	A		O	R	G		R	O	L	L
H	E	A	T		I	M	A		T	R	A	P
M	A	D	E		L	A	Y		S	E	W	S

Puzzle 36

U	P	I	N		O	P	T	S		M	G	M
M	O	N	A		B	E	E	T		A	L	A
P	E	C	S		E	I	N	E		N	U	T
			C	R	Y		E	V	E	N	T	S
D	O	N	A	T	E		T	E	N			
A	D	O	R	E	D		S	N	E	A	K	
D	O	T								M	A	J
	R	A	R	E	R		M	A	R	I	N	E
			E	X	E		E	V	E	N	E	D
S	M	O	O	T	H		A	A	H			
E	D	U		E	E	L	S		E	G	G	S
E	S	T		N	A	I	L		A	L	O	T
D	E	S		T	R	E	Y		T	O	D	D

Puzzle 37

M	E	T	A		S	C	H			J	E	D
E	A	R	N		T	U	E		R	A	M	A
G	R	I	T		R	E	M		A	V	I	D
A	L	B	I	N	O		A	V	I	A	T	E
			C	A	B		N	A	N			
M	P	H		W	E	B		N	E	R	D	Y
D	E	E	M		S	I	S		D	A	R	E
S	P	R	A	T		B	O	W		T	S	P
			R	O	D		L	A	N			
E	D	I	T	O	R		O	R	I	G	I	N
M	A	T	H		I	B	M		N	O	T	A
U	R	S	A		L	E	O		T	R	O	Y
S	K	Y			L	E	N		H	E	N	S

Puzzle 38

O	A	T			P	A	H		A	L	L	I
C	P	A	S		A	N	A		L	E	A	F
T	O	T	E		C	D	S		E	I	N	S
A	P	A	C	H	E		S	I	X			
			R	E	S	A	L	E		M	S	G
S	A	L	E	M		G	E	R		A	O	L
P	L	O	T		M	R	S		T	U	T	U
R	I	O		R	A	E		A	R	I	S	E
Y	E	P		A	N	E	M	I	A			
			Y	T	D		A	D	I	D	A	S
M	I	T	E		A	N	I		N	E	R	O
O	N	A	N		T	N	N		S	P	A	Y
S	K	I	S		E	W	E			P	B	S

Puzzle 39

I	L	E	T		M	E	D		S	P	I	T
M	I	M	E		S	K	Y		A	L	F	A
O	M	I	T		G	E	E		T	O	S	S
K	E	R	R			D	R	E	I			
			A	T	L			U	N	C	A	P
O	D	D		R	O	P	E	R		O	J	S
C	U	E		A	B	O	V	E		L	A	S
T	A	N		D	E	R	E	K		A	R	T
A	L	G	A	E			R	A	P			
			U	R	L	S			I	C	B	M
M	O	R	N		I	N	C		T	O	R	Y
D	O	N	T		P	A	H		A	N	I	N
S	P	A	S		S	P	A		S	E	G	A

Puzzle 40

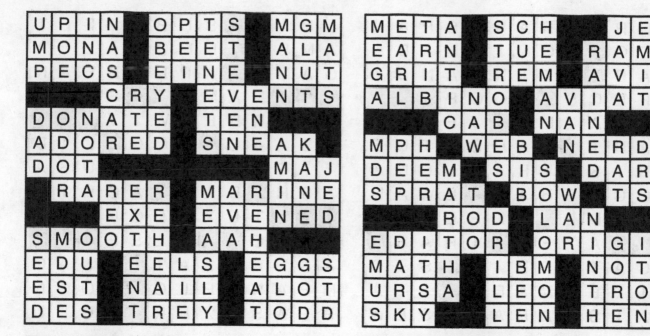

O	R	R		B	R	A	S		S	P	A	N
R	E	O		L	O	N	I		H	A	D	A
G	A	P		A	T	T	N		A	N	D	Y
	P	E	C	S			O	O	P			
			A	T	M	S		J	E	S	T	S
B	A	R	T		O	A	R	S		T	U	E
I	R	I	S		T	R	A		L	E	N	A
D	O	C		S	H	A	G		E	W	A	N
S	W	E	D	E		H	E	R	E			
			A	X	E			I	R	A	S	
S	C	A	T		R	B	I	S		S	I	C
L	I	F	E		M	A	D	E		I	T	A
O	A	T	S		A	H	A	S		S	E	W

Puzzle 41

L	U	I	S		S	U	B		P	F	F	T
A	M	B	I		H	M	O		A	L	L	A
G	A	M	E		A	P	B		B	E	A	N
			R	A	M	S			S	A	N	K
P	I	E	R	R	E		W	I	T			
I	S	A	A	C		D	O	C		C	I	D
T	I	C		A	L	O	N	E		U	S	A
A	S	H		D	A	H		A	C	R	I	D
			T	E	X		E	G	R	E	T	S
L	I	T	E			K	L	E	E			
A	S	H	E		F	A	T		S	L	A	G
M	E	A	N		E	L	O		T	O	O	N
P	E	W	S		Z	E	N		S	U	L	U

Puzzle 42

C	H	I		O	R	A			B	E	L	A
O	U	T		M	A	G	I		R	A	I	N
L	E	S	S	E	N	E	D		E	V	A	N
			I	N	K		C	I	N	E	M	A
S	T	I	R	S		L	A	D	D			
H	O	G	S		F	A	R	E	A	S	T	
H	E	E		L	I	N	D	A		P	I	G
	S	T	R	A	N	D	S		L	U	L	U
			A	L	A	S		S	I	R	E	N
R	A	G	T	A	G		M	A	O			
O	B	I	T		L	E	A	R	N	E	R	S
B	E	L	L		E	L	L	A		B	O	A
E	L	L	E			M	E	N		B	B	C

Puzzle 43

P	T	A		S	O	F	A		A	C	D	C
Y	E	N		O	V	I	D		V	I	A	L
R	A	D		N	E	R	D		O	A	H	U
E	L	I	X	I	R		O	R	I	O	L	E
			M	A	T		N	E	D			
P	Y	L	E			M	T	V		D	D	S
J	O	A	N		L	E	O		L	O	O	P
S	U	P		F	E	W			O	H	M	Y
			M	O	O		F	L	U			
T	S	H	I	R	T		R	O	D	E	N	T
U	P	I	N		A	M	E	N		G	E	E
B	A	K	E		R	A	R	E		G	R	R
A	M	E	S		D	Y	E	R		Y	O	N

Puzzle 44

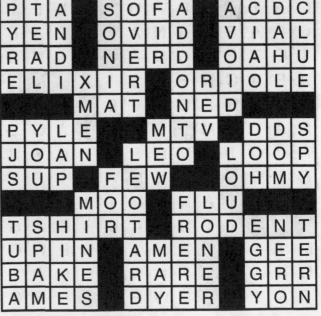

D	A	F	T		S	I	T		M	O	B	S
A	C	R	E		I	V	Y		E	N	Y	A
W	H	E	E		D	E	L		A	M	E	X
N	E	T	T	L	E		E	D	G	E	S	
			H	I	C		R	Y	E			
M	O	B		L	A	X		E	R	R	O	L
I	F	I			R	E	M			U	F	O
C	A	C	T	I		S	A	C		N	F	L
			A	P	T		L	P	S			
	S	A	V	O	R		T	R	E	A	T	S
D	U	N	E		E	Y	E		L	R	O	N
E	M	I	R		N	O	S		M	O	N	O
C	O	N	N		D	U	E		A	N	E	W

Puzzle 45

T	A	M	P		D	O	I		N	O	V	A
B	L	E	U		A	S	K		A	L	A	S
S	E	N	T	E	N	C	E		S	I	N	K
P	C	S		S	T	A		M	A	N	E	S
			E	T	E	R	N	A	L			
L	I	D	S			S	A	Y		N	O	T
A	P	O	L	L	O		W	A	R	S	A	W
V	O	W		O	N	S			P	A	R	A
			A	N	A	H	E	I	M			
S	L	A	N	G		A	L	S		O	R	G
H	O	P	I		I	S	L	A	N	D	E	R
O	L	E	S		R	T	E		B	O	N	O
O	L	D	E		K	A	N		C	R	O	W

Puzzle 46

O	R	I		C	A	B		A	R	M	O	R
P	A	N		A	R	E		L	E	O	N	E
T	V	A		M	I	D		T	A	L	C	S
S	I	N	C	E				O	C	T	E	T
			B	O	A		P	S	T			
O	F	F	S		R	U	E		S	I	L	T
N	R	A			A	S	S			S	A	W
E	O	N	S		B	E	T		A	H	S	O
			H	I	S		S	O	X			
R	I	P	E	N				N	E	A	R	S
A	D	I	E	U		L	O	S		S	E	A
M	E	E	T	S		A	W	E		O	A	R
P	A	R	S	E		Y	E	T		F	D	A

Puzzle 47

A	C	E	S		A	M	I		A	B	R	A
M	E	O	W		S	O	N		S	U	E	T
P	O	N	E		O	T	S		I	L	E	T
			D	A	N				A	B	L	Y
A	L	L	E	G	E		M	A	N			
L	O	O	S	E		B	A	D		I	D	A
M	I	A		N	E	A	T	O		C	A	P
A	N	N		D	N	A		R	E	E	V	E
			H	A	D		L	E	N	S	E	S
C	A	P	O				E	R	A			
O	W	E	S		G	P	A		C	R	A	M
B	O	L	T		E	L	S		T	U	G	S
B	L	T	S		M	O	E		S	M	O	G

Puzzle 48

P	A	C			D	D	S			H	I	C
I	C	O	N		A	Y	E		B	O	N	E
A	T	T	E	N	D	E	E		O	N	O	R
			V	I	E			E	X	E	R	T
L	A	P	E	L		S	I	T	E			
I	G	O	R			H	E	A	R	S	T	
P	E	N	S		P	E	R		S	E	A	N
	S	E	A	L	E	D			H	A	R	E
			Y	E	N	S		F	O	S	S	E
S	P	A	D	E			P	O	R			
L	E	V	I		P	E	A	R	T	R	E	E
E	L	I	E		R	E	D		S	U	N	G
W	E	D			O	K	S			B	E	G

Puzzle 49

B	E	G			A	D	J		B	L	O	B
A	X	I	S		L	O	O		R	I	P	E
J	E	S	T		L	A	B		I	M	E	T
A	S	T	U	T	E			Z	E	B	R	A
			C	A	N	A	D	A				
E	D	I	C	T		D	O	G		E	N	G
K	E	N	O		B	O	W		S	W	I	M
E	L	K		S	U	B		I	N	E	P	T
				P	R	E	S	T	O			
S	H	E	L	F			M	O	O	L	A	H
H	U	G	O		M	I	A		P	O	L	O
E	G	G	O		U	S	S		S	I	L	L
D	E	S	K		M	P	H			S	A	Y

Puzzle 50

D	A	D	A		D	A	M	S		C	D	S
I	M	A	C		N	C	A	A		L	E	T
B	O	T	H		A	C	I	D		O	F	A
S	K	E	E	T		O	N	A		S	T	Y
				I	E	R		T	H	E		
I	D	O		L	A	D	D		I	O	W	A
S	O	V	I	E	T		A	C	T	U	A	L
A	G	E	R		A	E	R	O		T	R	I
		R	E	C		M	E	N				
A	H	S		R	T	E		S	A	L	T	S
H	E	E		A	I	R	S		C	I	A	O
M	A	E		S	K	I	N		C	A	R	A
E	R	R		S	I	L	O		T	R	A	P

Puzzle 51

L	A	S	H		A	S	S		P	S	S	T
M	D	S	E		L	O	S		I	T	O	R
N	O	T	A		D	O	N		E	Y	R	E
			D	E	A	N		T	R	E	E	S
A	P	R	O	N		E	P	I	C			
L	E	A	V	E		R	E	C	E	S	S	
T	A	K	E		T	O	T		B	E	A	T
	T	E	R	R	O	R		A	R	E	N	A
			H	O	W	L		T	O	N	G	S
S	T	E	E	D		A	R	M	S			
C	O	R	E		P	T	A		N	A	S	A
U	T	I	L		R	E	L		A	M	I	N
D	O	E	S		O	R	E		N	A	T	S

Puzzle 52

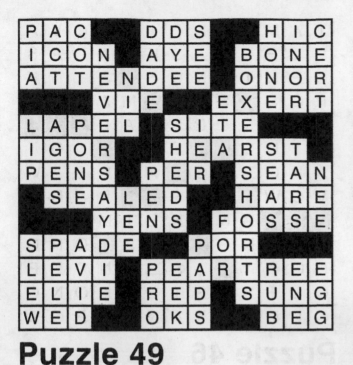

P	J	S			A	M	O	K		B	I	D
I	O	U	S		R	E	N	O		O	N	O
P	E	N	N		A	M	E	R		S	D	I
			U	P	T	O		E	P	C	O	T
T	R	I	B	E			V	A	T			
H	O	P		G	A	Y	E		A	P	P	T
A	T	O		S	P	E	N	D		R	A	H
T	O	D	D		A	N	T	E		O	N	A
			U	R	L			S	E	W	E	R
L	A	T	H	E		S	K	I	D			
I	Q	S		A	G	U	E		D	A	S	H
S	U	P		R	O	L	L		Y	M	C	A
T	A	S		S	O	U	P			Y	I	N

Puzzle 53

A	T	T	N		B	O	N		A	M	B	I
T	H	R	U		I	P	O		D	I	E	D
T	E	E	N	A	G	E	R		O	R	S	O
A	M	Y		W	O	N		F	R	E	T	S
			G	E	T	E	V	E	N			
P	I	T	T			D	I	T		P	L	Y
E	A	S	E	U	P		M	E	T	E	O	R
I	N	K		M	O	T			V	A	N	S
			A	P	R	O	P	O	S			
S	T	O	P	S		M	O	W		E	G	G
H	A	R	P		T	A	I	L	G	A	T	E
O	R	E	L		I	T	S		I	S	O	N
T	A	M	E		M	O	E		N	Y	S	E

Puzzle 54

A	M	C		R	O	D			T	I	N	Y
N	A	H		O	R	E	L		O	N	E	I
T	I	E		D	E	C	A		S	C	A	N
E	N	A	M	E	L		Y	D	S			
		T	A	O	S		E	R	E	C	T	S
U	N	E	A	S	E		R	E	S	E	A	T
S	O	D								A	P	U
E	L	O	I	S	E		A	R	I	S	E	N
S	O	N	A	T	A		B	O	R	E		
			G	U	T		S	T	E	L	L	A
A	F	A	R		I	G	E	T		E	U	R
P	A	R	E		N	I	N	E		S	A	O
O	B	I	E			S	T	N		S	U	N

Puzzle 55

C	A	W			C	B	E	R		S	H	A
O	P	E	D		I	O	W	A		T	I	S
L	E	E	R		D	R	A	T		I	R	K
E	X	P	E	L		E	N	T	I	C	E	S
		I	D	I	G			Y	A	K		
U	R	N		L	O	I	N		M	I	T	T
R	U	G		T	O	D	A	Y		N	A	W
L	E	W	D		P	A	P	A		T	R	I
		I	R	S			A	R	C	H		
O	R	L	E	A	N	S		N	O	E	L	S
V	O	L		N	O	N	O		S	M	U	T
I	P	O		T	R	I	B		T	U	N	E
D	E	W		A	M	P	S			D	A	M

Puzzle 56

S	P	F		I	F	S		D	E	V	I	L
L	O	A		N	I	H		O	P	I	N	E
U	P	I		D	R	Y		D	I	S	C	O
M	E	R	C	I				G	L	E	A	N
			B	A	S		C	E	O			
A	Y	E	S		T	H	Y		G	A	L	L
D	E	N			R	E	C			P	I	T
J	A	V	A		A	W	L		S	P	U	D
			N	N	W		E	E	K			
T	O	N	T	O				V	I	S	T	A
A	T	O	L	L		B	Y	E		T	E	L
B	I	N	E	T		B	O	N		A	S	P
S	C	O	R	E		C	U	T		G	T	O

Puzzle 57

T	E	E	S		A	H	E	M		T	W	A
A	X	L	E		L	U	S	T		H	A	W
O	P	E	C		L	E	S	S		R	Y	E
S	O	M	E		E	Y	E		C	U	S	S
			D	R	Y		N	A	N			
R	O	M	E	O		I	C	I	N	E	S	S
I	F	I		P	A	C	E	R		R	O	E
M	A	C	H	E	T	E		E	A	S	Y	A
			E	S	S		D	D	T			
S	W	A	Y		T	U	E		T	O	N	S
P	H	D		V	A	S	E		I	V	A	N
O	O	O		O	K	E	D		L	E	N	O
T	A	S		W	E	D	S		A	R	O	W

Puzzle 58

P	O	K	E		S	C	O	T		M	I	A
E	K	E	S		T	O	D	O		I	T	S
P	I	E	S		R	O	S	Y		S	C	H
	E	L	A	T	E	S			A	C	H	Y
			Y	A	P		R	E	X			
C	H	A	S	M		G	E	N	E	T	I	C
B	U	S		A	L	O	F	T		I	C	U
S	T	A	R	L	I	T		R	A	C	E	D
			R	E	V		F	A	R			
C	A	R	S			C	A	P	O	T	E	
A	P	E		T	O	E	S		M	O	N	A
P	A	T		R	U	N	T		A	R	C	S
O	L	D		A	R	T	S		S	A	L	K

Puzzle 59

B	R	A	T		P	H	I	L		P	U	T
L	O	S	E		R	U	D	E		U	R	I
T	Y	P	E		I	N	S	T		P	A	M
			M	U	M			M	A	P	L	E
S	W	I	S	S		T	E	E	N	Y		
P	I	N		C	O	R	N		O	L	I	N
U	S	A	F		R	E	C		N	O	D	E
D	E	L	I		B	A	L	E		V	O	L
		A	N	G	S	T		S	H	E	L	L
A	F	T	E	R			B	E	A			
W	A	H		A	L	L	Y		R	I	F	T
L	I	E		S	O	O	T		E	V	E	N
S	L	R		P	A	G	E		S	E	W	N

Puzzle 60

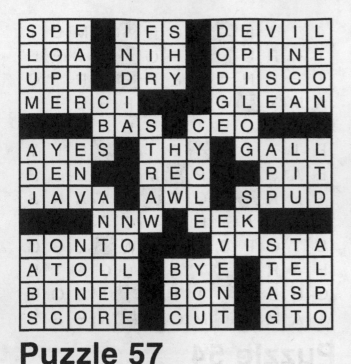

L	I	P	S		S	L	O	B		D	O	S
P	L	E	A		H	A	I	R		U	P	C
G	L	A	D		Y	U	L	E		D	E	A
A	S	K	E	D		R	E	E	L	E	C	T
				O	V	E	R	D	O			
A	B	C		M	E	L			S	A	C	K
T	O	U	P	E	E		F	O	S	S	I	L
M	A	D	E			A	R	K		H	A	M
			O	L	I	V	I	A				
I	R	O	N	O	R	E		Y	O	D	E	L
N	O	W		C	A	N	S		R	I	C	E
D	O	E		A	Q	U	A		I	M	O	N
Y	T	D		L	I	E	D		G	E	N	T

Puzzle 61

T	E	N	N			B	C	D		S	A	M
S	P	E	A	K		R	E	A		M	N	O
P	A	T	T	I		U	R	N		I	N	N
				M	U	T	E			L	O	O
L	M	N			N	E	A		D	E	Y	
T	A	I	P	E	I		L	O	Y			
D	E	P	O	T				M	E	R	G	E
			R	A	D		A	S	S	E	T	S
	K	A	T		E	P	I			P	O	P
I	N	D			C	A	R	T				
N	E	D		M	R	I		S	H	A	F	T
C	A	T		P	E	N		K	O	A	L	A
A	D	O		H	E	E			T	H	U	D

Puzzle 62

H	U	G	S		U	F	O	S		L	I	P
I	N	A	N		T	R	A	P		E	V	A
S	O	L	I	T	A	I	R	E		M	A	T
			D	U	H			C	L	O	N	E
P	O	S	E	R		O	R	S	O	N		
A	R	M		F	I	N	E		A	L	F	A
I	C	E	D		Z	E	E		M	A	I	M
D	A	L	E		O	A	K	S		W	R	Y
		L	E	N	D	L		N	O	S	E	S
A	T	A	R	I			P	A	R			
B	U	R		C	A	N	O	P	E	N	E	R
E	R	A		E	K	E	D		O	B	E	Y
T	N	T		R	A	T	S		S	A	K	E

Puzzle 63

I	N	N			C	A	W	S		S	E	T
L	E	A	K		A	T	I	T		E	V	E
L	A	M	E		D	R	N	O		M	I	R
S	T	E	E	R		I	S	R	A	E	L	I
			N	I	B	S		M	C	S		
S	S	T		T	I	K	I		H	T	T	P
T	E	E	T	E	R		S	L	E	E	V	E
N	C	A	A		D	A	L	E		R	A	W
		R	K	O		R	E	N	T			
S	C	I	E	N	C	E		T	I	N	T	S
L	O	N		T	O	T	S		C	O	O	L
A	L	T		A	D	O	S		S	I	D	E
G	T	O		P	E	O	N			R	O	W

Puzzle 64

S	N	I	P		R	C	A			D	N	A
C	A	R	E		A	O	L		C	R	E	W
U	N	I	T		T	O	E		R	E	A	L
M	U	S	I	C	A	L	C	H	A	I	R	S
			T	U	T		S	A	N			
G	P	A		P	A	W		Y	E	A	S	T
U	R	N	S		T	E	D		S	O	L	D
M	E	N	L	O		B	E	D		K	O	S
			A	N	T		S	U	N			
C	O	U	N	T	R	Y	C	O	U	S	I	N
H	I	N	T		A	V	E		R	E	B	A
A	N	T	S		M	E	N		S	P	E	D
T	K	O			P	S	T		E	T	T	A

Puzzle 65

S	Y	N	C		A	R	C	H		C	C	C
H	E	I	R		V	A	S	E		Z	O	O
H	A	L	O		I	W	I	N		A	O	K
			O	J	S			C	A	R	T	E
C	H	I	N	A		D	U	E	L			
R	O	W		N	O	A	H		E	A	R	P
A	W	A	Y		H	M	O		X	R	A	Y
M	E	S	A		N	E	H	I		M	I	L
			L	A	O	S		S	T	Y	L	E
E	T	H	E	L			C	H	A			
B	E	E		I	D	L	Y		B	R	A	D
B	R	R		G	E	E	S		L	A	I	R
S	I	B		N	E	X	T		E	D	D	Y

Puzzle 66

H	E	R	E		S	H	A		S	P	I	N
A	D	A	M		M	O	S		C	O	C	A
M	U	N	I		A	R	K		O	K	A	Y
			N	H	L				L	E	N	S
A	P	P	E	A	L		M	U	D			
N	A	O	M	I		R	I	G		T	A	D
D	I	P		R	H	O	D	A		I	C	U
Y	R	S		D	O	W		N	A	K	E	D
			C	O	G		A	D	M	I	R	E
C	Z	A	R				M	A	O			
L	A	T	E		C	H	E		E	M	M	Y
O	N	I	T		R	U	N		B	R	E	D
P	E	P	E		Y	T	D		A	I	D	S

Puzzle 67

M	A	S	C		S	C	I		W	H	A	T
O	C	T	O		O	U	R		H	O	S	S
P	E	S	O		N	B	A		I	O	W	A
			L	P	G	A		O	T	T	E	R
A	S	C	O	T		G	O	R	E			
L	E	A	N	S		O	R	D	E	R	S	
S	A	G	E		H	O	G		L	O	T	S
	T	E	S	T	E	D		D	E	T	E	R
			H	I	F	I		O	P	E	N	S
O	L	S	E	N		N	A	S	H			
R	U	L	E		U	G	H		A	N	D	I
B	A	I	L		P	J	S		N	O	O	N
S	U	D	S		C	R	O		T	R	E	K

Puzzle 68

R	D	S	■	L	E	G	■	■	S	A	G	A
Y	E	P	■	A	L	O	E	■	A	K	I	N
E	L	E	C	T	I	O	N	■	T	A	N	S
S	A	C	H	E	T	■	T	W	A	■	■	■
■	■	■	E	X	E	■	R	E	N	T	S	■
A	M	Y	S	■	■	V	E	T	■	R	I	G
P	E	A	S	■	F	E	E	■	C	O	G	S
P	A	L	■	P	R	E	■	■	A	N	N	A
■	T	E	A	S	E	■	A	P	U	■	■	■
■	■	■	T	I	E	■	R	A	S	P	E	D
S	O	S	O	■	S	T	O	N	E	A	G	E
O	X	E	N	■	T	O	M	S	■	T	O	N
D	O	P	E	■	■	Y	A	Y	■	E	S	S

Puzzle 69

D	I	M	■	T	R	O	D	■	S	O	D	A
O	L	E	■	R	O	D	E	■	T	T	O	P
N	I	T	■	A	L	D	A	■	E	I	N	E
S	E	A	N	C	E	■	■	L	A	C	E	S
■	■	■	O	T	S	■	W	O	K	■	■	■
L	I	F	T	■	■	B	A	G	■	G	I	G
B	L	U	E	I	N	T	H	E	F	A	C	E
S	L	R	■	T	R	U	■	■	A	B	U	T
■	■	■	S	T	A	■	A	B	S	■	■	■
P	L	A	T	O	■	■	A	R	T	I	S	T
O	A	H	U	■	F	O	R	A	■	N	Y	E
O	V	E	N	■	I	D	O	S	■	T	N	N
H	A	M	S	■	T	E	N	S	■	L	C	D

Puzzle 70

C	C	C	■	S	T	P	■	■	S	E	N	D
A	P	O	■	T	I	E	S	■	O	V	I	D
S	A	T	■	A	C	E	T	Y	L	E	N	E
A	S	T	O	N	■	N	O	V	A	■	■	■
■	■	O	T	C	■	■	L	E	R	N	E	R
A	N	N	I	E	■	W	E	S	■	E	L	O
F	I	G	S	■	L	E	N	■	N	A	I	L
A	N	I	■	M	I	T	■	O	C	T	A	L
R	E	N	T	A	L	■	■	R	A	F	■	■
■	■	■	E	R	A	S	■	T	A	R	P	S
I	D	O	N	T	C	A	R	E	■	E	I	N
S	A	W	S	■	S	L	U	G	■	A	P	U
P	Y	L	E	■	■	T	E	A	■	K	E	G

Puzzle 71

F	A	T	S	■	A	B	C	■	L	O	V	E
C	O	V	E	■	P	O	R	■	E	B	A	Y
C	L	A	P	■	P	G	A	■	T	I	N	E
■	■	■	I	T	A	■	M	A	T	T	E	R
E	C	L	A	I	R	■	P	I	E	■	■	■
G	L	O	■	N	E	W	■	D	R	A	M	A
G	A	G	■	■	L	A	M	■	■	R	A	W
S	N	O	U	T	■	R	A	F	■	U	K	E
■	■	■	T	H	E	■	E	L	A	T	E	D
S	A	L	M	O	N	■	S	U	B	■	■	■
E	X	P	O	■	D	D	T	■	B	L	U	E
L	E	G	S	■	O	U	R	■	O	O	P	S
F	L	A	T	■	W	H	O	■	T	O	I	L

Puzzle 72

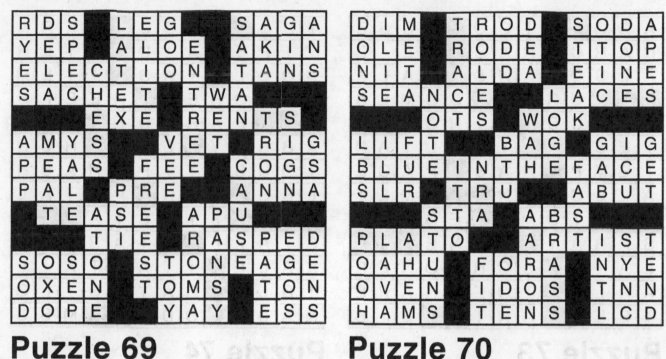

A	G	O			I	C	U			S	S	E
N	A	R	C		R	A	S		S	E	A	L
A	L	S	O	R	A	N	S		T	A	L	K
			U	R	S	A		D	O	M	E	S
E	P	I	C	S		D	I	N	O			
T	E	S	H			I	T	A	L	I	A	N
T	E	M	P		H	A	S		P	A	G	E
A	L	S	O	R	A	N			I	M	E	T
			T	O	M	B		E	G	A	D	S
S	P	R	A	Y		A	C	N	E			
L	A	I	T		S	C	H	O	O	N	E	R
A	R	L	O		T	O	E		N	A	P	E
T	S	E			A	N	T			B	I	B

Puzzle 73

T	D	S			C	C	C		O	K	R	A
Y	I	P	E		A	I	D		P	I	E	R
N	O	E	L		T	A	S		I	T	E	M
E	N	C	O	R	E			R	E	E	F	S
			P	A	R	A	D	E				
A	B	B	E	Y		L	I	D		H	U	N
I	O	U	S		T	I	P		H	A	S	H
L	B	S		O	W	N		P	E	T	A	L
				F	I	E	S	T	A			
S	T	A	F	F			T	A	R	M	A	C
K	A	L	E		I	T	A		T	A	I	L
I	D	L	E		G	A	Y		S	I	L	O
N	A	S	T		O	D	S			M	S	G

Puzzle 74

S	A	G	S		C	E	E		D	E	A	R
E	L	L	E		A	R	M		A	S	I	A
E	L	E	C	T	R	I	C		D	O	L	T
M	A	N		R	A	C	E	R		T	S	E
			S	E	T		E	I	N	E		
P	A	S	T	E	S		S	N	A	R	E	S
A	R	E	A						M	I	S	T
T	I	A	R	A	S		E	L	E	C	T	S
		S	E	N	T		S	I	S			
S	A	C		T	R	A	C	E		B	A	G
E	X	A	M		E	L	O	N	G	A	T	E
A	L	P	O		S	L	R		S	L	A	T
S	E	E	P		S	S	T		A	D	D	S

Puzzle 75

O	P	A	L		M	A	O		P	I	N	G
R	I	S	E		A	M	C		A	R	I	A
A	S	S	T		P	O	T		Y	A	N	G
L	A	N	G			R	O	O	M			
			O	L	G	A		R	E	S	O	D
L	B	S		O	I	L		A	N	I	M	E
A	L	O	H	A	S		O	C	T	A	N	E
S	A	L	O	N		A	W	L		M	I	D
T	H	E	S	E		N	E	E	T			
			T	R	A	Y			R	E	D	D
D	I	M	E		L	O	G		A	W	A	Y
E	V	A	S		U	N	S		P	O	L	E
L	Y	E	S		M	E	A		S	K	I	D

Puzzle 76

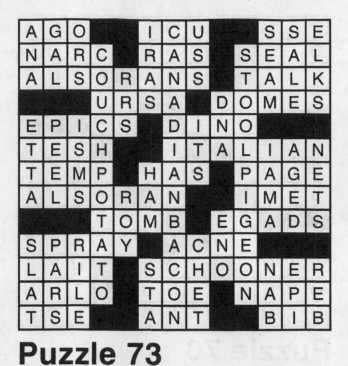

O	R	B		S	A	G			K	A	T	E
L	E	E		O	K	A	Y		A	V	I	D
D	E	E		U	R	G	E		B	I	D	E
E	L	P	A	S	O		L	O	O	S	E	N
			V	A	N		L	A	B			
M	I	R	O			W	O	K		D	O	S
O	V	E	N		H	O	W		D	E	N	T
O	Y	L		B	O	N			E	Y	E	D
			P	E	N		D	A	M			
S	A	L	U	T	E		I	N	S	T	E	P
C	H	A	R		S	N	A	G		O	X	O
A	S	I	S		T	Y	N	E		R	I	O
N	O	D	E			E	E	L		N	T	H

Puzzle 77

P	I	T	S		E	V	A		R	O	T	O
I	R	A	N		S	I	N		A	K	I	N
N	A	T	O		T	E	D		S	I	N	E
			R	N	A		E	X	C	E	S	S
A	S	S	E	N	T		S	E	A			
S	P	Y		W	E	D		S	L	E	D	S
I	A	N			S	U	E			V	O	W
A	S	C	I	I		O	Y	L		I	T	A
			N	I	L		E	Y	E	L	E	T
G	O	A	L	I	E		L	E	X			
U	R	G	E		D	D	E		A	S	H	E
S	C	O	T		G	O	T		M	A	A	M
T	A	G	S		E	M	S		S	W	I	T

Puzzle 78

F	A	T	E		T	O	P	S		T	O	E
A	P	A	L		O	R	A	L		A	P	T
N	E	T	S		S	A	D	E		G	U	T
			I	N	S			P	O	S	S	E
R	E	S	E	E		A	S	T	O			
A	L	E		E	A	R	P		P	S	S	T
S	I	L	L		L	O	A		S	O	L	O
P	A	L	E		M	A	Y	S		R	U	G
			S	C	A	R		A	S	T	R	O
S	A	L	S	A			S	O	P			
A	L	S		S	A	R	A		A	B	L	E
S	T	A		A	N	A	S		R	E	A	R
H	O	T		S	A	N	S		S	A	M	S

Puzzle 79

A	P	E		O	P	E	N		S	C	U	D
D	I	T		M	I	N	I		P	O	S	E
D	A	H		I	L	E	T		O	M	E	N
		E	N	T	E	R		P	O	E	S	Y
B	O	R	E	S		G	I	R	L			
E	W	E	S		N	Y	S	E		L	P	S
A	L	A	S	K	A		A	S	L	E	E	P
D	S	L		I	N	D	Y		R	O	T	E
			C	L	U	E		T	O	N	E	D
A	C	O	R	N		S	A	U	N	A		
W	I	N	E		K	A	R	L		R	B	I
O	A	T	S		A	L	L	I		D	O	N
L	O	O	T		T	T	O	P		O	P	S

Puzzle 80

D	E	C	O		S	L	I	T		L	B	S
O	A	H	U		T	I	N	A		I	O	U
I	S	I	T		A	L	E	C		V	A	N
T	E	A	S	E	R		R	I	S	E	R	S
				G	R	O	T	T	O			
L	T	D		G	E	M			N	O	A	H
C	O	I	N		D	A	D		Y	O	Y	O
D	E	M	O			H	E	Y		H	E	W
			P	L	E	A	S	E				
A	P	P	E	A	R		I	N	T	A	C	T
J	A	R		L	I	A	R		E	Q	U	I
A	T	O		A	C	N	E		R	U	S	E
X	E	S		W	A	G	S		M	A	P	S

Puzzle 81

A	M	O	S		I	D	S		L	O	B	E
S	E	A	T		L	E	O		E	V	A	N
A	T	T	A		L	A	N		S	A	N	G
N	E	S	T	L	E		A	I	S	L	E	
			E	E	G		R	A	E			
W	A	G		N	A	T		M	E	S	A	S
E	V	A			L	A	S			A	C	T
E	A	S	E	D		N	A	M		T	E	N
			R	E	A		D	O	T			
	S	T	A	L	L		N	O	O	S	E	S
S	H	E	S		A	B	E		A	E	R	O
H	O	N	E		R	A	S		S	T	A	B
H	O	T	S		M	R	S		T	A	S	S

Puzzle 82

L	I	N	E	R		L	S	D		R	I	O
A	D	A	G	E		I	T	O		O	R	I
T	O	T	A	L		T	U	G		S	A	L
			D	I	E	T			B	I	T	E
F	U	R		C	A	L		B	L	E	E	D
L	P	S			R	E	M	I	T			
A	S	T	E	R	N		A	N	S	W	E	R
			L	O	S	E	R			A	M	A
S	T	A	K	E		L	I	U		H	U	G
W	A	G	S			D	A	B	S			
E	L	I		F	O	E		O	U	T	D	O
E	I	N		L	A	S		A	M	O	U	R
T	A	G		O	F	T		T	O	T	E	D

Puzzle 83

A	T	O	P		A	R	R		S	H	O	P
S	O	L	E		D	O	E		T	A	L	E
H	Y	D	E		M	D	S		A	L	E	S
			W	R	E	S	T		L	O	S	T
S	C	R	E	E	N		A	C	E			
P	R	E	E	N		N	T	H		O	F	F
C	O	D		A	M	B	E	R		O	R	E
A	P	O		M	A	A		O	O	H	E	D
			M	E	T		A	M	U	S	E	S
I	D	L	E		I	S	L	E	T			
S	O	Y	S		N	O	G		L	I	M	A
I	N	N	S		E	S	E		E	C	O	N
S	E	X	Y		E	A	R		T	H	E	N

Puzzle 84

D	O	A			B	A	S	E		S	I	P
E	A	R	S		A	M	E	S		E	A	T
E	T	T	A		A	P	P	S		E	T	A
			M	A	S	S		E	A	S	E	S
A	S	P	E	N			A	S	I			
R	O	E		T	R	E	Y		L	A	D	S
C	R	T		S	I	R	E	S		L	O	O
S	E	E	R		L	A	S	T		E	N	O
			A	T	E			A	S	S	E	T
P	A	S	S	E		S	T	Y	E			
A	L	A		S	H	A	H		T	A	S	S
S	A	N		L	A	L	A		S	A	I	L
S	S	E		A	M	E	N			A	N	Y

Puzzle 85

E	A	R		S	I	F	T		S	O	D	A
K	I	A		C	O	L	A		A	L	A	N
E	N	V		A	N	O	N		F	E	S	T
S	T	E	A	L			G	R	E			
			C	A	B	S		A	R	U	B	A
O	B	I	E		L	O	E	W		S	A	P
W	E	A	R		U	R	N		P	E	R	T
N	A	T		P	R	E	Y		I	D	E	S
S	U	E	D	E		R	A	I	N			
			Y	R	S			D	E	A	N	S
F	O	R	E		T	E	A	L		B	A	T
A	J	A	R		E	L	L	E		C	P	A
A	S	P	S		M	I	S	S		S	A	T

Puzzle 86

A	D	J		S	T	O	P		C	B	E	R
L	E	A		P	H	I	L		A	Y	E	S
L	A	N		L	U	N	A		M	E	E	T
	F	E	M	A		K	N	E	E			
			I	S	M		E	R	R	A	N	D
S	T	A	S	H	E	S		R	A	T	I	O
I	O	U			A	N	N			O	P	S
T	O	R	A	H		L	I	C	E	N	S	E
S	T	A	T	U	E		H	E	X			
			T	H	I	N		A	E	R	O	
M	A	K	E		G	O	E	S		O	H	M
I	V	E	S		H	O	L	E		S	I	R
G	E	N	T		T	K	O	S		S	O	T

Puzzle 87

G	O	B	I		F	E	Z		S	K	I	M
I	C	O	N		U	N	O		A	N	T	I
G	T	O	S		E	G	O		L	O	B	S
			I	T	L	L		N	O	T	E	S
P	R	I	D	E		I	F	S	O			
R	A	T	E	D		S	O	A	N	D	S	O
O	U	T			T	H	E			R	E	G
F	L	O	T	S	A	M		I	N	N	E	R
			R	A	G	U		D	O	O	N	E
M	O	N	E	Y		F	L	A	T			
A	H	A	B		U	F	O		B	E	E	P
I	N	T	L		R	I	G		A	L	V	A
D	O	S	E		N	N	E		D	I	A	L

Puzzle 88

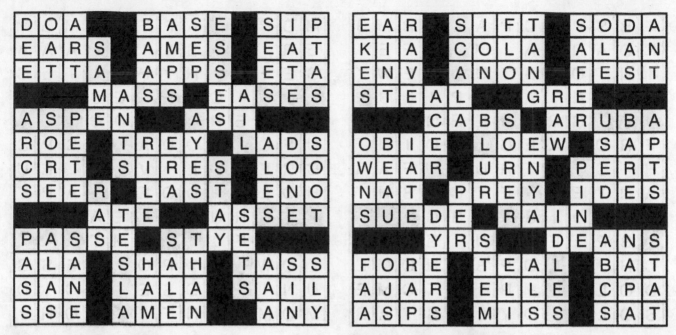

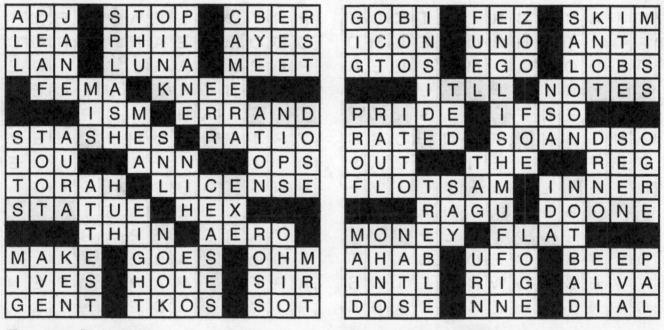

T	B	S	P		C	P	A		I	B	M	S
R	O	A	R		A	I	M		N	E	E	T
I	N	T	O		B	T	U		D	E	W	Y
B	O	S	N	I	A		S	P	I	N	S	
			G	R	R		E	E	G			
F	R	O		K	E	G		P	O	I	N	T
H	I	C			T	R	U			F	A	R
A	N	T	E	D		E	T	C		S	H	Y
			D	I	S		E	S	C			
	S	P	I	E	L		N	I	E	C	E	S
C	H	I	T		O	P	S		N	O	M	E
D	O	L	E		M	R	I		T	O	M	E
S	O	L	D		O	Y	L		S	T	A	R

Puzzle 89

M	O	P	E		A	P	T	S		M	G	M
E	R	I	E		S	L	I	P		A	A	A
G	E	E	R		H	Y	P	E		T	L	C
			I	C	Y			E	S	T	E	E
S	A	N	E	R		A	C	D	C			
U	F	O		Y	O	D	A		A	S	P	S
C	R	E	W		L	I	V		B	L	E	U
H	O	L	E		D	O	E	R		A	P	E
			R	U	E	S		E	A	V	E	S
A	N	S	E	L			G	M	T			
L	O	W		T	Y	P	O		B	E	S	S
U	N	I		R	O	S	E		A	C	I	D
M	O	M		A	N	T	S		T	O	R	I

Puzzle 90

F	I	B	S		C	R	T		T	K	O	S
E	D	I	T		H	B	O		E	L	M	O
D	O	D	O		A	I	M		L	E	E	R
			R	I	N				L	E	N	T
L	A	M	E	N	T		D	I	S			
I	R	I	S	H		M	O	N		U	S	S
E	M	T		A	M	E	N	S		Z	A	P
N	Y	E		L	U	G		A	L	I	V	E
			B	E	D		I	N	A	S	E	C
F	L	E	E				R	E	P			
D	I	V	A		C	E	O		S	K	I	T
I	V	E	S		O	W	N		E	I	N	S
C	E	N	T		W	E	S		D	A	N	K

Puzzle 91

P	R	Y		A	L	F	A		S	E	M	I
O	O	O		L	E	A	N		C	R	O	C
P	O	R		C	A	R	Y		A	I	D	E
S	T	E	N	O	S			U	L	C	E	R
			A	A	H		I	S	P			
T	R	I	M			U	M	P		H	E	Y
R	I	T	E	O	F	P	A	S	S	A	G	E
U	N	S		N	O	S			O	L	G	A
			D	U	E		S	S	T			
S	T	A	R	S			P	A	S	T	A	S
T	O	M	E		A	S	O	F		A	L	I
A	R	F	S		M	A	R	E		R	E	N
R	I	M	S		I	D	E	S		T	S	K

Puzzle 92

L	I	M	O		U	P	C			F	E	B
I	M	A	C		S	I	D		A	L	V	A
M	U	T	T		H	E	R		C	U	E	S
A	S	H	O	R	E		O	T	H	E	R	S
			P	A	R		M	O	O			
M	A	R	I	N	E	R		M	O	R	A	L
E	S	P			D	R	S			A	P	O
L	I	M	I	T		S	C	E	N	E	R	Y
			C	U	T		H	U	E			
D	E	M	O	T	E		O	R	A	T	E	D
I	W	I	N		N	F	L		T	E	R	A
M	A	S	S		T	R	A		L	A	I	D
S	N	O			H	O	R		Y	M	C	A

Puzzle 93

P	O	N	D		T	V	A		P	E	L	T
A	X	E	S		R	I	D		C	L	A	Y
W	E	L	L	T	O	D	O		T	E	M	P
S	N	L		A	W	A	R	D		C	E	E
			E	K	E		E	A	S	T		
I	S	R	A	E	L		S	M	A	R	T	S
N	E	E	R						W	O	O	L
S	C	H	L	E	P		O	P	E	N	E	R
		E	Y	R	E		N	E	D			
C	P	A		R	E	N	E	W		T	S	K
E	A	R	P		L	O	I	S	L	A	N	E
L	I	S	A		E	S	L		A	T	O	N
S	L	E	D		R	E	L		G	A	B	S

Puzzle 94

U	C	L	A		D	E	E	R		J	E	T
P	O	O	L		E	Y	R	E		A	X	E
S	O	U	T	H	B	E	N	D		M	A	N
			A	I	R	S		S	T	E	M	S
S	H	E	R	P	A		Z	E	E	S		
N	O	V				N	E	A	R	B	Y	
L	O	E	B		N	O	D		M	O	O	D
	T	R	E	M	O	R				N	Y	E
		S	T	A	N		R	A	N	D	O	M
E	L	I	A	N		M	I	R	O			
G	U	N		I	D	E	N	T	I	C	A	L
A	B	C		A	U	L	D		S	O	O	T
D	E	E		C	O	T	S		E	L	K	S

Puzzle 95

O	R	E	S		A	C	E			S	K	A
W	A	R	T		R	P	M		S	O	U	L
E	N	G	R		S	U	B		C	A	R	P
S	T	O	O	G	E		E	X	E	R	T	S
			D	E	N		R	E	N			
L	A	T	E	R	A	L		S	T	R	I	P
I	G	O			L	E	N			B	R	R
T	O	N	A	L		M	A	L	A	I	S	E
			M	A	I		R	E	L			
A	S	S	I	G	N		R	O	B	O	T	S
P	I	E	S		A	M	A		E	D	I	T
P	R	E	S		N	I	T		R	I	D	E
T	E	M			E	S	E		T	E	E	N

Puzzle 96

T	S	E		H	E	R	O		I	N	C	A
H	O	T		E	V	E	R		S	E	A	R
O	T	C		L	E	A	R		S	I	L	K
		E	V	E	N	S		R	U	L	E	S
L	A	T	I	N		O	B	O	E			
I	C	E	S		O	N	E	S		O	A	T
S	T	R	E	A	K		N	E	E	D	L	E
A	S	A		A	R	I	Z		K	O	L	A
			A	H	A	S		S	E	M	I	S
S	T	A	B	S		A	S	I	D	E		
A	I	R	E		B	I	A	S		T	U	B
K	N	O	T		L	A	G	S		E	P	I
S	A	N	S		T	H	E	Y		R	I	B

Puzzle 97

A	M	P	S		P	A	M			M	I	R
C	A	L	E		U	M	A		C	E	D	E
I	M	O	N		L	M	N		A	R	I	D
D	A	D	D	Y	L	O	N	G	L	E	G	S
			S	A	T		A	T	L			
A	M	I		M	A	O		E	A	T	A	T
N	I	K	E		B	R	R		S	A	G	A
G	L	E	N	N		R	A	D		C	O	B
			C	O	D		M	S	G			
F	A	R	A	W	A	Y	P	L	A	C	E	S
R	I	B	S		R	E	A		P	U	L	P
E	R	I	E		T	A	G		E	R	M	A
D	E	S			S	H	E		S	L	O	T

Puzzle 98

C	E	L	S		T	R	E	S		D	O	S
P	O	S	T		H	E	A	P		U	R	I
U	N	D	E	R	O	A	T	H		E	E	G
			R	O	M		S	E	A	S	O	N
A	M	A	N	D	A		A	R	I			
N	O	I	S	E	S		T	E	M	P	O	
G	O	D								A	P	R
	S	E	R	F	S		S	C	E	N	E	S
			A	L	T		T	A	L	E	N	T
S	E	T	T	E	R		A	N	D			
U	Z	I		E	A	G	L	E	E	Y	E	D
I	R	E		C	T	R	L		R	A	G	U
T	A	D		E	A	R	S		S	M	O	G

Puzzle 99

P	I	G	S		I	W	A	S		M	C	S
A	T	I	T		N	O	U	N		A	Y	E
S	O	S	A		T	O	G	A		T	S	P
			G	R	R			R	H	E	T	T
S	A	L		N	A	U	S	E	A			
P	S	I		A	N	N	E		S	L	O	P
A	W	E	S		S	I	N		P	A	P	A
M	E	N	U		I	T	S	A		C	A	L
			E	S	T	E	E	M		K	L	M
T	A	S	T	E			L	Y	E			
A	L	L		D	I	C	E		B	O	S	S
P	E	I		A	I	R	S		B	A	K	E
S	G	T		N	I	T	S		S	K	I	P

Puzzle 100

O	K	S		P	C	S		M	A	G	M	A
P	A	T		L	E	D		I	D	E	A	S
E	R	A		A	L	I	E	N	A	T	E	S
R	E	L	A	T	E		R	I	P			
A	N	E	W		B	A	N		T	A	R	P
		M	E	L		C	I	D		L	O	B
C	H	A		S	P	R	E	E		O	M	S
N	E	T		D	I	E		S	T	N		
N	E	E	R		A	S	H		O	G	L	E
			I	A	N		E	R	A	S	E	R
A	R	I	S	T	O	T	L	E		I	N	A
R	E	N	E	E		I	L	L		D	I	S
C	A	D	R	E		S	O	Y		E	N	E

Puzzle 101

T	W	O	S		H	E	H		P	L	U	M
R	I	F	T		I	V	Y		R	A	S	P
I	N	F	O		T	O	P	N	O	T	C	H
P	E	S	O			N	E	B				
			D	O	W	N		A	T	T	I	C
H	U	N		H	E	E	D		R	O	S	Y
E	N	I	G	M	A		I	G	U	A	N	A
R	I	G	S		R	S	V	P		D	O	N
E	T	H	A	N		P	E	S	T			
				U	F	O			R	O	I	L
O	P	P	O	N	E	N	T		O	R	C	A
A	S	I	F		U	G	H		T	S	K	S
F	I	A	T		D	E	Y		S	O	Y	S

Puzzle 102

H	E	N	S		H	E	F		S	A	G	A
I	B	E	T		I	L	L		A	T	O	M
G	A	R	R		T	E	E		B	L	O	C
H	Y	D	E			V	E	I	L			
			W	E	T			N	E	P	A	L
P	G	A		R	A	P	I	D		U	P	I
E	U	R		O	X	I	D	E		T	O	M
A	R	C		T	I	T	L	E		S	P	A
S	U	S	H	I			Y	D	S			
			I	C	B	M			C	R	O	C
T	H	I	N		R	E	B		O	I	L	Y
R	A	N	G		A	I	R		T	O	G	A
A	I	D	E		G	R	R		S	T	A	N

Puzzle 103

H	E	R		S	S	W			B	O	O	R
A	V	E		H	E	A	L		A	U	D	I
D	E	C	R	E	A	S	E		T	R	I	O
			I	B	M		C	L	O	S	E	T
S	C	U	B	A		R	A	I	N			
C	A	P	S		A	E	R	O	S	O	L	
H	M	O		S	T	E	R	N		N	I	P
	E	N	T	I	T	L	E		T	E	E	S
			I	D	E	S		H	O	I	S	T
L	E	N	T	E	N		L	E	M			
O	P	A	L		D	I	S	A	S	T	E	R
N	I	T	E		S	C	A	R		O	L	E
I	C	E	S			Y	T	D		T	K	O

Puzzle 104

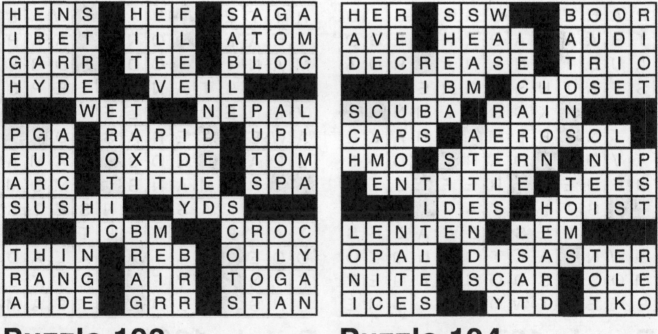

M	C	S			A	C	T	S		C	C	C
B	L	A	B		I	H	O	P		L	O	O
A	O	N	E		R	A	T	E		A	D	O
S	T	E	E	L		L	O	N		P	E	P
			N	I	K	E		T	N	T		
O	L	E		V	A	T	S		P	R	A	Y
R	O	L	L	E	R		A	F	R	A	M	E
B	L	E	U		L	A	K	E		P	C	T
		M	G	M		P	E	E	P			
A	C	E		I	C	E		S	O	R	T	S
V	A	N		T	A	M	E		T	O	O	L
O	P	T		T	R	A	M		S	I	N	O
N	O	S		S	E	N	T			L	E	G

Puzzle 105

O	P	T			S	T	A	T		O	N	T
A	I	D	S		P	A	R	E		H	E	H
T	E	S	T		A	G	E	S		M	A	I
			O	P	S			T	E	S	T	S
S	C	O	P	E		R	A	Y	S			
W	A	D		L	I	E	S		L	A	M	B
A	M	I		E	S	T	E	S		B	A	A
T	E	E	N		L	I	C	E		R	R	S
			F	R	E	E		A	M	A	S	S
S	C	A	L	E			D	N	A			
W	A	R		A	M	M	O		T	S	P	S
A	R	K		C	A	A	N		S	O	I	L
B	A	S		T	O	Y	S			S	A	O

Puzzle 106

P	A	N	E		H	U	G	S		S	I	D
T	R	A	M		A	S	A	N		E	G	O
A	U	D	I		N	A	N	A		R	O	T
S	T	A	T	U	S		G	R	E	E	T	S
				K	O	S		L	M	N		
N	I	N		E	L	M			M	A	L	E
A	V	O	W		O	A	R		A	D	O	S
G	E	N	E			R	E	F		E	T	C
		S	T	L		T	A	C				
R	E	E	S	E	S		S	C	A	L	E	S
O	W	N		A	L	T	O		N	O	L	O
M	O	S		S	O	O	N		A	G	E	R
E	K	E		T	W	O	S		S	O	M	E

Puzzle 107

R	I	T	E	S		B	A	S		W	A	S
I	N	A	L	L		O	N	A		A	A	H
M	A	N	I	A		O	D	S		D	R	E
			S	T	A	N		S	T	E	P	S
V	E	N	E	E	R		L	E	I			
A	W	E			E	R	A	S	E	D		
L	E	A	D		N	O	S		R	A	M	A
		R	O	M	A	N	S			M	O	M
			L	A	S		I	N	S	E	T	S
T	A	L	E	S		D	E	E	T			
O	D	E		T	A	I		S	A	L	A	D
F	I	N		E	V	E		T	R	I	T	E
U	N	S		R	E	D		S	T	E	A	M

Puzzle 108

S	H	O	T		U	Z	I		A	I	D	S
P	A	C	E		F	I	R		S	N	U	G
A	N	T	E	L	O	P	E		I	S	N	T
				I	S	A		G	A	T	E	S
B	A	R	O	N		D	E	E	M			
A	B	O	R	T		E	N	L	I	S	T	
H	E	M	I		B	E	G		N	O	O	K
	S	E	E	R	E	D		C	O	N	G	A
			N	A	N	O		A	R	S	O	N
N	A	S	T	Y		O	O	P				
O	S	H	A		A	D	H	E	R	E	T	O
D	I	E	T		P	A	M		K	N	E	W
S	A	D	E		T	H	Y		O	V	A	L

Puzzle 109

A	P	B		O	N	A	N		T	G	I	F
P	O	E		N	O	L	O		R	O	S	E
U	M	A		A	R	O	W		E	O	N	S
	P	R	A	I	S	E		T	E	N	T	S
			F	R	E	S	N	O				
M	I	N	I				P	R	I	E	S	T
I	N	A	R	U	T		R	A	N	C	O	R
S	C	H	E	M	E				C	O	P	Y
				P	L	A	S	M	A			
G	L	A	S	S		R	A	I	S	E	D	
L	E	I	A		C	E	L	S		D	O	M
I	N	N	S		P	A	V	E		G	T	O
B	A	T	S		U	S	E	R		Y	E	P

Puzzle 110

E	L	M			E	N	D		S	C	A	B
L	A	Y	S		R	A	E		T	H	R	U
M	I	N	T		O	P	S		Y	A	M	S
S	T	A	Y	E	D		S	I	X			
			L	E	E	R	E	D		P	C	T
M	C	G	E	E		O	R	S		A	A	A
Y	A	R	D		R	U	T		L	I	S	P
T	K	O		H	A	S		T	O	R	T	E
H	E	W		A	C	T	I	O	N			
		O	W	E		O	P	E	R	A	S	
F	E	T	A		C	A	N		R	O	M	P
H	O	O	F		A	M	I		S	U	M	O
A	N	N	S		R	C	A			T	O	T

Puzzle 111

T	H	E		S	L	A	Y		S	W	A	M
Y	E	A		L	O	D	E		L	A	V	A
P	M	S		A	S	S	N		A	N	I	N
E	S	T	A	T	E			O	B	E	S	E
			L	E	S	S	E	R				
A	D	A	M	S		L	C	D		P	A	C
P	O	P	S		C	O	O		P	O	L	O
B	I	T		M	A	P		S	L	E	E	T
				C	R	E	A	T	E			
L	S	A	T	S			O	R	A	T	E	S
O	H	N	O		M	O	R	E		E	L	K
S	E	T	A		R	O	T	E		D	I	E
S	L	I	D		T	H	A	T		S	E	W

Puzzle 112

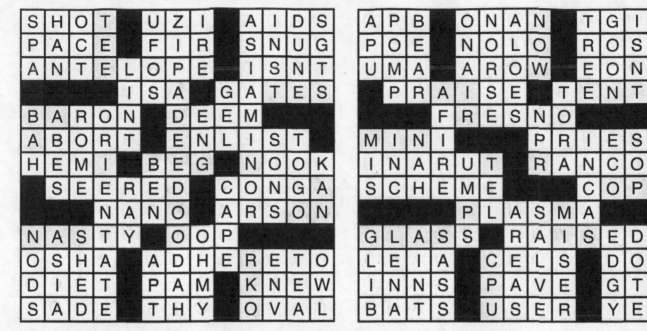

T	W	I	G			U	M	S		A	R	C
A	H	E	A	D		P	E	R		N	E	A
T	O	R	S	O		P	A	S		K	L	M
				A	C	E	D			L	A	P
M	G	M			P	R	O		T	E	X	
A	R	A	B	I	A		W	H	Y			
D	E	C	A	F				E	N	R	O	N
			T	S	P		S	M	E	A	R	S
	N	A	H		A	N	I			F	D	A
S	O	D			G	I	S	T				
W	O	O		C	O	N		R	O	A	R	S
I	S	P		A	D	J		Y	A	H	O	O
G	E	T		B	A	A			R	A	M	P

Puzzle 113

W	H	O	A		T	I	M	E		D	O	M
H	E	I	R		A	S	A	N		I	K	E
O	S	L	O		L	A	N	A		M	E	T
			U	S	O		I	M	P	E	D	E
N	E	L	S	O	N		L	O	O	N		
A	L	I	E	N	S		A	R	D	O	R	
N	I	P								V	A	T
	A	R	N	I	E		A	N	G	E	L	A
		E	A	R	N		C	O	O	L	E	R
C	L	A	M	O	R		T	D	S			
H	A	D		N	I	N	O		P	I	E	D
I	V	E		I	C	E	R		E	G	G	O
C	A	R		C	O	T	S		L	O	O	T

Puzzle 114

C	A	N		A	P	P			S	T	E	P
U	S	O		R	A	I	L		T	U	B	A
D	I	S		C	I	T	E		A	B	B	Y
	S	E	V	E	R		T	R	I	E	S	
			I	D	S		H	U	N			
R	O	A	M			B	A	N		P	J	S
U	A	W		I	D	O	L	S		R	E	O
N	F	L		D	E	W			M	E	T	S
			T	O	T		G	S	A			
	P	R	O	S	E		A	L	I	A	S	
M	O	A	N		S	O	M	E		S	A	M
R	O	V	E		T	I	M	E		I	V	E
I	R	I	S			L	A	P		F	E	D

Puzzle 115

T	H	U			J	A	W			P	I	E
W	E	S	T		A	B	E		B	O	S	C
O	N	E	H	O	R	S	E		O	N	T	O
			I	R	S			A	D	D	O	N
I	C	I	N	G		P	U	N	Y			
L	E	G	S			A	N	G	E	R	S	
L	E	E	K		A	N	I		N	I	L	E
	S	T	I	F	L	E			G	L	U	E
			N	E	I	L		C	L	E	R	K
S	H	I	N	E			M	A	I			
W	A	R	E		R	O	A	D	S	H	O	W
A	T	A	D		A	H	S		H	O	W	E
Y	E	N			G	M	T			R	N	S

Puzzle 116

F	B	I		A	L	T	A		A	M	B	I
C	A	N		G	A	R	B		L	O	A	N
C	R	T		I	N	O	R		L	O	R	D
	N	E	I	L	D	I	A	M	O	N	D	
		R	T	E			H	A	W			
A	S	E	C			D	A	S		S	C	I
M	U	S	H	R	O	O	M	C	L	O	U	D
P	E	T		A	R	T			Y	A	P	S
			I	F	I			C	N	N		
	C	O	T	T	O	N	C	A	N	D	Y	
L	O	N	E		L	I	A	R		S	A	D
C	L	A	M		E	L	S	E		O	R	S
D	E	N	S		S	E	A	T		S	N	L

Puzzle 117

J	A	R		A	M	A			T	H	A	W
A	T	E		T	A	X	I		Y	O	R	E
M	O	S		W	R	E	N		R	O	U	T
		T	E	A	K		A	D	A	P	T	S
S	M	E	A	R		T	R	O	N			
G	O	A	T		E	R	U	P	T	E	D	
T	V	S		B	L	A	S	E		M	E	A
	E	Y	E	L	A	S	H		L	I	A	M
			J	O	S	H		S	A	N	D	S
S	E	L	E	C	T		L	O	D	E		
E	X	E	C		I	D	O	L		N	E	W
P	E	A	T		C	O	N	E		C	R	O
T	S	K	S			H	I	S		E	N	O

Puzzle 118

N	B	C			O	F	F			G	A	P
N	O	P	E		W	A	R		P	O	R	E
W	A	R	D		L	A	Y		L	E	F	T
			G	P	S			T	E	R	S	E
N	I	N	E	R		I	D	E	A			
I	V	O	R	Y		T	A	N	D	E	M	
N	A	G			C	A	B			W	O	W
	N	O	R	M	A	L		S	T	O	V	E
			H	O	L	Y		I	R	K	E	D
T	W	A	I	N			M	N	O			
I	W	I	N		F	H	A		O	W	N	S
L	I	M	O		B	I	C		P	I	T	A
T	I	S			I	C	H			T	H	Y

Puzzle 119

O	H	M	S		M	I	C		S	L	O	W
F	O	O	T		I	C	U		T	O	R	E
F	E	T	E		L	Y	E		R	U	E	D
			V	A	L				A	T	M	S
S	O	B	E	R		M	A	R	Y			
I	K	E		C	L	O	V	E		P	H	D
F	L	A		T	A	L	O	N		L	O	A
T	A	R		I	N	A	W	E		A	N	Y
			I	C	E	R		G	E	N	E	S
E	S	P	N				Q	E	D			
T	H	A	T		A	F	T		I	S	P	Y
C	O	L	E		R	B	I		T	I	L	E
H	E	L	L		R	I	P		S	C	O	T

Puzzle 120

C	R	O	P		L	O	L		C	E	L	L
H	O	H	O		I	F	I		R	I	C	O
A	L	M	S		B	A	T		A	N	D	Y
P	E	S	T	E	R		E	B	B			
				L	A	U	R	A		G	A	P
S	W	A	R	M		S	A	N	T	A	F	E
K	I	T	E		M	I	L		R	Y	A	N
I	R	O	N	M	A	N		T	I	E	R	S
P	E	P		A	R	G	U	E				
			P	C	T		N	E	S	T	E	D
S	I	Z	E		I	D	I		H	I	V	E
K	N	E	E		N	O	T		I	N	A	N
Y	A	N	K		I	C	Y		P	E	N	T

Puzzle 121

T	A	P			E	M	S			P	U	B
I	G	O	T		L	O	G		Y	O	G	A
S	E	D	I	M	E	N	T		O	O	H	S
			M	A	C			P	U	L	S	E
O	A	R	E	D		T	H	A	R			
W	W	I	I			R	E	S	E	T	S	
L	E	S	S		G	U	N		S	O	P	H
	D	E	M	U	R	E			O	B	I	E
			O	P	E	R		O	V	E	N	S
A	L	A	N	S			F	H	A			
H	U	G	E		F	L	A	M	I	N	G	O
O	B	E	Y		L	I	T		N	A	I	R
Y	E	S			Y	D	S			P	G	A

Puzzle 122

H	M	O		E	S	C		M	O	U	N	T
B	A	N		S	I	P		A	R	T	I	E
O	N	E	S	T	A	R		R	A	I	N	S
			H	E	M			I	N	L	E	T
C	A	C	H	E			N	O	G			
U	S	O		M	E	G	A		E	M	M	A
B	A	R		S	A	I	N	T		A	I	R
A	P	E	D		C	L	U	E		U	R	I
			H	U	H			R	U	L	E	D
H	O	G	A	N			P	M	S			
E	V	E	R	T		O	R	I	E	N	T	S
F	E	R	M	I		N	O	T		A	O	K
T	R	I	A	L		O	D	E		G	P	A

Puzzle 123

I	C	E	D		P	A	S		S	A	M	S
M	O	L	E		U	N	O		H	O	O	P
O	P	E	C		M	A	X		A	N	D	A
K	E	G		C	A	L		S	H	E	E	R
		A	H	A		O	W	N	S			
P	A	N	A	M		G	E	E		S	Y	N
U	N	C	L	E	S		E	E	Y	O	R	E
B	Y	E		L	T	S		R	E	U	S	E
			C	O	P	A		E	S	L		
S	P	L	I	T		H	I	D		M	I	G
W	A	I	T		P	A	C		N	A	D	A
A	C	M	E		A	R	K		A	T	O	Z
B	E	E	S		H	A	Y		B	E	L	A

Puzzle 124

B	I	N		S	A	O			A	B	C	D
U	M	A		I	R	K	S		D	I	O	R
N	U	T		R	E	S	T		E	L	M	S
	S	E	V	E	N		R	U	P	E	E	
			O	N	T		O	F	T			
S	E	A	T	S		M	N	O		M	B	A
I	D	L	E		R	A	G		R	O	A	D
R	U	T		S	A	X		S	O	D	A	S
			A	I	R		A	T	O			
	S	P	I	T	E		R	A	F	T	S	
A	P	E	D		S	H	I	N		A	W	L
P	O	R	E		T	O	E	D		R	I	O
B	T	U	S			E	S	S		S	T	Y

Puzzle 125

M	A	S	T		I	S	I	S		S	P	F
T	A	T	E		M	I	S	T		P	E	A
S	A	P	S		A	B	L	E		A	N	D
			T	U	G		A	V	E	R	S	E
A	M	P	E	R	E		N	I	P			
P	E	A	R	L	S		D	E	A	L	T	
R	N	S								Y	O	U
	S	T	P	A	T		L	A	S	E	R	S
			O	R	E		A	R	I	S	E	S
E	A	S	T	E	R		S	E	E			
A	H	A		N	E	S	S		S	K	I	M
R	A	Y		O	S	L	O		T	A	D	A
L	B	S		T	A	O	S		A	T	I	P

Puzzle 126

C	I	D		S	T	Y			C	H	O	W
A	R	R		H	U	E	S		E	U	R	O
P	S	I		I	N	T	L		S	H	A	W
		L	A	N	E		E	V	A			
	P	L	A	T		N	E	A	R	E	R	
N	I	T	R	O		O	P	T		Y	O	N
P	E	E	P		K	O	S		M	E	G	A
R	C	A		D	A	N		A	B	O	U	T
	E	M	P	I	R	E		T	A	P	E	
			L	E	A		P	O	S	E		
F	L	U	E		T	O	O	N		N	I	T
L	I	Z	A		E	D	G	E		E	N	V
A	L	I	T			S	O	S		R	N	S

Puzzle 127

O	J	S		A	D	O		E	R	E	C	T
T	O	O		T	I	N		L	E	V	E	E
S	E	T	T	L	E	S		O	N	E	N	D
			H	E	S			P	E	L	T	S
L	I	B	Y	A			P	E	W			
U	S	A		S	P	R	Y		S	E	L	L
G	I	N		T	E	A	R	S		O	O	O
E	N	G	R		W	H	E	E		N	O	W
			E	D	S			D	E	S	K	S
A	B	A	C	I			W	A	D			
M	E	T	E	R		N	A	T	U	R	A	L
E	V	A	D	E		F	I	E		U	K	E
R	Y	D	E	R		L	T	S		M	A	X

Puzzle 128

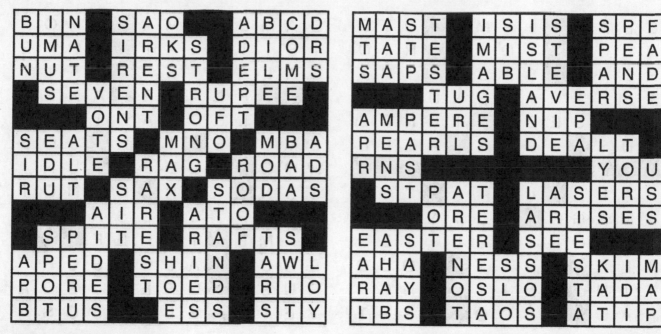

E	P	A			I	B	M	S		O	T	C
R	E	S	T		T	O	I	L		R	I	O
R	E	P	O		S	P	C	A		I	R	A
A	R	E	T	H	A		E	N	D	E	A	R
T	E	N	S	E	D			T	E	N	D	S
A	D	S		L	E	N	S		A	T	E	E
				P	A	N	T	S				
P	A	L	E		L	E	I	A		T	O	A
I	M	A	G	E			L	I	N	E	N	S
R	E	T	O	R	T		E	L	I	T	E	S
A	L	E		R	U	S	T		T	O	D	O
T	I	N		O	N	I	T		E	N	G	R
E	A	T		R	E	D	O			S	E	T

Puzzle 129

D	A	M	S		I	M	A		S	H	O	P
I	S	I	T		L	A	T		P	O	P	E
G	A	L	A		I	S	P		L	A	I	T
			P	L	A	T	E		A	X	E	S
N	A	I	L	E	D		A	C	T			
E	M	C	E	E		I	C	H		J	O	B
W	O	O		R	O	D	E	O		U	N	I
S	S	N		A	N	A		O	R	N	O	T
			P	T	S		U	S	H	E	R	S
M	A	M	E		T	H	R	E	E			
E	G	O	S		A	U	G		S	U	R	F
R	U	S	T		G	R	E		U	S	D	A
V	E	T	O		E	L	S		S	O	S	A

Puzzle 130

A	N	D	A		S	A	M		C	H	I	N
B	O	A	T		E	P	I		A	U	N	T
C	T	R	L		R	R	S		L	E	C	H
D	E	N	A	L	I		E	L	F			
			S	A	F	A	R	I		A	P	B
H	O	N	E	Y		B	L	T		B	E	A
A	X	I	S		S	O	Y		R	E	E	D
R	E	N		S	T	D		B	E	L	L	E
M	N	O		T	I	E	R	E	D			
			J	A	N		O	N	R	U	S	H
C	U	T	E		G	O	O		E	C	H	O
U	R	N	S		E	L	M		S	L	U	G
P	I	N	T		R	D	S		S	A	T	S

Puzzle 131

U	M	P			Z	A	P			F	D	A
G	O	O	F		U	S	A		S	E	A	L
H	E	E	L		L	A	M		P	E	R	M
			E	M	U			M	I	L	E	S
O	W	N	E	R		O	T	I	C			
R	O	O	T	S		D	O	T	E	L	L	
B	E	G			C	O	W			Y	A	Y
	S	O	O	N	E	R		G	E	N	R	E
			G	A	L	S		O	I	N	K	S
S	H	A	R	P			G	T	E			
T	U	B	E		C	R	O		I	N	F	O
O	R	B	S		H	I	D		O	I	L	Y
P	L	Y			A	B	S			H	A	L

Puzzle 132

S	E	C	T	■	A	M	E	S	■	I	M	A
D	E	E	R	■	C	E	D	E	■	R	A	N
I	L	L	A	T	E	A	S	E	■	E	N	D
■	■	■	D	A	S	■	■	D	A	N	E	S
S	A	B	E	R	■	M	A	S	S	E	■	■
O	R	I	■	■	T	A	B	■	A	C	T	S
F	I	G	S	■	A	R	C	■	P	A	R	A
T	A	C	O	■	B	I	D	■	■	R	O	Y
■	■	H	O	R	S	E	■	S	T	A	T	S
S	T	E	N	O	■	■	M	I	R	■	■	■
H	O	E	■	A	P	P	A	R	A	T	U	S
O	N	S	■	S	L	O	T	■	M	E	S	A
E	Y	E	■	T	O	T	E	■	S	E	E	D

Puzzle 133

B	O	N	E	■	A	L	G	A	■	D	R	S
A	X	E	L	■	C	O	A	L	■	E	E	E
R	O	B	E	■	R	A	S	P	■	C	A	R
■	■	■	C	H	E	F	■	H	B	O	M	B
P	A	S	T	E	■	■	G	A	B	■	■	■
F	R	O	■	R	I	S	E	■	C	O	M	A
F	A	B	■	S	C	A	N	T	■	S	O	P
T	B	S	P	■	A	C	E	R	■	A	S	P
■	■	■	J	A	N	■	■	A	B	Y	S	S
L	A	P	S	E	■	M	A	Y	A	■	■	■
O	N	O	■	S	C	A	B	■	L	A	I	R
T	K	O	■	O	O	Z	E	■	S	I	R	E
S	A	L	■	P	O	E	T	■	A	M	E	X

Puzzle 134

G	T	O	S	■	E	Y	E	D	■	G	P	A
O	H	O	H	■	D	E	C	O	■	L	A	B
R	A	Z	E	■	A	T	O	Z	■	O	R	B
Y	I	E	L	D	S	■	L	E	E	W	A	Y
■	■	■	■	O	N	L	I	N	E	■	■	■
U	P	C	■	G	E	L	■	■	L	A	M	B
M	E	O	W	■	R	A	S	■	S	U	E	T
P	A	P	A	■	■	M	A	Y	■	G	N	U
■	■	■	N	E	P	A	L	I	■	■	■	■
B	E	A	T	L	E	■	I	N	S	E	R	T
T	A	B	■	L	A	C	E	■	L	U	A	U
U	R	L	■	I	R	O	N	■	O	R	I	G
S	L	Y	■	S	L	O	T	■	G	O	D	S

Puzzle 135

M	P	H	■	A	T	M	■	■	S	H	I	P
T	E	A	■	P	H	D	S	■	P	I	S	A
V	A	T	■	N	E	S	T	■	A	R	M	Y
■	R	E	F	E	R	■	R	A	C	E	S	■
■	■	■	R	A	E	■	E	X	E	■	■	■
E	A	S	Y	■	■	H	A	I	■	S	N	L
L	I	P	■	S	E	E	M	S	■	H	O	E
S	L	Y	■	L	A	W	■	■	P	E	N	T
■	■	■	H	A	S	■	D	S	L	■	■	■
■	S	T	A	G	E	■	A	T	O	M	S	■
S	P	I	T	■	L	U	R	E	■	A	O	K
S	U	R	E	■	S	P	E	W	■	M	A	I
T	R	E	S	■	■	C	D	S	■	A	K	A

Puzzle 136

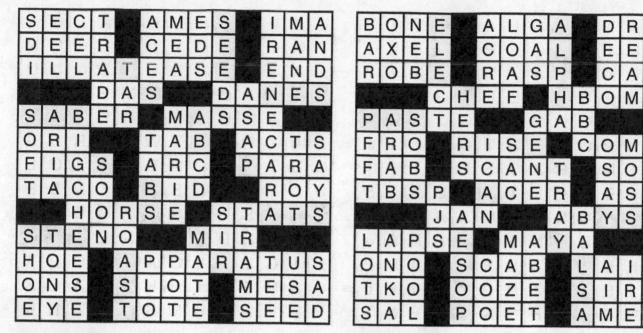

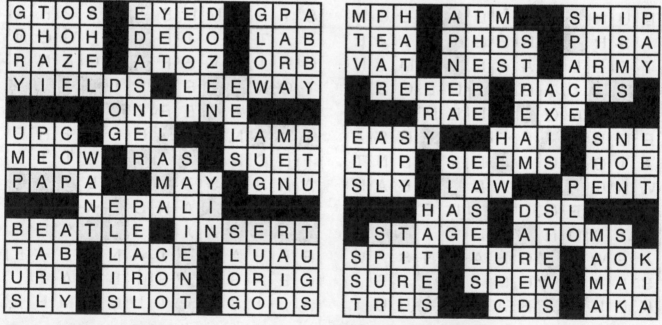

T	A	L	L		S	L	A	P		T	I	S
O	P	I	E		C	A	R	L		A	L	I
B	E	N	T		A	I	R	Y		M	I	T
E	X	E	S		D	D	E		G	E	E	S
			G	P	S		S	G	T			
C	A	N	O	E		S	T	R	E	E	T	S
E	I	N		R	A	I	S	E		T	A	I
E	L	E	M	E	N	T		T	S	A	R	S
			C	S	I		M	A	A			
P	A	C	S		M	I	A		S	H	A	W
I	K	E		S	A	S	S		S	A	M	E
T	I	E		A	T	N	O		E	V	E	L
A	N	S		L	E	O	N		D	E	N	T

Puzzle 137

C	A	T	S		H	E	E		A	L	G	A
E	A	V	E		O	Y	L		L	O	O	N
L	A	S	S		H	E	F		B	O	N	D
			A	B	O	O		M	E	T	E	S
S	H	A	M	U		F	O	R	E			
E	A	T	E	R		T	W	I		R	D	S
C	U	T			C	H	E			A	O	L
S	L	Y		M	O	E		R	I	N	S	E
			S	U	N	S		A	D	D	E	D
S	T	A	N	D		T	O	M	E			
L	I	C	E		L	O	A		A	B	R	A
O	N	M	E		I	R	K		L	A	O	S
P	E	E	R		U	M	S		S	A	N	K

Puzzle 138

B	U	N		L	A	D	D		P	L	U	M
I	S	H		O	R	E	O		S	I	Z	E
T	E	L	L	T	A	L	E		A	M	I	N
			I	T	B	E		G	L	O	S	S
D	R	A	N	O		T	H	E	M			
R	O	B	E		F	E	A	R		N	S	A
A	T	O	N	C	E		R	E	S	E	N	T
W	H	O		M	E	A	D		T	E	A	M
			P	O	L	S		H	E	D	G	E
B	I	S	O	N		T	H	A	I			
A	S	W	E		C	H	A	I	N	S	A	W
S	L	A	M		O	M	I	T		I	D	I
K	E	N	S		B	A	L	I		D	D	T

Puzzle 139

S	T	S		M	D	S		C	A	P	R	A
E	A	T		T	I	P		A	R	G	O	N
C	H	I		V	E	E		S	C	A	N	S
T	O	N			S	A	L	T				
S	E	G	A		E	R	S			F	A	D
			N	H	L		D	E	S	I	R	E
T	B	O	N	E				B	E	T	T	E
A	R	R	E	S	T		A	B	E			
B	A	D			A	H	S		K	I	S	S
				A	X	E	S			S	U	P
R	E	H	A	B		I	A	N		L	I	E
C	E	A	S	E		S	I	B		A	T	L
A	L	I	S	T		T	L	C		M	E	L

Puzzle 140

G	L	E	E		M	O	P	E		A	S	P
M	E	A	L		E	V	E	S		G	N	U
T	I	R	E		L	E	A	P	Y	E	A	R
			V	E	E	R		R	I	D	G	E
A	D	H	E	R	E		R	I	P			
R	E	I	N	S		I	N	T	E	N	S	E
F	E	D			S	O	S			U	A	W
S	T	E	T	S	O	N		L	A	D	L	E
			R	A	W		C	A	D	E	T	S
E	D	S	E	L		M	A	Y	O			
R	E	L	E	A	S	E	D		P	H	A	T
G	P	A		M	O	L	E		T	O	T	E
O	P	T		I	N	S	T		S	P	A	N

Puzzle 141

W	E	B	S		O	M	S		G	U	L	P
A	L	O	T		T	A	P		O	H	I	O
G	E	R	E		T	S	E		A	U	T	O
E	M	E	R	G	E		E	I	T	H	E	R
			N	O	R		D	R	E			
I	D	I	O	T	S		S	K	E	T	C	H
D	O	I								U	N	I
I	C	I	C	L	E		A	T	T	E	N	D
			L	A	D		W	A	H			
A	R	M	A	N	I		A	G	R	E	E	D
C	E	O	S		B	R	R		A	L	M	A
D	E	N	S		L	E	D		S	M	U	T
C	L	A	Y		E	D	S		H	O	S	E

Puzzle 142

C	H	E	T		L	I	P		A	S	O	F
H	A	L	O		U	S	C		R	E	A	R
I	N	K	S		L	O	S		M	A	K	E
			S	P	U	N		F	A	L	S	E
R	U	L	E	R			G	O	D			
A	N	O	D	E		H	E	R	A	L	D	S
S	T	U			K	I	M			U	A	W
H	O	T	S	P	O	T		P	A	N	D	A
			W	A	S			O	R	G	A	N
R	E	B	E	L		L	E	W	D			
A	X	E	D		S	A	D		E	D	D	Y
P	E	L	E		P	I	G		N	O	I	R
S	C	A	N		F	R	Y		T	A	G	S

Puzzle 143

A	C	C	T		I	S	M			B	L	T
H	O	U	R		I	C	Y		O	A	T	H
M	E	T	E		I	O	N		U	N	D	O
E	D	E	N			P	A	C	T			
			T	R	U	E		E	L	B	O	W
T	I	C		O	K	S		L	A	R	G	E
A	T	H	O	M	E		B	E	W	A	R	E
C	L	A	R	A		F	U	R		N	E	D
O	L	D	E	N		E	N	Y	A			
			G	O	A	D			C	O	M	P
M	I	S	O		M	O	B		I	K	E	A
I	T	O	N		F	R	Y		D	I	L	L
C	O	W			M	A	E		S	E	T	S

Puzzle 144

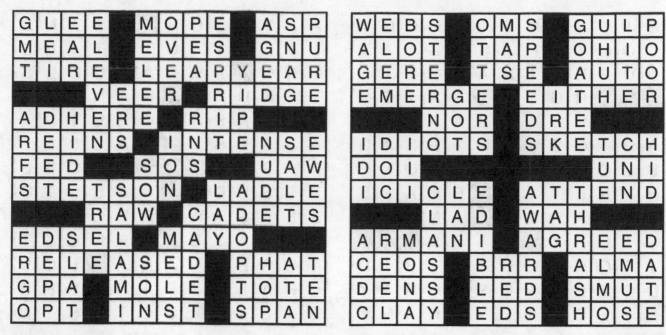

B	I	O	S		U	Z	I		E	G	G	Y
C	O	O	T		R	A	S		S	L	A	V
D	U	P	E		I	N	A		C	U	T	E
			R	U	S	E		B	A	T	E	S
C	R	I	E	S			Z	A	P			
A	U	T	O	S		T	O	T	E	B	A	G
S	L	O			F	L	O			O	X	O
H	E	R	E	T	I	C		P	E	A	L	E
			A	R	R			I	N	T	E	R
S	T	O	R	Y		R	I	P	S			
I	R	O	N		O	U	T		I	B	I	D
D	O	Z	E		A	D	S		G	R	A	Y
E	Y	E	D		K	E	Y		N	A	M	E

Puzzle 145

A	F	T		S	C	H			S	A	N	D
L	I	E		T	A	U	T		T	I	E	D
I	N	N		A	R	E	A	C	O	D	E	S
T	E	N	U	R	E		R	A	N			
		E	K	E	S		O	R	E	I	D	A
A	S	S	E	S	S		T	A	S	S	E	L
P	A	S								O	B	S
P	S	E	U	D	O		S	E	E	S	T	O
S	E	E	S	A	W		C	R	O	C		
			A	T	E		E	R	N	E	S	T
T	O	P	B	A	N	A	N	A		L	O	U
U	R	A	L		S	P	I	N		E	R	R
B	A	L	E			O	C	T		S	T	N

Puzzle 146

L	O	T	T		A	S	I		B	I	D	S
E	U	R	O		T	K	O		U	T	A	H
I	S	O	N		L	A	T		T	O	N	Y
S	T	I	G	M	A		A	E	T	N	A	
			U	R	N		S	S	E			
R	O	S	E	T	T	A		C	R	E	P	E
A	R	A	T		A	V	E		F	R	E	D
M	E	O	W	S		A	S	S	I	S	T	S
			I	E	R		S	A	N			
	P	A	S	T	A		A	L	G	O	R	E
B	O	L	T		D	A	Y		E	B	A	Y
L	O	V	E		A	R	E		R	O	L	E
T	H	A	R		R	I	D		S	E	E	R

Puzzle 147

R	U	B		G	L	A	D		S	I	N	G
E	N	E		R	I	T	E		A	T	O	P
F	I	E		A	T	M	E		R	O	T	S
	T	R	I	P			D	I	G			
			B	E	E	S		N	E	R	D	S
A	C	M	E		C	H	A	D		Y	A	K
R	O	U	T		H	E	H		T	A	T	E
K	I	N		P	O	E	M		G	N	A	W
S	L	I	C	E		N	E	H	I			
			U	G	H			I	F	S	O	
B	A	R	R		U	S	E	R		O	K	S
I	V	E	S		L	U	R	E		A	L	A
C	A	V	E		L	E	N	D		R	A	G

Puzzle 148

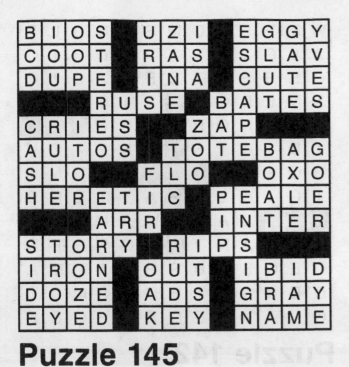

O	B	S	■	S	A	G	■	■	S	H	U	N
L	A	T	■	A	N	A	S	■	L	A	N	A
D	Y	E	■	L	O	L	L	■	A	T	O	N
■	■	P	E	O	N	■	O	F	T	■	■	■
■	P	A	W	N	■	A	G	A	S	S	I	■
M	O	S	E	S	■	R	A	T	■	N	S	A
U	R	I	S	■	W	I	N	■	M	A	L	L
M	E	D	■	G	E	E	■	S	A	K	E	S
■	S	E	R	I	A	L	■	O	R	E	S	■
■	■	■	A	L	L	■	O	N	C	E	■	■
D	R	A	T	■	T	W	I	N	■	Y	E	S
A	C	N	E	■	H	O	L	E	■	E	L	S
B	A	Y	S	■	■	E	S	T	■	S	O	W

Puzzle 149

F	A	D	■	T	H	U	■	■	C	L	E	F
E	X	E	■	L	O	N	■	M	O	O	L	A
N	I	L	■	C	O	T	■	R	O	B	I	N
D	O	H	■	■	P	I	G	S	■	■	■	■
■	M	I	X	■	L	E	M	■	■	H	R	S
■	■	■	M	B	A	■	T	O	L	E	D	O
P	O	L	A	R	■	■	■	W	O	R	S	T
C	A	E	S	A	R	■	O	L	D	■	■	■
S	K	A	■	■	K	E	N	■	E	E	G	■
■	■	■	■	C	O	N	S	■	■	D	E	C
S	N	A	F	U	■	D	A	S	■	G	E	L
H	A	B	I	T	■	E	L	K	■	A	S	I
E	Y	E	R	■	■	D	E	Y	■	R	E	P

Puzzle 150

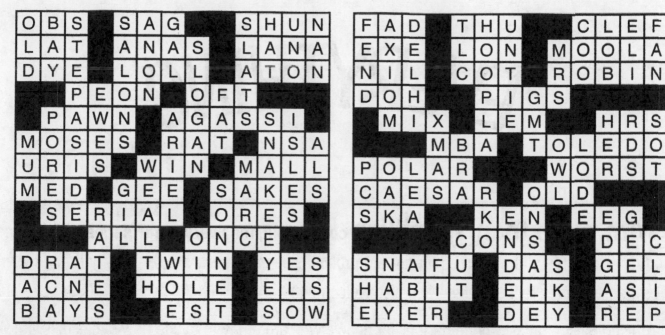